Signs Becoming Signs

Advances in Semiotics

Thomas A. Sebeok, General Editor

OUR **Signs**

PERFUSIVE **Becoming**

PERVASIVE

UNIVERSE **Signs**

INDIANA

UNIVERSITY Floyd Merrell

PRESS

Bloomington & Indianapolis

The paper used in this publication meets the minimum requirements of
American National Standard for Information Sciences—Permanence of
Paper for Printed Library Materials, ANSI Z39.48-1984.

Manufactured in the United States of America

Library of Congress Cataloging-in-Publication Data

Merrell, Floyd, date.
    Signs becoming signs : our perfusive, pervasive universe / Floyd
Merrell.
       p.   cm. — (Advances in semiotics)
    Includes bibliographical references and index.
    ISBN 0-253-33746-1 (alk. paper)
    1. Semiotics. 2. Peirce, Charles S. (Charles Sanders), 1839–1914—
Contributions in semiotics. I. Title. II. Series.
P99.M42 1991
401'.41—dc20
                                           90-49160
                                          CIP

1 2 3 4 5 95 94 93 92 91

CONTENTS

It is a mere accident that
we have no memory of the
future.
—Bertrand Russell

It is a poor memory that
remembers only backwards.   **Preface**
—White Queen to Alice

This book is a somewhat belated outgrowth of *Semiotic Foundations: Steps toward an Epistemology of Written Texts* (Indiana University Press, 1982). The title of that book might at the outset strike some as either embarrassing or a misnomer. I would suggest, however, that it escapes both charges, even though by the skin of its teeth. Actually, the term *foundations* hardly appears in that text. The underlying thrust of my argument was that semiotics should allow of no "foundations," as traditionally conceived, that is. If "foundations" there must be, they should set the stage for an evolutionary view, and if so, then they must also be subject to the same evolutionary pressures they propagate.

At the heart of Peirce's philosophy lies the notion that inquiry must be an evolutionary, self-corrective process. The terms *evolution* and *self-correction* refer to Peirce's concept of *community*. For Peirce the will to know is gauged not by the individual but by the entire collection of individuals seeking knowledge by negotiating that tortuous evolutionary road to truth. There are no guarantees, however, for each community, like the members of which it is composed, cannot but remain fallible to the end. Peirce believed that there are no truths so true that they could never become, at some other time and place, false. But solace is to be had given that the community of individuals, if sincere seekers, are by and large self-corrective, and hence generally more right than wrong. And since, Peirce maintained, one must begin somewhere, with instincts, beliefs, common sense, or conjectures, invariably there is at the outset some presuppositional base— manifested as *expectations* in terms of individual and community practices— unruffled by doubt. So according to Peirce, if "foundations" there be, they are grounded not in propositions so true they can never become false but, rather, in propositions that for the time being are not subject to doubt. Indeed, Peirce was one of the first to enter the battlefield against foundational knowledge in the sense of an atemporal, ahistorical perspective arrived at from the depths of the privileged Cartesian cognizing intellect (Aune 1971; but for a counterargument see Almeder 1980).[1]

With this in mind, in this volume I highlight Peirce's themes of *process, evolution,* and signs generating signs (i.e., *semiosis*) throughout. In so doing I draw from a wide spectrum of disciplines. Such a radically transdisciplinary posture, I must admit, often induces averted gazes, shuffling of feet, nervous coughing, or flat-out knee-jerk reactions. After all, why should an apparently nice fellow find himself floundering about in this unruly sea of ambiguity without a sextant to mark out a clear direction? What can I say in response? I entered the academic rat race because I thought it would afford me the time to follow my curiosity. And it did so, taking me in the process far from my home base, wherever that was. I have no regrets. If anything, I believe my circuitous mental meanderings will serve to heighten the impact this volume may have on its readers—whoever they may be—for better or for worse. At any rate, I hope to have been able to leave the reader the map of a roughly charted territory. Whether I successfully fulfill this objective remains to be seen.

Briefly, I begin chapter 1 with the image of what Peirce terms an imaginary blank "book of assertions," the field of "nothingness" in a state of readiness for a succession of "cuts" (propositions) bringing a semiotic universe into existence. If generated over a sufficient period of time and with appropriate tenacity, a given series of "cuts" would in the theoretical long run culminate in the Ultimate or Logical Interpretant. This "theoretical long run" being infinite in extension, the arduous chore must remain indefinitely incomplete. If what is "real" is thereby rendered inaccessible, any "reality" to be had, I argue, can be no more than "semiotically real." Peirce offers a note of consolation, however, insofar as the "real" can be approximated asymptotically. One of Zeno's notorious paradoxes is thus ushered in—an infinitely converging series—with which Peirce maintained a certain infatuation to the end, and to which I refer repeatedly in the ensuing chapters.

The ubiquitous tension between the "actually real" and the "semiotically real"—which patterns that between our incorrigible ideals and our real capacities—is the likely culprit lurking behind a set of *complementarities,* not mere dichotomies, which will also surface and resurface throughout this inquiry: symmetry-asymmetry, timelessness-temporality, reversibility-irreversibility, continuity-discontinuity, infinite-finite, one-many. In this light, I initiate discussion of a pair of Peirce's key concepts, *vagueness* and *generality*, which, I suggest, are highlighted by the contemporary impasse brought about by the antagonizing conflict between relativity and quantum theory. The props are now set up for the drama to be unfolded.

In chapter 2 I introduce Charles Hartshorne's critique of Peirce's continuity thesis from the viewpoint of Copenhagen quantum mechanics. The long-term reason for my so doing is to demonstrate that Peirce is at least partly vindicated by recent interpretations of the quantum universe, especially those of David Bohm and John Archibald Wheeler, and from a macroscopic perspective, by Ilya Prigogine's nonlinear, irreversible universe of becoming through "dissipative structures." Peirce's notion of continuity is mathematical through and through, as is Bohm's interconnected wholeness of the universe. Moreover, as I shall argue in succeeding chapters, Wheeler's "participatory universe" is patterned by way of Peirce's subject-sign, or better, interpreter-interpretant, conjunction. And Prigogine's ongoing creative universe, the very laws of which are subject to evolutionary tendencies, is in important respects commensurate with Peirce's cosmological principles. In bringing these affinities to light, Peirce's relatedness between mind and nature, and ultimately his enigmatic and controversial "man $\approx$ sign" equation, enter full force to constitute a theme which will gain momentum in the remaining chapters.

Chapter 3 provides a brief interlude, during which Peirce's concept of sign growth and evolution will be given a preliminary contextualization within the complex twentieth-century intellectual milieu. Then, passing discussion of the recent development of the "physics of chaos" in chapters 4 and 5 serves as a stepping stone to an integration of Gilles Deleuze and Félix Guattari's dense, diffuse, and recondite but always provocative thought, Humberto Maturana and Francisco Varela's radical and semiotically grounded theory of living entities, and Prigogine's universe. Regarding the latter, order evolves from disorder, as disorder gives rise to entirely new forms of order. The one cannot exist without the other; there is no being without becoming, and no becoming without being.

Cognizance of this important point ultimately demands holistic rather than reductionistic thinking, which I use in chapter 6 in an attempt to institute a critique of some of the Grand Dichotomies of Western thought, which are perhaps to a certain extent necessary, though they are severely restrictive. The watchword becomes, over the long haul, *complementarity,* which implies *mediation* by way of Peirce's Thirdness, and, above all, *semiosis.* Peirce's cosmology is thus a long shot from the classical paradigm—though in certain respects the semiotic backwoodsman remained a child of his times. His unorthodox fusion of objectivism and idealism, monism and pluralism, continuity and discontinuity, infinity and finitude, places him squarely within much contemporary discourse, especially the view of an evolving, self-organizing universe.

With this in mind, chapter 7 pairs the Peircean doctrine of signs with speculation by many twentieth-century scientists, including Niels Bohr, Louis de Broglie, Arthur Eddington, Albert Einstein, Werner Heisenberg, and Erwin Schrödinger. Two distinct perspectives or modes of knowing enter the scene, intimate (intuitive) knowledge and representational (symbolic) knowledge, which bear on the centrality of language for the human semiotic animal and reveal the trend, especially in the West, toward rampant abstraction and alienation from the "real." This is, I contend, germane to Peirce's dialogic self-other interaction, as it is to a paradox stemming from the existence of self-consciousness effectively outlined by Schrödinger in *Matter and Mind* (1967). Indeed, the very Peircean idea of the universe as mind entails a paradox of cosmological self-reference rendering the universe inconceivable in terms of traditional logic, yet it is the natural product of the "logic of vagueness" Peirce occasionally promised but never delivered in discursive form—perhaps because it is well-nigh impossible to dress it in discursive form. At any rate, regarding Peirce's cosmology, *vagueness-generality,* a leitmotif threading its way throughout this entire disquisition, is commensurate, I argue, with the havoc wrought by Gödel and others with any and all claims to *consistent* and *complete* knowledge.

My story then culminates, in the final chapter, in an attempt ever so slightly to take a peek behind Firstness, to that lowermost point, "nothingness," preceding the initial "cut" in the "book of assertions," before essence and existence, indeed, even before truth and falsity have made their entry. The circle is thus closed: the end becomes the beginning and vice versa. The book in this fashion falls victim to the same paradox inherent in that to which it is addressed.

In a sense it should self-destruct. But it does not, I would suggest. Rather, it patterns our perfusive universe of *semiosis,* which, also hopelessly self-contained and self-referential, escapes its own self-destruction by the fact that, somehow, it paradoxically flows on.

If I may be so fortunate as to see my expectations reach fruition, this volume will soon flow into yet another companion piece, tentatively entitled "Self-Excited Signs: *Semiosis* in the Postmodern Age" (1990), the draft of which is complete and to which I refer occasionally in the pages that follow. (I really must apologize for referencing a manuscript in progress. But the two inquiries are so tightly intermeshed that I found myself falling victim to the temptation. At any rate, I fully expect to send the later piece off within a year of having completed this manuscript.)

Before proceeding, I wish to thank Myrdene Anderson and Virgil Lokke for their having graciously worked their way through this manuscript to uncover inexcusable errors and omissions. I wish also to acknowledge my appreciation to Tom Sebeok for his continuing support of my efforts. Permission for the many citations from the *Collected Papers* is gratefully acknowledged to Harvard University Press. A note of thanks must be extended to Purdue University for granting me a sabbatical during which time the first draft of this book was written. Above all, I would like to express my esteem for Araceli, without whose support, through the thick and thin of things, this volume would never have seen the light of day.

Signs Becoming Signs

ONE   *Asymptotically*

Getting There

I. THE TEXT OF THE WORLD. In the beginning, Peirce tells us, is the *monad*. The *monad*, the *dyad*, and the *triad*, corresponding to *Firstness, Secondness,* and *Thirdness,* make up what for Peirce are the fundamental categories of signs, of thought, of mind, and by extension, of the universe. I wish to begin by speaking of the monad in the most general sense: the Pure Monad. Accessible by neither analysis nor inferential reasoning, self-contained and self-sufficient, it can be assimilated only in one impossible, monolithic, instantaneous gulp. Peirce's description of this Monad coincides curiously with orthodox metaphysical accounts of the deity—a nonrelative totality without parts, devoid of spatial and temporal localization, and independent of anything other than itself. The fundamental difference is that the Monad is sheer potentiality, while the deity is usually conceived to be an actuality (Hartshorne 1952:221). The Monad does, however, entail the possibility for actualization of an inexhaustible multiplicity of entities. In other words, the "being" of Monadic quality as mere potentiality is a continuum without existence, for the existence of particulars is *dyadic,* while consciousness *of* and perceptual judgment regarding existent particulars is *triadic* (CP:6.197, 1.328).

Thus we have Peirce's conception of ongoing interaction between *continuity* and *discontinuity, possibility* and *actuality,* the *one* and the *many,* which will be evoked throughout this inquiry. The continuum of possibilities is necessarily nebulous and vague. Actuality, in contrast, is the force of existence which punctuates the undivided to produce discrete units. In this sense, continuity is tantamount to generality, and continuity and generality "are two names for the same absence of distinction of individuals" (CP:4.172). Peirce's Monad also bears on what he enigmatically called the "logic of the universe," or "logic of vagueness," which consists of the entirety of all possible "logics" as a whole, a continuum—unformalizable, we must presume—of a higher type more rudimen-

1

tary than classical logic. Upon duly considering the course of this logic, Peirce declares, we cannot but conclude that "it proceeds from the question to the answer—from the vague to the definite" (CP:6.189–92)—i.e., by the undifferentiated differentiating itself, homogeneity taking on heterogeneity, the cloud condensing into myriad ice crystals. Indeed, Peirce's three categories cannot be adequately considered without an acknowledging nod to the Monad.

But the nuts and bolts of our everyday world are far removed from this ethereal entity, which is the stuff of highest abstractions, mystical insights, and the wildest of dreams. Leaving the Monad as a Grand First aside for the moment, let us step down to the Firsts of ordinary mortals. Peirce, once again, offers a trope, which is, nonetheless, grounded in his "logic of the universe" and hence virtually as abstract as the concept of the Monad. The rise of the most primitive of categories, Firstness, entails the possibility of an initial "cut" in what Peirce called the imaginary "book of assertions," the domain of "nothingness," consisting of "separate sheets, tacked together at points, if not otherwise connected" (CP:4.512). The first sheet in this chimerical book, the standard "sheet of assertion," represents, by virtue of the "cuts" on its pages, "a universe of existent individuals," the various parts of the surface indicating "facts" *about,* or propositions asserted *of,* that universe. Peirce asks us to imagine "cuts" penetrating the surface of this sheet such that what is placed inside each "cut" is severed from the sheet itself (MS 455:10). "Cuts" can be made in the sheet enabling passage into successive sheets and into "areas of conceived propositions which are not [yet] realized" (CP:4.512). Subsequent "cuts" in these successive sheets can then allow entry into worlds which, "in the imaginary worlds of the other cuts, are themselves represented to be imaginary and false, but which may, for all that, be true, and therefore continuous with the sheet of assertion itself, although this [truth] is uncertain" (CP:4.512).

Commensurate with Peirce's thought, a given universe of discourse in the book of assertions is comparable to a particular "semiotically real" world—i.e., the realm, from within that universe of discourse, of "semiotic objects"—which, given Peirce's "convergence theory" of truth, stands a chance of at least approximating the "actually real."[1] Thus a universe of discourse can consist of a variety of statements regarded as (1) either true or false in terms of certain relations holding between them, whether they are empirical or not,[2] (2) patently meaningless or absurd,[3] or (3) fictitious and imaginary, whether Meinongian "objects" (i.e., square-circles, gold mountains [Parsons 1980]), Vaihingerian (1935) "as if" hypostats, counterfactuals (Lewis 1973), or everyday figurative language use (see also Merrell 1983).[4]

Peirce invites us to regard his initial blank sheet of assertion as a film upon which there exists the as yet undeveloped photograph of the "facts" (propositions) of the universe. But this cannot be a literal picture, he hastens to point out, for when we consider historically the vast range of partly to wholly incompatible "facts" that have been at one time or another asserted to be true, we must conclude that the book of assertions can be none other than a continuum since these "facts" must somehow "blend into one another" (CP:4.512). This continuum, like a topological space,

> must clearly have more dimensions than a surface or even than a solid; and we will suppose it to be plastic, so that it can be deformed in all sorts of ways without the continuity and connection of parts being ever ruptured. Of this continuum the blank [initial] sheet of assertion may be imagined to be a photograph. When we find out that a proposition is true, we can place it wherever we please on the sheet, because we can imagine the original continuum, which is plastic, to be so deformed as to bring any number of propositions to any places on the sheet we may choose. (CP:4.512)

In this manner, each "cut" corresponds to an area on the initial sheet of assertion where the actual state of things is signified. All successive sheets represent an indefinite set of potential "facts," or propositions, many or most of which can, at an indefinite time and place, become intermittently part of the "semiotically real." Peirce suggests that "in order to represent to our minds the relation between the universe of possibilities and the universe of existent facts, if we are going to think of the latter as a surface, we must think of the former as three-dimensional space in which any surface would represent all the facts that might exist in one existential universe" (CP:4.512).

This is indeed a significant visual metaphor. It suggests a method by which the evolution of *forms,* by the succession of "cuts," can be conceived in timeless fashion as if *in bloc*. There is a problem, however, regarding the distinction between *experience* and *intellection*. For example, according to Newtonian dynamics, to the question, "What is the distance traveled by an object that begins from rest and accelerates to a velocity of 40 ft./sec. in a time of 15 seconds?" the mathematical solution is elementary:

$$\text{Distance} = 1/2 \ vt = 1/2 \times 40 \times 15 = 300 \text{ feet}$$

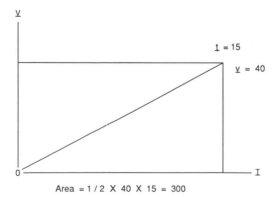

FIGURE I   Area = 1 / 2 X 40 X 15 = 300

But what is meant by the resulting statement "The distance the object travels *is* equal to 300 feet"? The copula, *is,* implies a timeless state of affairs, a Parmenidean universe in which everything is *there* simultaneously (Park 1980:22–35). This is a mummified rather than a living image, mechanical rather than organic, static rather than dynamic. It has hardly anything to do with the immediate quality of mind, of feeling, of sentience. We also could have solved the problem geometrically by plotting velocity against time along the Cartesian coordinates and determining the area of the triangle in terms of time and acceleration (see figure 1). But once again we would have a static form on paper far removed from the *experience of* acceleration. On the contrary, we could assimilate the two-dimensional graph in one perceptual grasp from our three-dimensional vantage point, just as a three-dimensional Spherelander could perceive a vast expanse of a Flatlander's world in an instant.[5] In this vein, M. C. Escher (1971:15) writes, regarding his prints, that

> Anyone who wishes to create a universe on a two-dimensional surface (he deludes himself, because our three-dimensional world does not permit a reality of two nor of four dimensions) notices that time passes while he is working on his creation. But when he has finished and looks at what he has done, he sees something that is static and timeless; in his picture no clock ticks and there is only a flat, unmoving surface.

Peirce's book metaphor, in like fashion, presents something akin to the Minkowski "block" interpretation of Einsteinian relativity, a conception, *sub specie aeternitatis* as it were, of the whole of signs, the Grand Monad—which from a critical vantage could threaten intellectually or conceptually to "spatialize" the ongoing temporal flux of *semiosis.* This point aside, though I shall return to it later, Peirce's notion of a *cut* marring the continuum of possibilities, besides its obvious relevance to a "Dedekind cut" bisecting a line (mathematical continuum), is tantamount to an organism's initial grasp of some-*thing* in the flux of experience. This cut entails *primordial negativity,* since that which *is* is separated from that which *is not.* In other words, the cut is a selection; *it cuts something* (as a First) and *distinguishes it* (as a Second) *from something else.* Then, as other cuts are exercised and combined into aggregates, they can become classified in the most general sense—with language in the case of human sign activity—as *objects, acts, events,* and *abstractions of thought.* Since the initial flux is a continuum, as with Peirce's book of assertions, there is potentially an infinity of ways to cut it up at partly to wholly arbitrarily selected joints. Hence any given set of cuts must be construed to be largely relative, for *the cuts always could have been made otherwise.*

Peirce's book of assertions evokes four important further considerations. First, the concept of continuity is strictly mathematical, and it bears on Peirce's doctrine of *fallibilism.* In fact, the continuum as pure potentiality is fallibilism objectified, for according to fallibilism, "our knowledge is never absolute but always swims, as it were, in a continuum of uncertainty and of indeterminacy" (CP:1.171). Commensurate with Peirce's fallibilism, his doctrine of *tychism* entails a universe of absolute chance, a potential containing an "aggregate of all possibilities that are consistent with certain general conditions." This potential is "greater in multitude than any possible multitude of individuals, but, being a mere potential, it does not contain any individuals at all. It only contains general conditions which *permit* the determination of all individuals" (CP:6.185).

We have here a distinction between the actualized aggregate of individuals, of Seconds, *to* consciousness, and the unactualized continuum of possibilities which are not yet available *to* consciousness as such, for as Firsts they remain unrelated to anything else. These two domains might be termed respectively the *selective* and the *nonselective,* and the *particulate* and the *nonparticulate,* domains. Given Peirce's continuity postulate, the nonselective, nonparticulate domain must eventually come under consideration, the former being circumscribed by the latter. It has been an error of traditional cosmological principles to infer that since the universe comprises particularities, it is itself something particular. On the contrary. Each representation of the circumscribed domain implies actuality (selection) only in consequence of the uncircumscribed (nonselected) domain. That which is actualized is necessary because it contains some things and excludes others; but the nonactualized is also necessary because of there being nothing that it does not contain. The actualized exists by virtue of not containing everything that is merely potential, in other words, by virtue of not containing that which might have been actualized but is not. The nonactualized exists by virtue of containing everything that remains or is absent from any given actualized domain. Quite obviously, in the actualized domain there will always be any given number of entities which *are not,* for without the absence *of something,* the domain of actuals is precluded from existing as a set of selected entities.

The second consideration is that of the very existence of discontinuity (the coming into existence of cuts, of particulate actuals) which disrupts the continuum. Peirce offers the example of a clean blackboard to represent "the original vague potentiality"—"nothingness" before Firstness (CP:6.203). The blackboard is an indeterminate multitude of possible dimensions, joints, and points, just as the ideal continuum is an indeterminate multitude of possible qualities. If we draw a line on the blackboard a discontinuity is produced, but this discontinuity is itself a continuity *complementary* with the continuity of the blackboard—that is, it is a line consisting of an infinite continuum of points. But the visible chalk mark is not really the line, for a line is mathematically of infinitesimal thickness. The mark can actually be conceived of as a narrow plane which severs and displaces a segment of the black surface:

> Thus the discontinuity can only be produced upon that blackboard by the reaction between two continuous surfaces into which it is separated, the white surface and the black surface. The whiteness is a Firstness—a springing up of something new. But the boundary between the black and white is neither black, nor white, nor neither, nor both. It is the pairedness of the two. It is for the white the active Secondness of the black; for the black the active Secondness of the white. (CP:6.203)

A cut in the continuum, like the initial mark on the blackboard, is the beginning of a series. It might be countered that such a discrete series, in conjunction with the original continuum, creates a problem. If along a line a cut is made equidistant between the beginning and the end—a theoretical impossibility, since ideally a line continues indefinitely—then another can be made halfway between the first cut and the end, and still another bisecting the final segment, and so on. And one of Zeno's paradoxes ensues, which is the result of contradictorily interjecting discontinuity into continuity.

Peirce, however, sees no problem here. Granted, from the view of the continuum, the road is endless. But from the view of the discontinuous series of events, Achilles suffers no embarrassment: after a few lengthy strides he easily overtakes his plodding counterpart. In fact, Peirce, in elaborating on his doctrine of *abduction,* argues that consciousness itself overcomes Zeno's quandary in that, "just as Achilles does not have to make the series of distinct endeavors which he is represented as making," so abductive inference, as it shades into perceptual judgment, and because it is subconscious, "does not have to make separate acts of inference, but performs its act in one continuous process" (CP:5.131; also 6.177–80). Let it not be assumed, however, that Achilles' path therefore takes on a "reality" more "real" than the continuum. For, according to Peirce, the continuum of possibilities constitutes the principal character of the universe (CP:1.62, 6.169–72).

The third consideration bearing on the book of assertions stems from this notion of the "real" and Peirce's "convergence" theory of knowledge. In Peirce's view, "truth" and the "real" are most adequately accounted for in scientific discourse. Science focuses on the general, on nature's regularities. Irregularity and disorder should ideally lie beyond its purview, hence according to Peirce they must be considered "unreal." Given the accumulation of our knowledge, the domain of the "unreal" is successively becoming smaller, and the "real" (the scientifically accessible) and the natural (the actual world) increasingly tend to coincide.[6] In other words, although certain problems will always remain to be solved, Peirce noted that the number of problems being put forth was on the increase, but so was the capacity for solving them. If the rate of increase of the latter were greater than that of the former, the probability of a given problem's eventually being solved would be favorable; otherwise the probability would be zero. Peirce believed the former state of affairs to be the case. In this sense knowledge will continue to increase, now receding, now proceeding, though over the long haul asymptotically approximating the "truth." One again, Zeno, in another garment.

Finally, the fourth consideration: Peirce's notion that ideas (another word for signs) spread continuously, which is also related to his law of mind and his conception of consciousness. The continuous spreading of ideas implies that all ideas affect all other ideas. As each idea spreads, though it loses intensity and power, it gains in generality and becomes welded with other ideas (CP:6.104, 6.143). By means of this continuity hypothesis, past ideas are connected to present ideas "by a series of real infinitesimal steps" (CP:6.109). This is ultimately made possible through the *mediacy of consciousness.* Consciousness must cover a temporal interval, for if not, it is hardly conceivable that we could acquire a sense of time. We are, therefore, forced to admit, Peirce asserts, that "we are immediately conscious through an infinitesimal interval of time" (CP:6.110).[7] In this infinitesimal interval, "not only is consciousness continuous in a subjective sense, that is, considered as a subject or substance having the attribute of duration, but also, because it is immediate consciousness, its object is *ipso facto* continuous" (CP:6.111, also 6.227).

However, consciousness *of* such and such cannot be immediate, a feeling, or Firstness, as it were. It is invariably mediate. For example, "we can never think, 'this is present to me,' since, before we have time to make the reflection, the sensation is past, and, on the other hand, when once past, we can never bring back the quality of the feeling as it was *in and for itself,* or know what it was like *in itself*" (CP:5.289). There is, consequently, no absolute simultaneity of Firstness, Secondness, or Thirdness *to* consciousness.

In addition to the continuous extension of mind and consciousness through time, Peirce's assertion of their extendedness through space paints a strange picture indeed. In fact, the mind's continuous envelopment of space forms the basis of Peirce's general law of mind which stipulates that minds, like ideas, "tend to spread continuously and to affect certain others which stand to them in a peculiar relation of affectibility" (CP:6.104). Peirce generalizes this hypothesis to the actors in a human community—and to all communities of organisms, for that matter—holding that there must be a community of feeling not only between parts of the mind but also between minds and minds (CP:6.133, 6.150–52).

Peirce's belief that consciousness and mind have continuous extension in space, that ideas and minds are connected continuously, and that feelings flow together with ideas and mind, flies in the face of the subjective/objective, sentiment/reason, body/mind, and other such stultifying dichotomies. In fact, if privileging there be in Peirce's metaphysics, it rests in feeling rather than intellect, in the heart rather than in the mind, so to speak. Peirce's contention that mental phenomena are governed by law "does not mean merely that they are describable by a general formula; but that there is a living idea, a conscious continuum of feeling, which precedes them, and to which they are docile" (CP:6.152). Consequently, mind is not to be isolated from its place in the totality of nature, and in its behavior clues can be discovered regarding the nature of the world. In fact, as we shall note in chapter 7, Peirce conceives the universe itself as mind in the process of development, and hence the possibility of knowing the universe depends on the notion that "human thought necessarily partakes of whatever character is diffused through the whole universe" (CP:1.351).

Two problems apparently ensue. In the first place, the "ocular metaphor," the mind as a "mirror of nature," which underlies the classical world view, surfaces. This metaphor has of recent been the focus of scathing criticism, and with a considerable degree of reason (see Bernstein 1983; Derrida 1974; Rorty 1979; Tyler 1987). I do not apologize for Peirce, though I must point out that in his anti-Cartesian posture he took a giant step toward deconstructing traditional metaphysics, as Derrida (1974:48) himself acknowledges. In the second place, a paradox becomes imminent, to which in chapter 7 I shall refer as the "Arithmetical Paradox." The mind, which is immanent, partakes of the universe, which is mind. In another manner of speaking, the set of all sets (universe) is a member (mind) of itself—and thus we appear to violate Bertrand Russell's (1910) proscription in his Theory of Logical Types. In what sense can the mind make of itself its own object such that it is both the observed and that which observes? Following G. Spencer-Brown (1979:105), this paradox might well be irresolvable, for the very physicist who describes the universe "is, in his own account, himself constructed of it. He is, in short, made of a conglomerate of the very particles he describes, no more, no less, bound together and obeying such general laws as he himself has managed to find and to record."

The universe sees itself in a mirror, which is it. But in order to do so, it must first *cut* itself up into at least one state that sees, and another that is seen.[8] Of course, the universe is inevitably itself, but in any attempt to see itself, it must make itself distinct from itself. In this condition it can be no more than an abstraction, partly false to itself, or as Nietzsche (1968:24) would put it, a fiction, or fable. What is more, when that aspect of the universe which has been cut is combined with what remains uncut, the selected with the nonselected, everything—possibility (Firstness), potentiality (Thirdness), and actuality (Secondness)—is paradoxically *there,* in the *now.* It all "exists" in simultaneity *in* the book of assertions, or, so to speak, *in* the text of the world.

II. STRIATED OR SMOOTH? This conception of "existence," though it ultimately and inexorably leaves us with an antinomy of Kantian magnitude, is not the real bugbear in Peirce's thought according to Charles Hartshorne (1973). He laments the fact that Peirce's belief in an actual continuum of possibilities as "real" as the actualities drawn from it prevented him from envisioning the importance of discontinuity as it is amply demonstrated in contemporary quantum theory. Hartshorne informs us that the continuous aspects in quantum physics are those of *real possibility,* while the discrete aspects are those of *actual happenings*. This fits Peirce's view, at least "when he was not blinded by his attachment to continuity." The problem supposedly is that for Peirce the continuous aggregate of possibilities and the set of actuals are coequal in the sense that they are both tantamount to, and modeled by, a mathematically dense continuum. In other words, "Peirce was beautifully clear as to the contingency of actuality as such . . . but somehow he was unclear as to the implied discontinuity of contingent actuality" (Hartshorne 1973:196).

Hartshorne argues that Peirce's *synechism,* the doctrine of continuity, erroneously entails a maximum of possibility: it keeps all of them open, hence it must be qualified as continuous rather than discontinuous action. In fact, Peirce pointed out that the possible, the general, and the continuous are ultimately the same (CP:6.189–92). In the spatial continuum (the *nonselective domain*) every conceivable size and shape can pop into existence, and the space-time continuum can hold every conceivable motion and change. In contrast, discontinuity (the *selective domain*) implies the exclusion of portions of these infinite possibilities.

And such an exclusion is, precisely, actuality. Hartshorne (1973:191–92), however, goes on to argue that

> either the actual world is every possible world in one, or it is not. If not, and few besides Spinoza have believed in the exhaustive actualization of possibilities, hence in principle there must be quantization, at least if the exclusion of possibilities is subject to any general rule or regularity. And why should this exclusion affect space but not time? In this, present quantum physics and relativity physics do indeed belong together. It is space-time, not just space, that characterizes reality.

Elsewhere, Hartshorne expresses his dismay that not only was Peirce unable to anticipate quantization in physics, but he believed in the existence of an actual continuity with enthusiasm. He justified his synechism by arguing that we must adopt the postulate that all possibilities are kept open as a continuous whole, otherwise some possibilities would be ruled out a priori. Hartshorne (1973:193) submits that this argument "involves a subtle confusion." Discontinuity as a principle "rules out nothing except the one infinitely extreme supposedly possible case, continuity." He then rather condescendingly suggests that perhaps in Peirce's effort to avoid nominalism he committed the "synechistic error" of affirming the continuity of becoming in which the past is a set of particulars (actuals), the future is potentiality, and the present somehow incorporates both.

For sure, both Peirce and Whitehead are disconcertingly realistic in the Platonic sense, the former regarding his "eternal objects," the latter his "Firstness." Despite their differences, however, they agree upon a "full blown" realism, which, William Reese (1952:225) points out, apparently employs the principle: "Whatever is needed to explicate reality must be granted a place within reality." Peirce and Whitehead's "reality" includes, in addition to actual existence, the mode of possibility and the mode of process—i.e., the actualization of possibilities, from "eternal objects" or "Firstness." For the nominalist, the possible cannot be a nonactual manifestation of the actual; in contrast, for Peirce and Whitehead, the actualization of particulars into "reality" implies what might be termed a "background," or an "underlying order," which is no less "real" than the existent set of actuals. A fundamental distinction between the possible and the actual rests in that the former is nonlocalized while the latter consists of presumably localizable singularities—with the attendant risk of what Whitehead (1925) calls the "fallacy of simple location." The former is "mutually implicative" rather than, as is the latter, "mutually exclusive" (Reese 1952:229).

From another perspective, nominalism asserts that the past categorically is no more; it remains outside the present, the product of an incessant passing through the instant of the "now." The philosphical realist, in contrast, would retort that the past, though past, is conserved in the present—contained within Peirce's Thirdness. Reese argues, and rightly so, I believe, that the nominalist regress of the discrete series of "nows" into the past *implies* a *potential infinity*. Like the number series, in a manner of speaking, it contradictorily implies infinity, for the series cannot be halted. However, supposing one to be capable of reconstructing the series of all past events, like traveling from zero through the negative numbers, or much like Borges's (1962:59–66) Funes the Memorious remembering his stream of sensory perceptions into the remote past—one still cannot recede further than the actual steps one has taken. In fact, throughout human history the infinity of steps cannot be actualized; there can be neither a conceivable beginning nor an end. According to Peirce, on the other hand, this contradiction of past times is avoided by assuming that all past events up to the present—although this implies an infinite number of events in the nominalist's view—compose one *Cosmic Event*. This totality is, we must suppose, continuous, and it can be subdivided indefinitely. Consequently, an infinitely receding series pointing toward an inaccessible first event presents no real problem, for Peirce at least.

Peirce attempted to circumvent the apparent dilemma further by arguing—albeit vaguely—that the possible is somehow "real" and that the past is equally "real." But this seems to fly in the face of common sense. Peirce's time and space as continuous and devoid of singularities obviously have no room for Secondness, that is, for actualities. They are exclusively Firstness, existing as a self-referential, self-contained whole. In other words, "a continuum which is without singularities must, in the first place, return into itself" (CP:6.210). Only thus can the series of reiterated cuts be initiated: in the sense of Spencer-Brown, the universe necessarily separates itself from itself in order that part of it may turn inward and distinguish itself from that which it *is not*.

Peirce (CP:6.211) offers the example of two intersecting lines, each of which is an infinite continuum of points (see figure 2). The intersection of the two lines is a singularity, something akin to a Dedekind "cut," which mars both continua. Peirce then severs the lines through that point and combines them at their extremity, which can be no more than an imaginary combination, since each line is presumed to continue indefinitely. Finally, an oval—the "ovum" of the universe—can be formed, which is in a sense both finite and unbounded and infinite and bounded; there is no beginning or end, yet one can begin or end anywhere (Boler 1964). The curve doubles back upon itself to describe an unlimited set of *possibilia*. Peirce reminds us that such a curve, which is theoretically invisible since it is infinitesimally thin, is "merely a Platonic world, of which we are, therefore, to conceive that there are many [worlds], both coördinated and subordinated to one another; until finally out of one of these Platonic worlds is differentiated the particular actual universe of existence in which we happen to be" (CP:6.208).

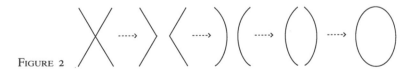

FIGURE 2

This ethereal realm is, of course, the continuum of possibilities, the undifferentiated *(nonselective)* domain before it has been mutilated with a *cut (selection)*. Peirce's notion of a *cut* in the *uncut* is remarkably commensurate, as I shall point out repeatedly in this inquiry, with Spencer-Brown's calculus of indications based on one symbol, ⌐, the *mark of distinction,* especially as it is interpreted by Francisco Varela (1975, 1979), Humberto Maturana and Varela (1980, 1987), and Louis Kauffman and Varela (1980). It is also closely related to what in *Semiotic Foundations* (1982) I call "boundaried spaces." We must be mindful, in this light, that Peirce was a mathematician and logician—which is to say, a semiotician—before he was a metaphysicist. Hence his conception of time and space *is* quite appropriately mathematical, though, given his place in the history of human thought, it remains in part commensurate with classical physics and Euclidean geometry. Consequently it conflicts with Hartshorne's conception of things, which appears to be more subjective, intuitive, and "commonsensical" than mathematical. Moreover, contrary to Hartshorne, as we shall observe in chapter 2, an important aspect of Peirce's thought, especially concerning First-ness, the Monad, is not antithetical to quantum theory according to one of its more creative interpretations. But before entering into that dialogue, I will present a few preliminary remarks on a crucial problem arising out of the contemporary scientific world view, especially regarding time, space, change, and objectivity.

III. NARY A GLIMPSE INTO ETERNITY. Against Peirce's notion of temporal and spatial continua, Hartshorne appears to follow Whitehead and William James according to whom Zeno's paradox of Achilles and the tortoise succeeds only in demonstrating that an alien property is interjected into the denseness postulate of time and space. A crucial issue of Zeno's paradox is whether or not the mathematical notion of continuity along a dense string of points is applicable to temporal succession. Whitehead and James, in this respect contrary to Peirce, assert that time does *not* possess the structure of a mathematical continuum. Their chief reason for this denial is based on their belief that (1) our conscious awareness of temporal order is *pulsational not continuous,* and (2) the order of the pulses is *discrete.* Specifically, James (1948:187) remarks that "the mathematical definition of a continuous quantity as 'that between any two elements or terms of which there is another term' is directly opposed to the more empirical or perceptual notion that anything is continuous when its parts appear as immediate neighbors, with absolutely nothing between." And Whitehead (1978:69), after favorably quoting James on Zeno, tells us that

> the modification of the "Arrow" paradox, . . . brings out the principle that every act of becoming must have an immediate successor, if we admit that something be-comes. For otherwise we cannot point out what creature becomes as we enter upon the second in question. But we cannot, in the absence of some additional premise, infer that every act of becoming must have had an immediate predecessor.
>
> The conclusion is that in every act of becoming there is the becoming of something with temporal extension; but that the act itself is not extensive, in the sense that it is divisible into earlier and later acts of becoming which correspond to the extensive divisibility of what has become.

Adolf Grünbaum (1967:48) raises two questions concerning James's and Whitehead's conclusions: (1) Does our awareness actually consist of a discrete series of pulses, of "nows"? and if so, (2) Is their postulated isomorphism of the perceptual and physical orders correct? Grünbaum argues extensively in favor of the first thesis, but he rejects the isomorphism thesis. In brief, he proposes that (1) awareness of the coming into existence of the thingness of the universe is mind-dependent, and (2) time and space in modern quantum theory *presupposes a dense continuum*—which is contrary, we shall note in chapter 2, to Hartshorne's interpretation of quantum theory as discretizing time and especially space, which becomes, he believes, grounds for his attack on Peirce. Grünbaum's first proposal, of course, has nothing new to offer. Its modern embodiment is found most notably in Hermann Minkowski's mathematical rendition of Einstein's special theory of relativity into the "block" universe which I mentioned above, a rather uncomfortably Parmenidean formulation. Time, according to this view, loses its movement; it is "spatialized," much like, on an exceedingly more mundane level, the problem of acceleration in figure 1. Consequently, time plays no part in this instantaneous clash of the universal symphony. Mathematician Olivier Costa de Beauregard (1981: 29) puts it trenchantly:

> In Newtonian kinematics the separation between past and future was objective, in the sense that it was determined by a single instant of universal time, the present. This is no longer true in relativistic kinematics: the separation of space-time at each point of space and instant of time is not a dichotomy but a trichotomy (past, future, elsewhere).[9]

In other words, according to this view, there is no knife-edge present moving along the linear race of time from past to future. All "events" in the "block" are at once both past and future—insofar as they are accessible to a given sentient organism along its "world-line"—as well as "elsewhere"—that which lies outside the organism's peceptual grasp, outside its "light cone," because of the finite velocity of light. This monolithic four-dimensional manifold is described by Hermann Weyl (1949:116) as a universe which "simply *is*, it does not happen. Only to the gaze of my consciousness, crawling upward along the life line of my body, does a section of this world come to life as a fleeting image in space which continuously changes in time." Consequently, the perceived universe is distinct, to a greater or lesser degree, for each individual along his "world-line." And the "elsewhere," lying outside his purview, bears witness that the universe cannot be accessible to any immanent observer. Time is relative to each observer, and change is dependent upon the mind-dependence of time. In Kurt Gödel's (1949:557) words:

> Change becomes possible only through the lapse of time. The existence of an objective lapse of time, however, means (or at least, is equivalent to the fact) that reality consists of an infinity of layers of "now" which come into existence successively. But, if simultaneity is something relative . . . reality cannot be split into such layers in an objectively determined way. Each observer has his own set of

"nows," and none of these various systems of layers can claim the prerogative of representing the objective lapse of time.

However, Grünbaum (1967:55) takes pains to point out the obvious: Minkowski's becomingless universe is a view *sub specie aeternitatis* in the first place, which makes no reference to anyone's particular "now." An event is becomingless in the sense that it occurs at a certain time, *t,* and within a static network of what we would ordinarily perceive to be both earlier and later. Hence becoming is tenselessly in a network of relations of timelike—from our perspective, at least—separation. Quite obviously, becoming as mind-dependent, following Minkowski's "block" universe and according to Grünbaum's contention, goes against the grain of James's and Whitehead's thesis.

This in an indirect way bears on Peirce's rather problematic conception of time, which I will treat briefly by way of a digression. Hartshorne points out that Secondness in the absence of Thirdness remains symmetrical and without direction. The asymmetry of time's arrow is the mere successive actualization of Seconds from the *possibilia* of Firstness. He argues that if the First, the Monad, were truly independent, then its successors and all other successors could be either First or Second to each other, and time would have no direction; it would be "spatialized," *in bloc* (Hartshorne 1964:461). However, Peirce at least hinted that time is the succession of genuine Seconds to Firsts which are actually relative rather than nonrelative. This presents the ambiguous condition of Firsts' being both relative and nonrelative, depending upon the perspective. But since Seconds are largely directionless, they depend on Firsts conceived to be relative rather than nonrelative in a more primordial sense. It is the Thirdness of consciousness which constructs time's arrow and hence asymmetrical temporal movement.

In other words, insofar as time is a pure continuum—in conformity with Peirce's doctrine of *synechism*—it has neither direction nor metric, and if the principles are to be attached to a definition of time, it must be by way of the content of time: what Peirce calls the law of mind gives the direction and flow of time from past to future. This law entails ideas affecting other ideas through relations of *asymmetry, transitivity,* and *irreflexivity.* In this case for two ideas, *A* and *B,* if the former is affectible by the latter, then it is later; if vice versa, then it comes before; if neither is affectible by the other, then they are simultaneous. Causality among ideas constitutes the basis for temporal direction (CP:6.127–31). But according to Peirce's "objective idealism," since matter is fossilized mind, and temporal order by way of mental processes establishes the direction of time for the physical world, time is mind-dependent. In this fashion, matter, as another form of mind, generates time, and since the individual mind—or minds—is *in* time, time is, paradoxically, *in* itself (see Murphey 1961:387–88).

If for Peirce mind gives direction to the physical universe, Einstein's belief in an objective world and the "block" interpretation of special relativity coupled with Gödel's idealistic interpretation of the "block" leads to the view that not only are all mechanical processes reversible, but in addition, the direction of time is mental. Or in the terms of this inquiry, we could say that the direction of time is "semiotically real" rather than "actually real"; it is mental in the broadest sense rather than purely physical (see CP:6.554, 6.68ff.).

On the other hand, quite understandably, while Peirce generally conceived space and time as continuous and absolute in the Newtonian sense, he never envisaged them to compose a four-dimensional continuum. Yet he approximated the concept of a space-time continuum in his suggestion that time is akin to a one-dimensional *hyperbolic* continuum in space. In this manner time and space are not exactly independent of one another (CP:1.273, 6.575). The nature of time thus manifests similarities with the nature of space, but with a major distinction: time, unlike space, cannot be symmetrical, because an entity cannot possess two contradictory properties simultaneously (CP:1.492–95, 1.501). That is to say, something cannot possess both x and non-x. However, it can, over time, first possess x and later non-x. Phillip can be both drunk and sober, provided the two Phillip events are separated by a temporal interval (CP:1.494). Peirce's more "general" logic, as well as his hypothesis of time, accounts for how an entity becomes. In contrast, that which never changes cannot exist *in* time.[10]

Regarding the second aspect of Grünbaum's argument—time and space as dense, not discrete—the question is posed as to whether Zeno's arrow and stadium paradoxes, both of which can be interpreted as directed against the continuity hypothesis of space and time, present the same challenge to quantum theory that Achilles did for the continuity thesis of motion and becoming. Grünbaum suggests that the initial assumption that this is indeed the case appears to be derived from the notion that quantum theory quantized physical properties which were continuous in classical physics. Speculations subsequently arose concerning the possibility of minimal increments of space ("hodons") and time ("chronons")—that is, discontinuous space and time in line with Hartshorne's notion.[11] This conjecture eventually led to naught. At best, according to Grünbaum (1967:111), "genuinely atomic space and time is nowadays a gleam in the eyes of hopeful speculative theoreticians."

In this sense, Peirce, for whom space in and of itself is continuous and without singularities, as is time, appears at the outset to lie midway between the discontinuity thesis and the continuity thesis (CP:6.82, 6.87). In another way of putting it, he is outside classical physics with one foot still caught in the door. Movement of something from one place to another in classical physics was defined as a change of spatial position with respect to a change in time. In relativity theory, in contrast, there is no such rate of change in the objective sense, for the observer is inextricably caught "within" one frame of reference or another, all frames of references being relative to some imaginary observer, or better, no observer at all. The rate of change of a space-time computation from within one reference frame would be available for computation from within another reference frame solely with respect to the relative movement of the second frame to the first one (Gerach, 1978). In other words, use of the term *movement* in relativity theory depends, like *simultaneity*, upon a *translation* from the language of the space-time computations of one reference frame to the language of the space-time computations of another reference frame. There can be no *absolute computation* or *description* of any universal phenomena—simultaneous *translation* of all languages into all other languages—from the vantage of an observer trapped "within" the system.

Yet, the Einsteinian notion of a possible mental instantaneous grasp of the whole as if it were in the eternal "now" testifies to the perseverance of mind constructs pointing toward systems of configurations with possible permutations as if permanence and stasis (monism) were more fundamental than movement and change (pluralism)—a topic that will engage us in chapters 6 and 7. But they are not. With due respect to Hartshorne's critique of Peirce, the prevalent world image created by the conflicting views of quantum theory and relativity resurrects the very continuity-discontinuity problem presented here, which has actually been with Western thought at least since Greek antiquity.

First and foremost, the continuity-discontinuity problem is germane to the limitations of language. Natural language, when used as if each word carved a granitic referent out of the world, is not only unreliable for a Parmenidean immutable universe, it is also entirely inadequate if reality is construed as Heraclitean flux or Peircean process. Natural language is an instrument primarily for specifying objects and their attributes, and secondarily what they do or what is done to them. Unlike mathematical language, it is obviously an incapable instrument for giving account of the four-dimensional universe of relativity. And natural language is certainly a poor candidate for providing a "description" of the fleeting events or happenings of the quantum world—the term in quotes is actually a misnomer, because it implies something relatively permanent, thus rendering itself to specification at a given point in time. Moreover, Louis de Broglie (1953:219), who is certainly not alone among twentieth-century scientists, tells us that scientific theories and even the most rigorous of *formal languages* they are embedded in are idealizations. These idealizations

> most likely become less applicable to reality as they become more complete, and hence, contrary to Descartes, nothing is more misleading than a clear and distinct idea, for if it is supposedly clear and distinct, it has no necessary bearing on reality, and if it supposedly has no bearing on reality, it is invariably subject to alterations.[12]

Peirce could not have said it better, this *semiosic* image par excellence. Like the world's furniture, signs and thought, thought-signs, whether ultimately dressed in natural or formal language, are destined to flow along an ongoing stream of perpetual displacement without the possibility of any given sign's being at any moment determinately *there* to be tacked down, contemplated, analyzed, known as it is in the *now* and as it will be in all future *nows*. This provokes knee-jerk reactions from even the most stalwart among us. We almost intuitively scream out for the comforting counterimage of hooks connecting signs to things, for determinate joints in the world. Yet, given the presently emerging view of the universe, of the mind, and of the human semiotic animal from a variety of disciplines, there appears to be no alternative on the distant horizon: the cloud of unknowing lingers above more ominously today than when de Broglie put his words on paper.

In addition to the limitations of language which have created innumerable conundrums and conflicts throughout the course of intellectual history, a preference for what Gerald Holton (1973) has called "themata" has also been a source of constant confusion and debate. For a case in point, Einstein and Bohr locked horns for years over something far greater than either of them: a complete and harmonious account of the universe (see Miller 1978, 1986). The *contrapuntal* give-and-take between these two mental titans was not a mere matter of equations. Rather, it involved the very nature of "reality" at its most basic. Einstein's world existed "out there"; Bohr's depended upon the observer's choice of observing equipment, which brought with it uncertain consequences. Einstein's ultimate "reality" was the "thema" of a space-time continuum; Bohr's came in discrete "chunks." And Einstein's intangible search for determinacy—"God does not play dice," he occasionally remarked—was countered by Bohr's adoption of Heisenberg's *uncertainty principle* and his own *complementarity*.

The notorious double-slit experiment, to be discussed below, uncannily patterns these two antagonistic views. The split beam, like the particle/wave duality itself, is "split-brained." As a particle, the electron is discrete, a no-nonsense, hard-core realist. It is left-brainy, so to speak. As a wave, it is right-brainy: smooth, continuous, holistic, a range of *possibilia*, a thought-sign rather than a thing-sign. The electron's hard-core manifestation generally follows classical mechanics, using variables appropriate for the notion of billiard balls: position, velocity, angular momentum, mass, time. Its soft-core manifestation uses continuous variables somewhat suitable for the effect of dropping a billard ball into a pond of water: wavelength, phase, frequency, amplitude. The real mind-bender is that the schizophrenic "electron" does not stand alone; both of its descriptions can be roughly applied to all "objects." In other words, it appears that the universe may ultimately be a contradictory collusion of two incompatible "themata," with no *translatability* between the languages used to describe each of them.[13]

Moreover, this incompatibility and nontranslatability between languages may well be paralleled by an incompatibility between modes of conception and perception, whether linguistically determined in the Sapir-Whorf sense or the product of everyday language use.[14] Idiosyncratic modes of perception and conception might play a greater role than is generally conceded. Peirce (CP:2.277) was prone to diagrammatic thinking. Popper (1974:182) confesses that he compulsively thinks in schemata. Einstein once claimed he first thought in pictures, thereafter translating his images into their equational form, while Heisenberg, Max Born, and others found concrete imagery disgusting (Hadamard 1945; Miller 1978).[15]

Of course such summary comparisons and contrasts are easily abused, and I will attempt to go no further. The point to be made is that, when all is said and done, and "themata" and nontranslatability of languages notwithstanding, we must concede that ultimately we cannot but "see" the world through filtered goggles. That is to say, to borrow German biologist Jakob von Uexküll's (1957) term, we are locked into our particular species-specific *Umwelt* (see also Thure von Uexküll 1982, 1985, 1986, 1988). Along a functional cycle or information-conveying loop, external signals enter and become internal signals, having been processed in the transition according to our particular capacities. Consequently, each organism, from the amoeba to Einstein, is limited not only to its unique *Umwelt* but also to its experientially unique *Innenwelt*. If an amoeba could write its own physics down on paper, it would differ radically from our physics. Notions of space and time would appear completely bizarre, perhaps entirely unintelligible, from one physics to another. It follows that the "world" of each species is ordinarily taken by that species to be a self-consistent and complete world by way of its particular *Umwelt*. It is for it *simply the way things are*. What lies outside its *Umwelt* does not exist.

In view of Peirce's continuity of mind through time, and the classical mechanics/relativity/quantum theory clash, J. T. Fraser's (1979:22–26; 1982: 30–31) formulation, inspired by von Uexküll, is worthy of note. Fraser divides the various *Umwelten* into *atemporal* (time cannot be recognized by the human being as such), *prototemporal* (time and space are distinguishable, but events and things are interchangeable—i.e., time is symmetrical), *eotemporal* (time is pure succession; it flows, but past-present-future cannot be clearly distinguished), *biotemporal* (that of sentient organisms), and *nootemporal* (beginnings and endings are recognized; self-consciousness and self-identity are possible). It hardly needs mentioning that *bio-nootemporality* and to a degree *eotemporality* are characteristic of the human *Umwelt*. The empirical bodies of classical physics belong to the reversible time of *eotemporality*. At a more basic level, electrons and other kindred entities are confined to *prototemporality,* and photons to *atemporality*.

Photons are in constant flux; their world is intrinsically chaotic and restless. Although from the photon's *Umwelt,* traveling at 300,000 m./sec., the universe would be bleak and dark, an entirely static state of affairs; it would be like the empty "book of assertions," the ultimate Monad containing everything as possibility and nothing as actuality. At the *prototemporal* level of quantum events, in contrast, enduring entities exist, though fleetingly. They resist the idea of permanence and continuity. Of necessity, quantum theoretical formulations generally divide the electron and its immediate cousins into their schizophrenic manifestations in order to make them somewhat intelligible for us from within our *eo-bio-nootemporal* framework, the wave-particle duality being the product of this split. This is fine insofar as it allows the physicist to get on with her equations and the high-school physics instructor to describe the world of *prototemporality* to her students. The electron can be *either* a particle *or* a wave but not both at the same instant. In this sense, the externally "real" is not the really "real" but the product of an *Umwelt:* it is a "semiotically real world." And what would the nimble electron have to say about all this? Most likely little or nothing at all. It is unaware of instants and of linear time. As far as it is concerned from within its *prototemporal* world, it is *both* a particle *and* a wave simultaneously, or *neither* a particle *nor* a wave. Take your pick.

Mind, and mind-generated time, in the sense of Peirce, apparently enter the scene at higher levels. Like *prototemporality,* the most fundamental aspect of the universe of Peirce's Secondness is motion and change in time—as picked up by the roving, restless mind. However, these particulars, viewed from within our *eo-bio-nootemporal Umwelt,* are gathered up into a rather dense concoction of *differences* made into *sameness* and even *identities:* tokens are "typized," individuals become universals, *haecceities* become *quiddities.* One must be aware, nonetheless, that in light of *semiosis,* rest and stasis are not primitive but evolutionary stopping points. They are the temporary repository of matter as effete mind, as habituated mind, for mind, in Peirce's cosmological framework, is primary.

This assumption, in light of the above discussion on the distinction between relativity and quantum theory, bears further commentary.

IV. ONE WAY OR MANY WAYS?: FROM *VAGUENESS* TO THE *FULLNESS OF THINGS.* The relativity concept implies continuous movement of a given entity along its "world-line" within the space-time manifold. The same seems to apply prima facie for movement as change in position during a time interval in classical mechanics. A radical distinction between the classical and the relativist views, however, consists in the latter's implication—as Whitehead insisted—that there can be no timeless localization of atoms, molecules, or elementary particles. There are no substantive singularities in the space-time continuum. If such material entities existed, they would exhibit the property of being cut off from the remainder of the universe; they would be limited to particular spatial ambulatory prisons.

But they are not. Rather, they are tantamount to the product of Peircean *cuts* or Spencer-Brownian *marks,* which are artificially exercised by particular minds, from the human animal to nonhuman organisms, in accord with particular *Umwelten*—those minds being themselves *cuts.* From the quantum theoretical view, the Copenhagen interpretation stipulates—though there is controversy in this regard—a wave "collapse" *(cut)* by an observer-instrument to produce a "particle," which can then be conceived as a discrete entity. In the John Archibald Wheeler (1977, 1980a, 1980b, 1984) rendition of the quantum world, remarkably in line with Peirce and Spencer-Brown, as we shall note in chapters 4 and 5, a *choice* is, so to speak, made. A *question* is then *asked* of the universe, and an *answer distinguished* to yield "stuff" in the space-time field. However, according to the field concept inherent in relativity theory as I understand it, what appears as discrete "stuff" is actually a "knot" in the continuum which is not an absolute singularity but is connected, hyperbolically or asymptotically as it were, with every other "knot" in the field. That is to say, the "warp" in the field's embrace of the "knot" curves hyperbolically without ever "cutting" itself off "entirely" from the field, much like the ripples of a pond which are a perturbation yet a manifestation of the pond's continuity (in general see Capra 1975). *Cuts* are, in this sense—and as Spencer-Brown takes pains to explain—artificial mutilations of the universe as an interconnected fabric.

Mendel Sachs (1988) presents an intriguing survey of the ongoing controversy surrounding the conflicting relativistic and quantum theoretical conceptions of the world. As I intimated above, through the ages, cosmologies have generally inclined toward one of two "themata": matter as discrete or as continuous. The most recent scientific revolution, in contrast, has not been able to shake its *schizophrenic* character. Relativity on the whole implies a continuum view of matter in terms of the field concept, while quantum theory is essentially atomistic, yet of a different sort from classical atomism.[16] In another, rather cryptic, way of putting it, and in light of Fraser's categories, Einstein's view is largely *eotemporal*—though devoid of the infinitely extended continuity of classical time and space. In contrast, Bohr's quantum theoretical view is largely *prototemporal*—though devoid of the observer/observed break inherent in classical mechanics (Fraser 1982:93–94). In a loose sense the probabilistic character of the *prototemporal* world is an evolutionary step between *atemporal* chaos and *eotemporal* determinism, the shimmering, scintillating vacillation of the *prototemporal* domain between particle/wave, *this/that*, having conjoined otherwise *inconsistent* antagonists (Fraser 1982:69–70).

Significantly enough, the quantum theoretical view is roughly commensurate with Peirce's (CP:5.505) concept of *vagueness,* which has no use for the principle of noncontradiction. In contrast, the continuous field of relativity is a counterpart to Peirce's *generality,* which renders the excluded middle impotent, though, from any given reference frame, information and hence knowledge must inextricably remain *incomplete*—it can be at best only approximated. *Vagueness* implies a *plurality* of possibles (Firsts) some of which will eventually be actualized (as Seconds) at different times and places. *Generality* calls for a synthetic grasp of that which is actualized with respect to those possibles that remain as such, though they could just as well have popped up instead. Were this synthetic whole to be had in one cognitive grasp, the Final Interpretant would be realized. This being impossible, a given sign of *generality,* an interpretant which is inexorably *incomplete,* is destined to pass away into its successor just as it emerged from its predecessor.

Now, to place this image within an even broader framework. The ultimate ramifications of the *semiosic* process—the Final Interpretant, Determinism, Law, Regularity, Habit, *Generality*—imply a continuous *(synechistic)* domain. This *semiosic* goal, the Final Interpretant, is not for the kingdom of this world, however. A perceptual—as well, we must suppose, as a conceptual—grasp of it will always remain unrealized—i.e., *incomplete*—for the immanent observer-interpreter-knower. On the other hand, pure indeterminism, pure chance, belongs to the *tychistic* field. It is unbounded; everything can possibly be and anything can presumably go. Consequently, since the noncontradiction principle does not apply, the system remains *inconsistent, vague.* Yet the immanent, finite observer-interpreter-knower persists in her push toward a modicum of certainty, determinacy, consistency, and clarity. Hence she naturally inclines to flee from *vagueness* toward *generality,* but without being able to either fall back on the one or reach the other.

The continuous, synechistic domain of Thirdness evinces symmetry between observer-interpreter-knower and observed-interpretant-known, and non-linearity. Such is comparable to relativity's four-dimensional space-time domain for the mapping of all components of the *semiosic* fabric within its enclosure. In contrast, the tychistic domain of Firstness is an open system of possibilities, a portion of which can be actualized into Seconds (elementary "particles")—recall the *selective* and *nonselective* domains, and Peirce's "book of assertions." This system entails asymmetry between observer-interpreter-knower and observed-interpretant-known, and linearity in terms of the stream of signs becoming other signs ad infinitum. Such is the separate spatial and temporal actualization of individual signs from within the indeterminate domain of possibilities. Roughly, such also is the universe of *complementarity* as defined by Copenhagen quantum theory.

The first system is, relatively speaking, *objective:* sign features are dependent upon their interpreters. Hence a sign, its interpretation remaining, as it were, indeterminate, leaves to the interpreter the right of pushing the determination of its interpretation toward completion for herself. The second system is relatively *subjective:* sign features depend upon other signs in order that their indeterminate interpretation may progress along the rail leading toward completion (CP:5.505). The *objective* view is reversible. The interpreter is separated (she separates herself) from the *semiosic* field, expanding her vision nonlinearly to encompass ever-broader parameters. Ultimately, the mind as sign can theoretically and potentially—though not in actual practice—become coterminous with the field of signs. As such both would have attained the final state of *generality*—Parmenidean stasis. The *subjective* view, in contrast, is irreversible. The interpreter is not separated from but is in inextricable interrelationship with signs, and, as it were, she interacts with another utterer or with her other self in an ongoing linear movement. Nothing is at a standstill. There is constant activity on both sides of the equation, between *this* and *that,* which are never equal to one another, for the interaction perpetuates itself—Heraclitean flux. But neither state in its totality, to repeat, is of this world of finitude: *we are victims of our own immanence.* The way of *generality* presumes some inaccessible "real world" embodying the Grand Truth; the way of *vagueness* allows for a picking and choosing of many little truths—all of them to a greater or lesser degree fictions, or fables.

Yet the fact remains that Peirce's doctrine of signs is a rather contradictory fusion of these two extremes. Ontologically he appears to be an idealist, though he holds to his faith in an objective world "out there." Epistemologically or methodologically he is a realist or objectivist, though his seeker of knowledge could never know the truth if he had it. He could not completely know it, as it were, because of the indeterminacy of meaning and therefore knowledge, which is reflected in the failure of the excluded-middle principle—that is, in the inevitable degree of *generality* in any and all determinations—and in the breakdown of the noncontradiction principle, which breeds *vagueness* of different sorts. Through the centuries various thinkers dwelling on human limitations from Heraclitus onward have arrived at the conclusion that the universe is *indetermined* and *indeterminate*. It cannot therefore be the object of total and precise knowledge, but only a partial and conjectural one, an image harking back ot Xenophanes and forward to Karl Popper, who occasionally delights in quoting the Greek. An indeterminate universe giving rise to indeterminacy of knowledge entails centerlessness, which has been a bane for those tirelessly in search of certainty and a soporific for those embracing segments of the spectrum, from wide-eyed liberalism to deconstructionism to hard-line relativism to full-throttle nihilism—not to mention Feyerabend's "epistemological anarchism." All disciplines have been flooded with what is conceived as this vice, virus, or vigor, depending upon the eye of the beholder. In the words of Lewis Thomas (1980):

> We have learned that we do not really understand nature at all, and the more information we receive, the more strange and mystifying is the picture before us. . . . There is no center holding anywhere, as far as we can see, and we can see great distances. What we thought to be the great laws of physics turn out to be local ordinances, subject to revision any day. . . . . It is, when you give it a thought, shocking.

Or as Peirce would say, nature is the ultimate "outward clash" which surprises. This "clash" can give way to mystery, or Einstein's "subtle is the lord." It has also awakened the West from the epistemological somnambulism Nietzsche (1968:2) anticipated in 1885: "Since Copernicus man has been rolling from the center toward X: the aim is lacking; 'why' finds no answer." Freud found the same "clash" in the unconscious, concluding that the "I" is not the master of its own vessel. Descartes's certainty becomes for Freud's unconscious, as for Peirce's *semiosis,* a sign perpetually displaced by other signs. Indeed, dreams, slips, lost memory traces, lapses are symptomatic of what Freud described as "overdetermined." But "determination" as used here has little to do with classical linear causality. Signs in this scheme have no simple one-to-one meaning. Rather, each sign points toward a nonlinear multiplicity of possible pathways, each with the hope of a pot of gold at the end. The sign is "determined" only in the sense that it was drawn from another sign, and that from another sign, and so on. This "determination" is perpetually open-ended, like that of language itself, of thought, of mental "objects," of the "real." Just as there are many ways, potentially an infinity of ways, of explaining a relatively rich and complex concept, so there is potentially an infinity of descriptions of both the positive and negative properties of a "semiotic object" "out there."

Regarding *vagueness* and *generality* further insofar as they bear on indeterminacy, consider, for a moment, the Tao. It is notorious that any idea of the Tao can be no more than vague and imprecise. Then how can it be defined? It cannot be, any more than other vague concepts such as mind, beauty, the good, freedom, and so on, which have confounded philosophers for centuries. If such "entities" or "things" or whatever we choose to call them are necessarily vague, then should not our idea of them be correspondingly vague as well? Any feasible response would appear to be affirmative. In such case the character of the idea would be a picture or mirror image of the "thing" of which it is an idea, hence by virtue of the logical positivist's picture theory of meaning the idea would be accurate rather than vague precisely because of its capacity for mirroring that which is vague.

In other words, the idea would be precise because it is a faithful picture, but imprecise because that which it pictures is vague. Furthermore, according to Peirce, the *idea of* the originary vague sign is itself a sign, and in such case, it must *resemble* it (iconically), *indicate* it (indexically), or *say* it (symbolically) by an inferentially grounded proposition or argument. If the picture theory is not acceptable—which it is not, in the framework of Peirce's semiotic—then *resemblance* is suspect. Indexicality and symbolism are not likely candidates either, for a "quite universal" concept or idea would as such be unrelated to an "other"; it would possess no Secondness or Thirdness. Then how comes it that this orginary universal sign is vague? Insofar as it is vague, it is like the Tao. Any precise idea of the Tao would be imprecise because of its very precision, hence it would be absolutely distinct from the Tao in that it is precise, but the Tao is not precise, hence the idea of it is insufficient. Any idea of the Tao must be as vague as is the Tao itself (Smullyan 1977:11–12).

Now, any respectable logical positivist would declare the proposition "The originary sign (Tao) is vague and general" to be neither true nor false but meaningless. Moreover, she would claim the ability to prove its meaninglessness by irrefutable logic, thus assuring us that it cannot fall into either the category of truth or that of falsity. In other words, following Peirce's idea that noncontradiction is ipso facto inapplicable to the vague sign and the excluded-middle principle to the general sign, our logical positivist would demonstrate that the proposition "The originary sign (Tao) is vague and general" is vague and general. And she would in a sense be correct. Not only is it vague and general and therefore by and large meaningless—according to her stringently limited notion of meaning—but it is absolutely yet indeterminately vague and general.

The vague sign, then, is *inconsistent* as well as *indeterminate* (truth or falsity is *undecidable*). And the general sign is *incomplete* as well as *indeterminate*. Indeterminacy is the character par excellence of the Monad, the unary sign, the icon, Firstness, as it is of the mediary sign, the symbol, Thirdness (CP:1.468).

V. IT BECOMES A MATTER OF THE SELF AND ITS OTHERS. Interestingly enough, according to currently accepted limitations on knowledge, and especially following Gödel, if a sufficiently rich formal system presents itself as *complete* and self-sufficient, then it has an *inconsistency* hidden away somewhere in the closet; and if it is *consistent,* then it cannot but be *incomplete.* From the broadest possible view, the *inconsistency* of *vagueness*—or by implication, the quantum theoretical formulation—prevents *completeness,* since something cannot be, to use our above examaple, both a particle and a wave. In

contrast, *generality* in the absolute sense demands *completeness* or nothing at all. But, as we have noted, there is no absolute *generality* in a finite world. Of course, from one reference frame an entity can appear as a particle and from another as a wave, but, since perspective is inevitably bound to particular reference frames, there can be no completeness *for* generality. On the other hand, though *vagueness* bans noncontradiction from its playground, it cannot entertain the actualization (into Secondness) of two inconsistent entities at the same instant: they are, so to speak, *complementary,* to be seen as one or the other alternately. Thus the inexorable *incompleteness* of *generality* and the *inconsistency* of *vagueness* are enforced. *Generality* and *vagueness* are in this manner themselves *complementary* at a more general level.

To take the analogy further, if I may be so permitted, the "quantum theoretical" or *vague* aspect of *semiosis* is *indeterminate* and *linear,* from First to Second. There must be a separate space-time property of each sign instantiation and its relation to and interaction with its "semiotically real" object. Such interaction implies, given Peirce's *pragmatic maxim,* contextualized action regarding the manipulation of signs. That is, before the truth of a given proposition can be established, we must determine its meaning, and to that end Peirce provided a criterion for meaning, his *maxim,* which states: "Consider what effects that might conceivably have practical bearings, we conceive the object of our conception to have. Then our conception of these effects is the whole of our conception of the object" (5.402).

What Peirce seems to be saying is that the meaning of a proposition is given in another proposition, and that in another, ad infinitum, all of them calling for some conceivable test, as a result of observable properties that one would expect under certain circumstances if the original proposition were true. Since the semiotic web is indefinite and, as far as the finite thinker is concerned, for practical purposes infinite in extension, the meaning of the original proposition, therefore, is destined to remain indeterminate.[17]

Moreover, such activity as called for by the proposition is subjective (i.e., mind-dependent). The "semiotically real" can itself be composed of *contradictory,* or *complementary,* alternatives, such as the switching of the two possible interpretants of a Necker cube as it flip-flops from face up to face down, and back again. In contrast, the "semiotically real object" and the "real object" will continue to be intransigently incompatible on certain points, for the finite community at least. There is saving grace, however, inasmuch as the sign and its "semiotically real object" can approximate (hopefully at least) the "real." Pragmatically speaking, then, each proposition can take on a particular context-dependent meaning, which is also dependent upon the context-dependent meanings of all related propositions, which, practically speaking, renders impossible any absolutely determinate meaning *for* some interpreter *in* a particular context.[18]

On the other hand, the "relativistic" or potentially *general* aspect of *semiosis* is, over the theoretical long haul of things, *determinate* and *nonlinear:* Thirdness. All sign entities in the semiotic field can theoretically be continuously mapped one onto another at certain points, hence the same space-time framework applies to them as a whole. Relations between signs are also theoretically "real"; they pertain to a given "semiotic reality." *Generality,* insofar as it applies to the "real," should be completely objective. This is, however, the *ideal* which can be no more than approximated. The "semiotically real" *general* sign is, and will always be for the finite mind, *incomplete.*

Thus the "clash" between First and Second, on the one hand, and Third, on the other, to yield "First-Second/Third," illustrates (1) *complementarity* relations between the two sides of the virgule, (2) the dual nature of the asymptote metaphor, and (3) inherent *inconsistency* and *incompleteness* of all "semiotically real" conceptions of the world. There appears to be a basic distinction, then, between *law* (Thirdness—and, by extension, the *general* laws of nature) and *rules* governing our *Umwelt*-generated perception and conception of the furniture of the world (items of Secondness as semiotic *actualizations* of the *possibilities* of Firstness). *Law,* that is, *law* as the final interpretant, the fullness of all things, requires reversibility (time symmetry), continuity, and determinacy regarding the flow of events. In contrast, our perceived and conceived world requires irreversibility, discrete events, and acausality (probability of happenings, natural selection, or, at the highest levels, selection by free will).

Law is the law of generation (of the Final Interpretant), which implies the end of the long trail having been reached, for every *would be* has been actualized as a *this-hereness.* The process is a fait accompli. The Minkowski "block" universe this concept evokes entails determinism, "objectivity" (subject/object), and limitlessness. On the other side of the ledger, *semiosis* is the ongoing flux of sign interaction. It is the locus of information to be processed—the "reading" of signs—during one's perceiving-conceiving the world, or, at the *micro-level,* during measurement in quantum theory. It is linear, irreversible, and time-dependent for the finite, limited, immanent observer, the subject-object dichotomy having been dissolved. The whole picture, including process and product, the stream of signs and its congealment, is possible solely by way of this Heraclitean conflictive interplay of opposites: the possible-actual on one side and *law* on the other, or Firstness-Secondness on one side and Thirdness on the other. In a nutshell, then, the *complementary incompatibilities* I have alluded to in the immediately preceding discussion are, once again, quite comparably those between quantum theory and relativity (see Sachs 1988; Pattee 1982).[19]

It is significant to note that Peirce struggled with a related complementary theme with respect to his two types of "other": (1) the interaction between the self and the social and physical *Other* "out there," and (2) the dialogue between the self and its *other* inner self. For Peirce the self does not attain a state of self-awareness—awareness of its *other* self—until it has erred regarding its perception and conception of the *Other* "out there." When this occurs, the self artificially extricates itself from everything else in the universe which leads, residually, to what it *is not* as an objective realm set in the context of time and space—and the Cartesian split suffers its first birth pains. Yet this move is necessary, though it need not necessarily be taken to its extreme manifestation.

That is, there can be mindfulness of self and/in the *Other* rather than self pitted *against* the *Other*. Indeed, this relationship, which can be written self/*other*// *Other*, is a double binary which generates a triad, and what is most significant, a complementarity relationship.

The self is a curious and unique some- "thing." One assumes in general that it somehow represents an "object," "I-me," which functions in the external world as do all other objects. Yet it is nonempirical. As an "object" it is at most only partly available to any form of sensory experience. It is chiefly the product of imagination: it is inferred. One problem is that the self is not unary but binary in nature, and in addition, like all signs, it manifests a trinary character. For Descartes self-consciousness is immediately intuited, and the self is autonomous: it is primary, existing independently of all external constraints. In contrast, Peirce's radically anti-Cartesian posture envisages a self which, like all signs, becomes external upon addressing itself to some other (CP:5.253; also Michaels 1977). In fact, it must determine some other, which is the task of all signs. In this sense, the self becomes aware of itself on becoming aware of what it *is not*, of the nonself, the *Other* (CP:1.324).

This becoming of awareness entails action/reaction, Secondness, the "real." During the rough and tumble of everyday life we are constantly "bumping up against hard fact." We develop habits and generate expectations, rather mindlessly taking things for granted as simply the way the world works. But the world inevitably sets up a resistance against our imposing ourselves upon it; it forces surprises on us, which constantly remind the self of what it *is not*. This notion of the "other, of *not*, becomes a very pivot of thought" (CP:1.324). Secondness is predominant in this scheme because it is essential to the very idea of "reality," for the "real" is that which "insists upon forcing its way to recognition as something *Other* than the mind's creation" (CP:1.325).

The "real" is *actual*, though of course it is *Other*. In conjunction with the self it makes up the other pole of a dyad. But the "real" is not immediately present *to* consciousness *as* such and such. Consciousness becomes aware *of* the "real" solely by trinary mediation—Thirdness—between itself and that *Other*, and by inference, as it were. That is, there is no time in the "present instant" for an inference, least of all for an inference concerning that very instant. An inference is possible only mediately, after the occurrence of a new event. This new event in the form of a surprise shocks one to attention such that one can then generate an inference regarding (1) the break between that which was expected and the event that is perceived to have occurred, and (2) the reason for such a break in the first place. Consciousness *of* must be mediate, Peirce argues, since the presence of the "real" has no respect for one's will or wishes; consciousness *of* is not merely dependent upon an act of volition. This implies that the immediately present is conative rather than perceptive. Consequently, consciousness *of* the "real" present is a perpetual struggle over what was expected and what is perceived actually to take place, the break between them evoking an incessant call for revamped expectations (CP:5.462).

One is in some sense immediately conscious of one's feelings, of course, but they are not feelings of a self-conscious *ego,* for the ego-self is inferred rather than immediate (CP:5.462). Peirce suggests that we are in command of no power by which an intuition can directly and immediately be known. An intuition must exist at some primordial first instant, and for it to be an intuition in the full Cartesian sense, apprehension *of* it *as* a cognition must occur at the selfsame instant; that is, it must be an event occupying no time. But since for Peirce, (1) any and all cognitions are always in a *process* of becoming and passing away, (2) it is impossible to know intuitively if a given cognition is not determined by a previous one, and (3) a cognition, like a perception, is not available *to* consciousness except mediately, then (4) there can be no apprehension of an intuition in the blink of an instant (CP:5.264–317).

Given that any cognition for Peirce is consciousness *of* an object *as* represented *to* self-consciousness, he means to say the same of one's knowledge *of* or consciousness *of* one's self. Such self-consciousness is not "a mere feeling of subjective conditions of consciousness, but of our personal selves. Pure apperception is the self-assertion of the *ego;* the self-consciousness here meant is the recognition of my *private* self. I know that I (not merely *the* I) exist" (CP:5.225).

Kant once suggested—and Peirce agrees on this point—that the retarded use of the "I" in children, since they manifest other powers of thought at an earlier age, was evidence of an undeveloped self-consciousness in them. When a child hears, say, a bell, she does not become aware *of* herself *as* hearing something which she herself *is not;* she is merely aware of some object which is making a sound. Or when she "wills" to move a table, she does not become aware *of* herself *as* desiring that the table be displaced, only that an object is fit to be moved (CP:5.230). The child soon discovers the relationship between objects "out there" and her own body as another object, which raises it to a level of importance and centrality. And later, after learning a language, the child is subject to sentences such as the warning "The stove is hot." And so long as she never comes into contact with the stove, she will not know whether it is actually hot or not. If she touches it, on the other hand, the sentence is verified in a striking way:

> Thus [s]he becomes aware of ignorance, and it is necessary to suppose a *self* in which this ignorance can inhere. So testimony gives the first dawning of self-consciousness. . . . In short, *error* appears, and it can be explained only by supposing a *self* which is fallible. Ignorance and error are all that distinguish our private selves from the absolute *ego* of pure apperception. (CP:5.233–35)

On so speaking of the *ego,* Peirce refers to the triad *feeling-volition-cognition.* Feeling is Firstness, quality. Volition is dual: force and resistance, agent and patient, *self* and *Other.* The shock of an unexpected event is volitional, the result of interaction between the self and the "real," which gives rise to dyadic consciousness *of* an *ego* and a *nonego* (CP:1.334–35). Cognition, or Thirdness, is the *process* of mediating between feelings and volitions. Metaphorically put: "Position is first, velocity or the relation of two successive positions is second, acceleration or the relation of three successive positions third" (CP:1.337). Peirce's analogy is apropos. Velocity is continuous, but there is merely change of position. In contrast, acceleration is continuous change *of* change; both position and velocity undergo successive alteration.

Quite obviously, feeling, volition, and cognition correspond to Peirce's tripartite sign. The *representamen* is immediate. That for which it stands, the *object,* is *other than* the self and subject to volition. And the idea to which the representamen gives rise is its *interpretant,* which entails cognitive activity. The object *of* representation is not the "actually real" but a "semiotically real object" represented by the sign, so the object of representation can be none other than another representation of which the first representation is the interpretant, and an endless train of representations can be conceived to have the "absolutely real" object behind it as a limit, which can no more than be approximated asymptotically (CP:1.339).[20] In brief, every interpretant becomes a sign-representation in the ongoing *semiosic* process. Like position, the sign *stands for* the "semiotically real object," which is moved along by the incessant transmutation of interpretants into sign-representations. And the interpretant, as mover, accelerates the sign, like the force of gravity at 32 ft./sec./sec. or the expanding universe which brings about the "red shift" phenomenon, toward the ideal limit.

This brings up the point, introduced above, that in addition to the external *Other,* there exists an internal one, the *other* self created by the passing of a sign into an interpretant, an interpretant into a sign, and the self of one moment into the self of another. The radical absence of the self from its *other* self, semiotically (i.e., symbolically) evidenced by shifters, creates not a stable but a restless *semiosis* incessantly sliding along the slope of signification. This renders the timeless identity of the self impossible: the self cannot be itself in the immediate present, but only what it *was not* during the moment past, and what it *not yet is,* what it *will be,* in the future moment.

However, the *Other,* above all, remains elusive. Regarding the sign triad, the interpretant is acknowledgment of the *Other* by way of mediation between representamen and object. But since it is itself another representamen whose interpretant is yet another one, ad infinitum, its self-identity incessantly conceals itself, and, as Derrida (1974:49) says of the signified, it is always on the move. The *Other* to which consciousness points via the interpretant is never fully present, though its presence is always felt, since the "real" represented by signs as the "semiotically real" remains as fugitive alterity and absence: "In the idea of reality, secondness is predominant; for the real is that which insists upon forcing its way to recognition as the mind's creation" (CP:1.326). The "real" conceived as *Other* is in this manner resistance, surprise, a subversion of exteriority against the self-conscious self.

But this sense of exteriority, of the presence of a *nonego* "which accompanies perception generally and helps to distinguish it from dreaming" (CP:1.332), is not merely a sense of the world "out there." It is the product, rather, of the *dialogic* self-*other,* "I-me," the "me" resting tenuously between the "I" and the "it," which constitutes the "real." Freud's (1925) concept of negation also bears on the "I-it" interaction. The prononoun *it* marks an irreversible loss of the self's self-presence, the self's "me" as absent from its "I." The child initially uses *it* to designate what will later correspond to its own displaced self. At this early stage there is no subject/object, no inner/outer. Gradually the "it" transmutes into "me" and becomes "outside" and "alien," in contrast to the "inside" and generally conceived "presentness" of the "I."

And thus Peirce's train of signs embodied in the "I-me" dialogue has lurched from the starting blocks. When one is thinking, the "I" uses signs by means of which to persuade the "me" that something or other is the case. In this activity,

> a person is not abolutely an individual. His thoughts are what he is "saying to himself," that is, saying to that other self that is just coming into life in the flow of time. When one reasons, it is that critical self that one is trying to persuade, and all thought whatsoever is a sign, and is mostly of the nature of language. The second thing to remember is that the man's circle of society (however widely or narrowly this phrase may be understood), is a sort of loosely compacted person, in some respects of higher rank than the person of an individual organism. (CP:5.421)

In other words, the immediate "I" as First (icon) refers to the object (index) or that which is the object of persuasion, in addressing itself to the *other,* the interpretant (symbol) in the process of "coming into life in the flow of time," which in turn becomes itself a sign with its own object (CP:2.274).

This *other-Other* concept is illustrated by the two "Borgeses" of that remarkable little tale "Borges and I" (1962:246–47). The sentient Borges (Borges$_1$) is the "subject" whose life "is a flight," for he loses more and more to the writer Borges (Borges$_2$), the "predicate." Borges$_2$, the fictional being who appears only in the mail, on lists of professors, or in biographical dictionaries, appropriates more and more of Borges$_1$, who retreats into ever-smaller subframes. At the precise moment when Borges$_2$ completely takes over, specific reference to either of the two disappears. THE BORGES (Borges$_1$ *and* Borges$_2$) now exercises his dominance. There is no longer any line of demarcation between "subject" *and* "predicate" ("object"). THE BORGES is self-contained and self-sufficient: he *is* as he *is*. As such there can be no inconsistency or incompatibility between the two because there is no external reference point from which to make a cut between the one and the other. But as such neither can any fictions—i.e., the fictional Borges$_2$—be constructed from "within" the system, for fictions require (1) the existence of two *partly inconsistent* frames, and (2) *incompleteness*, such that a potentially infinite regress of metaframes can theoretically be constructed (see Merrell 1983). The status of THE BORGES, then, is at the meso-cosmic level equivalent to the cosmic experience of the ineffable totality within which the self is contained. In this state, nothing is marked or cut, there are no frames, and hence fictionality (i.e., what the "real" in part is *not*) is no longer possible, for all simply *is*. There is no longer any dialogue.

Thus the self-*other* relation emerging from the self-*Other* entails separation *and* union. Self and *other* are from one vantage logically distinct entities. The self enters into *dialogue* with its *other* and that *other* with the self, as separate selves in mutual relation. At the same time, from an alternate vantage, self and *other* are one, continuous and inseparable, a self-referential unity. In this respect the relation is closed rather than open, like the self-*Other* relation. But the question arises: How can the individual self come into existence if the self-*other* is an indivisible whole? An answer might be forthcoming, once again, in view of Peirce's asymptote. Self-*other* as an indivisible whole appears in the sense of a tenuous approximation to that ideal goal, when all dialogue ceases, when total Oneness prevails, and Truth in all its plenitude is made manifest: the self-*other,* that is, the interpreter, at this point becomes coterminous with the ultimate interpretant.

In addition, there is an approximation in the opposite direction toward the ideal self-*Other* relation wherein the self itself has reached finality: it is an absolute absolutely set apart from the absolute *Other.* Yet, as an approximation, there is no more than an illusion of the categorical split between the one and the other; there is always at least a modicum of oneness in the self-*Other* interaction (much like the *Yin/Yang* complementarity, which likely influenced Bohr in the development of his quantum principle). In other words, self-*Other* does not entail the same ontological status as self-*other;* rather, the apparent objectivity of the self in this case is over the long haul an *idea,* an inference, an artificial construct. It is the manifestation of a whole arrived at by reflection on what the *that* is and why it is *other than this.* Solely the self-*other* state is capable of erecting the self-*Other* construct, but the self-*Other* must be acknowledged in terms of something *other than* what it otherwise would have been—i.e., when there is awareness of error. Without the self-*Other* there can be no scientific discourse. In fact, there can be no *dialogue* whatsoever from which the self-*Other* can arise.[21]

The observing self, then, is only apparently an autonomous subject, and the *Other* only appears to be an object "out there" and ready to be manipulated by the subject. Once more, there is neither exclusively one nor many, continuity nor discontinuity, but perpetual interplay between them. In contrast, there is an ordinarily *contradictory* yet *complementary* relation between self-*other* and self-*Other* which in turn *complements* the *complementarity* between self and *other* and self and *Other.* If self-*other* and self-*Other* were a continuous, inseparable whole, it would undoubtedly evince qualities comparable to the *Tao* of Lao Tzu. It would *be* simply *that which is,* outside all sensation of time, space, and "stuff." It would be ontologically prior to all existent things: a closed, recursively autonomous, symmetrical, timeless system—tantamount to the Minkowski "block" or the originary Monad. In contrast, combining the two pairs to form self/*other*//*Other* creates a *complementary* relationship. In one of his earlier formulations of complementarity, Bohr (1934:91) concluded that the concept "bears a deep-going analogy to the general difficulty in the formulation of human ideas, inherent in the distinction between subject and object." Since that time, there have been few discussions of the problem of measurement or the meaning of quantum explanations without invoking the mind (self-*other*) of the observer as an irreducible element.

This *schizophrenic* collusion of many and one, of holism and atomism, that is, this *contradictory complementarity,* an important aspect of contemporary thought especially regarding both the quantum world and relativity, is, most significantly, patterned in Peirce's own metaphysical *schizophrenia.*

T W O *Bohm's Tropology and*

Peirce's Typology

I. OF THE BUDDHIST SELF-REFLECTING STRING OF PEARLS. I engaged in the above digressions before returning to the thread of the Peirce-Hartshorne debate for a specific purpose. David Bohm's metaphysics, which I shall in this chapter relate to Peirce's doctrine of signs, cannot be divorced from the concepts of continuity and mind (or self-*other*). Nor does the mind/matter dichotomy apply. To put it rather cryptically, just as Einstein introduced us to the space-time continuum, so Peirce and Bohm, among others, and from within rather distinct conceptual frameworks, ushered in the mind-matter continuum.

At the outset I should point out that although quantum theory and relativity are incompatible on many counts, they share the fundamental premises that (1) the universe is an interconnected whole, a Monad; dichotomies of space and time, matter-energy and information, gravity and inertia, are actually different aspects of the same phenomena; and (2) there is no such thing as observing—setting oneself *apart from*—this interactive whole with respect to a neutral frame of reference; necessarily, irrevocably, and paradoxically, we are inside the fabric (Sachs 1988).[1] In other words, the *selected* cannot be coterminous with the *nonselected*. Since the early days of the Copenhagen interpretation, it has become evident that modern physics must divide the world not into things but into connections, that is, relations. The world consequently begins to appear "as a complicated tissue of events, in which connections of different kinds alternate or overlap or combine and thereby determine the texture of the whole" (Heisenberg 1958a:107).

Bohm (1957, 1977, 1980) has extrapolated this concept to the extreme. He reminds us that the classical notion of independent atoms making up the universe has been completely overthrown by modern science, hence it should now be asserted that an inseparable "quantum interconnectedness" constitutes the fundamental "reality," and that to conceive of independently behaving parts is

erroneous, for they are merely individual and contingent. This unbroken wholeness cannot be subject to localization, nor can it be explicitly describable: it is,
comparable to the pure Monad, simply *that which is*. Bohm painstakingly argues
that the undivided whole is—much like Peirce's initial (uncut) plastic book of
assertions—*n*-dimensional and atemporal, and it cannot be handled in any way
whatever by three-dimensional thought. Indeed, Bohm maintains that we must
now develop an entirely new conception of things more distinct from Descartes
than Descartes was from the Greeks.

The postulate of undivided wholeness is rooted in a strange feature of
quantum theory sometimes called "phase entanglement," which arises when two
or more entities capable of manifesting both wavelike and particlelike characteristics interact (see especially Herbert 1985). Whenever two such entities meet, so
also do their representative "proxy waves," which merge into a whole. Then,
after their momentum has carried them great distances apart, their wave phases
remain entangled in such a way that an interference effect on one entity will
instantaneously be transmitted to the other.[2] Ordinary waves, say, those of the
surface of a pond, do not become phase entangled because, unlike quantum
entities, they do not occur in what is called "configuration space." This space of
n-dimensions—rather than one, two, or three dimensions, such as waves along a
taut rope, on the surface of the pond, or sound waves, respectively—requires
three dimensions for each entity. Two entities reside in six-dimensional space,
three in nine-dimensional space, and so on. There is no upper limit. The
disconcerting feature of phase entanglement is that, on paper at least, there
appears to be action at a distance: in multidimensional space, action on one entity
can have an instantaneous effect on another, though information cannot pass
between them in the conventional form because it is, according to relativity
theory, limited by the speed of light. This apparently unexplainable phenomenon
is, precisely, the essence of Bohm's cosmology (Herbert 1985:168–72).[3]

Bohm's undifferentiated whole, which he terms the *enfolded,* or *implicate,*
order, is comparable to Peirce's ultimate Firstness or the Monad as what *might be*
before there is any originary *cut* and mediary consciousness *of* it. It is continuous
and self-contained; it entails the process of coming into being of the *thisness* of
things. On the other hand, the actualized world of particulars, the *unfolded,* or
explicate, order, is secondary to the primary implicate order, as is Peirce's
Secondness to Firstness.[4] The implicate order, Bohm tells us, indicates an entire
realm not hitherto afforded serious attention in physics, chiefly because it
demands an entirely new mindset. The equivalent of the unfolded or explicate
order was the focus of classical mechanics, whose analysis of phenomena into
separate points along the Cartesian coordinates constituted the general understanding of the universe. Relativity and quantum theory have not entirely
departed from these classical methods. In contrast, Bohm proposes that in the
most general sense, quantum theory calls for an exceedingly broader and more
fundamental conception than the classical paradigm: his implicate order. The
essential notion of movement, implicit in quantum theory, is, Bohm (1977:39)
argues, "not that of an object translating itself from one place to another, but

rather, it is a folding and unfolding, in which the object is continually being created again, in a form generally similar to what it was, though different in detail." Since the infinity of factors determining what an entity is at a given instant changes in the next instant, though ever so slightly, everything is in constant change, and nothing can remain identical with itself over time (e.g., *Shiva's dance*) (Bohm 1957:155). The explicate order, on the other hand, is mere appearance (e.g., *Maya*). It is abstracted from the implicate order on which it depends and from which it derives its whole form and set of characteristic relationships (Bohm 1977:39).

Bohm illustrates the relationship between the two orders with a metaphor. If we put some viscous fluid such as glycerine in a container, place a drop of insoluble dye close to one edge, and stir the mixture slowly with a mechanical device, the dye is "stretched" out in a circle until it seems to disappear. It is still *there*, but it is now *enfolded, implicate*. Merely because an entity is not empirically available to us—i.e., *nonselected*—Bohm hastens to add, is no guarantee that it is not "real"—and here the "realism" of Whitehead and Peirce, discussed in chapter 1, comes into view. Now if we slowly reverse the rotation of the stirring device, the drop reappears in its previous form. It has become *unfolded, explicate*. The important point is that during the entire experiment, the dye was part of the whole of things. While in its *enfolded (nonselected)* condition, it existed in an unactualized state. It was simply *there* potentially to become *explicated (selected)* (Bohm 1980:149–56). The combination of the *implicate order* (possibilities) and the *explicate order* (actualities) is what Bohm (1957:133–35) terms the *qualitative infinity of nature*. Much like Whitehead, he argues that there can be no end to the levels of interconnected networks, from the infinitely great to the infinitely small, such that there is no end to the number of perspectives. In fact, Bohm's implicate might conceivably be an explicate from somewhere else in another dimension.

In his early work, Bohm relates the qualitative infinity of nature to a *background* and *substrate* (recall Peirce's and Whitehead's concepts of "background" and "mutually implicative"). Every entity, however fundamental, depends for its existence on the maintenance of appropriate conditions in its infinite background and substructure. These conditions, in turn, are affected by their mutual interconnections and interactions with the entities under study, hence the explicate and the implicate cannot be separated. In this manner, the seamless fabric of the implicate exercises an influence on a set of explicate entities, and vice versa. This interaction Bohm (1957:144) calls the *reciprocal relationship*. Such a replete universe reminds one of the rabbinical idea of a scroll where the blank spaces take on importance equal to that of the actual ciphers.

Bohm (1980:186–89) also speaks of the implicate order as a higher-dimensional reality which projects into lower-dimensional elements to endow them with nonlocal and noncausal relationships. This higher-dimensional order obviously approaches randomness. But it is not absolutely random, because it possesses regularities capable of generating a myriad diversity of entities as space-time events. Nonetheless, as Bohm takes pains to argue, it is *n*-dimensional and atemporal, hence it cannot be cognized or handled in any fashion whatsoever by conventional thought and by the languages, both formal and natural, now used in physics. It is available solely to intuitive faculties, if at all. But, of course, we have already heard about such a higher-dimensional reality: Peirce's logic of *vagueness,* the *logic of the universe,* and Firstness as a *continuous cosmic whole,* all of which lie outside our own logic, analysis, and reason (CP:5.505–508, 6.185–213; also Smullyan 1952; McKeon 1952; Weiss 1952; Nadin 1982, 1983).

Bohm (1980:186–89) offers another visual trope for his nonvisual, and rather ineffable, higher dimension. Imagine two TV screens in a room showing a fish in a tank, one projected from the side of the fish and the other head-on. As we stare at the screens, we notice that when the fish on one screen moves slightly, the fish in the other instantaneously does the same, but at a 90° orthogonal to the first fish. Were we to be unaware that the two cameras were trained on the same fish from different angles, this behavior might be rather disconcerting. Obviously, there is no temporal cause-and-effect sequence, but some simultaneous interaction between the two bodies bringing about reciprocating movements. The problem is that we are viewing the TV screens as if each were a two-dimensional world, while the cameras, from a higher dimension, have created what appears to be an unexplainable phenomenon. This higher dimension, like the *background* and the *implicate order,* is inaccessible to linear reasoning.

Recall the above discussion of the graph constructed in figure 1 from the elementary problem of an object's acceleration in time. Spatially the lines on the sheet are two-dimensional, but they imply, along one of the coordinates, a third dimension: time. From our three-dimensional perspective this time dimension has no movement, it is entirely static. It is comparable to our own three-spatial plus one-temporal world conceived as the timeless Minkowski "block" lying outside our perceptual grasp. Or, to use Peirce's trope, it is as if a three-dimensional Spherelander were viewing the cuts on a given sheet from some point in the book of assertions, while a Flatlander, confined to the two-dimensional world of one of the book's sheets, would be incapable of such a perceptual grasp.[5]

Bohm elaborates on an even more intriguing trope, relating the combination of his implicate and explicate orders to a *hologram.* The hologram operates on the principle of interfering wave patterns. A laser beam is directed toward a half-silvered mirror in such a way that part of the beam passes through, striking a photographic plate, and part is reflected onto the object to be photographed. The light reflected from the object strikes the photographic plate at an angle with that part of the beam which passed directly through the mirror to produce a complex array of interference patterns. When the plate is developed and then illuminated, again with laser light, the object reproduced on the two-dimensional surface appears to possess the three-dimensional characteristics of the original object. The intriguing feature of laser photography is that there is no one-to-one correspondence between the parts of the photographed object and the parts of the photographic plate. Rather, the interference pattern of each region of the plate is equal to the whole. If the corner of a plate is broken off and illuminated, it will reproduce the entire object, though the smaller the piece the more vague the reproduced image becomes.

Actually, Bohm's hologram metaphor is a fixed image of the state of an electromagnetic field—a set of interacting waves—in the flat space containing the photograph. But this fixed state is not static. It is a shimmering, dancing bundle of standing waves in incessant movement. The sum of its myriad moves can be described as atemporal, yet there is pure change. In order that the hologram model be true to the combined implicate and explicate orders, which Bohm labels the *holomovement,* it must be conceived as both a static set of interference patterns and the unfolded three-dimensional image jumping in and out of the two-dimensional plane: it is perpetually enfolding and unfolding. The quantum formulation, Bohm argues, is precisely the mathematical description of this holomovement. But in quantum theoretical terms, there is no physical notion of movement in the ordinary sense. The physicist uses his mathematical metaphor because it produces results, but there is no meaning outside the mathematical symbols. In Bohm's words, on constructing a language with which to describe the implicate order, the holomovement must be

> considered as the totality in which all that is to be discussed is ultimately to be [foregrounded]. Similarly, in the algebraic mathematization of this general lan- guage, we consider as a totality an undefinable algebra in which the primary meaning of each term is that it signifies a "whole movement" in all the terms of the algcbra. Through this kcy similarity there arises the possibility of a coherent mathematization of the sort of general description that takes the totality to be the undefinable and immeasurable holomovement. (Bohm 1980:164)

The language of the holomovement, then, can be none other than algebraic, which is to say that it is imageless and by and large incompatible with natural language: as a whole it is a pure metaphor, or allegory if you will, of that which it signifies. Bohm discusses the possibility of "relatively autonomous sub-algebras" which entail aspects of the very general and undefinable "whole algebra." As each aspect of the holomovement enjoys only limited autonomy, so the sub-algebras are dependent upon the larger formulation. It is interesting to speculate that, just as Bohm's sub-algebras take on meaning in the context of research programs and only in regard to the general and undefinable whole algebra, so also what Peirce calls *subjective* (classical) *logic* exists only with respect to, and is dependent upon, the exceedingly more general and more complex *logic of the universe* (CP:6.189). With the holomovement, like the logic of the universe, a form of "objective reality" is in a sense restored: what *is not* (Firstness or Thirdness, both in their pure state continuous) is as "real" as what *is* (Secondness, actuality, discontinuity). The ongoing schizophrenia between particle/wave, matter/mind, continuity/discontinuity no longer exists in the clas- sical sense.

In order to qualify this assertion, we must return briefly to Hartshorne's critique of Peirce.

II. OUR RESTLESS WORLD. For Peirce, as we noted in chapter 1, time and space are continuous because they embody conditions of possibility, and since the possible is general, and generality is continuity, they are two names for the same absence of distinction. Peirce's failure to anticipate quantization in physics was a grave error, Hartshorne tells us—though this should actually be no surprise, for after all, the most eminent physicists of the nineteenth century failed in this respect as well. Hartshorne argues, as we have noted, that Peirce believed the past to be particular, the future irreducibly general or potential, and the present somehow both. Given, possibility entails futurity as such, which is commensurate with Peirce's *tychism* (the doctrine of chance). But Hartshorne (1973:193) observes that Peirce's indeterminism or tychism, rather than an arbitrary feature of his thought, was "central and essential to it." That might be fine and dandy, Hartshorne suggests. But, he warns, to say with Peirce "that possibility as well as actuality is real . . . is not to say that possibility is exhaustively actualized." Hartshorne goes on to state that Peirce's real problem is that "Peirce was beautifully clear as to the contingency of actuality as such and the continuity of possibility as such, but somehow he was unclear as to the implied discontinuity of contingent actuality" (Hartshorne 1973:196).

Contrary to Hartshorne, and in light of the above discussion of quantum theory according to Bohm's interpretation, space and time can quite legitimately be conceived as continuous: the former embodies the *potential* position of an entity and the latter *potentially* the instant of an event. The future in this regard is a continuous, *general* set of *possibilia* for contingent actualization in the present. Moreover, Bohm's qualitative infinity of nature represents a potentiality en-folded within the implicate order for an unlimited set of actuals, given an indeterminate lapse of time. In this regard, when Peirce is placed alongside Bohm, there is no call for claiming he proposed that the actualized world of empirical entities is at any given point in time continuous.

For Peirce, the coming into being of actual entities is contingent: *after having become,* they *are* discontinuous, but as contingent possibilities they *were-are-will be* continuous. And the conjunction of continuity *and* generality implies the absence of discrete actuals. Yet, over *unlimited* time, the becoming of actuals—in order to realize the Final Interpretant—would certainly constitute a continuous domain. The problem stems from Hartshorne's contention that Peirce affirmed (1) an actual continuity engulfing an infinity of entities, and at the same time (2) the continuous becoming or actualization of entities.

Statement (1) is in reality not the case, as Hartshorne poses it at least. Actualized entities constitute a discrete order whose existence is dependent upon a higher realm, the potential for future actualization. I speak here of fun-damentally the equivalent of Bohm's qualitative infinity of nature, *a composite of the implicate (nonselective) and explicate (selective) orders, of a continuous and discontinuous domain.* Peirce's continuous *logic of the universe* is copresent with entities actualized in the world at a given moment, and like Bohm's implicate order, it is infinite, and in a manner of speaking "actual," though not empirical. The vast majority of the entities in the *potentia* remain implicate at any given point in time, yet the possibility exists, however remote, for their being explicated somewhere at another time, hence the conjunction of *potentia* and indefinite time is unlimited (the term *potentia* is, as pointed out in chapter 1, section I, the Aristotelian term applied by Heisenberg [1958a] to the quantum world).

That is, the explication or actualization of entities is for Peirce a process of continuous becoming. Once having become, a given set of entities at a particular point in time and space can be no more than discrete. Yet over unlimited time and space, the total set of actualized entities must make up none other than a multitudinous whole—though whether or not it is dense might remain an open question. Hence (2) is somewhat deceptive, for though becoming, over the indefinite long haul of things, is continuous, that continuity, like the implicate order, is not empirically available.

Hartshorne (1973:194) argues further that the Heisenberg uncertainty principle cannot be effectively explained away by postulating "hidden variables."[6] At most, Hartshorne claims, the hidden-variables interpretation reveals the nonempirical characteristic of actualized entities and the statistical characteristic of possibilities. The only valid reason for accepting this interpretation is that otherwise there is no coherent logic for the notions of possibility and actuality. Peirce, we are told, argued for the impossibility of exact measurement, given continuous statistical variables, hence there could be no determinism. However, what he failed to recognize is that "if the world has both continuous and discontinuous aspects then, a fortiori, exact causal laws cannot apply. For the interplay of continuous and discontinuous aspects forbids such laws" (Hartshorne 1973:194). In support of his critique of Peirce, Hartshorne turns to the example of photons of light partly reflected and partly refracted when passing through a medium such as glass. A given photon's being either reflected or refracted is determined probabilistically by the angle of incidence, but since this angle can vary continuously, the discontinuity between reflection and refraction is explainable solely by a probabilistic account.

However, consider an alternative combination of continuity and discreteness: the *double-slit experiment*. A stream of electrons is fired at a thin sheet of metal punctured by two minuscule holes with a screen behind the sheet to detect the resultant pattern. If one hole is closed, some of the electrons pass through the other hole and strike the screen in a manner comparable to bullets from a machine gun passing through a hole in a barrier and striking a thick plank of wood behind it. They behave as particles. Now imagine that both holes are left open. We normally would expect there to be two patterns, one behind each hole, duplicating each other. But this is not the case. An interference pattern is set up in the space immediately behind the orifices which, on the screen, appears as if water waves had been passing through two slits in a barrier. The electrons, formerly behaving as particles passing through one hole, now act as waves interfering with one another after passing through two holes. The first trial demonstrated the electrons' discreteness, the second their continuity. And the mixture of the two entails the essence of Bohr's *complementarity principle*. In the first case classical laws inhere; in the second they do not. The first evinces the image of actualized entities in the present which make up a determinate past; the second, as waves, consists of a continuous set of statistical possibilities until they become actualized and take on their particle personality upon reaching the screen.

Bohm insists that this combination of classical and postclassical characteristics, a contradictory combination of causal and statistical phenomena, testifies to the incomplete nature of Copenhagen quantum theory. It is, he argues, the surface manifestation of a deeper, *subquantum level:* his implicate order of incessant flux, the laws of which are qualitatively different from those of the quantum level. Hence there is no reason why quantum equations describing either the wave characteristics or the particle characteristics should have any relevance at the lower level (Bohm 1957:111–16). If Bohm is correct, then this deeper level is every bit as "real" as the quantum level, though it contains no existing (that is, actualized) entities.[7] And, to extend our parallel, commensurate with Bohm's subquantum level, Peirce's *logic of the universe* as a continuous infinite or quasi-infinite realm of possibilities exists in the present as well as the future and the past.

Significantly, in this regard, like Bohm's holomovement, an important facet of this deeper logic is not formalizable with conventional algebras and calculi. And neither is the generality of Peirce's conditions of possibility in space and through time, which exclude exhaustively describable distinctions. I see no reason, then, for Hartshorne's somewhat disparaging remarks on Peirce. Quite frankly, either to criticize Peirce for his failure to divine the essence of Copenhagen quantum weirdness or to denounce Hartshorne for his apparent ignorance of Bohm's anti-Copenhagen interpretation would be baseless—though actually, Hartshorne's paper was published when Bohm was still relatively unrecognized outside a small group of practicing physicists. The fact is that Peirce's concept of continuity and originary Firstness *is* strikingly compatible, though he is not clear on some points, with the particular aspect of Bohm's quantum cosmology being discussed here.

Another aspect of Peirce's notion of continuity sheds broader light on the issue at hand. Peirce believed that the most convincing reason for his continuity postulate rests in its accounting for how an entity, be it mind or matter, can act continuously upon another entity (CP:1.170). Hartshorne retorts that the postulate of a finite number of events between two entities (or minds) does not discount the existence of internal relations connecting these entities, hence Peirce's notion of a continuous infinity of infinitesimals connecting them is cumbersome, contradictory, and unnecessary. The *potentiality* of events is continuous in space and time, *not their actuality.* Following Whitehead, Hartshorne tells us that if consideration is limited to the future potentiality of an entity, then it spreads out finally to pervade the universe; its actuality, on the other hand, is discrete. Although Peirce is vague on the spatio-temporal atomicity of actual events, the problem seems to be that he speaks of continuity at one level while Hartshorne refers to it at another level.

Regarding what Hartshorne conceives as Peirce's illegitimate collusion of temporal continuity and discontinuity, he elsewhere alludes to the absurdity of an infinity of experiences between two events, say, having breakfast and having lunch (Hartshorne 1964:469). I believe it is now quite apparent that this "dilemma" is also common to contemporary physics, and as far as the physicist knows at present, it might be endemic to the very nature of reality. For Planck light was of discrete *and* continuous character. Combining the wave mechanics of de Broglie and Schrödinger with Heisenberg's matrix mechanics, somehow electrons also seemed to be both continuous and discrete. Bohr's complementarity metaphysically brought the incompatible descriptions together, and P. A. C. Dirac even combined them mathematically (Sachs 1988).

But problems remained. In fact, Zeno's paradoxes, we have observed, are germane to the very issue. His immobile arrow in flight is predicated upon the idea that just as space can be conceived as consisting of an infinity of contiguous points, so time can be an infinite collection of contiguous instants. True, our experience of the arrow in flight appears to us to be strictly continuous, but perhaps it actually consists of William James's "drops of experience" which merge into one another to present the sensation of continuity. Then how can Zeno legitimately arrest the arrow in flight and then proclaim at the end of his argument that it never could have moved from one point to another in the first place? Physically the transition in question may be possible, but there is nothing to prevent Zeno's rendering it impossible by a sheer *act of mind*. On his so doing, the continuum is discretized by a contradictory mixing of two incompatibles, which is no problem for mind, though experience and intuition rebel against it (Dantzig 1930:124–27).

For example, in modern times the mind, via the calculus, can easily describe a continuous curve as a series of infinitesimal straight segments, an abstraction which is also no more than a skeleton of the world as perceived by our senses. And fortunately for us, a host of "real world" problems are solved by such *fictions,* which the mathematician has been trained to use for so long that he may come at times to prefer the substitute to the genuine article. Even the practical person who ordinarily demands at least the appearance of "reality" tends to regard mathematical terms not as symbols or thought—and much less fictions—but as images validly representing "reality."

Yet, Peirce's contradictory mixing of continuity and discontinuity, of infinity and finiteness, *is,* I would submit, quite appropriate to the task at hand. In the first place, independently of Richard Dedekind, and anticipating somewhat the work of Georg Cantor, Peirce established a logical distinction between finite and infinite collections, which was later to become the basis of set theory. The breakthrough was that an infinite set is equivalent to a proper subset of itself, whereas a finite set is not. For example, the set of natural numbers is equal to its many subsets, which can be illustrated by setting up correspondences:

$$
\begin{array}{lll}
1 <\!\!-\!\!> 2 & 1 <\!\!-\!\!> 2 & 1 <\!\!-\!\!> 1^2 \\
2 <\!\!-\!\!> 3 & 2 <\!\!-\!\!> 4 & 2 <\!\!-\!\!> 2^2 \\
3 <\!\!-\!\!> 4 & 3 <\!\!-\!\!> 6 & 3 <\!\!-\!\!> 3^2 \\
\quad \cdot & \quad \cdot & \quad \cdot \\
\quad \cdot & \quad \cdot & \quad \cdot \\
n <\!\!-\!\!> n+1 & n <\!\!-\!\!> 2n & n <\!\!-\!\!> n^2
\end{array}
$$

These series are paradoxical if one reflects on the meaning of the statment "Two (infinite) sets have the same number of elements." However, Cantor proposed that two sets could be considered to have the same (cardinal) number of elements if they are equivalent, which follows the ordinary usage of the term *set* quite closely. If a hotel has rooms with single beds only, and if there is an occupant for each room, one can say that there are the same number of rooms as people; whatever number is assigned to the collection of rooms must also be assigned to the collection of people.[8] By the same token, it follows that the set of even numbers is equivalent to the set of natural numbers, which goes against common sense as well as traditional mathematical conceptions.

Nonetheless, Cantor's contribution—which in part can be attributed to Peirce, though much of the latter's work in this regard awaited posthumous publication—was to illustrate that the statement "The whole is greater than any of its parts" is false when applied to infinite sets (for example, CP:6.115). This concept is embodied in the *Tristram Shandy Paradox*. Shandy labored for two years chronicling the first two days of his life, lamenting that at this rate no matter how long he continued to write, he would be further and further from the completion of his autobiography. To this Russell (1957:85–86) retorts: "Now I maintain that, if he had lived forever, and had not wearied of his task, then, even if his life had continued as eventfully as it began, no part of his biography would have remained unwritten." Finite and infinite sets, so it appears, are absolutely incompatible, which adds more brush to Hartshorne's bonfire.

However, we must note that, mathematically speaking, there are two kinds of infinity: *actual* and *potential*. And there are three basic kinds of series: *nondense and denumerable, dense and nondenumerable,* and *neither dense nor denumerable* (see Huntington 1929). Peirce's *possibilia,* like Bohm's *implicate* order, is an infinitely extended, *nonselective* domain each subset of which is equivalent to the whole. Peirce's *actuals,* like Bohm's *explicit* order, constitute a finite *selective* domain each subset of which is not equal to the whole, but which, given unlimited time, can in asymptotic fashion approximate the equivalent of the *implicate* totality. The first order, it would appear, is tantamount to the actual infinite; the second is potentially infinite in extension. These two domains also pattern the conflict, discussed above, between relativistic continuity and quantum theoretical discontinuity, or in another way of putting it, between the dense and the nondense, and the nondenumerable and the denumerable. The series of whole integers and a collection of nonoverlapping three-dimensional regions of space are dense and at most denumerably infinite. An example of a dense and nondenumerable series is the class of all nonterminating decimal fractions. A series which is neither dense nor denumerable is that of a line bisected *ad infinitum* in the impossible Zeno fashion to yield an infinite series of infinitesimal segments (however, Peirce was not in agreement with Cantor on all points [see Eisele 1979; Murphey 1961]).

The type of dense, nondenumerable series to which I wish to refer here is that of Dedekind continuity. Dedekind noted that a straight line consisting of an infinity of points is infinitely richer than the domain of rational numbers:

between each set of points there is an infinity of points, whereas there are gaps between rational numbers. The line is complete and continuous, while the series of numbers always remains incomplete and discontinuous. Dedekind then posited a "cut" in the line which severs it into two portions or classes, one to the left of the "cut" and the other to the right of it. It follows, he argued, that just as any point on the line severs it into two contiguous, nonoverlapping regions, so every real number constitutes a means for dividing all rational numbers into two classes which have no element in common, but which, in combination, exhaust the entire domain of rational numbers (Dantzig 1930:164–78).

Cantor's concept of infinity has its counterpart in the Dedekind theory. But there is a fundamental difference. Cantor discovered a property Tobias Dantzig (1930:148) calls the "self-asymptotic nature" of a convergent sequence, which can be illustrated by the following:

$1/2, 3/4, 7/8, 15/16, 31/32, 63/64, 127/128, \ldots \ldots$
$3/4, 7/8, 15/16, 31/32, 63/64, 127/128, 255/256, \ldots \ldots$
$7/8, 15/16, 31/32, 63/64, 127/128, 255/256, 511/512, \ldots \ldots$

Generation of this collection can obviously be continued indefinitely, with all sequences being asymptotic to one another. Noting that these sequences are asymptotic to the series of rational numbers, Cantor identified them with the real number series. In this light, Cantor's generation ad infinitum is *dynamic*. Numbers tend to grow beyond measure toward a limit. In contrast, Dedekind's line is *static;* it is *there, in bloc* for all time, and when punctuated with a "cut," though having suffered a mutilation, the left side and right side remain eternally the same, a continuum of points smoother than the richest vanilla ice cream. Cantor's set of convergent sequences, it hardly needs mentioning, is also directly relevant to Peirce's notion of the potential completion of the Final Interpretant and the approximation of knowledge to truth (see Rescher 1978).

In Peirce's conception of continuity, time eventually enters the scene. He believed that multitudes correspond to linear series, and that the potential aggregate of elements is infinitely greater than any aggregate of actualized elements. Yet, as a potential, it does not "contain" any elements at all. It only "contains general conditions which *permit* the determination" of elements (CP:6.185). This potential constitutes Peirce's notion of a "true continuum," which "is something whose possibilities of determination no multitude of individuals can exhaust" (CP:6.170). Drawing a set of individual elements from the potential can never exhaust it, though it can successively approximate it. Peirce adds that this nature of infinity does not spell out any categorical realm of ignorance on our part. Rather, we can have a vague idea of the totality. Take, for instance, the series of whole numbers. The aggregate of *all* such numbers cannot be counted within a given person's lifetime, nor can it be counted by an entire community of knowers short of infinite in number. But "though the aggregate of all whole numbers cannot be completely counted, that does not prevent our having a distinct idea of the entire collection of whole numbers. It is a *potential* collection, indeterminate yet determinable" (CP:6.186).

In this fashion, Peirce's concept of knowledge cannot but be very imperfectly realized so long as it is confined to *actual* entities. In contrast, an infinite community of knowers pools its resources into the infinitely distant future containing all possibilities theoretically to arrive, at last, at Truth. Ultimately the focus rests not on existent individuals but on classes of possibilities and potentialities, not on what *is* but on what *might be* and *would be*. In this sense also, and contrary to Hartshorne, possibility, as well as actuality, enjoys certain citizen's rights in the "real" world.

Further to demonstrate how mathematics pervaded Peirce's thought, this general notion also bears on Peirce with respect to his concept of *personality* and *consciousness*. Personality is like any general idea or an infinitely extended potential. It is not something to be apprehended in an instant; it must be lived in time. Nor can any finite duration of time embrace it. Nonetheless, in each infinitesimal interval of time "it is present and living, though specially colored by the immediate feelings of the moment" (CP:6.155). It is incessantly growing, developing *toward* some *end*. Hence there is reference to the future, but that future in terms of the *end* never arrives. Were it to be explicit in the *here-now*, "there would be no room for development, for growth, for life; and consequently there would be no personality" (CP:6.157).

Regarding consciousness, Peirce also evokes the mathematical notion of continuity.[9] He reasons that though a past idea cannot be in present consciousness but only in past consciousness, the idea can nonetheless be present insofar as it is always in a process of becoming past; it is always less past than any assignable date in the past, that is, if it is still in recollective consciousness (memory). This implies, Peirce concludes, that "the present is connected with the past by a series of real infinitesimal steps" (CP:6.109). Now this and other equally enigmatic statements are the prime focus of Hartshorne's critical remarks. How can we account for an infinite number of infinitesimal steps between breakfast and lunch? How can we even speak of infinitesimals and the nuts and bolts of the physical world all in one breath?

But Peirce continues undaunted. He points out the rather obvious: consciousness necessarily embraces a certain interval of time. If not, we could gain no knowledge of time, "and not merely no veracious cognition of it, but no conception whatever. We are, therefore, forced to say that we are immediately conscious through an infinitesimal interval of time" (CP:6.110). In this infinitesimal interval, not only is consciousness continuous in a subjective sense, but the object of consciousness, the idea in question, is also continuous, just as all signs (i.e., in their fulfillment as interpretants) and minds are continuous in the sense that they merge into one another and are thus welded together. In fact, this spread-out consciousness is patterned by the spread of its contents—in somewhat comparable fashion to the contemporary concept of space expanding as the universe, which contains space and is in turn contained by it, expands.

Peirce attempts to illustrate his heady idea of signs welded to signs, minds to minds, and consciousness to its contents with what are today known as the topological concepts of boundaries and neighborhoods. He asks the reader to imagine a surface bounded by a curve, say, a circle, to be half red and half blue. The red and blue surfaces, to exist as such, must have red and blue spread over them such that the color of any part of the surface is the color of its immediately neighboring parts. What color, then, is the boundary? Peirce responds that since "the parts of the surface in the immediate neighborhood of any ordinary point upon a curved boundary are half of them red and half blue, it follows that the boundary is half red and half blue" (CP:6.126). That is to say, to integrate Peirce's example with another of his thought experiments (CP:6.203–206), it can be said that the boundary, a line separating blueness (B) from redness (R), is actually neither B nor R: it is BR-lessness. However, this BR-lessness is precisely the property that unites B and R. So there must be some commonality shared by both B and R embodied in BR-lessness, which implies that it is somehow in some sense both B and R, which Peirce would deem "half B and half R."

This is a difficult pill to swallow, though it must be admitted that BR-lessness welds B and R together by *some* property, however vague, which they share. Such a property is metaphorically comparable to the Sheffer (1913) "stroke" function, to be discussed in more detail in chapter 4, the essence of which was anticipated by Peirce (Berry 1952; also Merrell 1985a, 1985b, 1987). The "stroke," "|", would indicate that BR-lessness denotes "*not both* not B and not R" or "*neither* B *nor* R." In such case BR-lessness would either oscillate between B and R—hence as Peirce says it would be half B and half R—or it would disclaim membership in either of the two surfaces—hence it would not evince any commonality between B and R and therefore could not be in possession of any power to combine them. It appears that if the latter were true, then there could be no meld of the two and they would stand as incompatible, with an insurmountable barrier between them (see appendix 1).

However, if we avail ourselves of Peirce's idea that consciousness has the capacity naturally and intuitively to overcome Zeno's Achilles and the tortoise paradox, this barrier is no *real* problem. Peirce observes that many scholars had thought it inconceivable that Achilles could pass through an infinity of points (or, following our example, lines separating a series of shades of blue and red). This, he remarks, "does not embarrass Achilles the least in the world, for his final effort carries him through a whole infinity of the points" (CP:2.27). In other words, during the temporal increment required for Achilles' final lurch, there is, according to Zeno's iterative slicing of time, an infinity of infinitesimal instants. And space, having been sliced accordingly, evinces an equal infinity of infinitesimal points. Achilles' final bound can therefore take him as easily through an infinity of space barriers as through an infinity of time barriers.

This introduces us directly to Peirce's exemplification of continuity in general by way of the model of time as continuous. Peirce frequently engaged in analysis in terms of time series. He also alluded to something like Cantor correspondences in reference to his idea that all signs, minds, and "semiotic objects" are welded together such that they lose their autonomy and identity. These series and correspondences include multitudinous collections that are transfinite, indeed, even beyond Cantor's *Alephs,* Peirce claims, in character. For example, the horizontal and vertical series

$$
\begin{array}{llll}
1 & -2 & -3 & -4 \ldots \\
1/2 & -2/2 & -3/2 & -4/2 \ldots \\
1/4 & -2/4 & -3/4 & -4/4 \ldots \\
1/10^{10} & -2/10^{10} & -3/10^{10} & -4/10^{10} \ldots \\
\bullet & \bullet & \bullet & \bullet \\
\bullet & \bullet & \bullet & \bullet
\end{array}
$$

increasingly becomes larger and larger in one direction and smaller and smaller in the other. There is no end. The series simultaneously shades into the infinitely great and the infinitely small. This principle of merging appears in many guises in Peirce's thought: growth, evolution, *semiosis,* consciousness, mind, color and sound intensity, instinct and reason, nature and culture, and above all, time. The successive variation (differentiation) is continuous, not discrete. Herein lies the essence of Peirce's "real" continuum of *possibilia* (the *implicate*) from which all things can be *explicated.* And herein Peirce's convergence theory of truth comes fully into view: the continuum (nonselective) domain plus the aggregate of all (selected) particulars, like Bohm's holomovement, is Peirce's true universal.

Peirce (CP:6.164–84) curiously defines his continuum as consisting in *Kanticity* and *Aristotelicity,* the first positing that there is at least one point between any two points, and the second that the infinite series contains every denumerable point that is a limit to the nondenumerable point in the system. *Kanticity* is proper to the Dedekind line; it is essentially *static,* all *there* all at once, to be cut according to the wishes and whims of the geometer. No other principle is necessary except the power of the mind to categorize entities along a definite scheme which is totally divorced from time. In contrast, *Aristotelicity* is Cantorian: *dynamic.* It entails a tendency to grow, to generate, to converge toward something. It necessarily moves within time. The first is time frozen (the Final Interpretant or Third), the second is pure chance, pure spontaneity (the Monad or First), which lends itself to the actualization of particulars in the "real" world. The first implies *legato,* a continuous harmonic unfolding (real numbers). The second implies a symphony of *staccato,* represented by successive punctuations in the continuum (natural numbers). Peirce at times appears to have hoped to wed the two by accelerating staccato until it merged into legato, thus explaining both away by their resolution into their opposites: a *conjunctionis oppositorum.* Whether he succeeded or not is, as far as I know, still an open question, Hartshorne's critique notwithstanding. The fact is, to repeat, that the continuity-discontinuity conflict with which Peirce and others struggled during the latter quarter of the nineteenth century and the beginning of this one has been abruptly foregrounded in the relativity theory–quantum theory logjam. To this theme I now return, as the dialogue between Peirce and Bohm continues to unfold.

III. THE PRIMACY OF MIND. To repeat, though quantum theory and relativity theory differ vastly on many accounts, in a deeper sense they share the implication of undivided wholeness. The Einsteinian space-time field is continuous, indivisible, particles being regarded as an abstraction from the field. They are singularities, or space-time "knots." A description of the relativity universe entails the structure of such singularities in the continuum field. In terms of the observer-observed relationship, the field of a particular singularity, constituting an object, merges, but not in simultaneity, with the field of the observer-as-singularity. This is actually a different sort of wholeness from that of quantum theory—e.g., the instantaneity of the "phase entanglement" interpretation discussed above in contrast to the nonsimultaneity of relativity. Consequently, in spite of their deep compatibility, relativity and quantum theory have not yet been effectively united to the general satisfaction of the scientific community, the chief reason being that extended structure has not been consistently introduced into relativity (Bohm 1980:111–39). Yet the concept of space inherent in relativity, as I understand it, is not entirely alien to Peirce's continuum of mind, especially in the sense that minds can influence one another mediately, not immediately, through their overlapping extendedness. And since the character of sign is that of the character of mind, mind itself being a sign, Peirce's notion of signs merging into one another becomes equally plausible (Hartshorne 1973:199).

A distinct relatedness between minds and the phenomena of the physical world exists in quantum theory. Recalling the double-slit experiment, if the electrons passing through one hole behave as particles, and if passing through both holes they take on wave characteristics, then how could an individual electron at the point of penetrating the barrier know that another electron was at the other hole in order to change itself into a wave? Somehow there must be an interconnection (e.g., "phase entanglement") between the particles approaching the metal sheet at different points. Quantum weirdness reaches a climax here. It marks the demise of classical objectivity: what happens to the electrons in the double-slit experiment is simply nonobservable in the ordinary sense. The electrons approaching the sheet appear to behave *as if* they were particles, but upon entering and leaving the holes they are like waves.

But actually they were waves all along, that is, if they went unobserved. For example, assume we are reduced in size sufficiently so as to be able to see individual electrons. Walking along in front of the sheet, we can see the swarm of particles obediently headed toward their destination. We reach the barrier and peer on the other side, expecting to see nothing—for, we assume, there is nothing but waves. To our surprise, an apparently chaotic array of particles heading for the screen meets our eye. What has happened? Our observing the "wave packets" has "collapsed" them into particles. In other words, the "electrons" were never electrons in the particle sense until they struck the screen, the interaction of which actualized them—i.e., the "wave packets" were "collapsed." What we thought were "particles" in front of the sheet were viewed as such only when we observed (interacted with) them. And when we assumed we would see "nothing" between sheet and screen, there was in reality "nothing" to see, but when we took a peek, electrons as particles jumped up to greet us. Quantum reality demonstrates that there is no objective world "out there": any world we can know is partly created by the observer.

The double-slit experiment illustrates quantum interconnectedness according to the original Copenhagen interpretation. Bohm, however, carried the interconnectedness idea a giant step further with his more general cosmology, which also, he believes, can incorporate the universe of relativity. From Bohm's holographic perspective, and with Hartshorne's critique in mind, it becomes apparent that there is nothing unbearably strange in Peirce's contention that minds "spread" and act on one another instantaneously. His law of mind stipulates "that ideas tend to spread continuously and to affect certain others which stand to them in a peculiar relation of affectibility. In this spreading they lose intensity, and especially the power of affecting others, but gain generality and become welded with other ideas" (CP:6.104). From what Peirce believes to be a spread of feeling found to occur in protoplasm, he generalized to the human semiotic animal, holding that feeling "has a subjective, or substantial, spatial extension" (CP:6.133). Further, "since space is continuous, it follows that there must be an immediate community of feeling between parts of mind infinitesimally near together" (CP:6.134). This explanation, Peirce asserts, coordinates the action of the nerve-matter of the individual brain with that between minds external to one another. Just as there is action between parts of the same mind that are continuous with one another, so one mind can act upon another, "because it is in a measure immediately present to that other; just as we suppose that the infinitesimally past is in a measure present" (CP:1.170).

A problem, however, rests in Peirce's belief that like signs, when thoughts, memories, and minds spread, they suffer a loss of intensity. Quantum wholeness is not a rerun of the Newtonian drama in which everything is instantaneously connected to everything else by means of a mysterious force—gravity—across distances. Gravitational connections diminish with distance according to the inverse square law, thus endowing nearby connections with overwhelming importance while distant connections become relatively insignificant. In contrast, quantum interconnectedness, undiminished by spatial and temporal separation, is altogether different. Phase entanglement indicates that an electron from a bench in Central Park can intermingle with another in Gorky Park as forcefully as it can with one of its neighbors from the same bench. In this respect alone, Peirce's action of one sign or mind on another appears to be strictly Newtonian. If Peirce was incapable of foreseeing the consequences of contemporary physics, it is principally in this regard, rather than his synechistic doctrine, as Hartshorne argues.

On the other hand, in light of Peirce's "law of mind," Bohm, drawing support from Karl Pribram, also suggests that the mind (consciousness) and physical reality are of one whole, and at the implicate level they are governed by a comparable "algebra."[10] Bohm notes that matter and mind (consciousness) evince certain commonalities, chief of which is their holographic character: both entail implicate and explicate orders.[11] First, various forms of energy, such as gravity, magnetism, light, and sound, constantly enfold information regarding the material world into particular regions of space. These energies are felt (Firstness) as the pull of gravity, the attraction of a magnet, light reflected from a stop sign which impinges on the retina, and an auto horn when one steps from the curb onto a street before an oncoming vehicle. Such information enters the sense organs and passes through *as* such and such (Secondness), which is then cognized (Thirdness). The structure of the information, in other words, is enfolded into the brain—somewhat comparable to music being enfolded into the grooves of a disk, later to be retrieved and reproduced by the speaker system. Hence, is not all matter, Bohm asks, tantamount to enfolded information from various energy sources? In Peirce's terminology, this is rather comparable to asking: "Is matter not truly effete (enfolded) mind?"

It is certainly plausible that the processing of sensory input resembles an image-constructing device analogous to holographic processes. Moreover, memory, according to Pribram's thesis, appears to be enfolded in comparable fashion, all over the brain rather than localized.[12] Bohm (1980:198) goes even further to suggest that "when the 'holographic' record in the brain is suitably activated, the response is to create a pattern of nervous energy constituting a partial experience similar to that which produced the 'hologram' in the first place."[13] If Bohm is correct, not only is the brain a repository of "mind-stuff," but so also is the entire body. Much in the Peircean sense, when one instinctively jumps back onto the curb upon hearing the auto horn, one has resorted to the reflexes of *habituated* mind. The body acted without there being any conscious and intentional will on the part of the mind to cause the body to so act. From human to ape, from horse to aardvark to amoeba and the plant kingdom, in the Peircean sense all such action on the environment is ultimately the product of jelled mind.

Peirce was critical of the notion, common during his day, that "an idea has to be connected with a brain, or has to inhere in a 'soul.'" This is preposterous, he charges. An idea does not belong to the soul; it is the soul that belongs to the idea. The soul does for the idea just what cellulose does for the beauty of the rose; that is to say, it affords it the opportunity to do its thing (CP:1.216). Thought, Peirce argues further, is not necessarily connected with the brain. Rather, it exists "in the work of bees, of crystals, and throughout the purely physical world; and one can no more deny that it is really there, than that the colors, the shapes, etc., of objects are really there" (CP:4.551). The lower organisms, as well as the physical world, as we have observed, are in one form or another different manifestations of mind. But Peirce goes even further still. When, say, a warm solution containing suspended Na^+ and Cl^- ions is allowed to cool and a seed crystal is placed in it, crystallization occurs, which is "mindlike" inasmuch as the ions are programmed with a "memory" to so behave.[14] All "physical stuff" is in this manner the conglomeration of "mind-stuff." Although Peirce generally admitted to the dependence of mental action on the brain, or on substance of some sort, that out of which mind arises and can manifest itself (CP:6.559, 7.586), he nevertheless always held that thought in general has "no existence except in the mind," and only as it is so regarded does it really exist (CP:5.288).

In short, Peirce's conception of things is actually less bizarre than the proposition that the mind actively explicates matter (i.e., the "collapse" of waves into particles), an idea propagated by the most speculative of the "new physicists."[5] It is also somewhat less bold than Bohm's notion that mind is an explicate parallel with that of matter. On the other hand, it bears on James Jeans's (1958:186) transformation of things into ideas when remarking that the universe is more akin to a Great Thought than the Newtonian-Cartesian Machine. At the same time it seems to hint at some sort of transformation of ideas into things in the grand style of Bishop Berkeley.

IV. MERELY AN ILLUSION?

IV. MERELY AN ILLUSION? Further to qualify Bohm's quantum interpretation for the purpose of relating it to the Peircean framework, let us return to his dye drop and glycerine trope. Suppose we put a drop of dye in the container and turn the stirring mechanism n times. We then place another drop nearby and stir n times once again, and we continue the process until a number of drops are enfolded into the viscous liquid. If we slowly reverse the turn of the mechanism, the drops will explicate as a succession of dots. Now suppose we turn the mechanism in the reverse direction, but so rapidly that the drops merge into one another to form what appears to be a solid object, a curved line, moving continuously through space. The development of this line appears to immediate perception to be the equivalent of a growing entity because the eye is not sensitive to concentrations of dye lower than a certain minimum: the observer is incapable of seeing the entire picture. Such perception, in Bohm's words, "relevates" (makes relevant, lifts up) a certain aspect of the apparent "reality." That is to say, it foregrounds the line while the rest of the fluid is seen only as a grey background against which the "relevated" object seems to be moving.

Bohm concludes that when his model is placed in a broad theoretical context, it is comparable to that which is relevated (lifted up, explicated) in our immediate perception. We begin with the holomovement, patterned by the *whole movement* of the dye and glycerine, which enables us to perceive the train of events. Then another system, the eye plus nervous system, including the limitation wrought by our persistence of vison, enables us to "see" an unbroken line when the individual drops are relevated in rapid succession such that they merge into one another. Otherwise, we would "see" only a series of dots when the rate of relevation is lowered considerably—bearing in mind that the holomovement is undefinable and unquantifiable, the dye and glycerine being merely a metaphor.

Bohm then compares his dye-and-glycerine narrative to a quantum context, an observation of tracks left by elementary particles in detecting devices such as a photographic emulsion or a bubble chamber. The tracks, which are the result of the particles' passage through the medium somewhat like the vapor trail left by a jet airplane, give the appearance of a continuous line rather than a series of dots, as did the dye drops. And, like the dye drops, the tracks are no more than an aspect appearing in immediate perception. In other words, the "track" as a collection of dots is not a line depicting any inherent movement of the electron. The electron does not move as such but is relevated (unfolded) and enfolded at successive spots along its apparent trajectory. The movement or line, as the Tantric Buddhists tell us, is a product of the mind; the mind makes the connections. Bohm warns us, however, that this is an artificial representation of movement described discontinuously. It is not a faithful replica of quantum jumps, since they tend to lead one erroneously to the conclusion that localized particles are capable of manifesting autonomous motion, which is irrelevant to the quantum universe as undivided wholeness.

The implicate coupled with the explicate order, moreover, bears further on Zeno's paradoxes of motion. In the implicate order, some ensembles unfold into the explicate as continuity (the dye drops emerging rapidly), and the unfoldment of others appears to be discontinuous (when the stirring device is turned slowly). Unfolding in this sense entails both continuity *and* discontinuity, such a combination apparently providing fodder for Zeno's arguments. But the problem, it would appear, is dissolved in Bohm's interpretation of the quantum world as unceasing flow, the *holomovement*. In illustrating his point, Bohm (1965) refers to Jean Piaget's studies in child psychology which, he suggests, demonstrate that our earliest experiences involve at least in part the implicate—an incessant, fluctuating enfoldment unfolding. After some time the child learns to mark out the equivalent of *distinctions* or *cuts* in the flux. Successive ruptures of the continuous whole made by her interaction with the world eventually serve to construct a model, a world map, following three-dimensional Cartesian space and time supposedly broken by a point, the "now." This becomes the nuts-and-bolts explicate world of everyday living. It is necessary for the socially sanctioned construction of one's "semiotically real" world, of course, but a stark abstraction from the whole, that is, the holomovement, of which the child is now generally oblivious.

Yet perplexing questions remain: If in the beginning everything was flow, then how was it possible to enact the first cut? This is the inverse of the arrow paradox: not only from within Zeno's venerable framework cannot the arrow shift from one temporal increment to the other, it never could have left the bow in the first place. Conversely, if everything is always already in flux, then from what position, point, or particular vantage can it be temporarily halted by a cut, since that position, point, or vantage could itself have been none other than a cut? Zeno, of course, fused continuity and discontinuity in order to carry out his proof, arguing that continuous motion perceived is illusory, and if discontinuity prevails in the absolute sense, then there can be no motion.

Recalling the above problem and its corresponding graph on the distance traversed by an accelerating object, science has traditionally viewed motion conceptually in this and all such problems as if the entire trip were present all at once. More complex scientific and engineering problems involve a more subtle calculus to differentiate, say, a curve into increasingly smaller units to approach an infinite limit: zero. By so fusing discreteness and continuity, it was assumed that Zeno's puzzles were laid to rest once and for all. In Dantzig's (1930:138) words, having determined to cling to the notion of infinitesimals in the calculus, "we have no other alternative than to regard the 'curved' reality of our senses as the ultra-ultimate step in an infinite sequence of *flat* worlds which exist only in our imagination." Quantum jumps reopened this can of worms, however, and the Eleatic paradoxes were once again foregrounded (Grünbaum 1967).

Bohm, unlike Peirce at times, and perhaps more than any other contemporary scientist, seems to appreciate the subtlety of Zeno's arguments—in fact, to an extent, in his denial of motion, Zeno approaches the implicate/explicate model. Bohm draws, in addition to his series-of-dye-drops model, from stroboscopic and tachistoscopic experiments such as two spots of light flashing on a screen in rapid succession, thus appearing to the observer as a continuous stream of light moving from the point of the first spot to the second one.[16] He then suggests that there is a similarity between the order of such immediate experience and the implicate order as it is apprehended by an abstractive act of mind. This reveals the possibility of a coherent mode of understanding the immediate experience of nature in terms of thought. For example, consider how motion is reduced to a set of points along a line. At a certain time, t_1, a particle is at position x_1, and at a later time, t_2, it is at position x_2. As pointed out in chapter 1, a formula for expressing the velocity of the particle between the two points, or a graph representing it, will be static, as if to say "now it is here, now it is there." There is no real sense of unbroken wholeness, of the *experience of* movement (Bohm 1980:198–201).

The calculus solves the problem differently. The time interval, t_1–t_2, and the change in position, x_1–x_2, become infinitesimal, and the velocity of the particles is defined as the limit of the ratio of the change in position divided by the change in time ($\Delta x/\Delta t$), as the latter approaches zero. Some reflection reveals, however, that this procedure is ultimately as abstract as the previous one, for neither is there any *immediate experience* of a time interval of zero duration, nor is it possible to see in terms of reflective thought what this could mean. Moreover, the calculus entails the notion of continuous movement, but quantum-level movement is discontinuous, so its application is limited to classical concepts (i.e., Bohm's explicate order, such as the movement of billiard balls), which provides at least an adequate approximation in the macroscopic world. Movement in the implicate order, on the other hand, does not involve this problem; it consists of nonlinear series of "inter-penetrating and intermingling elements in different degrees of unfoldment *all present together*" (Bohm 1980:203). This activity depends upon the whole enfolded order, which is continuous and determined by the relationships of copresent elements.

Bohm concludes that when we consider movement purely in terms of the implicate order, problems of the Zeno variety do not arise, because it is an outcome of this whole enfolded order determined by relationships of copresent elements rather than by the relationships of elements that exist to others that no longer exist. Through thinking in terms of the implicate order, one arrives at a notion of movement that is logically coherent and more properly represents our immediate experience of movement. Thus the sharp break between abstract logical thought and concrete immediate experience no longer needs to be maintained. Rather, the possibility is created for an unbroken flowing movement from immediate experience to logical thought and back again, and thus for an end to that obstinate, successive fragmentation (Bohm 1980:203).

Of course Peirce, unlike Bohm, did not enjoy access to contemporary logical and mathematical tools. Neither did he live during those years of turmoil when quantum theory was still in conceptual quicksand, which undoubtedly would have stimulated his thought immensely. This is not to say that had Peirce been born a century later the scientific community would have yet another maverick quantum physicist to contend with. Simply stated, Peirce, given not only his pioneer work in logic, mathematics, and the sciences but especially his trailblazing efforts on probability coupled with his infatuation with the problem of the infinite and the finite, continuity and discontinuity, foreshadowed certain key aspects of twentieth-century thought.

I refer most specifically in this context once again to Peirce's notion of continuity. The problem with Zeno's argument, Peirce (CP:5.335) tells us, is a self-contradictory supposition: that a continuum has parts. Yet Peirce uses this same contradictory combine repeatedly. A typical example is found in his comments on the succession of ideas (or thoughts). That one idea succeeds another is obvious, but we cannot be consciously aware *of* this succession. Why not? To understand the problem, Peirce asks how one Lockean idea can resemble another (CP:7.349). An idea contains nothing more than what is present to the mind in that idea. Two ideas cannot exist in simultaneity; hence what is present to the mind in one idea is present only at that particular moment, and it is pushed out of consciousness when another idea is present. They are, Peirce claims, mutually exclusive. Consequently, neither idea, "when it is in the mind, is thought to resemble the other which is not present in the mind. And an idea can not be thought, except when it is present in the mind. And, therefore, one idea can not be thought to resemble another, strictly speaking" (CP:7.349; also 5.289).

Is this mere sophistry? It might appear so at the outset. But if we conceive of time as a succession of instants, like the tick-tock of a clock or the jerks of the second hand on a watch, then Zeno lurks in the shadows, for how is it possible to go from the tick to the tock? On the other hand, if time is considered to be undivided flow, then how can a specific thought (idea, sign) jump into the mind and out again? In order to escape this apparent dilemma, Peirce proposes that if we assume what is present to the mind at one moment as distinct from what is present at another moment, then there must be a process present to the mind, and consciousness must run through the two moments, "perhaps indefinitely." In this manner, consciousness welds distinct increments together, each of them containing a definite thought (idea, sign). Hence consciousness must possess a duration, and if so, then there can be no instantaneous consciousness. All consciousness mediately relates to process. It follows, Peirce tells us, that

> no thought, however simple, is at any instant present to the mind in its entirety, but it is something which we live through or experience as we do the events of a day. And as the experiences of a day are made up of the experiences of shorter spaces of time

so any thought whatever is made up of more special thoughts which in their turn are themselves made up by others and so on indefinitely. (CP:7.351)

And synechism, Hartshorne's nemesis, resurfaces. Peirce's "indefinite continuity of consciousness" implies the perplexing notion that what was in the mind during the whole of an interval consists of what was in common in the contents of the mind during the composite parts of that interval, and so on, down to infinitesimals. Elsewhere, Peirce develops the same idea, but he enters from another angle:

> We must have an immediate consciousness of the past. But if we have an immediate consciousness of a state of consciousness past by one unit of time and if that past state involved an immediate consciousness of a state then past by one unit, we now have an immediate consciousness of a state past by two units; and as this is equally true of all states, we have an immediate consciousness of a state past by four units, by eight units, by sixteen units, etc.; in short we must have an immediate consciousness of every state of mind that is past by any finite number of units of time. But we certainly have not an immediate consciousness of our state of mind a year ago. So a year is more than any finite number of units of time in this system of measurement; or, in other words, there is a measure of time infinitely less than a year. Now, this is only true if the series be continuous. Here, then, it seems to me, we have positive and tremendously strong reason for believing that time really is continuous. (CP:7.348)

Here we once again confront Peirce's problem. Each state of consciousness is discrete, we would ordinarily assume, but in a year or less the number of states must be infinite in magnitude, hence they compose a continuum. But if this is the case, then how is it possible to get from one state of consciousness to another?— i.e., the impossibility of Zeno's arrow to proceed from point A to point B. To make matters worse, there is a Peircean counterpart to this dilemma in memory. Peirce (CP:7.674–76) tells us that there are no aggregate parts in memory, no absolute instants. All is flow; everything merges into everything else. There can be neither a first nor a last, for between each two potential moments of memory there exists an infinity of others. Hence memory entails an unlimited number of operations of the mind which lie below consciousness—in fact, the entirety of our past experience is, somehow, always in consciousness (CP:7.547, 7:674–76). But if this is the case, then once again, how is it possible for an item of memory to be abstracted? How can the first cut be made?

On this point Peirce is subjected to his most devastating attack from Hartshorne's bunker, and perhaps not without a grain of reason. As one incredulously reads Peirce's words, they can hardly appear to be anything but absurd. Infinity is not of this world, we tend to retort, it is merely a mathematical ideal. This was undoubtedly the reaction of Hartshorne, who, with Whitehead and others, contends that experience must come in least units, in packets. There is no need here to reiterate Grünbaum's (1967) "refutation" of the "bundle" theory of experience, since neither Peirce nor Whitehead nor Hartshorne offers direct empirical evidence for his hypothesis. It is consequently not wise to attempt to judge whether Peirce and Bohm are right and Hartshorne and Bohr wrong. Rather, a mapping between Peirce and Bohm merely demonstrates that in human thought throughout the ages, comparable ideas (i.e., "themata") recur.

I now turn to the most intriguing parallel between Peirce and Bohm in their attempts more adequately to account for the phenomenon of consciousness.

V. INTO THE INTERSTICES. As a result of some strange and rather bizarre "experiments" Peirce conducted on consciousness, and commensurate with his continuity postulate, he declared that consciousness is like a "bottomless lake" (CP:7.547; 7.553–54). Percepts are like rain on the continuous surface of the lake which *habits* (by contiguity) and *dispositions* (by resemblance) serve to authenticate. Those are suspended at various depths in the lake along a continuum. Ideas near the surface are readily available to the active mind, while those that lie at great depth are discernible only at the expense of great effort. A force comparable to gravitation—roughly following the inverse square law—indicates that the attraction of deep ideas is relatively slight, and hence with greater effort brought toward the surface. In addition, the mind can exercise control over no more than a limited area at each level; raising a group of ideas from the depths requires that others be pushed down. Related ideas exercise a selective attraction on one another. When one idea is at the surface, it creates a certain degree of buoyancy in other ideas. However, all ideas have a tendency to sink, to gravitate—i.e., become *embedded*—into oblivion. The aptness of this lake metaphor, Peirce concludes, "is very great."

Bohm's speculation on consciousness is relatively cautious and tentative, as it should be. At the outset, it must be mentioned that Bohm is well aware of the paradox inherent in his notion of consciousness: the very idea or intuition, and hence consciousness, of the holomovement is immanent; it is part of that very holomovement. Consciousness in this sense seems an impossibility, yet it exists. However, in Bohm's favor, this fact is no more or less enigmatic than Spencer-Brown's universe—as well as that of much Eastern philosophy—looking at itself in the mirror, which *is it* (perhaps the best we can do at this ground level is embrace the paradox and get on with the game).

For Bohm the flux of the holomovement is the implicate source of all forms, both physical and mental. The totality of existence, inanimate matter, living organisms, and mind, emerges from the enfolded. Consciousness, which includes thought, feeling, desire, volition, and so on, is thus placed, much in the sense of Peirce, on equal footing with matter. Consequently there is no fundamental distinction between Descartes's "thinking substance" and "extended substance" (Bohm 1980:196–208). "Extended substance" is ordinarily considered to be discontinuous, but the same cannot be so easily said of the former. A particular thought seems to be discontinuous, but thought itself functions as process. Bohm suggests that though the world "out there" can be most appropriately conceived almost exclusively with regard to its explicate qualities, the implicate should enjoy equal time in any discussion of the totality. And it is precisely mind, or consciousness, that gives us a conceptual handle with which to approach the implicate. If thoughts emerging into consciousness are construed in the same fashion as particles actualized from the implicate, we have an approximation to what Bohm is talking about. Moreover, memory, in line with Pribram's holographic model of the brain, remains enfolded, but an actualized remembrance, like a thought in consciousness, is an unfolding from the implicate (Bohm 1980:208).

Bohm is not clear on whether consciousness is a derivative directly from the ground, the implicate, or whether it is an epiphenomenon of matter, the brain. In either case, his consciousness as implicate order plus explicated thoughts bears likeness to Peirce's "bottomless lake" metaphor, especially in view of the fact that the implicate is a higher-dimensional reality than our three-dimensional physical world, and the lake (the implicate) as three-dimensional is a higher-dimensional source for derivatives at the two-dimensional surface.

Yet another commonality between Peirce and Bohm is found in their use of a music metaphor to account for consciousness. But first a word on music regarded as movement, or flux. Consider a polyphonic musical phrase, for example. It is a successive unfolding which must necessarily remain incomplete. At each particular stage a new moment is constituted by the addition of a new musical quality. But this is not mere addition ab initio without modification of what is already there. Rather, the quality of a newly arrived tone, in spite of its particularity, cannot but be tinged with the totality of the antecedent musical context which, in turn, is retroactively changed by the emergence of a new musical quality. The individual notes are not externally related to the whole as if it were a static block, nor does their particularity disappear in the undifferentiated continuum of the musical totality. The musical phrase is a successively differentiated whole which remains integrated in spite of its successive character; yet it remains differentiated, with its marked individuality, in spite of its characteristic dynamic wholeness. It is at once one and many, analog and digital, continuous and discontinuous. Musical experience perhaps comes as close to Heraclitus's "unity of opposites" as is possible from within the confines of human linear perception.

More specifically, Bohm, by reflecting on and giving careful attention to what happens in certain experiences, avails himself of music perception to illustrate his holographic trope. When one is listening to music, at a given moment a certain note is being played, but a number of previous notes are still "reverberating" in consciousness. The simultaneous presence of these reverberations is responsible for the directly felt sense of movement, flow, continuity. The notes must be of close proximity; listening to a set of them removed by a substantial time increment would destroy altogether the sense of a whole unbroken, living movement providing for aesthetic appeal. Bohm suggests that one does not experience the entirety of this movement by retention of notes during past moments and comparing them with the present. The reverberations are not memories but rather "active transformations" of what came earlier. Such transformations consist of a generally diffused sense of the earlier sounds with an intensity that gradually diminishes, as well as varied emotional responses, bodily sensations, incipient muscular movements, and the evocation of a wide variety of subtle meanings.

One can in this manner experience the direct flow of a sequence of sounds as they are enfolded into many levels of consciousness; the sounds interact to give rise to an immediate feeling of movement. That is to say, the notes, as unfolded Seconds in the air, return to their quality of Firstness in consciousness during the moment of aesthetic apperception. This activity in consciousness, Bohm (1980:199–200) continues,

> evidently constitutes a striking parallel to the activity that we have proposed for the implicate order in general. . . . [W]e have given a model of an electron in which, at any instant, there is a co-present set of differently transformed ensembles which inter-penetrate and intermingle in their various degrees of enfoldment. In such enfoldment, there is a radical change, not only of form but also of structure, in the entire set of ensembles . . . and yet, a certain totality of order in the ensembles remains invariant, in the sense that in all these changes a subtle but fundamental similarity of order is preserved.
>
> In the music, there is, . . . a basically similar transformation (of notes) in which certain order can also be seen to be preserved. The key difference in these two cases is that for our model of the electron an enfolded order is grasped *in thought,* as the presence together of many different but interrelated degrees of transformations of ensembles, while for the music, it is *sensed immediately* as the presence together of many different but interrelated degrees of transformations of tones and sounds. In the latter, there is a feeling of both tension and harmony between the various co-present transformations, and this feeling is indeed what is primary in the apprehension of the music in its undivided state of flowing movement.

When experiencing a succession of aesthetically pleasing sounds, Bohm (1980:200) concludes, one is *"directly perceiving an implicate order."* This order is dynamical in the sense that it is a continual flow into emotional, physical, and other responses that remain inseparable from the transformations out of which it is constituted.[17] Bohm compares his notion with a similar phenomenon concerning visual perception which offers the advantage of its being empirical. This entails studies of the effect of stroboscopic devices, mentioned above, giving the illusion of flowing movement between two light flashes as if they were analog rather than digital. In Bohm's terminology, the two visual images undergo active transformation as they are enfolded into the brain and nervous system, giving rise to emotional, physical, and other responses of which one may be only at most dimly conscious. These stroboscope experiments are comparable to the reverberation of musical notes in consciousness, the chief difference being that the visual images, unlike their auditory counterpart, cannot be resolved in consciousness to provide an aesthetically satisfying pattern. This suggests for Bohm that

> quite generally (and not merely for the special case of listening to music), there is a basic similarity between the order of our immediate experience of movement and the implicate order as expressed in terms of our thought. We have in this way been

brought to the possibility of a coherent mode of understanding the immediate experience of motion in terms of our thought (in effect thus resolving Zeno's paradox concerning motion). (Bohm 1980:201)

In Peirce's conception of things, space being continuous (the Newtonian view) in contrast to Zeno's construction of an infinitely converging discrete series, our experience dictates that Achilles encounters no barrier against his traversing an infinity of real infinitesimal steps. This, in light of Bohm and Peirce's auditory model, suggests that individual "events" (musical notes) from within the continuity of becoming can be cut out of the continuum, though their character is necessarily fictitious: their juxtaposition or coinstantaneity with other "point-events" along the line of becoming is an intellectual abstraction from the concrete world of experience. In contrast, the flow of musical experience is an unfolding of the enfolded, the becoming of a potentiality, a continuity which, unlike the mathematical continuum, cannot be abstracted without being mutilated. In Whitehead's (1925:54) words, "a note of music is nothing at an instant, but also requires its whole period to manifest itself." Durationless instants are mere ideal limits, arbitrary cuts in the dynamic continuity of becoming.

More specifically regarding Peirce's music trope, separate notes are for practical purposes considered with respect to their digital properties, while the melody is continuous. A single tone may be prolonged for an hour, a day, a week, and it exists *as it is* during each second of that time, present to the senses as if everything in the past were as completely absent as the future, since there would be no background against which the tone could be properly differentiated. In contrast, a melody consists of a succession of sounds striking the ear at different moments, and to perceive it "there must be some continuity of consciousness which makes the events of a lapse of time present to us" (CP:5.395). Of course we perceive the melody by hearing the separate notes, yet we do not directly hear it, for we hear only what appears to be present at a given moment, the remainder of the entire succession remaining unavailable to us at that particular moment. Peirce is addressing himself to two sorts of awareness, that is,

what we are *immediately* conscious of and what we are *mediately* conscious of, are found in all consciousness. Some elements (the sensations) are completely present at every instant so long as they last, while others (like thought) are actions having beginning, middle, and end, and consist in a congruence in the succession of sensations which flow through the mind. They cannot be immediately present to us, but must cover some portion of the past or future. Thought is a thread of melody running through the succession of our sensations. (CP:5.395)

In sum, just as the musical score exists in parts as marks on paper, each segment having its own submelody, so in the auditory perception of the piece various systems of relationship of succession subsist together between the same sensations. But once again, physical or spatial imagery unfortunately threatens to take over the trope. This is much the problem of describing quantum events in natural language. When is a "particle-event" a particle, and when is it a probability wave amplitude? The first is physical, spatial, digital, and "visualizable" in the imagination; the second is a continuous whole without predefined parts. The first is an individual in the conventional sense; the second is not: it is of "undulatory" or "pulsational" character, an imageless frequency of potentiality associated with a resultant mass once the wave has been "collapsed" into a "particle." The wave as wave manifestation is a "pattern." As Whitehead (1925:193) expressed it, such a "pattern"

> need not endure in undifferentiated sameness through time. The pattern may be essentially one of aesthetic contrasts requiring a lapse of time for its unfolding. A tune is an example of such a pattern. Thus the endurance of the pattern now means the reiteration of its succession of contrasts. This is obviously the most general notion of endurance . . . and "reiteration" is perhaps the word which expresses it with most directness. But when we translate this notion into the abstractions of physics, it at once becomes the technical notion of "vibration." This vibration is not the vibratory locomotion: it is the vibration of organic deformation.

Whitehead's terms *vibrational* and *pulsational* perhaps most adequately describe the sort of synthesis he strives to bring about between the particle/wave antithesis. Rather than movement in space as the displacement of one particle by another, Whitehead prefers *alteration of pattern*. Instead of the term *particle*, he prefers *event*. *Pulsational becoming* thus supersedes the matter/energy dichotomy.

All this is analogous—alas, analogies are the most we have to go on—to the dynamic structure of polyphony. In a contrapuntal fugue, two or more melodically independent movements, whether harmonious or dissonant, occur simultaneously. In this sense, and to appropriate Peirce's image, each component unfolds successively alongside the others, and all of them proceed toward the future while "overlapping," or "merging" into one another, but without sacrificing individuality and autonomy. These "alongside" and "overlapping" relations immediately evoke spatial connotations, though spatiality really has nothing to do with it. The dynamic union of the intertwined successivities is distinct from static spatial juxtapositions. It is cobecoming rather than coexistence, cofluidity rather than correlation. It is *n*-dimensionality packed into one-dimensional becoming rather than one-dimensional *relata* spread over three-dimensional space.

This *processual* and *relational* conception of *semiosis* as revealed in Peirce's river metaphor in conjunction with the music trope is apropos (CP:6.325).[18] Ever-changing, the river flows on, gradually carving out a channel for itself along the most economical route, settling down into *habit*, but a habit that is itself incapable of rest, for it is invariably subject to variation. An isolated part of this entire flow is meaningless: it must be considered as a *whole movement*, comparable to the movements of two accomplished pianists playing a fugue. They compose a coordinated whole; their fingers flow along the keyboard, their minds attending not to particular notes, fingers, or keys but to the whole. If a particular key on the piano is out of tune and one of the musicians for an instant focuses on the sound it discordantly produces, the flow may be disrupted, and the entire process is thrown into disarray. While within the flow, in contrast, the pianists' creative input can bring about variations, some of which improve the general rendition, but some perhaps not, and the process continues, though it is never the same as it was in previous recitals: *there is no absolute repetition.*

This flow of the fugue, this whole, is not describable as a mere concoction of atomistic events—i.e., pressure applied on certain keys at certain points along the linear stream as the piece is played in order to produce particular sounds. Nor is the piece itself merely a conglomerate of individual tones: *it is a whole.* To repeat Bohm's conclusion, when experiencing a succession of aesthetically pleasing sounds, one is *"directly perceiving an implicate order"* (i.e., Firstness, quality, feeling, tone), the essence of the Monad. It seems that, to paraphrase Leibniz, whether speaking of the holomovement or music, we are speaking of unconscious algebra.

Let us, then, probe deeper into this whole, this bottomless lake.

THREE   *The Tenuous "Reality"*

of Signs

I. OUT OF CONTROL? The holistic, nonlinear view suggested at the close of chapter 2 in conjunction with the notion that all processes consist of variations on a theme with no absolute reduplication has been, so to speak, "in the air." To cite merely a few examples, I have already referred to the relativity framework of a set of space-time "knots" flowing along the warps and woofs of the continuum and the quantum theoretical formulation of an interconnected web. In evolution, the variation-on-a-theme principle is described by Conrad H. Waddington's (1957) "chreodic paths" in the "genetic landscape," and more recently by Rupert Sheldrake's (1988a) "morphic fields."[1]

Evolution is now being described as "emergent systems" in a "self-organizing" universe (Jantsch 1980) and as "synergetics"—nonlinear cooperative interaction between evolving entities (Corning 1983; Haken 1978, 1980). In addition, we have the exuberant and at times quasi-mystical holistic view of Henry Margenau (1987; LeShan and Margenau 1982), the grand synthetic view integrating Eastern philosophy and Western science with cosmic consciousness (Wilber 1977, 1982; Hayward 1984, 1987; Peat 1987; Briggs and Peat 1984, 1989), and the more moderated "anthropic cosmological principle" (Barrow and Tipler 1986). Other "new sciences" within this emergent field deal with the appearance, development, and functioning of complex systems regardless of the domain of investigation to which they belong. They originated with general system theory pioneered by the likes of Ludwig von Bertalanffy (1968), Anatol Rapoport (1950, 1974), and Kenneth Boulding (1956, 1978), along with the science of cybernetics developed by, among others, Norbert Wiener (1948, 1950), W. Ross Ashby (1954), Warren S. McCulloch (1965), and Stafford Beer (1959).

Since the 1960s, investigators of complex systems have been joined and reinforced by nonequilibrium thermodynamics, via the work of Ilya Prigogine

(1980, 1981; Prigogine and Stengers 1984) and his followers; by cellular automata, with John von Neumann's (1958) pioneering work which later evolved into the autopoietic system theory of Humberto Maturana and Francisco Varela (Varela 1979; Maturana and Varela 1980, 1987); and by catastrophe theory and dynamic systems theory developed by René Thom (1975, 1983), Christopher Zeeman (1977), and Ralph Abraham (Abraham and Shaw 1982). It is becoming increasingly evident that these fields of intellectual endeavor—occasionally known collectively as "sciences of complexity"—may well offer a viable alternative to the classical model.

On the other hand, in the social sciences and humanities, the emerging world picture is suggested by various postures—to enumerate a few, antifoundationalism (Bernstein 1983; Rorty 1979; Rajchman and West 1985; Baynes, Bohman, and McCarthy 1987), textualism and textual undecidability (Derrida 1973, 1974, 1978), the new historiography (Foucault 1970; Hunt 1989; LaCapra 1983; White 1978, 1987), ethnography (Clifford and Marcus 1986; Geertz 1983; Tyler 1978, 1987), and sociology of knowledge (Bloor 1976, 1983; Radnitsky and Bartley 1987; Phillips 1973, 1977). The principle of variation on a theme as fundamental to languages, both natural and formal, the arts, and life itself, is nowhere more remarkably presented than in Hofstadter (1979) and Gombrich (1960, 1979), and in actual works by the likes of John Barth, Beckett, and Borges, e. e. cummings, Lewis Carroll, and Gertrude Stein, and Escher and René Magritte.

But actually, this holistic view, thanks to a few harbingers, has been slowly emerging for some time. In the seventeenth and eighteenth centuries certain mathematicians, among them Euler, Fermat, and Lagrange, developed abstract descriptions of nonlinear processes. This trend culminated in the nineteenth century in the so-called Hamilton-Jacobi theory, which provides a uniform framework capable of accounting for change emerging out of the totality—e.g., Bohm's implicate order—which suggests that the events (Seconds) of the world—the explicate order—are ultimately interpreted as the expression (Thirds) of an underlying unity. The clash between permanence and change, the one and the many, parts and the whole, also bears on the distinction between linear thinking and nonlinear thinking, and, by interpolation, between Saussurean semiological binarism and Peircean semiotic triadism (see Merrell 1991 for a critique of semiology from the vantage of Peircean semiotics).

Indeed, there is, as we shall note, a certain complementarity in these so-called oppositions. For example, in contrast to semiotics, Saussurean semiology, predicated on the principle of radical *differences*, tends toward binarism and linearity. *Langue* is antagonistic toward *parole*, and *synchrony* toward *diachrony*. Yet *syntagm*, which is more compatible with the right-hand side of these two dichotomies, does not always take a back seat to *paradigm*; it introduces a sort of *nondiachronic*, yet *nonsynchronic*, dimension to signification, interjecting irreversibility into the system. Rather than dynamizing the whole affair, syntagm stultifies it. Unlike *parole*, and especially Chomsky's *performance*, it does not effectively embody a capacity to generate an infinite diversity of messages within an equally diverse set of contexts (i.e., reference frames). On the contrary. Syntagm is like the acceleration problem in chapter I where movement is *there,* once and for all, as a static trajectory on a graph. Order prevails, and linearity inheres, true to the mathematics of differential equations in engineering, physics, biology, and economics.

Classical linear systems are by and large predictable in their behavior and attractive in terms of their relative simplicity. Smooth and continuous, they soothe the eye and mind. They most satisfactorily describe slow-flowing streams, electrical circuits, springs stretching continuously, machines operating normally, the pleasant movement of a piece by Brahms, Renaissance—as opposed to baroque—architecture, or language organized in a novel with customary patterns. The Saussurean view of language works fine during a particular synchronic "moment," when signifiers and signifieds fall into the phalangeal marching order that suits our longing for harmony and simplicity, for predictability and therefrom, perchance, control.[2]

Linearity does, of course, have its place. It can frequently be used to analyze complex systems into simpler ones. This is made possible by the fact that linear systems are reducible to collections of coupled differential equations corresponding to the interacting elements in the system. For example, the sound patterns produced by each instrument in an orchestra can be broken down by "Fourier analysis" into a complex wave of superpositions, and when these are combined with the complex wave of all other instruments, a linear pattern can be derived. This and other such computations lend credence to the classical tradition of conceiving the universe as a vast set of linear cause-and-effect sequences. Given relatively simple systems considered in isolation, this *approximation* has its validity.

However, such harmonious bliss is quite alien to a new arrival on the scene: the "physics of chaos," which is an extension of the study of complex systems.[3] Once the activity within a system reaches a high pitch, it takes leave of linearity and enters the more complex domain of nonlinear effects. A stream becomes turbulent, a circuit breaks down, an engine begins vibrating and finally blows, a concerto suddenly takes an unexpected turn, a novel reveals its multiply paradoxical navel, its *aporia,* at which point its expected meaning also vibrates to pieces. Such unexpected breakdowns are the essence of Hofstadter's (1979) chimerical self-destructing record player, which contains the equivalent of a double bind. It is like a Gödelian sentence causing a formal system to disintegrate when the crescendo reaches a certain peak. Actually, the same effect can be experienced with any cheap stereo. Gradual turning of the volume knob produces a linear response from the speakers, but if it is turned too far, nonlinearities in the circuit will cause a distortion in the output. These more complex systems, evincing radical perturbations, transformations, catastrophes, and violent evolutionary breaks, imply far more complex and more subtle processes which demand an account of the entire system, not merely its parts.

Nonetheless, we persist in our striving for order, harmony, simplicity.[4] Cause-and-effect schemes were successfully represented by linear differential equations from within the classical scientific framework. By the end of the nineteenth century, scientists were relying almost exclusively on linear equations. They were only remotely acquainted with nonlinear equations capable of modeling discontinuous breaks in a diverse range of phenomena (explosions, sudden changes in cloud formations or air currents, the fracture of a continental plate, a bridge or dam under pressure suddenly giving way). The problem was that such equations required techniques unavailable to investigators up to the 1970s. Today, nonlinear equations are used extensively. For instance, they can model *how* an earthquake occurs after irregular pressure along a fault line increases until a critical value is reached. What they cannot do is determine precisely *when* this will occur, for there is no linear cause-and-effect sequence allowing for predictability. If cause and effect there be, it is nonlinear, involving a numbing complexity of variables. Nonlinear equations model chaos, but they have demolished the dream of reductionist science, for virtually all vestiges of *control* have been lost.[5]

II. OR MERELY ORGANIZED CHAOS? "But Saussurean synchronicity," one might wish to retort, "does incorporate nonlinearity, and network 'causality.' As such, it lends itself to interconnectedness. Witness the chessboard analogy to language, for example."

This would be a distortion of Saussure, however. The synchronic slice out of the semiological salami is binary rather than trinary and polydimensional. And regarding a sentence's actualization into a syntagmatic string, it is linearly rather than multiply connected. Gilles Deleuze and Félix Guattari (1983:242) point out, rightly I believe, that Louis Hjelmslev's "glossematics"

> stands in profound opposition to the Saussurean and post-Saussurean undertaking. Because it abandons all privileged reference. Because it describes a pure field of algebraic immanence that no longer allows any surveillance on the part of a transcendent instance, even one that has withdrawn. Because within this field it sets in motion its flows of form and substance, content and expression. Because it substitutes the relationship of reciprocal precondition between expression and content for the relationship of subordination between signifier and signified.

In short, Hjelmslev's language is a free matrix; Saussure's is more akin to a Markov chain generator. The former destroys the notion of a linear stream of signifiers, which is also particularly highlighted in much of Jacques Lacan's writings. It allows for expression of the individual as a unidirectional trajectory within a social network, and, in addition, it allows for that individual's multiple lateral moves in unexpected directions within the entire interconnected, nonlinear fabric. It lends itself to tree structure as well as patterns, and to a binary *"this or that,"* or *"this and then that,"* as well as to an indecisive and vacillating *"either this . . . or . . . or . . . n,"* which, when carried out to a sufficient number of decimal places, becomes *"both and."*[6]

In fact Deleuze and Guattari's formulation is remarkably nonlinear. And, I might add, it is nonlinguistic; they find Saussure's language-based semiology especially unacceptable, preferring Peirce's "nonlinguistic semiotics" in much of their work (see in particular Guattari 1984). Deleuze and Guattari foreground the individual from within the whole, which has been shoved under the rug for so long because of the West's obsession with abstractions. In so doing, they contrast what they term the nonlinear, radically independent *schizophrenic* attitude via-à-vis the world with the linear behavior of the obsessively binary-goggled *paranoiac*.[7] Linear tunnel vision is *paranoia;* perpetual nonlinear breaks at orthogonal angles into unaccustomed pathways constitutes *schizophrenia*. A schizophrenic vacillation, *"either this . . . or . . . or . . . n,"* takes over from the paranoid *"this or that,"* or *"this and then that."* The schizophrenic's *molecular* indeterminacy takes precedence over a paranoid statistical *molar* certainty. The "binary machine" breaks down, and the multiply dimensional "schizophrenic machine," centered within its "semiotically natural" environment, replaces it. Deleuze and Guattari's schizophrenic experiences, both as an individual and as the entire species, the "semiotic world" in terms of *semiosic* production. He is an individual and everybody at one and the same time. Without plans, design, or vision, he mushrooms out into the "semiotically real" world metaphorically to encompass the whole.

As Deleuze and Guattari (1983:15) put it:

> The schizo has his own system of coordinates for situating himself at his disposal, because, first of all, he has at his disposal his very own recording code, which does not coincide with the social code, or coincides with it only in order to parody it. The code of delirium or of desire proves to have an extraordinary fluidity. It might be said that the schizophrenic passes from one code to the other, that he deliberately *scrambles all the codes,* by quickly shifting from one to another, according to the questions asked him, never giving the same explanation from one day to the next, never invoking the same genealogy, never recording the same event in the same way.

The schizophrenic is a nomad, a rebel. The paranoiac remains within the system, caught in a one-dimensional stream of labyrinthlike binary choices; there is no way out and no retrievable center. In contrast, the orthogonal schizophrenic's sidestep places him "outside," which is no transcendental quantum leap, mind you, but entails awareness of the binary wave-train head on: it is *as if* everything were there all at once, which endows him with the characteristics of every-body and at the same time no-body. Deleuze and Guattari's schizophrenic is also a pragmatist *par excellence*. That is to say, he is a *bricoleur*. He is in command of a hodgepodge collection of signs of related characteristics with a general but always transient rule of thumb for their use, and he goes about rearranging them in continually novel and different patterns and configurations: his language is a word-salad relating to a junkyard of "semiotic objects." As a consequence, he remains indifferent toward the methods of production and the product, or the overall result to be achieved. What is of interest is the doing, the process.

Two perplexities ensue from this account: (1) Deleuze and Guattari's use of the term *machine,* obviously of cybernetic origin, which they creatively interject among other technical terms, and (2) the question, "How can we account for the schizophrenic's *'either . . . or . . . or . . . n'* in terms of *semiosis?"*

Regarding the first perplexity, the problem with the term *machine* is that it tends to be construed as excessively binary and linear. It threatens to conjure up in the mind either an image of the mechanistic paradigm, developed in the eighteenth century with the notion of de le Mettrie's (1912) *l'Homme machine,* or the early cybernetics of Norbert Wiener and others, an offshoot of which was the Shannon-Weaver information theory, both of them remaining somewhat tinged with the classical model (see Campbell 1982). On the other hand, Deleuze and Guattari's *machine* is strikingly comparable to Maturana and Varela's (1980:136; 1987: 75–80) definition of the term: an entity in physical space qualified by its particular mode of organization capable of communicating with other entities by structural couplings—which implies a nonanimistic view foregrounding the inner dynamism of the entity. An organism, in contrast to a "machine"—insofar as the latter is presently known, though that could change in the future—is radically nonlinear in nature. And it is more "synchronic" than linear and causal in that patterns unfold out of a more general background of *possibilia* (the implicate order), something like the pianist revealing what was concealed in the musical score as she deftly moves her fingers across the keyboard. The score as *possibilia* is *there,* all at once, and the pianist enjoys the freedom of actualizing some—but never the totality—of those *possibilia.*

One might now retort that the term *synchronicity* reveals an antiprocessual, and hence anti-Peircean, posture. However, there is synchrony and there is "synchrony." My use of the word is divorced from the notion of a static Saussurean slice. Rather, it bears on Peirce's pre–First and Firstness—i.e., Aristotle's *potentia* as appropriated by Heisenberg, and, among others, by Bohm, in his attempt to articulate the implicate domain. The idea of synchronicity with respect to the Minkowski "block" is not tantamount to Saussurean "synchronicity," as some hopeful structuralists have speculated (for example, Jakobson, 1972). In the first place the "block" allows for no simultaneities; in the second, it is nonlinear rather than linear; in the third, commensurate with Hjelmslev's concept of language, any and all inhabitants remain *immanent*—a characteristic emphasized by Deleuze and Guattari.

According to the nonlinear equations of general relativity, Reimannian geometry provides the ground for all "matter" and "energy" which emerge as "lumps" or "knots" of curving time-space. A "knot" can remain relatively stable over a certain period of time, or it can ramble about, "colliding" with its neighbors. In whichever case it is never divorced from but is related to everything else in its environment, and even to the entire universe. What appear to be disparate objects of experience are actually interrelated and interacting emanations from a nonlinear field. The universe is in this respect like an organism in which each part is in some manner a manifestation of a single, undivided whole. Although the parts might appear to be the product of random Brownian-like motion, from a broader view, they compose an orchestrated ensemble.

Ilya Prigogine (Prigogine and Stengers 1984:186–87) uses the example of a colony of termites to illustrate this point. Each insect within the colony seems to be scurrying about at random with its minute piece of dirt, its activity unrelated to that of the other termites. Then, at some critical point the movement of the colony becomes coordinated, and a complex nest is constructed as if the entire collection of insects composed an organism with a blueprint in hand to guide it. It is as if a few "knots" came together to create order out of the vast sea of chaos. This is not exactly the case, however, as Prigogine repeatedly argues, for such order out of chaos is the natural process of all phenomena, be they inorganic or organic, unicellular or organisms of incomprehensible complexity.[8]

Various levels of organization are at work here, from *micro-* to *macro-levels*. The important point is that as a system develops, the level of organization does not always determine its structural complexity: higher levels are not necessarily more complex than their subsystems. At the molecular level, H_2SO_4 is considerably simpler than the atomic structure of H, S, and O, and their atomic structure is simpler than their subatomic level. A colony of cells is structurally simpler than the structure of each constituent cell, and the structure of that cell is simpler than the molecular structures of which it is composed. The structure of the termite colony, an ape society, or an ecological system is less complex than the biological and organic structure of each individual component. Simplicity and complexity, in this sense, depend upon the perspective; they exist in large degree in the eye of their beholder.

The hierarchy resulting from the evolution of more complex systems, especially living systems, not only is *structural* but manifests a certain nonlinear form of *control*.[9] At the termite colony level, the hierarchical chain of command exercises its control over the structurally more complex individual members of the colony. Less complex higher systems can then control more complex subsystems. Biophysicist Howard Pattee (1970, 1977, 1986) argues that at higher levels, irrelevant details of more complex subsystems are shunted aside in order to force the lower-level units into patterns of collective behavior independent of their structural workings as independent units. On the other hand, once a new hierarchical level has emerged, it tends horizontally to branch out, evolving into a progressively more complex system. Hydrogen is structurally less complex than uranium, adenine than RNA and DNA, ape colonies are less complex than human societies, and so on. Thus a new level is often marked by development into simplification, which then gravitates toward evolutionary complexification—though, I must mention, the destiny is teleonomic, that is, unforeseeable, as Deleuze and Guattari's schizophrenic has testified repeatedly.

However, when viewed as a whole, the vertical development of higher systems coupled with their horizontal evolution, especially when considering life processes, *tends toward* complexification, not simplification. And if sign behavior is, as Peirce asserted time and again, tantamount to life processes, we should expect sign processes to follow the general procedures of developmental simplification and evolutionary complexification (Salthe and Anderson 1989).

Let us, then, consider an example from Peirce: *natural language as symbol*.

III. THE GROWTH OF SIGNS. A proposition, Peirce demonstrates, is a compound sign containing two signs of less abstract sort: an *index* (the subject) and an *icon* (the predicate). In fact,

> It is impossible to find a proposition so simple as not to have reference to two signs. Take, for instance, "it rains." Here the icon is the mental composite photograph of all the rainy days the thinker has experienced. The index, is all whereby he distinguishes *that day,* as it is placed in his experience. The symbol is the mental act whereby [he] stamps that day as rainy. . . . (CP:2.438)

At the outset this seems straightforward enough. The icon as "mental composite photograph" and the index as *"that day,"* distinguished from all other days representing the speaker's memory store, expectations, and propensities, are a relatively complex system. The proposition or symbol as a "mental act" becomes merely an abstract stamp, a veritable caricature placed on an existing set of possible sensory, "semiotically real," and cognitive conditions. The icon is *possibility,* Firstness, what *might be* as related to the intricate set of all past happenings in the memory bank of the speaker. The index is Secondness, a *happens-to-be* in relation to all other "semiotically real" events, past, present, and future to come, whether "out there" or in the imagination. And the proposition, consisting of the interconnected icon and index, is Thirdness, what most probably *would be* in the event that a certain set of conditions, from an anesthetizing complexity of possible conditions, were to exist.[10]

But things are never quite so simple as we would like. Peirce goes on to point out that in the case of most relatively complex propositions, the subject-index pair is itself compound. In the sentence (a) "A sells B to C for the price D," A, B, C, and D form a set of four indices, and "_____ sells _____ to _____ for the price _____" is the icon or idea representing the set of indices. According to the sentence (b) "James Keys, who wrote *Only Two Can Play This Game,* is actually G. Spencer-Brown, author of *Laws of Form,*" the indices in question are linked to the same "semiotic object," though they are not identical or synonymous, since the two instantiations of the "semiotic object" are dressed in distinct semiotic attire and they are contextualized differently. The proposition brings the two indices together as a relatively simple whole, thus eschewing many of the possible instantiations of the "object" in question while focusing on that quality of the "object" relevant to the particular proposition.

On the other hand, (c) "Flying planes can be dangerous" contains an ambiguous index, the two "objects" being mutually exclusive. Disambiguation of the proposition eschews the myriad instantiations (composite photographs) of each of the incompatible icons, while foregrounding precisely that incompatibility in order to determine, in the context of its use, which of the two indices applies. When considering propositions (a), (b), and (c) in terms of the existing set of sensory, "semiotically real," and cognitive conditions, the labyrinthine complexity of natural language in regard to its *implicate* and *explicate, nonselective* and *selective,* dimensions begins to take effect.

However, we have hardly begun to scratch the surface. Peirce's "it rains" as a "mental composite photograph" (icon) of the sum total of the rainy days the utterer has experienced comes dangerously close to—if it is not itself the spitting image of—that long-venerated "picture theory," shot from the launching pad by Plato and brought to its aphelion with Wittgenstein's *Tractatus*. The picture theory—mind and/or language as a mirror of nature—came to predominate so thoroughly in metaphysical ventures that, as Richard Rorty (1979:12) remarks,

> It is pictures rather than propositions, metaphors rather than statements, which determine most of our philosophical convictions. The picture which holds traditional philosophy captive is that of the mind as a great mirror, containing various representations—some accurate, some not—and capable of being studied by pure nonempirical methods. Without the notion of the mind as mirror, the notion of knowledge as accuracy of representation would not have suggested itself.[11]

Rorty critiques Peirce's use of the phrase *"man's glassy essence"* (CP:6.270–71) on arguing that "a person is nothing but a symbol involving a general idea." Peirce propagates the erroneous idea, Rorty points out, that "man" is an essence trying to discover the essence of essence (nature). The universe, so this story goes, has produced minds that mirror the universe: the mirror mirrors itself within itself. The Cartesians, Rorty continues, erred in that they believed the mind tuned properly inward could divine the essence of everything, and the empiricists were on the wrong track in remaining true to Cartesian epistemology in their belief that the Inner Eye was capable of reduplicating everything "out there" (Rorty 1979:70–127). On the other hand, Rorty applauds cognitive psychologist Jerry Fodor (1975) for his postulating psychological states as propositional and computational rather than metaphorical or visual. If representation there be, the Chomsky-Fodor innateness thesis, according to which representation is generated by a mechanism "wired into" the brain, is rather plausible. However, confusion reigns between pictures and propositions—between retinal images (and their counterparts in the cortex) and such beliefs as "That's blue and square." The image is unmediated, and the belief put in propositional dress is a premise. To reduce an image to a proposition is contradictorily to fuse the two (Rorty 1979:252–53).

Rorty adopts a variant of Quine's "holistic" approach in order to get rid of the mirror-of-nature metaphor and visual perception. We are within the fabric of sentences, he tells us, and as such we cannot grasp the totality of things, hence we cannot know *how* the mirror works—if the mirror indeed existed—let alone know *that* it mirrors by faithfully describing *what* is mirrored. The most we can do is do what we do—using language within particular contexts—and hope for the best. All we have is a fabric of sentences. To say something is not necessarily to say something *about* something but simply to use language. In Rorty's (1979:371–72) words:

> We must get the visual, and in particular the mirroring, metaphors out of our speech altogether. To do this we have to understand speech not only as not the externalizing

of inner representations, but as not a representation at all. We have to drop the notion of correspondence for sentences as well as for thoughts, and see sentences as connected with other sentences rather than with the world. We have to see the term "corresponds to how things are" as an automatic compliment paid to successful normal discourse rather than as a relation to be studied and aspired to throughout the rest of discourse.

The upshot has it that there is no mirror but mirage, no representation but mediation.

In the first place, regarding Rorty's critique of the fusion and confusion of images and propositions, the former unmediated and the latter mediated, we have the fundamentals of Peirce's Firstness and Thirdness, iconicity and symbolicity. But the latter cannot exist without Firstness *and* Secondness (the "semiotically real"—not the "actually real"). This distinction between "semiotically real" and "real" is of utmost importance, for therein lies a most significant facet of *semiosis:* the two shall never meet for anything short of an infinite community of knowers. In the second place, another distinction I have mentioned, and will elaborate on repeatedly, is that between *vagueness* and *generality,* the former gravitating toward Firstness, the latter toward Thirdness. The image is destined to remain inexorably vague and to a degree inconsistent—therefore it is not merely a cloudy mirror to be polished to its lustrous best (truth). And propositions cannot but be, as generals, incomplete—therefore they will never directly say what the world *is.* In this sense "it rains" as a "mental composite photograph" cannot be a reliable mirror image but an approximation. And when couched in propositional form, *"that day,"* as an index "pointing" to the "semiotically real" world, makes up a premise—as Rorty would say regarding "That's blue and square"—which, coupled with a supporting premise and a conclusion, composes an *argument* (consisting of a *subject* and a set of *propositions).* But just as the mental image, or whatever we wish to call it, cannot but remain somewhat vague, and each proposition somewhat incomplete, so any and all arguments can never reach absolute fulfillment.

What, actually, would be the significance of a perfectly faithful mirror image? Returning to Rorty (1979:376), "The notion of an unclouded Mirror of Nature is the notion of a mirror which would be indistinguishable from what was mirrored, and thus would not be a mirror at all. The notion of a human being whose mind is such an unclouded mirror, and who *knows* this, is the image, as Sartre says, of God." This ideal unclouded mirror would be tantamount to the Final Interpretant—as I shall illustrate further in chapters 6 and 7—in its self-contained, self-reflexive, self-sufficient totality: The Ultimate Hologram. Available solely to some infinite entity, it must remain inaccessible *for* us in the Peircean sense. Hence we hardly need to worry about it, but best we should continue doing what we can do, as Rorty counsels. If Peircean "mirror of nature" there be, it is certainly no utopian dream in the Cartesian style. Rather, true to Peirce's mathematics- rather than language-based sign theory, as a mind construct it is "semiotically real" but perennially inaccessible to any collection of "semiotic objects" in the world "out there."

Consideration of this unclouded mirror ushers in Umberto Eco and his essay on mirrors in *Semiotics and the Philosophy of Language* (1984:202–26). Eco calls mirror images *absolute doubles,* which is not to say that they are icons, for, Eco argues, they are not signs in the full sense at all. A sign, according to Eco's theory, must be able to refer back in time or space to something which *is* what the sign at least in part *is not:* it must endow its user with the possibility of lying (Eco 1984:177–82). A mirror, in contrast, cannot be a presence in the absence of that to which it refers; it never refers to remote consequents. Thus neither can it be correlated with a content. Nor can it establish a relationship between types or generals, but only between tokens or individuals. As such it is never independent of its medium, and therefore cannot enjoy an interpretant: it simply *is what it is,* unmediated in the sense of sign-object-interpretant interaction.

But what is *absolute iconism* anyway? If it is not signness, then what can it be in Peirce's universe perfused with signs, if not wholly consisting of signs? In view of the preceding chapters, it is, like Rorty's unclouded Mirror of Nature, the impossible Final Interpretant. This unimaginable Interpretant, having taken in more and more until it included all, has become coterminous with the Pure Monad. The ideal continuum at one extreme is equal to the ideal continuum at the other extreme. I cannot overemphasize the fact that this Peircean conception of things is not the same as that ill-fated dream, that quest for the chimerical Mirror of Nature Rorty so effectively deconstructs. Peirce is exonerated at least in part by his illustrating time and again that we are within the holistic fabric of signs, with no map of the whole to guide us. Although Peirce did not take the final leap, he compellingly demonstrated that we need not expend needless energy toward realizing pretentious dreams, but, by way of critical dialogic exchange, collectively we can push on hopefully to become a bit more right than wrong. In this light, if the mirror does not produce a sign in the full sense when coupled with its image but affords a vague and delusory hope of reaching, somewhere and somewhen, that Grand Absolute Icon, the problem is that it promises infinitely more than it can deliver.

Eco suggests so much. The mirror image is a most peculiar case of the double: it is an *absolute double.* This explains

> why mirrors inspired so much literature; this virtual duplication of stimuli (which sometimes works as if there were both my body as an object and my body as a subject, splitting and facing itself), this theft of an image, this unceasing temptation to believe I am someone else, makes a man's experience with mirrors an absolutely unique one, on the threshold between perception and signification. (Eco 1984:210)

The apparent duplication of the body as both object and subject constitutes in effect a fusion, albeit imaginary rather than "real," of the long-standing subject-object dichotomy. It is precisely from this imagined absolute iconism inherent in the specular image that "the dream of a sign having the same characteristics arises" (Eco 1984:210)—and thus the Western obsession with ocular metaphors, the Great Mirror of Nature, the Inner Eye capable of reduplicating, in all its fullness, the world "out there." Eco writes further of mirrors as "rigid designators," concluding that there is a difference between mirror images and proper names in that the former is an *absolute proper name,* just as it is an *absolute double* and an *absolute icon.* The mirror image serves vicariously to bring to fruition the semiotic delusion of proper names' "being immediately linked to their referent (just like the semiotic dream of an image having all the properties of the object they refer to)," which "arises from a sort of *catopric nostalgia"* (Eco 1984:212). It also fulfills the obsession among many traditional cultures with "word magic"—the word becomes coterminous with the thing, hence to be in possession of a person's name is to be in possession of that person—as well as James G. Frazer's magic by likeness (metaphor-iconicity) and magic by contagion or contact (metonymy-indexicality).

Since we are destined to remain short of the Absolute Icon or Final Interpretant, (a) "A sells B to C for the price of D" cannot be a picture of the "real" transaction. Nor is it even a "picture" of the "semiotically real" event in question. It is merely a sentence among sentences, to be understood in the context of other sentences. "James Keys" and "G. Spencer-Brown" in proposition (b) cannot be mirror images of one another, given their unique context as tokens occurring in the linear stream of signs. And "Flying planes" in (c) dramatically reveals the semiotic uncertainty present in any and all systems whose obstinate push toward the absolute must remain as an infinitely receding horizon.

IV. SIGNS LOST AND SIGNS REGAINED. Actually, propositions (a), (b), and (c) are quite depthless and value-free in comparison to pregnant, value-laden propositions such as, say, (d) "The universe is a machine." Product of the Cartesian-Newtonian corpuscular-kinetic world view, this proposition embodies and at the same time lies behind an entire language-dependent and culture-dependent universe of discourse, from the hard sciences to the social sciences to the humanities, and it came to pervade, by the end of the nineteenth century and well into the present one, the arts and even many facets of everyday speech habits. In short, it became the tacitly presupposed universe *embedded* in the collective mind of the community, thus compelling *automatized* semiotic responses to certain conditions.[12] It became virtually unimaginable that the universe could be otherwise.

Our semiotic world is constructed by means of an elaborate succession of *cuts* or *marks* which eventually form a complex and relatively coherent set of categories: "This is a Mayan, not an Aztec, jade carving," "The humpback whales are endangered," "You've come a long way, baby," "The market plunged 59.3 points," "Have a good one," and so on. With continued use of categories in contextualized discourse, mindlessness sets in such that behavior becomes automatized, not entirely unlike that of the pianist in chapter 2. The good news is that without such categories the world would be devoid of much of its meaning *for* us. The bad news is that the mind tends toward stultification, toward *embedded* forms of sign generation and interpretation. In Buddhism, such mindless acts of signification, Peirce's habit of mind or thought (Boler 1964), are called the "Lord of Speech":

We adopt sets of categories which serve as ways of managing phenomena. The most fully developed products of this tendency are ideologies, the systems of ideas that rationalize, justify and sanctify our lives. Nationalism, communism, existentialism, Christianity, Buddhism—all provide us with identities, rules of action, and interpretations of how and why things happen as they do. (Trungpa [1973] in Langer [1989:11])

Shedding one set of categories and constructing a new set can be a disconcerting, even bizarre, experience, to wit, as illustrated by Borges's (1964a:103) ancient Chinese encyclopedia in which animals are put into apparently absurd pigeonholes, or by Einstein's equally strange *Gedanken* experiments. Deviation from such *embedded* pathways of least resistance must be a *mindful act,* a swim against the current, a negentropic force against a brain in the process of running down. In many Eastern philosophies, proper meditation techniques lead to such *de-automatization.* In the process old categories dissolve back into the *semiosic* soup, and the individual is no longer trapped by customary stereotypes and classes (Deikman 1966).

Actually, mindlessness entails a spectrum, from brute physical force to instinct to customary pathways of physical action to mental habits or styles of reason and reaction. As habit, it is Thirdness, or as part of another triad, *deduction.* Purely rational or deductive thinking serves to confirm old mindsets, rigid categories. On the other hand, the continuous flow of experience, or Firstness, presents the possibility of novelty; this is the realm of *abduction.* But an abduction is nothing unless it passes the test of Secondness, by *inductive* trials and tribulations. The trick, of course, is to maintain oneself in a state of readiness for mindful happenings. That, precisely, is how free flights of the imagination that develop into fruitful artworks, theories, inventions, technological innovations, and so on come about.

Further to place proposition (d), "The universe is a machine," in its proper context, let us turn to Thomas Kuhn's *The Structure of Scientific Revolutions* (1970). It is now generally accepted that scientific development follows definite patterns, whether or not they are those precisely specified by Kuhn. According to this theory, the train of information generation and processing in the sciences is nonlinear, marked by periodic bursts of creative activity ("revolutionary science") interspersed with periods of relatively routine research ("normal science"). During "normal science" (conducted by way of *habit,* Thirdness, that is, *embedded, automatized* semiotic activity), the received world picture is rarely questioned. Scientists content themselves with designing tests for existing theories, extending those theories to uninvestigated phenomena, and in general doing mop-up work.

However, "perturbations" eventually appear in the form of new evidence that fails to conform to expectations (Peirce's "clash" of Secondness). These perturbations, eventually breeding anomalies, accumulate and cast doubt on the soundness of the theoretical core of the world picture. When the conglomeration of perturbations exceeds a critical mass, the status of the paradigm begins to change: it no longer commands the blind allegiance of the more adventuresome scientists, while conservative investigators begin fighting rear-guard action to defend the anomaly-ridden theory. Eventually, by an imaginative flight of fancy (*abduction,* Firstness), some maverick scientist, usually young of age and outside the mainstream of "normal science," generates a radically novel theory partly to almost wholly incompatible with the received view. This new view is initially embraced by a minority group of scientists who then turn "revolutionary," and if the revolution is effective, the conventional theoretical edifice soon collapses. Only by such a revolution could the centuries-old dominion of classical physics have come to an end.

More specifically, the original formulation of the machine model, in Descartes's (1644:285–86) words, was: "I have described the earth and the whole visible universe *as if it were* a machine, having regard only to the shape and movement of its parts." This Cartesian-Newtonian trope, after becoming entrenched *(embedded* and *implicitly acknowledged,* via *habit),* was eventually transformed into "The universe *is* a machine," which served generally to govern the tacit—and at times mindless—behavior of the community. The citizens of the community tended to go along with their daily affairs, oblivious of the original *as if* clause in the "machine ≈ universe" trope, conducting their scientific activity *as if* this were simply *the way the world is.* In other words, the Newtonian revolution booted the language of science to a new level, which then branched out horizontally to become progressively more complex, eventually giving rise to perturbations. The linguistic system gradually became less stable, and finally virtually chaotic, until the appearance of a new world view, the Einsteinian revolution, which, as the mind of the scientific community became more accustomed to this new conceptual framework, revealed a new world of relative order.[13] In other words, the Newtonian set of symbols were morphologically transmuted into a new set: *symbols evince a tendency to multiply* (CP:2.302).

It is worthy of note that, in light of the above comments on hierarchization, the fundamental changes brought about by such "paradigm shifts" not only radically alter the basic constructs of science; they also simplify them—recall the words on simplicity and complexity in section II of this chapter. Relative simplicity replaces the labyrinth of perturbations and their accompanying anomalies that burdened the existing paradigm. The apparently comparative simplicity of an emerging world picture should not be construed as easily comprehended merely because it might appear at the outset less burdened with an undesirable cargo of complexity. Emerging paradigms are seldom if ever fully understood at the outset. As a rule they are many steps removed from the plane of observation and common sense—Copernicus's theory was dubbed "Copernicus's paradox" for a couple of centuries. Einstein's equation $E = mc^2$ is simpler than Lorentz's transformation formulas used by some physicists in their attempt to salvage the waning Newtonian world picture, but it required one to step up to a much higher level of abstraction in order to grasp it; hence it did not immediately receive wide acclaim. Much the same could be said, and examples given, of nonscientific endeavors.

To couch the above paragraphs more specifically in Peircean terms, originally, the sign, as proposition, or symbol—Descartes's "universe *as if it were* a machine"—was conceived to be a figurative, rhetorical device with which to generate a universe of discourse. As such the proposition, along with others, became an *argument,* the pinnacle of *semiosis* and the ultimate sign in Peirce's basic tenfold set of categories. During the early stages of the Cartesian world image, the argument entailed use of the sign *as* symbol with cognizance of the metaphor qua metaphor. This is the active mind at work, conception and cognition via the mediacy of Thirdness, a mind-dependent synthesis of signs and their "semiotic objects" by sheer intellection. However, with time, nonintellectual, nonconscious *habit* exercised its dominion. Consequently, what were previously conscious thought processes gradually submerge into the depths of consciousness to become less mediate, and more *as if* immediate.[14] Mind, tending to jell, becomes increasingly passive, toward, and finally reaching, the stage when it acts and reacts mindlessly. This, precisely, is the level of *tacit knowledge,* which approaches the *instinctive* domain of behavior.

Such habituation marks *embedded* sign use, and *de-generacy* of signs from symbol to index and finally to icon. In other words, the "universe *as if it were* a machine" becomes *indexicalized* such that the distinction between *this* (machine, which is empirically accessible in terms of its parts and functions) and *that* (universe, which is in part nonempirical but is rendered intelligible in relation to a machine) begins to fade. And ultimately, the once-proud proposition becomes *iconized* such that the universe is tacitly viewed as *that which is,* that is, *as if it were literally a machine*—though I do not wish to disparage iconicity, which is crucial to the *semiosic* process.[15] It is now *as if* the initial Cartesian trope were a *quasi-absolute icon,* a mirror image of the universe: something approximating the Mirror of Nature was artificially realized in the minds of many practitioners of science by the end of the nineteenth century.

At this point the system reaches out and bites its own tail. On the other hand, it is now open to the domain of Firstness, chance, spontaneity, possibility. Hence there can exist, once again, susceptibility to novelty by way of *abduction.* Indeed, the spontaneity of Firstness, of iconicity, is always grounded in the very nature of things. Without it there is no physical process, diversification, growth, development, or evolution. Chance and spontaneity at one extreme, and generality, habit, and law at the other have a meeting ground in common: one extreme entails the continuum of all possibilities, the other entails the continuous becoming of all that was possible. The end is the beginning and the beginning the end.

But actually, to repeat, there can be neither end nor beginning *for* finite consciousness. In the sense of Bohm (1986:196–201), *enfoldment* is timeless, *unfolding* is temporal. The temporal is a *becoming of being,* without *being*'s ever *becoming* a final and absolute state; the timeless ("synchronic") is the *being of becoming,* the substrate or background from which everything that is perceived and conceived arises without the possible exhaustion of *being* or the termination of *becoming.*

In another way of putting this, the generation of meaning, according to the examples I have given from a portion of Peirce's theory of icons, indices, and symbols, creates, so to speak, "knots" in the *semiosic* fabric. Such "knots" are nonlinear systems which can, by way of the flow of all "knots," evolve into forms that are to a greater or lesser degree maintained in spite of their being in a process of perpetual change. And through it all, the *semiosic* fabric prevails. It *is as it is,* though it is never exactly the same from one instant to the next. The Heraclitean (or Peircean) image of a river as the same yet different is once again apropos. The river maintains its general shape because it is never the same; it is constantly dying and being reborn by virtue of its flow. There are perturbations, undulations, debris that temporarily check the flow, minute eddies, and through periods of drought, flash floods, spring thaws, and so on, it suffers catastrophic shifts, some of them irreparable. Nevertheless, it is conceived as the same river, as a dynamic whole, and requires no artificial act of construction to give it life. It is self-sufficient, and in this respect it contains its own meaning.

Significantly, the patterns and perturbations emerging on the river's surface are the result of chance and contingency existing at a deeper level, the general background or, so to speak, *implicate order*. *Synchronicity,* as the term might be used in this context, is precisely such apparently time-bound chance happenings—that is, there is apparent chance at the surface, but necessity lies timelessly at the deepest of levels. The image of Peirce's "bottomless lake" of consciousness, which involves thought-signs at the surface that emerge from a deeper ground and are sustained by it, is germane here. Conjoining Peirce's metaphor with Bohm's trope, the mind contains in enfolded form the whole of this background, only a minuscule portion of which at a given point in time is available to consciousness, much like the enfoldment of a particular sign from the background containing the plethora of signs that otherwise could have been unfolded but were not (Bohm 1980:204–206). The "synchronic" domain, or "block" if you will, is the potential for all signs, all meaning, all "semiotically real worlds," generated from the implicate domain.

Understandably, therefore, each interpretant of a sign inevitably passes away into other signs whose successors necessarily contain within themselves some "memory" or "trace" of the signs that preceded them. These interpretants serve retroactively to determine what *will have happened* in order that that which *was* "earlier" might be made relatively coherent with that which *will be* "later." Every interpretant caught in the *semiosic* flow of things is, like a space-time "knot," interactively interrelated with everything else in one's mutually "causative" holistic fabric of signs: a given *Umwelt*-generated "semiotic world."

By a somewhat tangential route, I now turn to the second perplexity put forth in section II: how to relate Deleuze and Guattari's vacillating *"either . . . or . . . or . . . n"* to the *semiosic* process.

F O U R *Signs Becoming Mind*

Becoming Signs:

A Topological View

I. THE BINARY MACHINE'S FEET OF CLAY. One of the recent in-
fatuations with binarism has been the right-left brain hemisphericality. Admittedly, this dichotomy departs somewhat from customary binary thinking, since the
right brain already represents, by definition, holistic, synthetic, nontemporal or
multitemporal, and nonlinear processes.

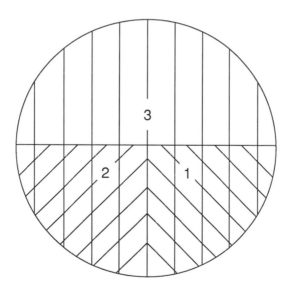

FIGURE 3

Consider, in this light, and for the mere sake of schemata, the brain to be
compartmentalized according to figure 3. Area 1 is the *sinister brain,* 2 the
dexterous brain, and 3 the *whole brain,* whose domain includes 1 and 2 in

addition to the zone it exclusively inhabits. In other words, we have (1) the "skillful" and "adroit," plus (2) the "pernicious" and "destructive," plus (3) "Nirvana" and "oblivion," the composite of which yields the self, or better, self-consciousness, which is neither absolutely individual and disjoined nor fused and conjoined, but somewhere in between. Area 2, according to stock interpretations of the split-brain phenomenon, is analytic, linear, sequential, causal, atomistic, and so on. Underlying all those rather sterile categories with which we are familiar such as male/female, outside/inside, logic/intuition, rationalism/empiricism, it entails essentially a binary mode of intellection, somewhat comparable to Saussurean-based binarism.

In this regard, 1 is not simply the opposite of 2. Rather, as the pre-Socratic philosophers—especially Heraclitus—interpreted such dualities, 2 and 1 should be understood in terms of what they *are not*. That is to say, in terms not of differences but of the interplay between different differences—or as Gregory Bateson (1972) was prone to put it, of differences that make a difference. Area 1 *is* 2 in the sense that dualities shape differences and differences combine to form wholes. And it *is also not* 2 in the same manner that 2 *is* 2. That is, 1 brings 2's sequentiality into an atemporal framework. Poststructuralist thinking, inspired by Nietzsche and propagated by Derrida, Foucault, and Lacan, among others, sets 1 + 2 off against traditional Platonism. Area 1 + 2 + 3, in addition, reveals a possible move outside the normal channels of thought and intuition found in 2, 1, and 1 + 2, toward the final self-referential, self-sufficient, self-confirmatory interpretant, which is inexorably destined to remain approximate rather than consummate.

The circle girding 3, 2, and 1 is significantly an icon of pre-Firstness. It is the beginning before the beginning, before the first *cut, mark, sign*. The ordinary generative progression is: 0 => 1 => 2=> 3. But since 3 is never final, there must needs be the possibility of reversion (by way of a Peircean *de-generacy* of signs) from 3 back to 0, which *in, by,* and *for* consciousness, is then mediately filled with the sequence of ciphers. And the ongoing cycle continues.

In his extensive commentary on Peirce, Hartshorne (1970:100–101) places a set of "metaphysical contraries" in two columns, the first corresponding to Seconds and Thirds, and the second to Firsts, the more relevant of which I have with certain variations reduplicated:

SECONDNESS-THIRDNESS	FIRSTNESS
(1) Relative, dependent.	(1) Absolute, independent.
(2) Becoming, nascent, being created.	(2) In being, already created.
(3) Temporal, succeeding some, preceding others.	(3) Nontemporal as: i. primordial, preceding everything. ii. everlasting, succeeding everything.
(4) Concrete, potentially definite, particular.	(4) Abstract, radically indefinite, universal.

(5) Actual, potential.

(6) Discrete.

(7) Singular, member.

(8) Singular event, so and so now, or in futurity, individual state.

(5) Possible.

(6) Continuous.

(7) Composite, group, mass.

(8) So and so through change, individual being.

Hartshorne observes, and rightly so, I believe, that what appears at the outset to be a set of dichotomies is actually enclosed in triadicities. In this he follows Peirce's implicit injunction: "Think in triads, not mere dyads." The latter are crude and misleading; the former, though indeterminate, are always evolving toward something. Regarding trinarism and binarism, merely to oppose concreteness and abstractness is fallacious. Both concepts are universals, and their very juxtaposition as a dichotomy tends to obscure the fact that concreteness is itself an extreme form of abstraction, and that an instance of concreteness is by no means the concept reiterated, but something new and richer.

Let us, in this light, redefine the ciphers, 0, 1, 2, and 3, in consonance with Hartshorne's formulation, to yield figure 4. Initially notice that the rectangle topologically evinces the construction of a Möbius strip. If we cut it out, double it, and give it a twist, thus connecting the 0 corner to the 1 corner and the 2 corner to the 3 corner, we have a two-dimensional surface warped in three-dimensional space such that at the junctures 0–1 and 2–3 "inside" becomes "outside," and vice versa. This is not insignificant, as we shall see, since in addition, at these same junctures, continuity becomes discontinuity, or the other way round, as the system finally doubles back and takes a gander at itself. The arrows of the two-way transformations represent the pathways of least semiotic resistance (*de-generacy, embedment, automatization,* confirmation, entropy) as well as the general push against the current (*generacy, de-embedment, de-automatization,* novelty, surprise, negentropy). The curved arrow from 0 to 1 represents a leap from what we may call the "greatest lower bound" to the simplest of cuts-signs, from the empty mind to thought-signs, from nothingness to somethingness.

Then, *semiosis (generacy)* can proceed from 0 => 1 => 2 => 3. The self-returning loops around each sign type depict *recursive reiteration* of the same sign folding back on itself (111, 222, 333). The arrows depict the *function* booting sign *generacy* up a notch toward the "least upper bound," to yield the natural classes of signs (112, 122, 222), though it can proceed directly from 1 => 3 to yield special sorts of higher sign types (113, 133, 333). And so on.[1] From 3, the culmination of a cycle, sign *generacy* can then be elevated to 1 at yet a higher level—it becomes another sign of a more developed type in the hierarchy. On the other hand, it can *de-generate* to a lower type, into either 1 or 2. Or, by a "catastrophe," so to speak, it can be canceled entirely to fade back to 0, into "oblivion" or "nothingness"—the empty sheet of assertion. The process then once again begins anew.

Very significantly, the Möbius strip is a necessary characteristic of figure 4, because the rectangle is radically asymmetrical. In contrast to the Aristotelian square of oppositions, the so-called semiotic square (Greimas and Courtés

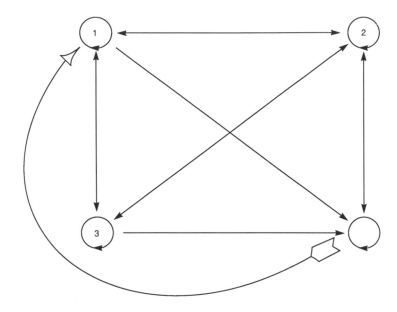

1 = FIRSTNESS, QUALITY, *MIGHT BE* (REPRESENTATION, ICONICITY)

2 = SECONDNESS, ACTUALITY, *HAPPENS-TO-BE* (OBJECT, INDEXICALITY)

FIGURE 4   3 = THIRDNESS, POTENTIALITY, *WOULD BE* (INTERPRETANT, SYMBOLICITY)

1982:308–11), or Piaget's (1953) psychological group, the three operations depicted by the horizontal, vertical, and diagonal arrows are not entirely symmetrical, reflexive, and two-way, but chiefly unidirectional, though not entirely irreversible. In other words, signs tend toward *semiosis*—sign *generacy* at increasingly complex levels—or they tend to *de-generate,* to gravitate toward a natural "sink": o.[2] Hence the one-way arrow from 1, 2, 3, to o, and from o to 1. And hence the radical asymmetry they imply.

Figure 4 takes on further import, given its particular topology, and especially in light of Jacques Lacan's theory of the unconscious (see Clément 1983; Turkle 1978). I refer to the so-called Schema R, a rectangular figure drawn on the flat page, which must be read, Lacan warns, in three dimensions, like the Möbius strip (Lacan 1966:531–83). J.-A. Miller (1966:175–76) adds that the Möbius quality of the schema renders apparent heterogeneity homogeneous. What would otherwise be a catastrophe is, so to speak, smoothed out. In short, discontinuity becomes, from another vantage, continuity, and symmetry becomes asymmetry. Elsewhere, Lacan (1977:155–56) uses another two-dimensional figure, called the "interior 8," which doubles back into itself. That is, the "interior 8" is continuous only up to a point, where the surface is folded in upon itself in three-dimensional space such that there are two intersecting fields:

Lacan places the libido at the point of the intersection as the field where the unconscious develops. This point is, Lacan claims, a *void*. It is commensurate with a mathematical point: *imaginary*. Potentially everywhere and yet no-*where,* it can be at one of an infinity of locations along the inner loop. We are told that this line, containing potentially an infinity of points, is the "line of desire" lying between "the field of demand, in which the syncopes of the unconscious are made present." More significant still, this "line of desire" is metonymous, that is, linear and asymptotic, since desire cannot be totally fulfilled (Lacan 1977:156). And here we note an obvious commonality between the point of intersection in Lacan's "interior 8" and a given point on the initial sheet of Peirce's "book of assertions." Moreover, the "interior 8" is comparable to what Peirce in his "existential graphs" calls a "scroll" (MS 450), which can be constructed in four operations (Roberts 1973:34n):

My introducing Lacan is not for the sake of defending or debating the value of his theory but to reveal the nature of his figure: its import for the present purpose lies in its abstract quality as a topological form, rather than in its substance or figurative meaning. Like the topology of Lacan's "interior 8," Peirce's "scroll," as one cut within another, represents a cut severing an area from the sheet of assertion and hence enacting a second severance. Thus a scroll:

can be read "P scrolls Q." It is the graph of material implication, "If P, then Q."[3] Q is the inner cut of the scroll, a second enclosure or area on a flat plane—the sheet of assertion. It implies something more than an imaginary sheet of infinitesimal thickness, however. It essentially includes two sheets (i.e., an additional dimension), since the cut allows a view of the successive page in the book of assertions. And with successive self-enclosing scrolls, an indefinite number of sheets (dimensions) become necessary (see appendix 1).

This is, I believe, significant. Neither is the scroll nor the "interior 8" merely symmetrical, reflexive, or reversible. They are, rather, like the Möbius strip embodied and enfolded in figure 4 by which the observer, traveling along his two-dimensional path, can alternate from "inside" to "outside." At the Spencer-Brownian level of pure form, the transformation "in" and "out" of dimensions renders the continuous discontinuous and the reversible irreversible. But unlike Spencer-Brown's *marks,* in the living context of particular "semiotically real" worlds, with each transformation there is never absolute reiteration. Something is always different: the difference that makes a difference. Here, as we shall observe in more detail in the next section, we have a model, or perhaps a *microcosm,* it would appear, of the essence of movement, change, novelty, and perhaps even time. As signs are piled upon signs, and erasure of signs (*embedment,* submergence into consciousness, memory loss) upon erasure, our navigation toward the ultimate interpretant in the universal sea of signs within which we find ourselves as immanent travelers has no end point short of infinity.

Nor can we enjoy the comfort of retrievable origins: signs are an *infinite regressus* as well as an *infinite progressus* (we are always caught in the *void* of Lacan's "interior 8" along the "line of desire"). In other words, denied complete knowledge of where we are in the signifying fabric, we have no recourse but to enter an *imaginary state,* the equivalent of Spencer-Brown's (1979) *imaginary value,* $\sqrt{-1}$, which, he suggests, is the generator of time in its most primitive form. Within this domain what *is not* enjoys its rightful place at the side of what *is*—Peirce's knowledge by virtue of *error*—as a guiding principle. Mere blind or animal-like reiteration is "truth" (what *is*) with instinctive or computerlike consistency, while awareness *of* difference, and above all *of* error, entails awareness *of* "falsity" (what *is not*). Pure reiteration is obliviousness regarding time; awareness *of* difference and error requires time, since at some point in the *then,* there *was* a rupture of the flow. For example, according to the "universe ≈ machine" model, with *embedment* there is an accompanying loss of awareness *that* a machine is in certain important respects *different from* the universe—the icon is tacitly taken for the genuine article, as if it were an *absolute icon.* Time is of no consequence; there is no difference that makes a difference. On the other side of the ledger, becoming aware at a particular point in time *that* the universe is in certain important respects *not* machinelike entails the process of *de-embedment,* a becoming of conscious awareness. The flow has been ruptured; something in the *now* is *not* what it *was.* Thus memory comes into play.

But how can smug instinctive, computer determinacy—or Deleuze and Guattari's paranoid *"this then that"*—potentially become worrisome, uncertain knowledge—the schizophrenic *"either . . . or . . . or . . . n"?* When blind *habit* becomes consciousness *of habit,* the semiotic machine can then become aware *of* the error of its ways in order to bring about a change in its "semiotically real" world. Such switches or dissipations pattern the *asymmetry, transitivity,* and *irreversibility* manifested in figure 4. And they lie at the heart of Peirce's dictum: *signs, and especially symbols, grow.* However, since the "real" can be no more than approximated asymptotically, a given community of knowers is ipso facto limited to one or another of the myriad possible "semiotic realities" of their own making—recall that Peirce was an "objective idealist" (i.e., a methodological realist but an epistemological and ontological idealist). Rather than the "real" and "truth" per se, we are forced to consider, so to speak, topology and relations per se. Awareness *of* this all-important feature of *semiosis* breeds awareness *of* myriad possibilities rather than tunnel-visioned assurance.

Fallible fledglings that we are, there can be no absolute provability, only refutability, as a result of error-awareness (of course, we have here once again the Peircean counterpart to Popper's "falsification" [see Freeman 1983; Freeman and Skolimowski 1974]). In the open space of truth there is no fulcrum point; but in the overpopulated jungle of error, a starting point can be found virtually anywhere, followed by a tenuously charted path hewn toward some unknowable end. Therein rests the beauty of Peirce's notion of *cuts* of variable size and shape made anywhere in the initial empty sheet of assertion according to one's whims, and Spencer-Brown's equally arbitrary *marks* and *indications* in conceptual space separating *this* from *that*.[4] Ultimately, *relations*—between *cuts* or *marks*—are paramount, especially regarding the necessity of time to Peirce's general scheme of things, which calls for irreversibility.

However, another rather random walk will be necessary in order further to illustrate the thesis of process, of irreversibility, being presented here, which will include a few words on Peirce as semiotician-mathematician-logician. Some commentators find in Peirce a unique contribution to the study of mind and language paralleling and at the same time illuminating the work of Frege, Russell, Wittgenstein, and others, and, in addition, a general framework for an integrated theory of culture (for example, Apel 1981). However, Peirce was actually far removed from the logical atomism generally prevalent during the first decades of this century. Though Christopher Hookway (1985:157–80) expresses worries about Peirce's outmoded, classical theory of perception, Hartshorne (1983:88–92) assures us that with his theory of mathematico-logical relations, the "logic of relatives," Peirce took a step toward superseding classical subject-predicate logic (see MSS 516–17, 532–37, 544–45, 547–48). To say "P is Q" implies a dyadic relation, which is sufficient in the event that the copula is taken to be the equivalent of identity. But where relatives are concerned, dyadic relations are inadequate. "P is sad," "P sees," and "P gives" are clearly incomplete. "P" is saddened by what? What does "P" see? What does "P" give and to whom? Such predicates imply dependence or relativity, especially in light of Peirce's *pragmatic maxim,* as discussed above.

Russell, Hartshorne (1983:88) remarks, "took over the logic of relatives, largely from Peirce, and neatly missed the ontological point." For Russell the subject of a relational proposition is not relative but absolute: the only logical requirement is the subject and its own monadic predicate. Russell followed Hume insofar as for both of them "reality" consists of a succession of fragmented and stationary states, each being what it is at its particular moment and independent of all other states. Two states, A_1 and A_2, are logical absolutes; they are related symmetrically. Each is a Peircean First to the other, hence there is no concept of linear, irreversible progression from one to the other. The relations are entirely reversible (a notion which, interestingly enough, Borges [1962:217–34] takes up, with the aid of Hume and Berkeley, and extrapolates to the extreme in his celebrated "The New Refutation of Time").[5]

This static notion of relations allows no Secondness or Thirdness. Secondness offers at least an initial introduction to asymmetry, thus excluding two radical doctrines: Hume's and Russell's perceptual atomism or absolute pluralism, and an extreme form of monism in the sense of Francis Bradley. Secondness is the actualization of a possibility, of Firstness, and it points toward Thirdness. Firstness as what *might be* becomes what *is,* which will invariably have some successor drawn from it by Thirdness, or conditionality, what *would be* under certain circumstances. In this light, Hartshorne (1983:88–89) concludes:

> It seems close to obvious that without Secondness there can be no understanding of what it is distinctively to be a caused or conditioned phenomenon, and without Firstness there can be no understanding of what it is distinctively to be a cause or condition, and that without a third and intermediate relation between sheer dependence and sheer independence there can be no understanding of time's arrow, the contrast between the already settled, decided past, and the not yet decided, needing-to-be-decided—yet not merely indeterminate—future.

Russell's perceptual atomism also entails immediate "knowledge by acquaintance," a form of pure intuitionism by way of a dyadic relation between knower and known, which was the focus of repeated attacks by Peirce (Bernstein 1964:167–68). Moreover, the Kantian flavor of Peirce's work—i.e., that the mathematically "real" is the ontologically ideal—coupled with a lack of sympathy for the logician's program of reducing mathematics to logic, sets him apart from the analytical school (Rescher and Brandom 1979:104–25).

But above all, and as I have suggested, Peirce's notions of *vagueness* and *generality,* which roughly coincide with *inconsistency* and *incompleteness* in the sense of contemporary logic and mathematics (Rescher and Brandom 1979), render him highly suspect from the vantage point of those hotly in pursuit of certainty. Vagueness, for Peirce, is "the antithetical analogue of generality." A sign is *general* in that it "leaves to the interpreter the right of completing the determination for himself," and it is *vague* in that it leaves its interpretation "more or less indeterminate, it reserves for some other possible sign or exception the function of completing the determination" (CP:5.505).[6]

In this sense, to repeat, *vagueness* defiles the purity of the principle of noncontradiction as *generality* does that of the excluded-middle principle. This is the inverse of Russell's view that the excluded middle rather than noncontradiction is restricted by vagueness (Cohen 1962; Gallie 1952). Analytic philosophers and logicians are prone to agree that natural languages are *vague,* thus their interest in constructing a precise ideal language. In contrast, those with a desire to encompass a more *general* sign system within their purview find it essential, usually after a number of fits and starts, to entertain the idea that *vagueness* is implicit in any and all forms of semiotic representation (Nadin 1983:159–64).[7]

Following Peirce, the *vague* is generic to *possibility;* the *general* is generic to *necessity* (CP:5.448, 5.459, 5.505). Possibility is the condition for the generation of individuals, of Seconds, while necessity includes individuals. An individual "determines nothing but itself or always determines itself in determining anything else," while something "which can of its nature determine something else without being itself determined" is a general (MS:899). Semiotically speaking, *vagueness* is distinguished from *generality* insofar as a vague sign, qua indeterminate, leaves its further interpretation to some other sign or experience. Denying such completion of its interpretant to the interpreter, the sign will always remain *for* the interpreter "semiotically real," an incomplete manifestation of the "actually real" (CP:5.447, 5.505). Insofar as generality leaves further interpretation of the sign to the interpreter, the sign may approach near-universality, though it will never reach that point in a finite world. In this sense, a vague sign toward the "greatest lower bound" is a *remote universal,* while a general sign, toward the "least upper bound," is a *near universal* (see McKeon 1952:243–45).

Apparently, then, Peirce's *vagueness* and *generality* exist at opposite poles: Firstness and Thirdness, *tychism* and *synechism*—in other words, with regard to figure 4, *toward* 0 at one extreme and *toward* 3 at the other. Pure *vagueness* (the *not-yet-selected*) is that which is not clearly and precisely felt, sensed, understood, comprehended; it entails uncertainty (chance), leaving things open to the possibility of inconsistency—hence vagueness abrogates noncontradiction. On the other hand, pure *generality* (the *having-been-selected*) is that which is ideally applicable to everything, to the whole. Fusing individuals through some real or imagined commonality between them, generality must remain inexorably incomplete, since for Peirce a grasp of the totality, *sub specie aeternitatis,* will never be at hand—and hence it does away with the excluded-middle principle.[8] We have, once again, the *selected* with respect to the *nonselected,* what *is* with respect to what *is not,* the "*This, then that . . . n*" juxtaposed with "*Either . . . or . . . or . . . n*"—and here, the problem posed in chapter 3 thus comes to the fore, which will be fleshed out further in chapters 6 and 7.

On the other hand, Secondness, lying between the two extremes, is the reactionary "clash" of the world "out there." In its pure form, nothing more than a succession of particulars set apart by their differences, even though they may be well-nigh infinitesimal as they impinge upon the senses. They are *haecceities*—Duns Scotus's term Pierce used often—in the most radical sense. Like Borges's (1962:59–66) supernominalist in "Funes the Memorious" who was shocked to discover that others considered a dog seen from the front one moment and from the side at a later moment to be the same dog, such pure particulars play havoc with the idea of identity: there are only myriad similarities and differences.[9] That is to say, identity and contradiction—i.e., classical binarism—are no more than a hopeful figment of the mind.

II. ON THE INCOMPATIBILITY PRINCIPLE.

The distinctions having been outlined between Firstness (possibility, chance, spontaneity, vagueness), Secondness (particularity, *haecceity*), and Thirdness (necessity, habit, regularity, generality, law) are thus related to the previous discussion of Spencer-Brown's calculus, Peirce's existential graphs, and general topological forms. And, as we shall note, they can help to account for the lack of symmetry in figure 4. Consider an individual, say, a, in light of Henry Sheffer's (1913) "stroke" function, which has been variously related to Peirce's "ampheks," his "logic of relatives" (Hartshorne 1970:206–10), and his logic of "statements" (Berry 1952; also see appendix 2).[10] The stroke, "|," written in an expression as "$a|a$," can be defined as "not both" or "neither," which yields $-a$. From this point the other notations of classical logic, as well as the other calculi and logics in question here, can be generated according to the following roughly equivalent categories (see Roberts 1973):

SHEFFER	CLASSICAL	SPENCER-BROWN	EXISTENTIAL GRAPHS
$a\,|\,a$	$-a$	$\overline{a} = $ ▦	(a)
$(a\,|\,a)\,|\,(a\,|\,a)$	a	$\overline{\overline{a}} = a$	((a)) $= a$
$a\,|\,b$	$-(ab)$	$\overline{ab} = $ ▦	(a b)
$\overline{a}\,|\,\overline{b}$	$a \wedge b$	$\overline{\overline{ab}} = ab$	((a b)) $= ab$
$(a\,|\,b)\,|\,(a\,|\,b)$	$a \vee b$	$\overline{\overline{a}\,\overline{b}}$	(a)(b)
$(a\,|\,\overline{b})\,|\,(a\,|\,\overline{b})$	$a \rightarrow b$	$\overline{a\ \overline{b}}$	(a (b))

[where ▦ denotes the unmarked, unboundaried, the empty "book of assertions"]

Let it first be noted that in Peirce, Sheffer, and Spencer-Brown, a single notation is used to generate all the notations of classical logic. This is indeed significant. It ushers in an element of parsimony, of elegance predicated on negation and on the "not yet decided, needing-to-be-decided," but "not yet merely indeterminate," possibility of Firstness. Regarding sign relations as they have been described thus far, let us use this primitive form of calculus with only one symbol, a. Assume Firstness to be represented by an uncertainty between actualization into a Second of two different possible instances of a, a_1 and a_2, the first instantiation preceding the second one by a temporal increment. The expression of the two possible instantiations is (a₁ a₂) bearing in mind that *neither a_1 nor a_2* has yet been actualized, but, since both a_1 and a_2 are in a state of suspension or readiness to be actualized, the equation becomes (a₁)(a₂) . Conditions of symmetry exist between a_1 and a_2; there is no priority or privilege of one over the other. Secondness, which demands, in its purest form, *distinguishability* between each instantiation of a, is expressed by the equation

$\left(\boxed{a_1 \quad a_2}\right)$, indicating that a_1 *and then* a_2 were actualized (recall that Second-ness introduces a primitive form of asymmetry). Thirdness, signified by implication $\left(a_1 \boxed{a_2}\right)$, finally introduces asymmetry, irreversibility, and "time's arrow"—though the arrow in the expression has no bearing on ex-perienced temporality, it is at this point merely a primitive logical constuct. Recalling Hartshorne's (1983:88–89) words, Firstness ushers in independence, Secondness dependence (relationality), and Thirdness "the contrast between the already settled, decided past, and the not yet decided, needing-to-be-decided— not yet merely indeterminate—future." That is, a_2 is not what it *was* but what it *is*, which necessarily includes a *trace* of that part of it which *was* but no longer *is*, and what *is* is subject to anticipation of what potentially *will be* in the future.

If we correlate the three categories as described here and their respective expressions with figure 4, we have figure 5. Category 1 is the feeling of what *might be* the case, 2 is the *action*, the *effect*, of that which *is* the case, and 3 is the *representation (signification)* of that which *would be*, or *will have been*, the case in the event that certain conditions are in effect. Category 1 implies "either *this* or *that* but not both," 2 "*this* and then *that*," and 3 "if *this* then *that*." While 1 is mere atemporal oscillation between symmetrical entities, 2 is linear, hence asymmetrical and temporal, but solely in the sense of pure succession, and 3 attains, in contrast, the highest degree of asymmetry. In other words, disjoined terms are symmetrical, the binary operation of combining terms is temporal but

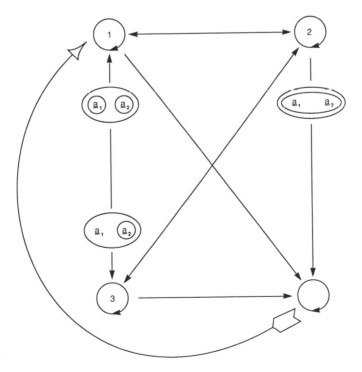

FIGURE 5

purely linear, and, with the triadic relation, true asymmetry and hence irreversibility or temporality begin to exercise their force. Thus we have, potentially, the becoming of the *"either . . . or . . . or . . . n,"* of consciousness *of* error, and subsequently the transitory switch—catastrophe—to a different level of signification. And thus it is that *symbols begin to grow.*

Hartshorne (1970:206) argues rather convincingly that asymmetry or one-wayness is attained at the most fundamental level with Thirdness. This comes about in its greatest defining power through Sheffer's function, since *not both* and *neither nor* (conjoint negation) are (as Peirce knew well) the only functions each of which, taken singly, is capable of defining all the other logical symbols. In this fashion, roughly, the defining power of logical functions varies inversely with their symmetry. (Significantly, Howard DeLong [1970:31] notes that Peirce is an exception to most innovators of mathematical logic who knew little about stoic logic and its focus on the Liar Paradox and material implication, both of which were germane to Peirce's work.)

This function becomes the domain of the *either/or* which Deleuze and Guattari's schizophrenic subverts by affirming both disjoined terms, thus stretching the *either/or* out to *"either . . . or . . . or . . . n."* It is also Beckett's (1955:176) elaborate system of affirmations and negations, characteristic of which is: "It is midnight. The rain is beating on the windows. It was not midnight. It was not raining." Differentiations become finer and finer: the staccato approaches legato, digitality approaches continuity, that is, generality, the undifferentiated. Exclusive disjunction makes a move toward inclusive and relatively unfettered disjunctions.

Now, following Deleuze and Guattari (1987), let 1 in figure 5 be called *disjunctive synthesis,* 2 *connective synthesis,* and 3 *negatively conjunctive synthesis* (Deleuze and Guattari call these three operations "productive recording," "production of production," and "productive consumption" respectively, as necessary concepts in their practice of "schizoanalysis"). As feeling (iconicity), *disjunctive synthesis* is immanence. It is not an inclusive or restrictive use of signs but their fully affirmative, nonrestrictive, exclusive use. It is a disjunction that must remain disjunctive, yet there is still the possibility of affirming both terms of the disjunction. Their affirmation is made possible by their very disjointness, their distance: one is not necessarily restricted by excluding it from the other—recall Peirce's mark on the blackboard from chapter 1. This is in itself paradoxical, though a paradox whose two horns both *differ* and are *deferred* temporally: an oscillatory *"either . . . or . . . or . . . n,"* instead of the simple binary *either/or* (Deleuze and Guattari 1987:78). What we have here is a *superposition* of the one *and* the other. Such superposition is rather comparable to Heisenberg's (1958a:167–86) view of the wave function of quantum reality as a tendency for something, Aristotle's *potentia,* the coexistence of a set of possible states. Or in Popper's (1982) terms, remarkably similar to Peirce, it is the mathematical representation of a certain *propensity* (i.e., a *habit*).

The idea of superposition can be roughly modeled by the Necker cube in a state of readiness for oscillating between P (face up) and Q (face down), which is tantamount to indeterminable iteration, like a wave-train: $\lfloor P \rfloor Q \lfloor P \rfloor Q \lfloor P \rfloor Q \lfloor P \rfloor$

(Comfort 1984; Kauffman and Varela 1980, Kauffman 1980). The superposition, or the mere possibility of *sign disjunction*, makes way for the construction of a "semiotically real" domain, P-Q, such that for any sign, S, S obtains in this domain if and only if it obtains as a semiotic equivalence with, or a subset of, either P or Q. Such sign domains represent, in Rescher and Brandom's (1979:10) terms, *superposition, sign disjunction* (non-noncontradiction), *inconsistency,* and *overdetermination* (or in Peircean vocabulary, *vagueness,* which corresponds to Firstness).[11] The notion of superposition evokes, significantly enough, the quantum world or *prototemporality,* as described above. Overdetermination breeds the conditions for a sign interpreter's becoming conscious *of* contradiction, inconsistency, paradox, and anomaly—i.e., that which was not expected, which causes surprise, and opens up the possibility of abductive leaps. Thus overdetermination entails interpreter-interpretant interaction. The interpreter is a participant rather than a passive recipient, and the interpretant becomes an actor in the *semiosic* drama rather than a mere object to be acted upon.

Category 2, *connective synthesis,* is a linear, binary coupling of "machines," which reveals the other side of the coin: a pure succession of signs. For example, Deleuze and Guattari's "desiring machines"

> are binary machines, obeying a binary law or set of rules governing associations: one machine is always coupled with another. The productive synthesis, the production of production, is inherently connective in nature: "and . . . " "and then . . . " This is because there is always a flow-producing machine, and another machine connected to it that interrupts or draws off part of this flow. . . . And because the first machine is in turn connected to another whose flow it interrupts or partially drains off, the binary series is linear in every direction. Desire constantly couples continuous flows and partial objects that are by nature fragmentary and fragmented. (Deleuze and Guattari 1983:5)[12]

The "couplings" or connections are both biological (ontological, physiological) and social, both individual and collective, *molecular* and *molar.* The whole of technical machines is an organized system of production, whereas the human biological machine as a whole consists of a *molar,* aggregate level of organization, with its respective parts functioning at a *molecular* level (see also Merrell 1990).[13] In whichever case, everything is coupled with everything else either physically or mentally (i.e., sign-things or thought-signs). That is, everything is a machine: something coupled with something else in the sense of *this* and then *that,* as succession, as *eotemporality,* in contrast to the *prototemporal.*

Moreover, this "coupling" is closely related to what might be dubbed "quantum chaos," following Bohm, and "phase locking," both of them nonlinear phenomena. In Bohm's implicate order as a quantum potential, each electron-to-be-explicated is in a state of perpetual quivering, a sort of infinite sensitivity, since it is interconnected to all other potential entities in the holomovement. The entire quantum potential dictates an electron's behavior in terms of an unimaginably intricate manifold, which, according to Bohm, is entirely determinate, though, given the complexity of the whole system, it must be for the mind short of anything but infinite capacity, completely unpredictable. Phase locking occurs when a set of oscillators gradually alter the frequency of their oscillations such that they begin resonating in harmony. A remarkable example of phase locking in nature is that of a group of fireflies which, at what appears to be some predetermined moment, begin coordinating their electrical impulses to bring about an illumination of their abdominal sections. "Jet lag" is a more familiar example. The biological clock is phase locked into a frequency dictated by the twenty-four-hour day. The disorientation experienced during jet lag is due to the body's attempt to adjust itself to a different twenty-four-hour pattern (for an excellent study of phase locking regarding the cardiovascular system, see Winfree 1987).

At this juncture I must also emphasize that Deleuze and Guattari's "machine," though comparable to, as I pointed out in section II of chapter 3, is not to be confused with that of Maturana and Varela (1980), who highlight the "autonomous," "autopoietic" character of the living organism as a "machine." Maturana and Varela focus almost entirely, indeed in hedgehog fashion, on the *autonomous* aspect of the living organism as a homeostatic "machine." In this sense, an autopoietic entity is viewed as that which is "distinguishable from a background, the sole condition necessary for existence in a given domain." The nature of this entity and the domain in which it exists "are specified by the process of its distinction and determination; this is so regardless of whether this process is conceptual or physical" (Maturana and Varela 1980:138). In this fashion, the "machine" subordinates its environment to its own self-maintenance, retaining in the process its identity through an active compensation of the changes it undergoes. It is thus definable in a topological space consisting of a network of processes of production, transformation, and destruction of self-reproductive components that, through their interactions and transformations, constantly regenerate the network of processes that produce them.

On the other hand, according to my reading of Deleuze and Guattari's "machine," the closed domain of processes and relations specifying it by no means dictates total autonomy. Rather, it is also open to its environment. There is a constant exchange of material, energy, and information, which serves to alter "machine" as well as environment in the process, a conclusion that coincides roughly with the work of, among others, Ilya Prigogine regarding the nature of systems in interaction with their environment (see Jantsch 1980). Deleuze and Guattari (1983:1–2), with their characteristic rhetorical aplomb, write further of "machines" thus:

> Everywhere *it* [the *Id*] is machines—real ones, not figurative ones: machines driving other machines, machines being driven by other machines, with all the necessary couplings and connections. An organ-machine is plugged into an energy-source-machine: the one produces a flow that the other interrupts. The breast is a machine that produces milk, and the mouth a machine coupled to it. The mouth of the anorexic wavers between several functions: its possessor is uncertain as to whether it is an eating-machine, an anal machine, a talking-machine, or a breathing-machine (asthma attacks). Hence we are all handy-men: each with his little machines. For every organ-machine, an energy-machine: all the time, flows and interruptions.

They allude to Molloy in Beckett's novel, who continually transfers his sixteen sucking stones from one pocket to mouth to another pocket, a continuity of action corresponding remarkably to a mathematical group. This is an ideal example of process, the process of production. But the coupling is binary, between machines of distinction rather than successive differentiation. This "production of production" is inherently connective in nature. It is serial, and asymmetrical, yet atemporal in the sense of experienced time. Nevertheless the machines in their composite are flow machines, that is, process machines. The binary series is linear, and it produces continuous flows and objects that become over the long haul fragmentary and fragmented. This "sinistral" function, the production of *I* and *you, we* and *they, good guys* and *bad guys, capitalism* and *communism,* etc., corresponds to the cipher two, to indexicality, to the finger that points, to superordinate and subordinate, to the *other* and the *Other.* It marks the establishment of Deleuze and Guattari's *territoriality.* And, whereas it is *eotemporality,* there is hierarchization but as yet no definite asymmetrical, temporal one-wayness. There is no more than Newtonian pushes and pulls the composite of which is devoid of real direction.

Category 3 in figure 5, *negatively conjunctive synthesis,* or "production of consumption," is, so to speak, the *via negativa* giving rise to all that *would be* (Thirdness). As Deleuze and Guattari put it, this synthesis is the moment of awakening—an abductive leap as a result of thwarted expectations coupled with a conjecture, a hypothetico-deductive gamble—when one exclaims: "So that's what it is!" But there is no finality here, no ultimate determinacy, for all is tentative and tenderly fallible. It is in this sense ultimately *conjoint negation: "neither . . . nor . . . nor . . . n,"* or *"not both this . . . and that . . . and that . . . n"*—and here, once again, we have Sheffer's "stroke" in a new garment. It is a "vessel" or "matrix" (not a mere "hole" to be filled) through which a potentially infinite series of signs can pass. This is the prototypical *schizophrenic*—the Nietzschean subject who passes through a series of states and who identifies himself with each and every one of them: *"every name in history is I"* (Nietzsche 1969:347). The self becomes displaced and spreads itself out along the entire circumference of the circle, the center of which has now been abandoned. In Whitmanesque fashion it becomes everybody and everything, it becomes tantamount to the universe: its universe. "No one," we are told, "has ever been as deeply involved in history as the schizo, or dealt with it in this way. He consumes all of univeral history in one fell swoop. We began by defining him as *Homo natura,* and lo and behold, he has turned out to be *Homo historia"* (Deleuze and Guattari 1987:21).

Given this perpetual displacement in time and space, the schizo is not in possession of his own self. He can be something or somebody solely by being something or somebody else. He is a *nomad;* his messages are indeterminately *polyvocal;* there is no stationary mooring, all is in a transient state. Consequently, he is *racial* (he belongs to all races), without exercising binary racism in the sense of the dyadic 2, for everything is relative to everything else. But this is not an "anything goes" enterprise, no logic of chaos, but a "nothing goes" game of successive cancellation; or better, it is *"neither this . . . nor . . . nor . . .*

n," which is not linear but expands in all directions simultaneously (and we have nonlinearity as opposed to the linearity of 2).

We are thus speaking of *sign conjunction by negation* which is characterized in terms of *underdetermination* (continuity), *incompleteness,* and *schematization* (Rescher and Brandom 1979:9–10), or what Peirce terms *generality.* Progressive underdetermination deals with familar circumstances so made familiar by (mindless) *habit:* commonplace or easily imaginable objects, acts, or events which are by their nature incomplete insofar as part or all of those objects, acts, or events have become so familiar that they are submerged *(embedded, automatized)* and no longer part of the experience *of which* one is conscious. Schematic or undetermined worlds contain blanks or blurs that remain unspecified or undefined, but which, by successive additions to a given world, can become increasingly more specifiable and defined. "This project," Rescher and Brandom (1979:5) tell us,

> seems especially plausible in a framework of *emergent* properties within a situation of temporal development which produces a succession of different "worlds" (or world-states) in such a way that the successive transitions move matters from the more to the less schematic. (That is, the earlier worlds are schematic with respect to properties, dispositions, or laws that only appear on the scene later on.) This perspective is posed by the sort of evolutionism from simple to more complex worlds or world-states envisaged by Herbert Spencer and C. S. Peirce in the latter part of the 19th century.

The move toward complexification with an accompanying proliferation of interpretants, of successive differentiation toward continuity or generality, is precisely the push into futurity of Thirdness. In this conception of generality, given the conjunction of a pair of sign domains, for a particular sign, S, S obtains in conjoint domains if and only if S obtains in *both* domains, though it can be the case that S obtains in *neither* of them. That S can obtain in *both* domains is important. As signs merge into signs and minds into minds within the field of *semiosis,* not only does the excluded-middle principle tend more often to make a hasty retreat, but also, since the features of individual signs have become foggy in the process, a set of signs or a given sign can come to embrace, in the minds of their users, wider and wider domains of signification.

That S might obtain in *neither* of the two domains is also crucial, since it is solely by a process of elimination that 3 in figure 5 can exist in the first place. Category 3, as symbolicity, as at least partial arbitrariness, *re-presents* what tentatively *is* by representing at least in part what *is not.* But since what *is* must be taken only provisionally, what *is not* is as ontologically fuzzy and indeterminate as what *is.* Everything must remain to a degree fuzzy, as if there were strange goings-on—though the overriding tendency, indeed a longing, is to put a stamp of finality on *it.* As such, 3, as the "least upper bound," as nonlinear and continuous, bears on *synechism.* And it is necessarily the prototype of *semiosis* insofar as its lack of completion perpetually calls for, in fact demands, either a getting along swimmingly or a floundering about in the unruly sea of signification. As generality or continuity, therefore, the excluded-middle principle tends to languish, and even fall into impotence.

Conjoint negation ($a_1|a_2$ or $-[-a_1 \wedge -a_2]$), therefore, marks the radical shift into Thirdness, which, mediating between 1 and 2 and at the same time stepping outside their zones of influence into its own light of day, provides unlimited possibilities. It is like Deleuze's and Guattari's wandering, deterritorialized schizophrenic. She is free to penetrate any plot of topological terrain, moving to and fro, resisting identification with anything in particular and representing nothing in general. She is unfettered by binds, knots, tangles, traps, and impasses. Significantly, the schizophrenic of conjoint negation owes nothing to society, to the "reality" into which society has interjected her: she is free of that awful web of inculcation, injunctions, and interdictions.

In short, if, in figures 4 and 5, 0 is *atemporality,* 1 is *prototemporality,* and 2 is linear *eotemporality,* then the nonlinear, apparently disordered, indeterminate, and fallible nature of 3 opens the doorway allowing for the initial glimpse of *bio-nootemporality.*

III. ORTHOGONAL LEAPS. At a higher level of abstraction, consider a more advanced specification of figure 5. Let 1 be defined as $\sqrt{-1}$—*superposition* implying the possibility for *prototemporal* oscillation or iteration in the manner of a continuous wave form by an operation on a pair of states: $+1$ and -1, or P and Q. Let 2 be defined as a purely linear, *eotemporal* succession of either positive or negative values (i.e., iterative affirmation or negation in the sense of *"this, then this, . . . n"* or *"not this, then not this, . . . n"*). And let 3 be defined by either $[1|1 = -1]$ or $[-(-1 \wedge -1) = -1]$ (i.e., *conjunctive negation* such that $+1$ and -1 can be both affirmed and denied). These relationships can be diagrammed by what is called an "Argand circle," which incorporates the function of the imaginary number, $i (= \sqrt{-1})$, in the two-dimensional Cartesian plot (see figure 6). The y axis is represented by $+\sqrt{-1}$ (i.e., i), and $-\sqrt{-1}$ (i.e.,

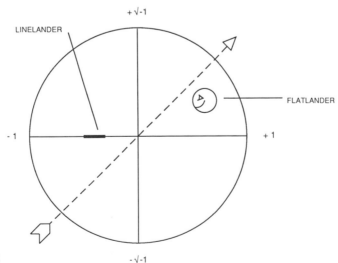

FIGURE 6

$-i$), and the x axis by -1 and $+1$. This can be all clear to us in a flash, like the graphed acceleration problem in chapter 1, since we see it from a three-dimensional perspective and from an angle *orthogonal* to the two-dimensional plane.

Imagine, in contrast, our Flatlander dwelling on this two-dimensional plane. It would be for him well-nigh impossible to create a mental image of the entire circle, let alone draw it. An imaginary one-dimensional Linelander would not even be able to see any succession of iterants from his particular locale along the imaginary axis. Traveling along his lineworld, he might conceivably experience some sort of change in the primitive sense of a worm in a worm hole creeping forward and with tunnel vision experiencing something remotely the equivalent of "now this, now this . . . " For a three-dimensional being this aboriginal type of sequentiality has nothing to do with temporality: the Linelander's trajectory is as far as he is concerned all *there* all at once, as if *in bloc*. That is, the x axis containing the whole integers is no more than artificially "temporal" as pure sequentiality, with -1 representing the past, 0 the "now," and $+1$ the future.

What we need is a "time's arrow," which, precisely, is represented by the arrow orthogonal to the Argand plane. This arrow allows a three-dimensional grasp of the plane all at once, as if from a perspective *sub specie aeternitatis*, of what may be termed *abstract* or *imaginary time*. However, assuming the eye of an observer to travel along this "time line" would imply the production of "real" or concrete "sensed time," as if the plane itself, along with the eye, were receding back into the horizon indefinitely. In other words, "time's arrow" calls for a third axis—that of solid geometry—dynamizing the whole affair and

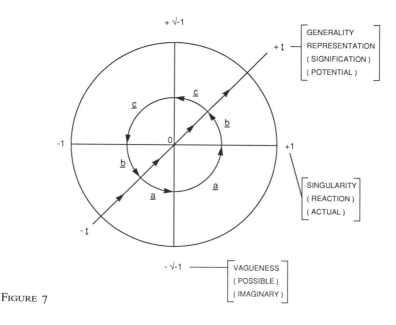

FIGURE 7

providing for a transition with respect to the original axes. The two-dimensional Argand plane plus one dimension of time becomes roughly analogous to the Einsteinian four-dimensional space-time manifold of three spatial dimensions and one temporal dimension. And the eye moving into the horizon along "time's arrow" in figure 6 becomes tantamount to an entity's "world-line" within the Minkowski "block."

Such pseudotemporal transitoriness coupled with switches from one axis to another to afford complementary grasps of things is illustrated in figure 7, to be viewed as a sphere, where the arrows represent the operations in the rectangle in figure 5 bringing about a transformation from one mode of signification to another. Each operation is a 90° orthogonal switch, and the sphere itself represents the "greatest lower bound," o. From the o point, entry can be made into the interior of the sphere from the imaginary axis $(+\sqrt{-1}, -\sqrt{-1})$ from which there is accessibility to other axes. Operation a $(+\sqrt{-1} \rightarrow +1)$ is comparable to physicist John Wheeler's (1980a, 1982, 1984) *complementarity, choice, and selection,* which allow for the exercise of *distinguishability,* bringing about a *phase change* and a "collapse" producing a thought-sign, sign-thing, or particulate entity, which, by way of operation b—mediary Thirdness $(+1 \rightarrow +t)$—leads to *irreversibility, temporality* (that is, *bio-nootemporality*). Operation c $(+t \rightarrow +\sqrt{-1})$ returns the process to Firstness, to the axis of possibility, of chance. Significantly enough, when considering the midpoint of the sphere to be moving along the infinity of its "point-worlds" on the "imaginary" time axis orthogonal to the Argand plane, it becomes evident that the "sphere" is in reality a "hypersphere" (see Kauffman and Varela 1980 and Kauffman 1986 for a discussion of the hypersphere with respect to the dynamics of Spencer-Brownian forms).

Moreover, the orthogonal moves are the metaphorical equivalent of a twist along the Möbius strip which changes "inside" to "outside," right-hand to left-hand, end to beginning. Just as two trips around the Möbius strip return us to our original state, so operations a-b-c-c-b-a are a return to the same axis. This is fundamentally the set of operations depicted by Bryce S. DeWitt's (1968) "popular" rendition of what is called "Smale's Theorem"—the details are not relevant here—which illustrates that a two-dimensional sphere can be turned inside out via a differentiable homotopy of immersions in three-dimensional Euclidean space. DeWitt accomplishes his task through the set of topological transformations from a point to a point in figure 8, which in essence describes a torus and then turns it inside out, thus illustrating that the inward-turned two-dimensional manifold manifests no clear-cut "inside/outside" dichotomy. All is continuous, as Thirdness, generality, a temporal and mediary collusion of the values of the possible (as Firstness) and the singular (as Secondness). Given the similarity between the fourth and sixth stages of DeWitt's transformations and either Peirce's "scroll" or Lacan's "interior 8," it is reasonable to suppose that just as $\sqrt{-1}$, the Möbius strip, or the torus, is capable of an "inside-outside" self-returning cycle-oscillation, so also with thought-sign and thing-sign reiteration. The very important difference is, of course, that, regarding such reiterations as time-bound, asymmetrical, and irreversible, thus nothing *is* exactly as it *was.*

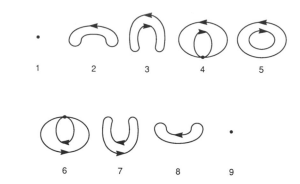

FIGURE 8

"So what's the point?" someone asks. "Isn't all this mere idle palaver? Can one arrive at a worthwhile conclusion with such apparent trivia?" Perhaps not. On the other hand, it may be well to point to what were once considered useless toys for the mathematicians' playpens such as hypercomplex numbers, which later attained a certain application, namely, Hamilton's *quaternions*. As the name implies, quaternions are four-term numbers constructed out of one real and three other units, which can be interpreted as directed quantities (vectors) in three-dimensional space. Quaternions have enjoyed a very useful role in the mathematical treatment of rotation of three-dimensional space about an origin, much like the figure 7 topology. Such rotary extensions have proved handy in certain formulae of relativity theory—the "Lorentz transformations" in the four-dimensional Minkowski "block," as well as in quantum theory.[14] Nothing, it would seem, is so far-fetched that it will be eternally barred from the "semiotically real." I cannot be so presumptuous as to claim I have resolved any fundamental problems with my own very modest contribution. At most, perhaps I have been able to offer a brief glimpse into the vast realm of *semiosis* from a slightly different angle. What I also believe I may have illustrated is the important Peircean notion that *semiosis,* the field of signs perpetually transmuting themselves into other signs, is a self-referential, self-organizing whole. In this regard signs manifest the same function as all living organisms (Varela 1979; Maturana and Varela 1980, 1987; Jantsch 1980).

IV. BACK ON *TERRA FIRMA,* OR, OF WHAT IS "REAL." Lévi-Strauss's myths that speak themselves through "man," Heidegger's language bringing about its self-realization through us, Derrida's "we are always already in the text," Wittgenstein's "the limits of my language mean the limits of my world," and Peirce's "I am the sum total of my thought-signs," all testify in one form or another to the nonlinear, asymmetrical, irreversible, multiply in-formed "semiotics ≈ life" equation that has been vaguely suggested throughout this disquisition. However, there is a problem here. Pierce's conclusion that the whole of "reality" is in a sense a universe of signs appears to contradict the distinction I have made between the "semiotically real" and the "real." To repeat

Peirce's comments of 1906, there are two kinds of *indeterminacy:* (1) *indefinite-ness* (vagueness) and (2) *generality,* in regard to which we are told that

> the former consists in the sign's not sufficiently expressing itself to allow of an indubitable determinate interpretation, while the [latter] turns over to the interpreter the right to complete the determination as he pleases. It seems a strange thing, when one comes to ponder over it, that a sign should leave its interpreter to supply a part of its meaning; but the explanation of the phenomenon lies in the fact that the entire universe, embracing the universe of existents as a part, the universe which we are all accustomed to refer to as "the truth"—that all this universe is perfused with signs, if it is not composed exclusively of signs. (CP:5.448n)

If the universe is "composed exclusively of signs," if signs constitute all of "reality" that can be represented by other signs, whether as mere possibility or as law dictating what will be actualized, then need there be no boundary between the "semiotically real" and the "real"? A boundary of sorts *does* exist, however. In order to get a better handle on the distinction between the two uses of "real" here, I shall turn to Pierce on *propositions as representation*—i.e., representation not in its twentieth-century empirical positivist sense but with respect to the "semiotically real"—hence a more appropriate term might be *signification* (the "production of meaning"), also a synonym for *semiosis* (Greimas and Courtés 1982:299).

The general proposition "All solid bodies will fall in the absence of any upward force or pressure" is of the nature of Peirce's "representation." Nominalism, Pierce points out, would hold that that which is represented is not identical to that which is "real." He concedes that what is "of the nature of a representation is not *ipso facto* real. In that respect there is a great contrast between an ideal of reaction and an object of representation. Whatever reacts is *ipso facto* real. But an object of representation is not *ipso facto* real" (CP:5.96). On the other hand, Peirce diverges from the nominalist thesis in his belief that a general proposition stating what *would happen* under certain circumstances is of the nature of representation; it refers to experiences in futuro, which may or may not be experienced, and which may or may not serve to confirm the proposition, given Peirce's fallibilism principle—I refer the reader once again to Peirce's *pragmatic maxim.* Hence, when Peirce asserts that "really to be is different from being represented," he means that

> what really is, ultimately consists in what shall [in the long run of things] be forced upon us in experience, that there is an element of brute compulsion in fact and that fact is not a mere question of reasonableness. Thus, if I say, "I shall wind up my watch every day as long as I live," I never can have a positive experience which *certainly* covers all that is here promised, because I never shall know for certain that my last day has come. But what the real fact will be does not depend upon what I represent, but upon what the experiential reactions shall be. (CP:5.97)

Ultimately, the matter comes down to Peirce's asymptotic approximation to some *perpetually undefinable truth* on the part of the entire community, not the individual.

Another way of putting Peirce's concept evinces a rough analogy with Popper's (1972, 1974) thought, namely, his triad of Worlds.[15] The orange-yellow flame produced by an NaCl solution subjected to a Bunsen burner flame, as a possibility, a feeling, a quality, as an impingement on the senses, though there is not yet conscious acknowledgment *of* it, is Firstness (Popper's World 1). The mode of conditionality of the NaCl solution, its *would be,* is Thirdness, or law. The law is essentially the habit or real probability by virtue of which a particular future occurrence will (or will not) take place (Popper's World 3). The orange-yellow flame produced by the solution thus enjoys a "reality," though it would possess this "reality" even if Na never manifested itself *for* any observer *as* an orange flame.

In other words, it possesses Thirdness as law or habit more or less determining how a particular NaCl solution *would behave* under certain conditions. Comparably, the proposition "If this NaCl solution were subject to a Bunsen burner flame, it would produce an orange-yellow hue" is, we generally suppose, "real" (i.e., "true") in terms of sodium's general behavior. If put to the test, that "reality" can be confirmed by virtue of what actually appears *to* consciousness, or what consciousness, mediately as it were, and in interaction with the "real," *selects* and *distinguishes* from among the entire set of possible percepts (the impact of Secondness) (Popper's World 2).

However, the NaCl solution as a "semiotic object" of the proposition in terms of the hue produced on combustion is "real" only insofar as it is, in the theoretical long run, determined by other signs (i.e., the nature of ions in solution, the properties of Na and Cl, their relation to other alkalis and halogens, chemical spectroscopy, etc.) (see note 17 of chapter 1). It is not the "actually real" dynamical object which serves to determine signs as such, but the "semiotically real" which is determined by other signs as such. This mediary rather than immediate nature of Secondness, as I have argued elsewhere (Merrell 1985a), is an absolutely essential component of Peirce's doctrine of signs. The universe as we can possibly know it, then, is a "perfusion of signs," and as far as we can know, it may be "composed exclusively of signs." In sum, whatever is "real" has no intelligible status except insofar as it is determined by the *process of significa-tion* (i.e., Peirce's "representation").

Against the nominalist postulate that what is signified cannot be a mirror image of the "real," Peirce argued indefatigably that all is in theory knowable, though it can be known absolutely solely in the theoretical long run. Peirce points out that if what lies behind that which is signified is never itself given in the signified, then any attempt to characterize it would entail the contradiction of attempting to signify the unsignifiable, to know the unknowable (CP:5.257, 5.312). Peirce admits that though knowledge of things in themselves is entirely relative to human experience and to the nature of the mind, "all experience and all knowledge is knowledge of that which is, independently of being represented" (CP:6.95). Even lies "invariably contain this much truth, that they represent themselves to be referring to something whose mode of being is independent of its being represented" (CP:6.95). Yet, he also admits, "no proposition can relate, or even thoroughly pretend to relate, to any object otherwise than as that object is represented" (CP:6.95). All knowledge, then, is knowledge of the "semiotically real," of particulars generated by finite individuals or human communities—they are invariably tinged with *vagueness,* while the proper "real" objects of knowledge are *generals* to which knowledge aspires but will never reach absolutely. To repeat, knowledge is always and invariably a *process of representation,* or in terminology more proper to this inquiry, a *process of signification.* Peirce promises that the "real" will surely someday be ours if we persist with sufficient tenacity, but we will never live to see that day. Hence a *boundary* will always exist between the "real" and a given "semiotically real" world.

Peirce's "realism," guaranteeing that sufficient efforts expended to know the "real" will achieve success in the theoretical long run, is based on mathematical principles justifying probable inference: that the character of an aggregate may be determined by a large enough sampling of the parts (CP:2.102, 2.785, 5.110). This *probable* end as the result of a collective enterprise is a sharp contrast to the *necessary* goal of the solitary Cartesian mind introspecting absolute truths. In the former the effort to know is limited by the intensity and duration of the inquiry; the latter is a purely nonhistorical, rational process, whose limits are defined by the ability to avoid contradictions, for a contradiction inevitably leads to a failed attempt to achieve a necessary conclusion (Thompson 1952). However, Peirce's dilemma is that of a paradox not entirely unlike the tu quoque arising out of the Cartesian leap of faith in reason. If, as Peirce asserts, nothing is absolutely incognizable, then how can he know it? Peirce was aware of this problem, and he even insisted that his principle of the ultimate cognizability of all things rested on grounds for which no reason could be given. He openly conceded that

> the assumption, that man or the community . . . shall ever arrive at a state of information greater than some definite finite information, is entirely unsupported by reasons. There cannot be a scintilla of evidence to show that at some time all living beings shall not be annihilated at once, and that forever after there shall be throughout the universe any intelligence whatever. (CP:5.357)

To put it pithily, the belief that nothing is incognizable is itself based on an incognizable premise. In essence we have the paradox: "'nothing is incognizable' is incognizable." By extension, regarding self-consciousness, it can be stated from the Peircean perspective that "'the self is not incognizable' is incognizable," which places the self, the cognizing mind, in the same grab bag with all signs. The self can know its own introspecting self no better than it can know the "real," which is to say that it can know itself in theory but not in practice.

And we are once again reminded of Peirce's enigmatic "man ≈ sign" equation—a topic to be taken up more thoroughly in chapters 6 and 7 in the guise of "mind ≈ sign." If the universe "is profused with signs," then we, ourselves, are signs. We naturally tend to read this equation with incredulous eyes. It appears demeaning, even in a sense humiliating. Signs surely must exist to suit our purposes?

However, if we return for a moment to Peirce's remarks on *vagueness* and *generality*, we begin to comprehend the interaction between signs and ourselves on an equal basis. Further determination of the vague sign is left up to the sign's interpretant; further determination of the general sign is chiefly the responsibility of the interpreter. Since a corpus of signs invariably contains signs which are either vague or general or both, and since all ideas (thoughts) are signs, a given corpus of ideas must evince vagueness and generality (CP:5.448). Determination of the signifying corpus must depend on a collaboration, and mutual interdependence, between interpreter and interpretants; hence, like the observer-observed pair of quantum theory, they are inseparable. Indeed, they are in a sense coterminous. They are, themselves, composed exclusively of signs.

As Peirce puts it, "the fact that every thought is a sign, taken in conjunction with the fact that life is a train of thought, proves that man is a sign" (CP:5.314). We inhabit, we are, a world of vague and general, inconsistent and incomplete, signs. Hence according to Peirce's objective idealism, the "semiotically real" domain is, ipso facto, methodologically and epistemologically *real*, yet ontologically *ideal* insofar as the "semiotically real" will never become identical with the "real" in our finite world. Therefore we collaborate with signs "out there" and with thought-signs "in here" toward completion of their (our) determination.

In this manner, Peirce attributed a certain organicity to signs. Whereas earlier he declared that "the word or sign which the man uses is the man himself" (CP:5.314), by 1892 he had backtracked somewhat with the suggestion that "every general idea [thought-sign] has the unified living feeling of a person" (CP:6.270). Yet in spite of Peirce's apparent *realism*, he never could escape the *objective idealist* imperative of maintaining a distinction between the subject-mind as architect of signs and the subject-mind as object of knowing. One still tends to retort from the gut, however, that even though a sign, a thought-sign, or a general idea possesses the same qualities of feeling we attribute to a human being, there must be some very fundamental difference between a person and a sign. Since an interpretant is determined by its respective sign (representamen), it must exist apart from its interpreter. But were it possible for an interpretant to be *absolutely* determined by its sign, its object would be a self-contained univocal singularity: there would be no latitude on the part of the interpreter, who would at this point necessarily become indistinguishable from the interpretant; *she would become, herself, the ultimate interpretant*. Fortunately we do not run this risk, for, that ultimate interpretant being inaccessible to us, we will always remain to a greater or lesser degree *apart from* the sign we are in the act of interpreting. Nonetheless, we are inexorably partly interjected *into* it:

> Whenever we think, we have present to the consciousness some feeling, image, conception, or other representation, which serves as a sign. But it follows for our own existence (which is proved by the occurrence of ignorance and error) that everything which is present to us is a phenomenal manifestation of ourselves. This

does not prevent its being a phenomenon of something without us, just as a rainbow is at once a manifestation both of the sun and of the rain. When we think, then, we ourselves, as we are at that moment, appear as sign. (CP:5.283)

Peirce seems to imply that every interpretant popping into consciousness is subject to further determination by the interpreter who is, herself, a further representation of that selfsame interpretant.[16] A distinction can be made solely as a result of ignorance and error, which raises the interpreter's consciousness to an awareness of something *other than* herself. It follows, Peirce argues, that in the same manner the laws of nature influence matter. A law is a general, a Third, in contrast to an existing object, which is simply a blindly reacting entity to which all generality, representation, and signification is utterly foreign: the general law is oneness, which sets the parameters for the behavior of individual material entities, the many. Its oneness is indivisible, and the manyness of the individuals remains incompatible with it, yet they are determined by it. This, Peirce remarks, is the "great problem of the *principle of individuation* which the scholastic doctors after a century of the closest possible analysis were obliged to confess was quite incomprehensible to them" (CP:5.107). Peirce's concession to a tinge of mysticism in his response to this problem is perhaps inevitable: the universe must possess, he suggests, the characteristics of an utterer who, in dialogic fashion, interprets her own utterances. Peirce continues:

Analogy suggests that the laws of nature are ideas or resolutions in the mind of some vast consciousness, who, whether supreme or subordinate, is a Deity relative to us. I do not approve of mixing up Religion and Philosophy; but as a purely philosophical hypothesis, that has the advantage of being supported by analogy. Yet I cannot clearly see that beyond that support to the imagination it is of any particular scientific service. (CP:5.107)

Elsewhere, Peirce might appear to be a candidate for the Intellectual Club of Unbridled Speculation on suggesting that the universe is a Supreme Symbol. Like an idea, the universe is a representamen "working out its conclusions in living realities." And since every symbol must have, "organically attached to it, its Indices of Reactions and its Icons of Qualities," which exercise the fundamental role as subject and predicate of the symbol (proposition), they comprise a *Text,* the "Universe being precisely an argument," which, though at present incomplete, if given indefinite unfoldment, can potentially be played out in the long run (CP:5.119). The universe as argument is both utterer-representamen and interpreter-interpretant, which is to imply that, viewed as a timeless whole, somehow it contains both its argument and its own counterargument.[17] It is tantamount to $\sqrt{-1}$, the Möbius strip, or the torus, which, when turned inside out, becomes its mirror image—recall Eco on the mirror image.

This notion also implies Peirce's description of the process of thought as *dialogism* (CP:6.338). While I have briefly discussed the dialogical nature of *semiosis* elsewhere (Merrell 1990), it takes on special importance in the present consideration of the one and the many, the whole and its parts, continuity and discontinuity. Peirce makes a gallant effort to articulate the distinction between absolute truth (the one) and that which an individual might take to be the truth (one among the many). First, nobody is absolutely an individual. Rather, her thoughts are what she is always engaged dialogically in "saying to herself," that is, "saying to that other self that is just coming into life in the flow of time. When one reasons, it is that critical self that one is trying to persuade; and all thought whatsoever is a sign, and is mostly of the nature of language" (CP:5.421).

Second, one's circle of society as a collectivity "is a sort of loosely compacted person, in some respects of higher rank, than the person of an individual organism" (CP:5.421). Combining these two points, one is led to the conclusion that the self is constantly displaced by its *other*, which perpetually presents, so to speak, a counterargument to the self which the self in turn must counter, an ongoing process tending toward habit. On the other hand, the self dialogues with that collective *Other*, the community, which, if the dialogue were interminable, would culminate in the final community opinion regarding the "real." These two processes "render it possible for you—but only in the abstract, and in a Pickwickian sense—to distinguish between absolute truth and what you do not doubt" (CP:5.421).

In other words, one self is the utterer-representamen, the *other* is the interpreter-interpretant (or critical self) which is constantly emerging into the flow of time. In this manner, the self-*other* interaction is incompatible with "real" (experienced) time, though not abstract (imaginary) time. But since at the very moment the self enters "real" time it leaves its role as interpreter behind and becomes the utterer, the first self, the self of, so to speak, *différance* in the sense of Derrida (1973), that other self, as interpreter-interpretant, must ultimately sink into the abstract along with Absolute Truth. That is to say, if the critical self (as individual and as community) is destined ultimately to embrace Absolute Truth, though this cannot be realized in "real" time, that Absolute Truth must be distinguished from all particular signs, habits, and beliefs entertained by any given individual in its dialogue with its individual and collective *other*.

In this sense the ideal critical and collective self is an abstraction from the "semiotically real" world as such and "real" time as such. This characterization of the *other* self, however, can be articulated only insofar as it is related to the known or phenomenal self, the first self, especially in light of the fact that it partakes of the nature of sign. The phenomenal self at the center of the sphere in figure 7 can shrink to a point, or it can project itself outward into indefinitely expansive space and indefinitely future time. It does so in dialoguing with its own *other*, which constantly engages in generating countersigns (propositions, arguments) in response to the signs the first self puts forth. In this fashion the self plus its *other*, upon expansion, encompasses more and more of the community dialogue. But since the individual can never be identical with the whole, the community *Other* is always "out there," generating its own countersigns (propositions, arguments), which serve to reveal the individual self's errors of its ways. The *Other* constitutes a repository of community knowledge, a particular "semiotic reality." As this "semiotic reality" becomes increasingly general, the outer sphere undergoes expansion, though over finite time and given anything less than a community of infinite capacities, the sphere's boundaries are destined to remain indeterminate.

There is apparently an inconsistency in Peirce's thought here: the other-worldly critical and collective *Other* appears to be somehow partly, though in the theoretical long run wholly, outside time and space in contrast to the concrete thisworldly time- and space-bound phenomenal self. This attests to a host of conflicts (scholastic realism and pragmatism, objectivity and idealism, common-sensism and mathematically abstract theoretical formulations), all of which are rather contradictorily embraced by Peirce's umbrella label *objective idealism*. It also bears witness to the inevitable *vagueness* and *generality* of all signs with which the universe is apparently perfused. Yet there is so intimate a connection between the *Other* and the individual observer (self plus *other*) that they cannot be divorced. The community *Other*'s "semiotically real" world and the world of the individual (subjective) observer are, in a manner of speaking, incomplete or foggy mirror images of one another. That is to say, the *effect* of the "real" along the x axis in figure 6 makes up the *Other*'s "semiotically real," while the imaginary (y axis), which is individual and subjective, serves to generate, as it slides along the time axis by recursion and oscillation between *this* and *that*, potentially an infinite variety of "semiotically real" worlds, each of them affording a tenuous grasp of the "actually real."

A given "semiotic reality" is thus perpetually displaced as a result of the interaction at their meeting point of the individual, subjective, and imaginary generation of signs by the self-*other*, on the one hand, and on the other, the *Other*'s world of forms "out there." The traditional opposition between *episteme* and *doxa* must now be viewed as a struggle between complementarities, as an interaction which creates "reality" as such. The *imaginary* is no longer to be understood as a mere fiction that contrasts with the "real." Rather, it is an integral part of the "real" itself, essential not only to its representation as signification but to its very composition. And the "real" cannot exist as such without being able to see itself at once as neither *this* nor *that*, *this* or *that*, *this* and then *that*, and both *this* and *that*. Self, *other*, and community *Other* are the instruments by means of which the "real" engages in this self-reflective dialogue.

Such intrigues and enigmas are most likely inevitable in any and all holistic configurations.

FIVE *Mediating Fallibly*

I. THE MIND'S STAGE, AND ITS ACTORS. Peirce's *objective idealism* is a strange concoction indeed. Methodological (and epistemological) realism coupled with ontological idealism: something akin to physicist Arthur Eddington's (1958a:xi–xix) desk as an uninterpreted complex of sensations (the positivist's reality) and as a reified construct (a swarm of electrons). This distinction entails a transition from the perceived world at the edge of consciousness to the realm of mental constructs subject to human creative capacities and logical combinatorial principles. The one somehow, and hopefully, finally confirms the other, and the other the one.

A question, however, must be asked: "What would the 'real' be without minds to construct it?" This problem combines methodology (and epistemology) as well as ontology. Kant, of course, rooted both of these branches in general metaphysics. Ontology must rely on faith not methodology, and methodology in the final analysis relies on ontology, which is to say that over the long haul it relies on theory, itself ultimately based on faith—we see what the theory lets us see, Einstein (in Heisenberg 1971:63) once said. For Peirce, as I have repeated throughout, "reality," that is, the myriad collection of all possible *Umwelt*-generated "semiotically real" worlds, reflects "mind-stuff." Or perhaps better stated, the "real" *is mind-stuff* (Eddington 1958a, 1958b). But since this "mind-stuff" is never static and never terminal, we must be satisfied with the admission that "reality," as we can know it "semiotically," has many faces; these faces are changed without our consciously altering our "mind-stuff," even in spite of our concerted effort to arrest such change. (As the early Wittgenstein [1961:6.43] trenchantly put it, the happy man and the sad man live in two different worlds.)

On the other hand, if this "mind-stuff" and the "laws of nature are ideas or resolutions in the mind of some vast consciousness," to requote Peirce, then we are placed in yet another pickle—of which Peirce was well aware. At the outset the notion that our minuscule minds are actors on the world's stage appears to present no problem. Or does it? If we take physicist John A. Wheeler's (1980a, 1980b, 1984) quantum cosmology at face value, we as actor-participants bring the *world-as-recorded-world* into existence. In other words, the world as a whole lifts itself by its bootstraps. This is tantamount to a Grand Interpreter saying what the world *is* as a Grand Interpretant, but in order that this be made possible, Interpreter and Interpretant must be coterminous. They merge one into the other to compose the unthinkable Cosmic Sign—they cannot be separated as Manley Thompson (1953) takes pains to do in his critique of Peirce.

Assume, for a moment, that the totality of the universe upon which this ultimate interpretant bears is serial. At a given point there are n interpreter-interpretant couplings. If a particular coupling under consideration is added to the preceding ones in the series, it can be enumerated $n + 1$, and upon so being taken into account, it becomes integrated: $n + 1 = n$. This synthesis then calls for an additional signifying act, $((n + 1) + 1) = n$, an act corresponding to the last series, n, under purview. But in order to hold that series in a conceptual grasp, another act is required: $(((n + 1) + 1) + 1) = n$, and so on. The series is infinite, hence it can be taken in one instantaneous conceptual gulp solely by some inconceivable infinite mechanism or organism.[1]

However, we can introduce a counterfeit "temporal-logical operator" into the series, thus exercising a *cut*, a "now," which creates a distinction between before and after. If the "now" is arbitrarily placed at the instantiation of a given interpretant, t_0, then what occurs after that point can presumably be marked out as something other than what went on before in the n series. The sequence can be written $n_{t-1}/n_{t0}/n_{t+1}$, where the latter, as a Second, maintains its individuality vis-à-vis the whole. The problem here, as we have observed regarding Gödel's (1949) interpretation of the Einstein-Minkowski "block" universe, is that, when considering all possible series for all possible interpreters, what for interpreter x is n_{t-1}, for interpreter y can be n_{t+1}, and the notion of "now" thus loses its significance. Everything exists as a static set of simultaneities (i.e., J. M. E. McTaggert's [1927] B-series). All series and all "nows" are *there, in bloc.* Thus the paradox inherent in the series cannot be eliminated except by artificial means. Any "semiotic reality" capable of embracing this series is the result not of "time" or "logic," traditionally conceived, but of "reality" according to its "block" interpretation. This "block" accounts for moving objects not in the Newtonian sense of classical mechanics but in terms of Einsteinian "world-lines." By the same token, it would appear, the ongoing *semiosic* process of signs transmuting into other signs can be conceived as no more than a vast static set of series in what might be called the "semiotic block," the trajectory of each sign being described as a minuscule curve within the whole Parmenidean package.

Consequently, from this monolithic conception of things, the ongoing web of multiple sign series can lay claim to citizenship rights in the same "block." Signs, or better, interpretants, if conceived as following their respective "world-lines" like physical objects in the space-time continuum, necessarily form potentially an infinite set of series. Any interpretant referring to the "block" is therefore by definition part of the "block." If we artificially interject "time" into this operation, it can be said that when that very interpretant used to interject "time" comes into existence, in the *next* instant it will be part of the timeless "block." If history is conceived as the successive generation of interpretants, then any and all interpretants regarding the existence or nature of the "block" also become, in the *next* set of instants, integrated into the "block," therefore they are part of the domain to which they refer.

In contrast to this "block" idea, to which I have frequently alluded in this inquiry, and more in line with Peircean *semiosis,* ontologically the determination of specific state properties of an object at the quantum level is a profound switch from the classical paradigm, though its ramifications bear on the universe as an interconnected web, which, like the relativity concept, also harks back to a holistic cosmological view. It is now time to be more explicit regarding this apparent contradiction.

The subjectivity inherent in the quantum theoretical conception of the universe, I must first emphasize, exists at the *micro-level (prototemporality)*— Eddington's desk as a swarm of particles. The *macro-level* physical objects of everyday living *(eotemporality)*—Eddington's desk as an object upon which to write—are generally regarded as existing independently of any and all observers. The fact remains, however, that observation entails at least partial creation— though minute it may be—of the physical aspects of nature (see especially Herbert 1985). This aspect of quantum theory is indeed a profound revolution in Western thought. It does not presuppose Berkeleyan metaphysical idealism according to which the furniture of the world exists only insofar as it is perceived and continues its existence in the absence of any human being, for it is in the mind of that monolithic spirit, God. In the quantum theoretical sense, an electron as a discernible object exists in the physical world apart from any human or divine being's thought or perception of it. What does not exist independent of its being observed (interacted with) is the particular set of physical variables pertaining to the electron as a function of the act of observation (interaction).

In Wheeler's (1984) terminology, the *choice, selection,* and *established distinction* determine the nature of the electron—that is, its being *recorded as* such and such at a particular point in time *for* some observer and *put to use for* some purpose. Otherwise, the electron is simply *there,* in an abstract sense. The observer decides what property of the electron is to be measured, and in the act she becomes, in a manner of speaking, an attribute of the potential state of the electron, thus bringing about an "eigenvalue" for that property, though without necessarily being able to determine either which "eigenvalue" will result or precisely what the state will be after observation. In another way of putting it, the apparatus tells the system what properties are to be measured, and the system responds accordingly. The *choice* made by the observer-interpreter determines what is to emerge from chance. In this sense, the "uncollapsed" continuum (Firstness) is independent of consciousness until a *choice* is made and something *selected,* then the system is "collapsed" (into Secondness) and *put to use.*

To couch this more directly in semiotic terms, the sign generally leaves completion of its interpretation, and thus the specification of its interpretant, to the discretion of the interpreter, though she can never bring the interpretation to absolute completion, nor can she know precisely which of the probable immediate interpretants will pop up next. What she can do is *choose, select,* and *distinguish this* interpretant from *that* one, and *put it to use* or commit it to memory (*record* it) for later use. In this sense also we see that a slash is necessary between the "semiotically real" and the "real," the latter being tantamount to the universe independently of whatever signification may be attributed to it, and the former being dependent upon the community—or as Wheeler (1980b:154) puts it, the *joint product* of the community—and hence it is inexorably tinged with a degree of subjectivity, in spite of any force exercised by the "real" through its instantiations in the *here* and *now* as Seconds.

The classical view depicted the universe as evolving from some initial set of conditions toward some presumably teleological end, whether the human semiotic animal is part of the whole scene or not. The quantum picture plays havoc with that idea: at the *micro-level* the universe is altered, as a result of observer-observed interaction, in ways that are statistically but not deterministically predictable. Hence there is no teleology definable a priori. In comparable fashion, given the indeterminacy of a particular interpretant's development, we cannot know what the future of our "semiotically real" holds in store for us. In lieu of a universe as somehow marching to the tune of an established set of initial conditions, it must now be conceded, as we shall note in the following sections, that, whether speaking of the *micro-level* or the *macro-level* of the "semiotically real," the whole of the universe is constantly being (re)generated at each juncture according to unpredictable twists and turns. In the process some sort of order somehow and suddenly appears out of chaos: there can be no totally presupposed or calculable future state of affairs.

The Necker cube model as a *micro-level* superposition which can be, upon inspection, "collapsed" into one of two potential states is relatively clean and easily spit-polished for illustrating the essence of "quantum logic," and it introduces a flexibility quite lacking in classical mechanics (see Comfort 1984:66–86). At large-scale *molecular,* and especially *molar,* levels involving particles in the order of 10^{10} and upwards, however, things become so messy that for practical purposes one may assume that the older determinism can by and large be retained: the system is governed in somewhat deterministic fashion in terms of statistical aggregates. Yet the existence of statistical rather than determined events at the small scale allows for the ubiquitous possibility of novelty. For example, at a given point in time an indefinite number of molecules in a pan of water at room temperature will reach the requisite kinetic energy to be converted to their gaseous state, thus part of the water constantly undergoes evaporation. If a sufficient number of the molecules were suddenly to reach the requisite kinetic energy and the water began to boil, no physical law would actually be violated, though the probability of this occurrence is virtually zero.

This possibility for novelty at the *micro-level* calls for qualification.

II. A SIGN COLLAPSED BECOMES/IS ANOTHER SIGN: FROM THE *MICRO-LEVEL* UPWARD. To repeat, no more than a minuscule portion of

the events in the universe consist directly of human observer-dependent properties. For each of Wheeler's phenomena that are *recorded* and *put to use* to become part of our "meaningfully real" or "semiotically real" universe, there are countless billions that go undetected. In this regard we are relatively insignificant, a mere handful of ants on the jungle floor. Nevertheless, with respect to *our* concept of the universe and of ourselves, our history, art, and all our intellectual endeavors, the physical universe as we conceive and perceive it is justifiably a matter of crucial importance *to* us. That which we *select* and *record* in the construction of our "semiotic world" constitutes what Wheeler (1984) calls "meaning physics," the ultimate stage of investigation of the universe. Questions must thus be asked concerning how basic *micro-level* action is related to our thought and behavior, that is, to semiotics in general.

I begin with reference to the uncertainty and openness such as that permitted by quantum theory for the determination of properties of natural systems, which do not allow the same self-guidance and self-will as does classical physics. Richard Schlegel (1980:225) argues that the subjective conviction people have of being able to exercise their free will and make a decision with respect to some kinds of behavior coupled with evidence of a remarkable degree of unpredicted behavior in others is consonant with the multistate possibilities quantum physics has discerned at the atomic level. It becomes reasonable, consequently, for a person to believe that, subject always, of course, to many inherent constraints, she is capable of determining her self's own properties, and that to a large degree what she is and does is of her own volition. Yet she is intrinsically a part of the natural world. Human ideals, values, and purposes, in this sense, may be regarded as rooted in nature, whereas in the classical-physics outlook they were considered to be mere epiphenomena at most, adjoined to our physical being but essentially belonging to a different order of existence.

Schlegel goes on to suggest that since we can acquire knowledge of a given "eigenstate" of a system only by observing it, our mediated awareness *of* it must be associated with a corresponding superposition of states in readiness for interaction, which I will term, following Schlegel's argument, a "semiostate" (i.e., the *micro-level,* or category 1 in regard to figure 5). A semiostate as a state of possibilities actualizable into consciousness is the "eigenstate" of a biological neurosystem which has generated, as a result of growth, experience, and education, a superposition of many possible states.[2] New states are constantly being formed by an organism in response to external and internal stimuli, some of which can be recalled, while others have been lost to memory (embedded). Or in Peirce's terms, at the *micro-level* of unformed *possibilia* (Firstness), there is a superposition of states of complex probability amplitude. The instantiation ("collapse") of one of these states into a "particle" (Second) corresponds to what, at that particular point in time and space, *is*. And a probability factor governs an aggregate of these "particles" in terms of what most likely *would be* under certain circumstances (Thirdness, the *molar* level).[3]

Now for a *Gedanken* experiment to illustrate the relative openness of the quantum view and its possible relevance to the *semiosic* process. At the *micro-*

level let I be the mediately conscious subject, let I^i be a particular *internal* semiostate (of self-*other*), and let I^e represent a semiostate (of self-*Other*) involving some aspect of the *external* world. The superposition of $|I^i>$ and $|I^e>$ can be described thus:

$$|I^i> = \Sigma_j |I^i_j> \text{ and } |I^e> = \Sigma_k |I^e_k>$$

$|I^i>$ is the immediate sensation, or feeling (First), of the organism's semio-system of some quality, with the concomitant readiness of that semio-system to "collapse," $|I^i_j>$, according to a probability function, Σ_j, into a semiostate, I^i (Second), which is then mediated to take on an interpretant (Third) and become a thought-sign. The subscript of Σ_j also marks the possible result of a *foregrounding* or *actualization* ("collapse") of $|I^e_k>$, some item of experience in the world "out there," defined by the probability function, Σ_k, into an empirical "semiotic object" (Second) as I^e. This *external* semiostate is then susceptible to mediated consciousness *of* it (Thirdness) by a concomitant *foregrounding* or *actualization* ("collapse") of $|I^i_j>$ into a particular semiostate, $I^i I^e$. Mind, $|m>$, as a sign, exercises a *choice* or *selection, pace* Wheeler, which entails a *distinction* (and subsequently the "collapse") of the combined superpositions, though the two do not occur in the same instant—i.e., somewhat comparable to the wave-particle complementarity. Combining the mediating $|m>$ with the internal and external components of the semiostate, we have: $I^i I^e m$.

In another way of putting it, the combined superposition is a juxtaposition and interconnectedness of things as *possibilia,* which corresponds to Fraser's *atemporal* domain. The "collapse" yields a particular sign which is then placed in relation to its "semiotic object." Subsequently it calls up a mediating sign, the interpretant, which in turn passes away into its *semiosic* successor. The conjunction of such signs and objects composes an aggregate, which, in its empirical manifestation, is commensurate with the *eotemporal* as a sheer linear succession of signs: *semiosis.* This succession, especially regarding human semiotic, entails the self or the sequence of interpretants, of *I*s addressing themselves to themselves (their *other*) as well as to their community and the "real" *(Other)* in an incessant Peircean dialogue. This entails the *biotemporal* (and potentially the *nootemporal*) realm evident in cell aggregates whose activity is coordinated toward some end. Such harmonious communities are best epitomized by those of insects and societies of more developed organisms—though any relatively complex developing organism evinces the same sort of harmonized "community" of cell aggregates as well. Most important, all these collections to a greater or lesser degree manifest mind, according to the Peircean framework.

In this manner, let *otherness (other-Other)* be an operator, O, acting on the *combined* superposition to produce mind (as sign) thus:

$$|m> = O <\Sigma_j |I^i_j> + <\Sigma_k |I^e_k>$$

Mind as sign is not exactly a singularity, since it is interconnected with other mind-signs: it is a "compound sign" (see Merrell and Anderson 1989a). Neither is it necessarily formed by only one of the superposed states, since, marginally at least, and mediately as it were, the mind can be conscious of more than one sign. This characteristic of mind bears on Polanyi's (1958, 1966) *focal* and *subsidiary* awareness as a component of *tacit knowing* (also Merrell 1982, 1983, 1990). For instance, while on the sofa in the pleasant surroundings of one's home, one may be reading a book. Attention to the marks qua marks on paper exists only subsidiarily (as qualities or Firsts), while focal attention is directed toward them as marks qua symbol-signs which refer to something they *are not* (Seconds), and ultimately toward their meaning (interpretants, Thirds). At the same time, the sensation of a purring cat at one's side on the sofa, the ticking of a clock nearby, the hum of the refrigerator in the kitchen, are all part of one's subsidiary awareness, which can quickly be booted up to focal attention if the clock stops, or the cat leaves in search of a more exciting pastime. If this occurs, the cat and clock are signified by the "collapse" of external signs, while attention to the sequence of events in the book one is reading involves successive "collapse" of internal signs (in this regard, see Bohm and Peat [1987:75–84] on tacit or "subliminal" language use in scientific discourse and the problems it caused in articulating the quantum world).

The operator, governed by *otherness,* ranges from *biological demand* to *social need* to *individual desire.*[4] Biological demand is what *is* in the *here-now.* It constitutes that which is necessary and necessarily reiterated as part of one's action and reaction to inevitable sensations; it constitutes, in a manner of speaking, the Secondness function of the operator. For example, in a state of physical discomfort due to a drop in the temperature, images of the thermostat, an open window, or a sweater in the closet are conjured up as |m> states pointing toward a remedy for the inconvenient state of affairs. In contrast, social need, experienced as the compulsion to behave according to community conventions and standards, to accumulate a requisite set of material goods for the sake of status, to undergo certain sacrifices in order to reap future gain, involves the probability of such and such ensuing if specific conditions are met. It is a *would be,* the counterpart to Thirdness, which Peirce often viewed as a continuum of inferences much like a cable: though certain of its strands might be defective, its overall strength will stand up to the test (CP:1.137–39, 4.531, 6.595). The "conclusions" of a train of thought, action, and events stemming from social need are in this respect highly probable, and if one follows them effectively to their end, one is relatively assured of certain benefits. Individual desire is another story altogether. It includes gratuitous mental play, sheer "musement," which holds little relevance to the world of practical affairs. It is a *might be,* a mere possibility from the tossing ocean of pure chance. Whatever emerges in the mind during this largely supererogatory activity is akin to the *abductive* act (Firstness). Nothing is predetermined or determinate here. Everything *is as it is* for the moment: a monad. And for that moment it is self-contained and autonomous with respect to the world "out there."

Of course there can be a dynamic interplay between signs generated by biological demand, social need, and individual desire, as well as constant oscillation between focal and subsidiary awareness *of* them. While I can be preoccupied with a toothache, a loud noise may suddenly cause me to jerk my head in the direction from which it came in an attempt to identify it. Then, realizing it was a backfiring engine from a nearby car with a faulty muffler, my memory takes me back to a time in my childhood when I was playing with firecrackers on the Fourth of July. The toothache foregrounds $|I^i>$, the exhaust explosion an alternative $|I^e>$, and the recalled event, another $|I^i>$, all occurring in rapid succession at focal and subsidiary levels in the mind, $|m>$. And all these instances of foregrounding are through and through *semiosic,* involving the "collapse" of one sign marked by the almost instantaneous emergence of another sign, as they dance in and out of consciousness. It reminds one of a set of Necker cubes flip-flopping back and forth.

Interestingly enough, Schlegel (1980:227), after illustrating how possibly the physics of elementary processes might lead to a better understanding of the flow of consciousness, concedes that, though there is yet no experimental basis on which to claim psychophysical validity for his proposal, nonetheless

> it can illustrate that the fact of observer-dependence has significance far beyond the establishment of new concepts of physical property and causal behavior for the individual atomic-level particles. To the physicist those novel ideas alone are of immense import. But just as Newtonian physics brought a new way of thinking to all the sciences, and frequently with great success, we likewise can expect that quantum theory recognition of the role of the observer will lead to new understanding in domains where the mechanical impersonal physics was strikingly helpless.

In this sense, the initial immediate experience (Firstness) of signs could be regarded as arising in some manner at a rudimentary neurological *micro-level.* This would discount the theory of mind-brain parallelism, and to an extent the theory that mind happenings are epiphenomena of brain happenings. It does imply a hierarchical and increasingly complex chain of command from brain happenings to mind happenings, with neither being at all separable from the other (Hofstadter 1979).[5] According to this third alternative, what one experiences and feels and intuits (as Firsts) is no less "real" than what one consciously perceives (as Seconds) and interprets (as Thirds).

An actual swan, as (1) a thought-sign, (2) the word *swan,* or (3) a "semiotic object" "out there," is no less "real" *for* us than (4) the feeling or metaphorical image *of* a swan. All four are equally signs and all are equally "mind," whether in thought or condensed into the crystallized, effete, "real" thing; that is, they are "semiotically real." Furthermore, a poet with an inclination toward "swan-feelings" can create an image every bit as "real" as an actual swan in yonder pond, water rushing over the drop at Niagara, a tree in a deep ravine stretching its branches toward the sun's path, or a mass of granite which, subject to untold pressure over the centuries, is transformed into gneiss. All are of the nature of things (that is, signs) and of the nature of "mind" in general. Demand, need, and desire, consequently, are dispositions commensurate with this nature of things. Drinking when thirsty, donning the clothes that will meet with peer approval, and free flights of the imagination either follow or deviate from *habit.* If they move along in automaton fashion, habit has exercised its hegemony. If they deviate slightly, then perhaps that particular habit was not concordant with its environment and context, and the "clash" of Secondness has made its presence known.[6] If they deviate radically, then there has been a somewhat random dip into the pool of chance, of that vast realm of possibilities offered up by Firstness. In whichever case, the flow of signs continues on; happenings pile upon happenings in what often appears to be an accidental succession but which, as Schopenhauer mused, can often be seen, in retrospect, to have been composed according to a consistent plot.

Just as the observer—usually unwittingly—plays a crucial role in determining the properties of a physical micro-state, so the interpreter aids the interpretant along its weary road toward completion. Whether speaking of mind in relation to the physical-state disposition of a biological organism, or of mind as interpreter either of signs or of itself since it is also a sign, the same conclusion inheres: the Cartesian split has suffered a dissolution. Brain-mind, like particle-wave, or sign-interpretant, composes an utterly ineffable, incomprehensible whole—unsayable and unknowable primarily because language, as Bohr indefatigably pointed out, is incapable of giving it full account. That is to say, just as responsibility lies with the interpreter in determining the character of the interpretant, if that determination were to reach finality, which it cannot, there would then be no distinction between interpreter and interpretant. The sign, in all its fullness, would be an indivisible, completely transparent, dense continuum of meaning.

However, in our "real world" of polluted rivers, pizzas, concrete jungles, beer commercials, congested traffic, and videos, given the radically indeterminate nature of the interpretant and the interpreter's fallibilism, whichever interpretation happens to be foregrounded is so foregrounded at the expense of a myriad array of other interpretations that could have been foregrounded but must remain in the background on to an indefinite future. Semiotically speaking, whichever eigensign happens to pop up is every bit as ephemeral as, at the micro-physical level, any other eigensign, for the sign, that is, its interpretant, almost immediately merges back into its respective semiostate, or perhaps some other one, to yield another probability of occurrence which then gives birth to yet another sign. And so one, and so on.

Although a given interpreter might conceivably be able to reconstruct in every detail the "semiotic universe" of the community to which she belongs, this construct would still not be everything, for, in the first place, she must at least in part be set *apart from* the field of signs in order to get on with the job of sign procreation—as Bohr (1934:119) wrote of physics, "the new situation . . . has so forcibly reminded us of the old truth that we are both onlookers and actors in the drama of existence." And in the second place, when finally the interpreter might have concluded her task, that "semiotic universe" *would have expanded, and hence evolved, into some new order*.

This role of the observer-participant in determining the properties of the "semiotically real," or concomitantly of the interpreter in determining the interpretant, is foreshadowed in Kant's *Critique of Pure Reason* (1781) according to which the subjectively endowed modes and categories of thought and perception generated by the mind give knowledge its general structure. The knowledge I speak of here is *Umwelt*-dependent, corresponding to the "semiotic world," rather than the *Ding-an-sich,* which set the stage for the dialogue between knower and known in the construction of this world. Kant, an inspiration especially to the younger Peirce, also had a definite bearing on the turn contemporary cosmology has taken.

In this light, I now focus on the interpreter as an actor on the stage of her "semiotically real" world, which consists of a multiply variegated "collapse" of signs making up a component of the "real," the target of all cosmologies.

III. A HOLISTIC PARADIGM OF MIND BEFORE ITS TIME.
Peirce's cosmology is the most enigmatic aspect of his thought; it evinces a speculative intrepidity absent in most of his other writings. An important, perhaps the most momentous, facet of this cosmology is Peirce's thesis that all things are constantly in a process of evolution toward some new order, and that the interpreter-interpretant takes on an axial role in this evolution. This view of cosmic evolution, when coupled with Peircean semiotics, is the culmination of myriad semiostates, which, in light of the concept of *asymmetry* and *irreversibility* developed from figure 4, mutually interact in a collaborative effort to keep the self-organizing *semiosic* dynamo in motion. And, as I shall argue in this chapter, this is strikingly commensurate with Prigogine's hypothesis of an irreversible, self-organizing universe.

Peirce's work on cosmology dates from 1890 on, when he was at the apogee of his creative endeavors and at the same time that he was placing strictures on unduly rampant metaphysical speculation. His raising cosmological problems and attempting to solve them apparently stem from two branches of his general interests: (1) the universal application of laws to radically diverse phenomena, and (2) the stalemate science had apparently reached (Turley 1977:64–65).

Although in general isolated from the intellectural mainstream of his time, Peirce was nonetheless at the forefront of some of the controversies surrounding problems evolving from classical mechanics, especially the question of determinism. Peirce argued repeatedly that (1) determinism is fallacious in regard to the emerging concepts of *evolution, increasing complexity, human consciousness,* and *reason,* and (2) an entirely mechanistic universe is incompatible with the notion of *growth, development,* and *decay,* all irreversible processes (CP:1.174, 6.14, 6.72). Evolution must imply a general trend toward increasing diversity, which, Peirce remarks, "is *the* most intrusive character of nature" (CP:1.159). Such diversity—the focus of Prigogine and the "physics of chaos" in the contemporary scene—cannot be accounted for with classical laws dictating strict uniformity and "*one* determinate result" while prohibiting any and all originary variations as the product of a truly creative universe (CP:1.159, 6.553). Peirce remarks, and rightly so, that the ultimate and invariant laws of nature were regarded by the determinists as "hard, ultimate, unintelligible" facts, the "why and wherefore of which can never be inquired into." To this, he argues, a sound logic "will revolt, and will pass over at once to a method of philosophizing which does not barricade the road of discovery" (CP:6.60).

Peirce comes close to labeling nineteenth-century mechanistic discourse, as did Whitehead after him, a "mystical chant" over ultimately an unknown and unknowable universe. Regarding consciousness, if, as the determinists claimed, the extramental universe behaves in strict accord with the laws of mechanics, the sole role remaining for consciousness must be that of a passive spectator, "a perfectly idle and functionless *flâneur* of the world, with no possible influence upon anything—not even upon itself" (CP:1.162). Peirce resisted treatment of consciousness as merely another mechanism in a clockwork universe. Quality, feeling, and *quale*-consciousness are simply not reducible to quantitative data like billiard balls rolling down an inclined plane.

According to Peirce's cosmology, indeterminacy and chance—his doctrine of *tychism*—are equally as important to the inner workings of the universe as law, though the evolution of the universe is gradually playing out the range of possibilities while regularity is on the increase in a more or less inverse proportion. This domain of *possibilia,* corresponding to Firstness, also bears indirectly on Peirce's doctrine of continuity. Since Firstness consists of a quasi-Platonic realm of qualities or feelings, Peirce believed it to be through and through mental in nature. This conception is in keeping with Peirce's continuity thesis insofar as, if matter is fossilized mind, like tychism (and Bohm's implicate), it holds a potentially infinite continuum of possibilities. And, since mind is highly flexible in comparison to matter, its laws hardly seem to be laws, there is such freedom of movement. Although there are grounds for distinguishing between mind and matter, the distinction is in degree rather than kind. Peirce's psychical interpretation of matter is idealistic, not of the subjective idealist variety, but that of "objective idealism," which is the "one intelligible theory of the universe that matter is effete mind, inveterate habits becoming physical laws" (CP:6.25, also 6.148, 6.158, 6.268).

Peirce calls this psychophysical interpretation of the universe *hylopathy* (CP:6.24). We are told that something of the general nature of feeling pervades the universe. This daringly speculative leap is actually neither pantheistic nor animistic, though it is anthropomorphic. And it is through and through *semiosic:* matter and mind, living and inanimate, human and nonhuman, share *signness* above all, since the universe is in all probability composed of signs in its entirety. In this conception of things, it follows that just as mind, that is, consciousness, is a sign, everything, living as well as nonliving, possesses consciousness in varying degrees, since "what is meant by consciousness is really in itself nothing but feeling" (CP:7.364).

As I suggested above following Schrödinger (1967), activity which drops out of consciousness to become tacit or unconscious, and finally to become part of phylogeny, has to do not with a conscious/unconscious slash but with myriad levels of consciousness—i.e., Peirce's trope of consciousness as a bottomless lake. This is yet another of Peirce's reasons for throwing darts at the Cartesian dichotomy between *res cogitans* and *res extensa*. He argued that the most we can expect from the mechanical laws is the acceleration of material objects, and if the mind/matter split is enacted, then mind, being of an entirely distinct genre, is rendered forever unintelligible and inexplicable.

In addition, Peirce continued to nurture the belief that the system of nature enjoys an affinity with thought—that is to say, with logic. But the "logic" he speaks of in this regard is not that of the relatively restricted traditional variety. While it is true, he concedes,

> that the whole universe and every feature of it must be regarded as rational, that is as brought about by the logic of events, . . . it does not follow that it is *constrained* to be as it is by the logic of events; for the logic of evolution and of life need not be supposed to be of that wooden kind that absolutely constrains a given conclusion. (CP:6.218)

This general conception falls in line with objective idealism, which sets for itself the task of discovering what is "intelligible and reasonable in the universe at large" (NE, IV:378). In fact, the very search for such an understanding of the universe presupposes objective idealism: belief that nature is commensurate with good thinking, which is in turn commensurate with the *logic of events,* of *evolution,* of *life*. The whole enterprise is circular, which does not necessarily discount objective idealism or Peirce's metaphysics in general, since both, unlike Cartesian discourse, are capable of embracing such infinite regresses as germane to the nature of the universe. Peirce's notion that thought, and by interpolation the mind, enjoy an affinity with nature, which he variously calls insight, instinct, and genius, should enable us eventually to discover "the Thirdness, the general elements," of the universe (CP:5.173). The evolution of knowledge via the community must be the case in order that it be consistent, Peirce asserts, with the general evolution of the psychophysical universe.

This evolutionary view places Peirce squarely within the contemporary milieu of theoretical science with the likes of Prigogine and Wheeler, as well as Bohm, according to which the only feasible account of the laws of nature for uniformity in general is to suppose them the results of evolution.[7] They are thus neither absolute nor obeyed with precision. They are invariably tinged with a degree of "indeterminacy, spontaneity, or absolute chance in nature." Peirce continues:

> Just as, when we attempt to verify any physical laws, we find our observations cannot be precisely satisfied by it, and rightly attribute the discrepancy to errors of observation, so we must suppose far more minute discrepancies to exist owing to the imperfect cogency of the law itself, to a certain swerving of the facts from any definite formula. (CP:6.13; also 6.201)[8]

To repeat, as the realm of possibilities in the cosmic game of chance are gradually being played out, the universe is becoming more lawlike. Yet, to the extent that cosmic habits have not reached predominance, chance and spontaneity continue to resist encroachments. And since psychical phenomena resist habituation with the greatest effort, and given the perpetual *de-embedment* of *embedded* and *automated habits,* the mind's frequent tendency to diverge from regularities represents a swim against the evolutionary current. In this sense hylopathy and tychism are inseparable: the former without the latter is dead; the latter without the former is empty of meaning. Tychism, absolute chance, nonetheless implies a universe in which consciousness and mind are fully integrated; hylopathy, rather than universal order in obedience to static classical laws, demands an uncertainty factor enabling consciousness and mind to remain actively involved *with(in)* the universe.

Ultimately, it appears, though *semiosis,* like the quantum universe in general, is mind-dependent, the mind, itself bound within the field of *semiosis,* brings about evolutionary changes and at the same time is the victim of those changes. The mind is in part the author of *semiosic* evolution, yet it cannot foresee its evolutionary path, for it remains within *semiosic* evolution. The game is inexorably played from inside, but there is ordinarily no awareness of this insideness; from within, it always appears that an unlimited number of possibilities are there for the taking. Hence the mind "collapses" the semiostates of its universe of its own volition, yet it is itself a semio-system "collapsed" by/within the field of *semiosis;* it is free and it is not free, fortunately, on account of its own finitude—and its blissful ignorance (see appendix 3).

IV. FROM THE PARTICULATE AND MOLECULAR TO THE MOLAR WITH A VENGEANCE.

"But," one asks, "surely there is a set of determinable constraints in the workings of the mind, perhaps most adequately specifiable in terms of linguistic constructions such as those sought by Chomskyan linguistics?"

Perhaps. And perhaps not. What the present state of fallible knowing suggests is not only that the world is radically indeterminate at the lower levels, but that chaos may well lie at the very roots of all forms of what we generally take to be order. This places the traditional notion of order irretrievably beyond the boundaries of predictability and explanation. Order can be modeled, but not directly known or predicted. It becomes well-nigh impossible to speak of constraints within this context. Nonetheless, Tursman (1987:115–31) proposes the following constraints stemming from Peirce's metaphysics: (1) *the most general constraint on the laws of nature,* the logical *illative relation* of arguments (what *would be* the case—Thirdness—comparable to material implication), which requires *a certain set of initial conditions* (see Tursman [1987:72–74] on the *illative relation*), (2) *monotonic constraints* (the imperative, or irreversible)—comparable to the Second Law of Thermodynamics: birth, growth, death, (3) *mind-body interface constraints* (the *apparently* irreconcilable differences between the mental and nonmental), and (4) *limitations at the atomic level.*

Upon discussing (1)–(4), I wish to place Peirce in a somewhat more contemporary light than Tursman does—though this is not meant to reduce the importance of his disquisition. Constraint (1), the *illative relation,* a *would-be* exigency of Thirdness, is relatively clear-cut when one attends to Tursman's first example: if NaCl were added to H_2SO_4, the result *would be* a different salt, Na_2SO_4, and a different acid, HCl. When we shift from inorganic to certain organic reactions, however, less regularity enters the picture. Yields from particular reactions are based on percent averages, since they do not go to completion. More complex problems arise with another of Tursman's examples, the harmonic notion of a pendulum swing which is describable by a precise equation. When considering friction, the earth's force of gravity, and other diverse perturbations, which Tursman duly notes, a pendulum swing undergoes a potentially infinite number of variations which are nonlinear rather than linear, and indeterminate rather than determinate.

This observation, to the chagrin of Peirce scholars coveting a modicum of finalist determinacy vaguely suggested in some of his work, places us directly within the field of "chaos physics." Phenomena such as pendulum swings now go by the name, coined by David Ruelle (1980), of *strange attractors* in *phase space* (Davies 1988:44–51). Phase space is generally composed of as many variables (or dimensions) as are needed to describe a system's behavior. As a variation of the acceleration problem graphed in figure 1, assume you begin accelerating in a sports car with a stick shift. Each time you change gears you must release the pressure on the accelerator pedal, then resume the pressure when the proper gear ratio has been established. This causes the vehicle's acceleration to wane, followed by a renewed surge. Figure 9 demonstrates, as did figure 1, that the corresponding phase spaces look different on a graph than the actual trip "feels." The "feeling" as Firstness and the action as Secondness have their

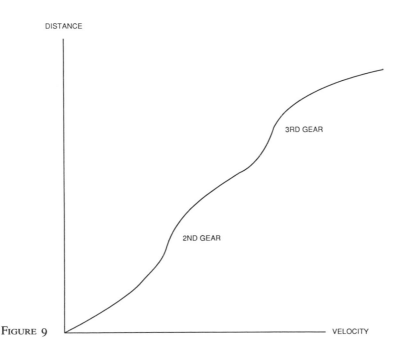

DISTANCE

3RD GEAR

2ND GEAR

FIGURE 9

VELOCITY

Thirdness realized as a graph (a type of *hypoicon*, the diagram [CP:2.276f.]), which becomes a metaphor (a higher type of *hypoicon*) of the experienced sensation. The graph, as Thirdness, is radically abstracted. Yet it is a helpful *map*, especially insofar as it reveals that the car's trajectory is much less smooth and orderly than might be expected.

A more dramatic example of phase space consists of a measure of the instantaneous state of a periodic process such as that of the pendulum. Pendulum swings are normally in one-dimensional space: back and forth. A graph of such moves consists of all the necessary information of the system: the moving pendulum gradually slowing down is reduced to a single point when it comes to rest. A given swing of the pendulum can be graphed timelessly to represent the system during one of its cycles (see figure 10). It is as if at one instant the pendulum were located at a point, and with each successive instant the point moves along its circular trajectory until it reaches its original position. Since the dynamic system is in constant change, the point's position is constantly altered. The entire history of the system can thus be charted by the imaginary moving point, which, like a "world-line" within the Minkowski "block," or the acceleration problem represented on a graph, traces a static trajectory through phase space with the passage of time.

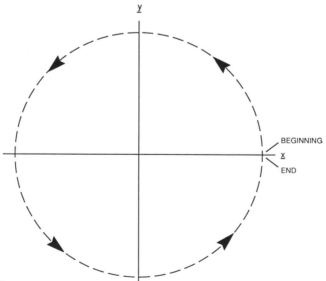

FIGURE 10

The set of point-instants, in short, is plotted along the Cartesian coordinates. For a free-swinging frictionless pendulum, the variables are position and velocity. When the pendulum begins its swing, the velocity is zero at a point along the *x* axis, and as it reaches its highest velocity at the bottom of its arc, that velocity is represented by a point on the *y* axis. Then the pendulum slows to a standstill once again at a point on the *x* axis opposite from the beginning point, and finally, as the negative swing on the opposite side of the *y* axis reaches the initial point, a circle is described. And everything is in order. If friction is taken into consideration, the pendulum steadily loses energy, and the point's trajectory describes a spiral gravitating toward an "attractor," the 0 coordinate in the graph, which indicates the pendulum's eventually coming to a rest.

However, things never quite conform to our ideals. That is to say, Peirce's *illative relation,* when regarding the distinction between the "semiotically ideal" and the "semiotically real"—to say nothing of the "actually real"—is not as determinate as we would like. It has to do with that incommensurability between the "mind-stuff" of the emerging world model and the "physical-stuff" of the classical mechanistic-deterministic universe. In the present context the nemesis of Western thought which could well be termed *turbulence,* that telltale sign indicating the prominence of "mind-stuff," has been everywhere evident, though it generally has been pushed under the rug by most great philosophers and physicists. Recently, as I suggested briefly in chapter 3, the turbulent activity playing havoc with the entrenched classical paradigm has gradually been pulled out of the closet. From Mandelbrot's (1982) fractals we learn that the universe is more cloudlike than clocklike. From Prigogine and the "physics of chaos" we are forced to concede that wild, unpredictable patterns are more fundamental—not to mention more interesting—than the well-scrubbed security of Newton's equations. Take the everyday example of a faucet in your kitchen. If you open the valve slightly, water courses out in a smooth flow, hissing slightly; open it a bit more and a to-and-fro rhythm commences; then turn the knob more, and another, less orderly frequency takes over, and finally, the even flow becomes chaotic.[9]

For an illustration of such "chaos," if a perturbation is applied at the anchor point attaching the pendulum to an otherwise stable source, after a few swings it will begin an apparently sporadic behavior that will become wilder with each oscillation rather than eventually reach a stable point. The attractor is in some sort of undefined motion: it has become a *strange attractor.* The movement is now never quite periodic with respect to an antecedent oscillation and a successive oscillation. There is always a *difference:* the pendulum never exactly repeats itself in a periodic loop, but rather, with each cycle its swings become wilder and wilder. The consequent nonlinear loops and spirals are infinitely deep. They never quite join and never quite intersect, yet they remain within a finite phase space (see figure 11).

The implication of this and other such phenomena is that the world's fastest supercomputers are incapable precisely of tracking the trajectory of the point in phase space tracing out the life of not-quite-periodic motion around a strange attractor. In the typical euphoria experienced by a number of scientists working with strange attractors, David Ruelle (1980:137) exclaims: "I have not spoken of the esthetic appeal of strange attractors. These systems of curves, these clouds of points suggest sometimes fireworks or galaxies, sometimes strange and disquieting vegetal proliferations. A realm lies there of forms to explore and harmonies to discover."

The very important point is that strange attractors irreparably muddy the waters of the classical world. Nature becomes radically unpredictable, an inordinately fickle mistress. This tends to aggravate those physicists searching for

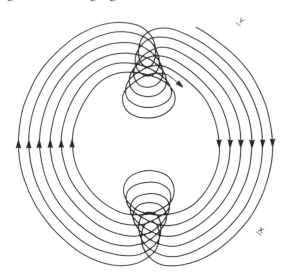

FIGURE 11

a harmonious universe, especially since phase space, it seems, is so pregnant with possible happenings as to be well-nigh incomprehensible. "It always bothers me," Richard Feynman (1967:57) remarks in a complementary context, that "it takes a computing machine an infinite number of logical operations to figure out what goes on in no matter how tiny a region of space, and no matter how tiny a region of time. How can all that be going on in that tiny space? Why should it take an infinite amount of logic to figure out what one tiny piece of space/time is going to do?" Here, quite lucidly, we sense Peirce's lifelong obsession with infinite regresses and other paradoxes of infinity. A given set of initial conditions, though it could be absolutely specifiable—which it cannot be, as Peirce argued and as the "physics of chaos" has demonstrated—would not lead to determinable and determinate knowledge regarding any and all future events. Knowledge must in this regard always remain *vague,* hence *contradictory* and *inconsistent* at the level of Firstness, and *general,* though *incomplete,* at the level of Thirdness. That is, knowledge is as *unspecifiable* as it is *indeterminate.* This, I am afraid, plays havoc with the *would be* of the *illative relation.* Since, given "chaos physics," a vast number of important phenomena are unpredictable, it appears as if in certain respects the circle has been completed, the *continuity of generality* has gravitated toward the *continuity of vagueness,* and *law* becomes a strange bedfellow of *chance.*

But there is a certain consolation regarding Tursman's *monotonic constraints,* or the imperative of irreversibility. Suffice it to reiterate that Prigogine (1980; Prigogine and Stengers 1984) and his associates have argued quite successfully for *asymmetry* and *irreversibility* not only at the *macro-scopic, molar* level of the Second Law of Thermodynamics (of *generality,* Thirdness, *semiosis*) but also, as we shall note in more detail below, at the *molecular, particulate,* and even *micro-level* (of *vagueness,* semiostates), and in the inorganic as well as the organic realm (or in the Peircean sense, the living as well as the nonliving, mind as well as matter). Prigogine, like Peirce, foregrounds *becoming*. Pluralism is in this context highlighted over monism. In contrast, Western thought has traditionally foregrounded *being*. Parmenides, the Stoics, da Cusa, Spinoza, the German idealists, Bradley, and McTaggert have generally held that propositions should be directed toward one subject: substance, essence, the absolute.[10]

However, a few preliminary words before engaging directly with Prigogine. Toward the end of the nineteenth century, Ludwig Boltzmann demonstrated that classical particles described by reversible equations can be made to fall in line with the irreversible universe of entropy. Then came the quantum debacle. Unlike the classical mechanical and thermodynamic views with which Boltzmann contended, the two complementary quantum worlds are truly at odds. Before a "collapse," the multiple possible solutions to the Schrödinger equation exist in simultaneity; time is reversible, and the potential "particle" is spread over the wide area. After interaction, and after the particle is detected, time takes on meaning. The mathematical description before the "collapse" is generally considered to be the most fundamental; after the "collapse" the system is no longer in its pristine, pure form.

Prigogine disagrees with this interpretation. He attempts to place the irreversible, yet timeless, picture of the quantum universe *(prototemporality)* on equal footing with the reversible, yet time-bound, picture of thermodynamics *(eotemporality)*. In accomplishing this task he evokes two concepts: (1) *symmetry breaking* and (2) *nonlinearity*. The first introduces irreversibility and time. According to the classical conception, symmetry lies at the heart of the universe. Space has no up or down, forward or backward: complete democracy prevails. And time has no necessary arrow. "Reality," however, breaks such symmetry. For example, a pair of dice can be placed in mirror-image symmetrical relation one to the other. Then if they are tossed, the symmetry is broken. The numbers are no longer lined up parallel to one another, and most likely two different numbers will be showing. This marks a direction for time. Something occurred, which resulted in a different state of affairs, and for there to be such an occurrence, the previous symmetry must have been broken. Comparable happenings at the quantum level muliplied by a number to the order of 10^{10} give an indication of the complexity of broken symmetry.

But mere symmetry breaking is not enough. If, as Prigogine—along with Bohm—believes, everything interacts with everything else, then all happenings, from the quantum level upward, are nonlinear rather than linear. Nonlinear equations are far more forbidding than their linear counterparts. Linear equations change in proportion to a change of one of the variables. Nonlinear equations, in contrast, may manifest a gradual change, then at some unexpected point there is a sudden breakdown, and a totally distinct situation arises. It is like the straw that broke the camel's back; a certain threshold is crossed and the animal collapses with the addition of a minuscule addition to its load. René Thom's (1975, 1983) catastrophe theory is appropriate here. His seven models illustrate how, for example, two dogs meet, test each other with snarls, bared fangs, and aggressive postures, then a catastrophe occurs when one of the two animals moves across some boundary, and a fight ensues.

Symmetry breaking, irreversibility, and nonlinearity are keys to Prigogine's radical view, predicated on (1) *openness* of systems, (2) *exchange of energy, material,* and *information* with the outside environment, and (3) *far-from-equilibrium conditions* that lead to *fluctuations* and *dissipative structures* by way of *symmetry breaking* and *nonlinearity.* The very term *dissipative structures* seems at first blush contradictory: structure is ordered, while with dissipation, order disintegrates. The fact of the matter is that dissipative structures exhibit two characteristics. When near-equilibrium prevails, order diminishes (particularly in isolated systems), but when far-from-equilibrium conditions are present, order can emerge out of apparent chaos. This occurs when a system proceeds, through fluctuations and symmetry breaking, until a threshold level, a *bifurcation* (critical) *point,* is reached, and the system progresses to a new form of order. Such processes require open systems continuously taking in energy, material, and information from their environment and maintaining a continuous expulsion of entropy as dissipation or waste. The system thus constantly renews itself: it is self-organizing. It retains its identity by perpetually changing. Such order from chaos cannot be adequately captured by the popular label "negentropy," mind you. Dissipative structures do not generate something from nothing; they reorganize themselves and their environment such that they minimize entropy within their own system. In fact, like the entropy principle, dissipative structures not only are irreversible and time-bound, they also bear witness to the impossibility of absolute stability.

Non-self-organizing systems and self-organizing systems roughly correspond to Maturana and Varela's (1980) distinction between *allopoietic* and *autopoietic* entities. A bicycle is allopoietic. It must be propelled by an outside force, and if it breaks down it cannot replace its own defective parts. It can do no more than decay if abandoned by its owner. A living organism is autopoietic— though I use this term with the reservations outlined in chapter 4. Each of its cells, and the entire organism as an aggregate, is open to its environment. It takes in energy and material, renovating itself by transforming the subsystems within it, from microbes to molecules to atoms, and expelling entropy as waste. Through this incessant change it is able to maintain a form of identity, having set itself *apart from* its universe, as *this,* a *mark of distinction* indicating what is *not this* (the remaining part of the universe).

From Prigogine's view, somewhat at variance with Maturana and Varela (Jantsch 1980), what is most important is not the autopoietic entity but the *autopoiesis,* not the "thing" but "happenings," not *being* but *becoming*—that is, not the sign but *semiosis.* The entity maintains itself in the processual stream of events by constantly balancing the need to guard against self-destruction (a molar catastrophe, total dissipation, death) and the need to remain open to its environment such that it can perpetually renew itself. It is like a sprinter who thrusts his body forward at the finish line and, losing his balance, can maintain himself upright solely by continuing to stumble forward. Order is generated in an impending sea of chaos, there is becoming without stable being, *semiosis* without any final interpretant that can be nailed down in the *here-now*. As for the sprinter, there is no turning back; the process is irreversible.

Examples of order out of chaos are legion, from *micro-* to *macro-levels*. From the "collapse" of a complex wave amplitude into a "particle," to atoms, to molecules, and finally to bio-molecules generated out of dissipative structures. From the most primitive of cells—prokaryotes and eukaryotes—emerging from their environment as autopoietic entities, to slime molds which act as an aggregate of individual cells, but in the scarcity of food merge into a single corporate being which moves across the forest floor; from insect colonies, to animal herds, to primate societies, and to human communities: order is successively generated out of chaos. A city emerges in the desert, as if springing up spontaneously, its multiple arteries connecting it to other cities which serve to import energy and material and export waste, its massive landfill bearing witness to its constant expulsion of entropy. The move is invariably, with fits and jerks, toward the "semiotically ideal," toward equilibration, stabilization, the ultimate pie in the sky being absolute order (see table I, appendix 3). But the "semiotically real" and "real" worlds of broken symmetries, dissipative structures, and far-from-equilibrium conditions constantly beckon: *eros* is disrupted by *thanatos*, harmony by dissonance; what was hopefully to be one becomes many, and vice versa.

Thus, interpretants emerge from signs, and they in turn pass away into their successor signs along the *semiosic* stream of things. The flow continues, as eddies and ripples unfold and die away, passing once again into the enfolded. At some region the process becomes turbulent. There is uncertain vacillation; a bifurcation point has been reached. The slightest change in external conditions—some interpreter becoming aware of a sign's reverse side—pushes the fluctuation unpredictably in one direction or the other. Without warning a relatively autonomous *semio-system* emerges, an ordered system simultaneously *apart from* and *part of* the general flow: a sign has pushed itself, drawing in its interpreter, and at the same time its interpreter has pushed it, toward an ephemerally stable vortex, a whirlpool of signification, which is then faced with further fluctuation and change.

In the Prigogine sense, the sign can survive only by remaining open to the entire flow of signification. In fact, signification literally flows through it, allowing it to maintain a degree of self-identity while it is in perpetual becoming. Yet its very openness somehow endows it with a certain resilience: it changes but does not change. Its resistance to change is through the flow; it changes because of the flow. It is stabilized, for it allows the flow to flow through it; but it is only relatively stable, since the flow renders it unstable. Its very stability is instability in that it depends upon its environment, and without it, its environment would suffer a loss. It *is* and *is not* the same sign; it *is* and *is not* a different sign at each moment. Its signness is destined to remain caught in an incessant, reiterative coming into being and going out again.

V. THE PARTING OF THE WATERS. As a result of the work of Prigogine and others, that underlying current, the tradition of Heraclitus I have either indirectly or deviously alluded to, has been resurfacing over the past few decades. A tolerance for contradiction, inconsistency, indeterminacy, and paradox is on the upswing.

More in a Peircean vein, the Parmenidean-Heraclitean conflict is monism pitted against its age-old antagonist, pluralism. For the monist everything is continuous and "spacelike." Within this "space," something and its contradiction cannot coexist. In contrast, the pluralist, relying on a temporal perspective, retorts that something can be one thing at one time and another at another time. Hence there need be no restriction to noncontradictory fireworks, for time is capable of healing any and all distinctions: the *vagueness* inherent in the generation of particulars along the stream of time. According to the monist, spatiality implies dynamic relatedness between things consisting largely, though not exclusively, of symmetrical and asymmetrical relations such as *larger than* and *smaller than,* which lie outside the notion of temporal irreversibility. The pluralist argues that if one wishes to interject a single subject into a temporal framework, one must concede to asymmetry and irreversibility, which necessarily introduce becoming.

A car, the monist declares, is considered in everyday discourse to be the same car even though ten years past it was new and now it has been totaled in a wreck. Temporally speaking, however, there is an irreversible facet of the car's existence which cannot be accounted for in the monist's framework. The wrecked car *was* a new car. That much is generally assumed. But when the car *was* new there was no absolute certainty that it *would become* on this particular date a wrecked car. The monist attempts to destroy directional order by claiming that just as the wrecked car *has been* a new car, so the new car *will have been* a wrecked car, which evokes Wheeler's (1984) (and Lyotard's [1984]) use of the *future anterior*. The past but not the future is in principle (disregarding obvious human limitations) knowable in detail.

This, then, is an important aspect of the temporal versus spatial distinction in Peirce (for further discussion, see Hartshorne 1970:chap. 9). The problem is that, from the broadest possible vantage capable of including both conceptual frameworks, things seem to be placed in a timeless frame wherein the universe, as an always already completed whole, is looking at itself. It thus creates itself—it *has* created itself, *will have* created itself—by lifting itself (which is always already a foregone conclusion) by its own bootstraps—also Wheeler's assumption, it would appear. Be that as it may, we are, all signs are, immanent, and as far as we can be concerned, we are participating with the universe in its self-organizing enterprise. Indeed, Wheeler's apparently timeless image coupled with Bohm's dynamically fluctuating but nontemporal holomovement appears at the outset to be a far cry from the temporal irreversible, processual characteristic of Prigogine's view of things.

Although each is preoccupied with his own set of problems, nonetheless the work of Prigogine and Wheeler is united by two common, rather Peircean threads: (1) rejection of empiricism in favor of a mindlike universe, and (2) acceptance of an open, nondeterministic, participatory universe (recall note 7 of this chapter). In this respect, Peirce's categories evince, apparently contradictorily, a static view of Firstness, but it perpetually cedes ground to Secondness and Thirdness, hence to temporality. Iconicity is roughly commensurate with a static point in a phase space, a collection of points, or the entire trajectory as a line (cf. column B of table 1 in appendix 3). It is all *there;* it simply *is* as it *is,* atemporally one of an infinity of possibilities that *could have been* but *are not.* Temporal irreversibility in the full sense begins with indexicality, the generation of particulars involving action and reaction, which are two-way, yet linear, as are vectorial forces. Temporality of a sort is at least introduced here, though it remains cyclical and reversible.

True irreversibility in the Prigogine sense is the playground of symbolicity, which, following from the asymmetry principle developed in chapter 4, is capable of breeding random, unpredictable, infinitely differentiated oscillation. Granted, it is law, habit, regularity, but with each reiteration there is always a degree of difference. Each reentry introduces variation, change, and change of change. Nonlinear, *n*-dimensional, and temporally irreversible, symbolicity paves the way for differences that make a difference. This is no counterpart to mere memory, reiteration, identity, or rote learning but, in a manner of speaking, creative *deutero-learning* (Bateson 1972). Just as *symbols grow,* so they constantly resubmerge in the *semiosic* soup. And just as "life," whether speaking of Prigogine's reactions (as a result of dissipative structures) or Manfred Eigen's (1971; Eigen and Schuster 1979) hypercycles, is also characterized by the universe's general signness in the Peircean sense, so also "senescence" and "death" are inevitable stages of all phenomena, whether of life or of signs. Yet the exact path (i.e., of some hoped-for teleology) is never exactly known. When a given change of change will occur is never predictable; when the end will arrive nobody can foresee.[11] Hence in the Prigogine and "chaos physics" conception of irreversibility, Peirce's *illative relation* implied by a set of initial conditions cannot be determinate.

Peirce was privy to this idea, but he did not take the final leap. His failure in this regard is evidenced further in Tursman's third category, the *mind-body interface constraints.* Peirce attempted to substantiate his belief that mind acts on matter as well as vice versa with the image of mind as an endless series of events and matter as a beginningless series of transformations, with an infinite series between the two (CP:4.611). He illustrated his point with the graph of a spiral whose curve starts at $r = 1$ (which for practical purposes is beginningless when conceived from "within" the spiral, since there is an infinity of spiraloidal differentiations) and coils outward toward $r = 2$, describing an endless series of revolutions before it reaches that point (hence $r = 2$ can be construed as an endlessly receding horizon). The "outer" series depicts mind ("representation") and the "inner" series depicts matter ("being"). Although there is an infinity of real gradations between "being" and "representation," this, Peirce asserts, "shows that although it be true that Being immediately acts only on Being and

Representation immediately acts only on Representation, still there may be two endless series, whereby Being and Representation act on one another without any *tertium quid*" (CP:8.274).

The indeterminable extremities of Peirce's example possibly testify to the lack of information regarding initial conditions which ultimately renders his *illative relations* conditional. The problem is more complex than immediately meets the eye, however. During Peirce's latter days, Henri Poincaré, a sort of predecessor of "chaos physics," observed that, given classical mechanics, if the initial conditions of the universe were known, the conditions of the universe at a given succeeding moment could be predicted. But even if all natural laws no longer held any secret for us, those initial conditions could be known in no more than *approximate* fashion. If such an *approximation*

> enabled us to predict the succeeding situation with the *same approximation,* that is all we require, and we should say that the phenomenon had been predicted, that is governed by the laws. But it is not always so; it may happen that small differences in the initial conditions produce very great ones in the final phenomena. A small error in the former will produce an enormous error in the latter. Prediction becomes impossible and we have the fortuitous phenomenon. (Poincaré 1914:68)

On an exceedingly less complex scale, this is the pendulum problem. Assuming one begins measuring the swings *in medias res* without knowledge of the set of previous swings, the first swing measured is slightly deviant from the previous swing, though the investigator cannot be aware of it. But she does notice that the second swing is slightly deviant with respect to the first, that the third is also deviant with respect to the second, and that this second deviation is slightly larger than the first one, and so on, such that the last swing measured will result in a greatly magnified deviation when compared to the first few measurements. The oscillations have become, in a word, unpredictable, chaotic.

This conclusion appears to contradict Peirce's belief that the universe is becoming more lawlike and less contingentlike. It could be said in Peirce's defense, however, that regarding the pendulum problem, we are speaking of islands of exception to phenomena that generally follow classical rules—and Peirce, we must be mindful, was understandably prone to follow classical mechanics, though he often broke rank. Such islands are necessary for a universe of becoming, for life itself: life as an aberration, a deformity in an otherwise well-oiled cosmos. Thus it appears that along the great chain of command between living and nonliving entities, and between brain processes and mind processes, there must be, to use Douglas Hofstadter's (1979) terms, a conglomerate of "strange loops" (his counterpart to "strange attractors") along a "tangled hierarchy." In short, just as Poincaré's timely observation plays havoc with the orderly classical universe, so does life as aberrant behavior, as *semiosis.* Peirce's spiral model is wise in at least this respect. Aware that the mind-body interface was little understood during his time—and the same can be said today—the model suggests that there is no discernible distinction between mind processes and body processes. All are of the order of *autopoiesis, of dissipative structures.* If, as Peirce asserts, matter is effete mind, then mind, like the organic system giving rise to it, is also self-organizing, as are signs in general.

Finally, Tursman refers to Peirce's *limitations at the atomic* (or we might say in the context of the present discourse, the *particulate*) *level,* category four. Tursman rightly notes that the classical atom either has or does not have a particular property. Thus the excluded-middle principle and noncontradiction apply. Peirce's logic approaches the atom from another vantage: its properties consist of a set of "real" possibilities which become partly actualized at a given point in time and space (compare to Bohm's *implicate* and *explicate*). Since actuality cannot exhaust possibility, any and all observations are selections as a result of choice. And given indefinite time and possibilities of actualization, an atom subjected to successive perceptual grasps can be expected to display unexpected states, growth, development, and decay. It will be in a state of incessant change, as pure possibility it will have no true identity, for identity pertains to Secondness (NE, III:758). Consequently, Tursman (1987:130) observes,

> the properties of the atom are not expected to obey the law of excluded middle or the law of non-contradiction. The properties of the atom are expected to obey the law of continuity. Peirce frequently pointed out that no part of a continuum has to be or is wholly *A* or wholly not-*A*. Neither the law of excluded middle nor the law of non-contradiction applies to *anything* general and the atom is general except at that moment of observation at which point it becomes fully determinate. The atom is, then, except at the moment of observation, a general or collection of real possibilities. Upon the occasion that the atom is observed, that is, upon the occasion that an actually existing state of the atom is observed, then there is a discontinuity and the laws of excluded middle and non-contradiction apply to the atom.

Here, I believe we should take Tursman's taking Peirce at face value at face value. As Peirce conceived it, classical logic, with its tenuous foundations and its delusions of grandeur, would be superseded at a deeper level by more general "logic of vagueness" which precedes the level of semiostates and allows for movement toward *generality.* Secondness imposes binary existence on forms, but the laws of the growth of signs permit existents, which, as Seconds, must conform to the laws of classical logic in order to evade those laws (CP:1.488). And, outside even the laws of sign growth lies logic in the most *vague* sense, the logic of chance, spontaneity, freedom, and potentiality, which, Peirce proclaimed during one of his Hegelian moments, must ultimately annul itself: "For if it does not annul itself, it remains a completely idle and do-nothing potentiality; and a completely idle potentiality is annulled by its complete idleness" (CP:6.219).

In other words, at the "greatest lower bound," given chance, spontaneity, and freedom—*vagueness*—it would appear (contra Tursman) that the constraints in the neighborhood of the atom as the juxtaposition of semiostates are hardly constraints at all. For (*pace* Wheeler via Bohr) the universe of signs is radically participatory: from the "completely idle potentiality" some-thing is spontaneous-ly brought into signness. On the other hand, given habit, regularity, law—*generality*—in its final and complete form, the universe of signs is static, it annuls itself: regarding the totality, for every force (sign, argument) there is an equal but opposite force (sign, counterargument), such that in their composite they are "mutually cancellatory." Hence if the potentiality is idle, it remains null; if it is active, the sum of all possible actions yields the null set—the Peircean counterpart, to be sure, of Wheeler's (1980a, 1980b) cosmic equation, "$0 = 0$," according to which everything cancels everything else to leave the pure Monad, that which *is as it is*. This, the equivalent of the universe as Utimate Interpretant, returns us to the beginning: Tursman's conception of constraint by way of the *illative relation*. If every *would be* were to have reached finality, as such there would hardly be any chance, spontaneity, or freedom at all! How can this conceptual cul-de-sac be accounted for?

In the first place, we must bear in mind that what the Monad (implicate, idle potentiality) *is* cannot be known *as* any-*thing*. Only the plurality of actualized Seconds (explicates), perpetually in the play of action and reaction, bifurcating the world into *thisness* and *thatness*, can be known, albeit partially. Knowing, by extension, is *semiosic*, ongoing, and irreversible. But knowledge is not accessible through mere Secondness alone. What can be known is known through mediative Thirdness. That limited *whole* of knowing is the knowing itself, not the known, which implies an asymmetry between the (knowing) mind and (known) matter, and which can perhaps be understood solely through Peirce's psychophysicalism. Mind and matter depend on one another asymmetrically. Mind depends upon matter asymmetrically for its very existence, and matter depends upon mind asymmetrically for the properties it may be endowed with at a particular time and place. All in all, we would like to conclude, asymmetry, irreversibility, temporality, plurality, ceaseless change must win hands down, for without it, we are back to complete generality, "$0 = 0$," or the pure Monad, which as an absolute is also absolutely unknowable.

Assuming "$0 = 0$" were to be the case, either one of two situations would most likely be in effect. The first would be a static domain; the second would be a state of constant change without there being any change of change, which is to say the same thing from the totalizing perspective. Consider, for example, Schrödinger's notorious *Gedanken* experiment concerning his live/dead cat.[12] Suppose the experimenter wants to assure herself of a "democratic" state of affairs according to which the cat enjoys equal rights with any and all potential observers from outside the box. She screws some hinges on the inside such that the cat can open the lid inward to observe (actualize) his observer, and she puts another set of hinges on the outside such that the observer can lift the lid to look at the live-or-dead cat. The problem is that now the door can be opened from neither the inside nor the outside. Everything *is* as it *is*, without the possibility of any change. We have an uncanny *meso-level* thought experiment of a *micro-level* condition patterning the totalizing equation, "$0 = 0$." This is tantamount to Peirce's (or Spencer-Brown's) undifferentiated domain before time and before ordinary logic, "the utter vagueness of completely undetermined and dimension-less potentiality" (CP:6.193). In this domain, the superposed "live cat/dead cat" is destined to continue on into the indefinite future without there being a "collapse" into Secondness.

Suppose another experimenter decides on an alternative "democracy" by removing the hinges altogether, thus endowing all parties concerned with complete freedom. But now the lid "collapses" on the superposed "live cat/dead cat" eigenfunction such that one of the two potentialities is actualized, but neither can be actualized in such a way that it stands *for* something *to* someone *in* some respect or capacity. In the sense of Wheeler, neither cat could be *recorded* and *put to use* for such and such a purpose *by* some observer. In fact, if the universe as perceived—interacted with—by any entity is nothing more than a mere bundle of disjoined events, then nothing in the universe could *be* as such: the *originary cut* leading to an interpretant could never have been made *by* someone. As the Eastern mystics have said for centuries, the universe, as unformed, unfixed, and uninterpreted by consciousness, is completely devoid of meaning. In other words, there could be no more than a buzzing array of unrelated sense-qualities (Firsts), which are no-*thing* definite. Peirce writes of this realm of precognition thus:

> Even if you say it is a *slumbering* feeling, that does not make it less intense; perhaps the reverse. For it is the absence of *reaction*—of feeling *another*—that constitutes slumber, not the absence of the immediate feeling that is all that it is in its immediacy. Imagine a magenta color. Now imagine that all the rest of your consciousness—memory, thought, everything except this feeling of magenta—is utterly wiped out, and with that is erased all possibility of comparing the magenta with anything else or of estimating it as more or less bright. That is what you must think the pure sense-quality to be. Such a definite potentiality can emerge from the indefinite potentiality only by its own ritual Firstness and spontaneity. Here is this magenta color. What originally made such a quality of feeling possible? Evidently nothing but itself. It is a First. (CP:6.198)

Wheeler's (1980a) own answer to the problem is to place a pliable hinge on the lid of the box housing Schrödinger's eigenpussy so it can be opened from either side. Now there is no predefined hierarchy. But neither is there any symmetry. Rather, a *decision* is made by the community, there is a *selection*, something is *distinguished* from something else, the lid is opened from outside, the cat is observed *as* such and such, and a "semiotic world" comes into existence. The cat has no say in the matter. This appears fine and dandy for one near-instantaneous observer-observed interaction. However, since it appears that in Wheeler's *total* picture everything in the universe *has been, is,* and *will have been* always already, the system, though in a sense asymmetrical, must be also atemporal. That is, when either the dead cat or live cat is *put to use* by the signifying community, the entire past history of Schrödinger's feline fantasy *will have been* determined in the present by this solitary semiotic act. And if *recorded*, which it must be, future history will also *have been* jelled once and for all. There is no doubting that Wheeler's alternative is "democratic," but only if regarded as a cosmic whole: once again, "o = o." Pluralism becomes, from the broadest possible vantage, monism, and monism has no true identity without pluralities. Chance becomes necessity and vice versa. The dilemma remains.

However, for both Wheeler and Peirce, the only "semiotically real" perspective is that of each member of the community and of the community as a whole from "within." This *immanent* perspective gives a picture of the universe as ongoing, a self-organizational, irreversible, and temporal becoming. In another way of putting it in regard to table 1 of appendix 3, a particular individual or a finite community of individuals can at a given point in time and space be aware of no more than segments cut out of the middle of columns A through E, like the eye that is limited to a minuscule portion of the frequencies making up the entire energy spectrum. This image testifies to our fallible immanence as it does to our propensity constantly to push beyond.

It also returns us to Prigogine's thesis. Given Heisenberg's uncertainty, Bohr's complementarity, Bohm's infinitely complex holomovement of top-down and bottom-up mutual interaction and effectuation, and Wheeler's participatory universe in view of Schrödinger's *Gedanken* experiment, it is not possible to speak of constraints or limitations at Tursman's atomic level but of an intricate web of interaction. Upon Prigogine's entry onto the scene, the role of randomness and chaos in the creation of structure conjures up a universe in which the *meso-* and *macro-levels* are less determinate than in the classical, and even the quantum, pictures. Prigogine's "new uncertainty principle" demolishes the last vestiges of classical predictability and control with the injection of randomness, fluctuation, symmetry breaking, and far-from-equilibrium conditions into a once neatly wrapped and tied package. There are no longer any linear cause-and-effect sequences. Rather, as we learned from Poincaré, a *micro-level* perturbation in a far-from-equilibrium state is capable of becoming magnified finally to throw the entire system into disarray. This is like a young lad who, from a bridge overlooking a flooding river, tosses his beer can into the water, which causes a slight perturbation, the ripples of which bring about a degree of turbulence some yards downstream, which increases finally to reach a threshold which is crossed, a dike gives slightly, then disintegrates, and a town is devastated.

This is not mere figment of the imagination, but a possible series of events according to Prigogine—and in his own way, Wheeler (1984), I might note. Like Heisenberg's *micro-level* uncertainty, Prigogine's uncertainty also plays havoc with classical reductionism, especially of the sort propagated by Jacques Monod (1971). This becomes less a limitation or constraint than a promise of creative possibilities. The open character of the universe or the universe of signs, its history, the possibility of an infinity of unexpected happenings—the "clash" of Secondness on consciousness—should generate anticipations rather than the vision of impending tragedy. Heraclitus has his day. The universe as ongoing flux takes precedence over the universe as oneness, stasis, order for all time.

"o = o," fixedness, the Parmenidean way, is actually not of the living world but depends upon ab-straction, acts of the intellect divorced from the flow of experience, as if the ab-stracter enjoyed a position *sub specie aeternitatis,* completely divorced from the hustle and bustle of everyday living (recall the graph in figure 1). Here we reencounter the problematic collusion of time and timelessness, finitude and infinitude. In Prigogine's view, life is continuity, invention, irreversibility, evolution. Intelligence (i.e., the mind), in contrast, fragments, isolates, abstracts, and stultifies process. Mind cannot comprehend life, and biology can do no more than caricature it. Solely intuition, feeling (Firstness), is capable of knowing it. Classical science was Medusa-like, converting the world into lifeless, inorganic, mineral substance. The "new science," on the other hand, is process-oriented—which for Peirce was the principal characteristic of mind in the first place.

Relativity retains the classical propensity to spatialize time, to intellectualize or idealize process. Neither Einstein's nor Schrödinger's equations mark a fundamental distinction between past and future. A "world-line" within the "block" can proceed as easily in one direction as the other, and standing waves know no "time's arrow." In contrast, the ancient Aristotelian view places primacy on a tendency to become rather than static being, a propensity toward constant transience rather than that which eternally is (Prigogine 1983:65ff.).

Yet, in Peirce, Bohm, Prigogine, and Wheeler, there remains a strange conflict between process and that which is held timelessly in check. At each bifurcation point in a system's past, a *choice* was made, a *distinction* marked out, and something was *actualized,* which canceled all the other possibilities forever. Time is inexorable, yet what is past is there, timelessly, what is future lies timelessly in wait, and what is present is what *is.* Briggs and Peat (1989:145) explain the apparent dilemma thus: "The dynamics of [Prigogine's] bifurcations reveal that time is irreversible yet recapitulant. They also reveal that time's movement is immeasurable. Each decision made at a branch point involves an amplification of something small. Though causality operates at every instant, branching takes place unpredictably."

This mixture of *necessity* and *chance, constraint* and *freedom, generality* and *vagueness,* Thirdness and Firstness, constitutes the history of a system. A system dampens many *macro-level* variations—thus they appear to follow classical laws—but fortunately for us all, *micro-level* flexibility and creativity remain relatively unfettered. Small-scale changes, by amplification, stand a chance of becoming large-scale changes. Such amplification is a characteristic, par excellence, of sign systems. A bee enters a hive and does a dance which sets hundreds of insects in motion. At some unpredictable moment the proper signal is forthcoming, and the apparently random movements of a colony of termites become coordinated. Napoleon gives an order and an entire army is mobilized. An unexplained disorder is found on the U.S. president's nose, and the stock exchange suffers a setback. Whether or not the mixture of timeless and temporal terms can be reconciled is not the question. It is a matter of abolishing these and other such dichotomies altogether—as we shall note in the following chapter.

This, on a grand cosmic scale, is the thrust of Peirce's fusion of matter and mind accompanied by the abolition of life against intellect, process against stasis, chance against necessity, and time against timelessness.

Yet, after all is said and done, one must concede that, given Peirce's fascination with paradoxes of infinity, Bohm's implicate order all there at once, and Wheeler's self-reflexive, self-excited universe which somehow always already *will have been* constructed, a perhaps inevitable lingering inclination—nostalgia?—seems to remain toward the One.

SIX *From a Broader Point*

of View

I. ALONG THE GREAT DIVIDE. In view of the last section of chapter 5, Peirce's "man-mind ≈ sign" equation, which, when extrapolated to the limit, becomes "cosmos ≈ sign ≈ mind," bears further commentary. Peirce grounds his (1) *objective idealism,* (2) *tychism,* and (3) *synechism* on the assumptions that, to recap, (1) all that *is* is mind, matter being congealed mind, (2) all originary actions are a matter of pure vagueness and chance, and (3) actions tend increasingly toward continuity and generality.

Peirce took pains to point out that his "everything is mind" postulate coincides with the experimental evidence available to him during his day. In 1891 he attributed mind of a rudimentary sort to life-slimes and protoplasm. Given their reaction to certain stimuli, he argued, they feel, possessing a primitive form of consciousness, and hence they exercise the basic functions of mind. To the questions, "What mechanistic framework can account for this phenomenon?" and "What molecular composition can possibly cause feeling, mind, and consciousness?" he responded that an answer cannot be easily forthcoming, since mind is (pluralistically and *nootemporally*) irreversible, while inanimate matter, according to classical laws, is (monistically and *eotemporally*) reversible (CP:6.127). Yet mind and matter constantly engage in interaction. In fact, mind, from a *complementary* vantage, *is* matter, and vice versa (CP:7.370, 8.168). It would be a mistake, we are told,

> to conceive of the psychical and the physical aspects of matter as two aspects absolutely distinct. Viewing a thing from the outside, considering its relations of action and reaction with other things, it appears as matter. Viewing it from the inside, looking at its immediate character as feeling, it appears as consciousness. These two views are combined when we remember that mechanical laws are nothing but acquired habits, like all the regularities of mind, including the tendency to take

habit itself; and that this action of habit is nothing but generalization, and generalization is nothing but the spreading of feelings. (CP:6.268)

This implies that the mind/matter dualism must be tossed in the trash can in favor of synechism. For everything, Peirce argued time and again, is continuously related to everything else such that "all phenomena are of one character, though some are more mental and spontaneous, others more material and regular" (CP:7.570). Rejecting the mind/matter dichotomy thus, we once again appear to be driven to *hylopathy,* otherwise termed *monism* (CP:6.24). One cannot, it seems, embrace both pluralism and monism at the same time. Nevertheless, Peirce repeatedly tried to plunge between the Scylla of the impossibility of conceptualizing the monadic realm and the Charybdis of myriad particulars between a consummate Firstness-Thirdness on the one hand and the ultimate nominalist extension of Secondness on the other. This enigmatic "monistic" inclination must be further qualified.

Peirce's remark of 1891 that the traditional form of Cartesian dualism "will hardly find defenders today" was, in retrospect, rather optimistic. However, in his fellow pragmatist William James—whom he on occasion severely criticized—we find another champion of the idea that subjectivity and objectivity are fused, if not hopelessly con-fused. James writes:

Let us take outer perception, the direct sensation which, for example, the walls of these rooms give us. Can we say that the psychical and the physical are absolutely heterogeneous? On the contrary, they are so little heterogeneous that if we adopt the common-sense point of view, if we disregard all explanatory inventions—molecules and ether waves, for example, which at bottom are metaphysical entities—if, in short, we take reality on which our vital interests rest and from which all our actions proceed, *this sensible reality and the sensation which we have of it are absolutely identical one with the other at the time the sensation occurs. . . .* In this instance, the content of the physical is none other than the psychical. (James 1968:186)

James's intriguing, aberrant sort of "monism," though simple enough in principle, is still mind-boggling, for it implies that when the originary split *(cut, mark)* is exercised, our world, as well as our-selves, remains mutilated and no more than partial. As Spencer-Brown (1979:105) puts it, the world "is itself (i.e., as indistinct from itself)," but once the subject is separated from the object, the world has made itself "distinct from, and therefore false to, itself." This artificiality cannot be "real," since the total world always must be indistinct from itself, hence any further distinction will be illusory. Such "monistic," that is, nondual, consciousness, then, cannot itself be a clear and distinct idea or thought. Neither can it be put into words. Much as the Eastern sages tell us, it is pure, unadulterated experience. Ideas, thoughts, words—signs all—cannot iconically mirror it, indexically point to it, or symbolically represent it, for they are part of that very experience—thus Schrödinger's quasi-mystical words that apparently defy intellection. Monistic consciousness is not a luminous mass of mush. Indeed, it exists exactly as it does *for* pure experience, but not *for* signs perceived, conceived, and said *as* such and such. The dancer and the dance are one, the knower is simultaneously the known.

In Peirce's conception of things, the only feasible answer is that the phenomenon cannot be explained except indirectly by way of the concession that physical happenings are but underdeveloped manifestations of psychical happenings. Initially matter behaves according to pure chance, but it slowly takes on uniformity of action, continually evolving according to specific modes of habit formation that cannot be accounted for in mechanistic terms (CP:6.238–71; also 6.301).

The upshot is, then, that the universe of mind ultimately coincides, as a final interpretant, with the universe of matter (CP:6.501; also Holmes 1964). Mind is not merely the outgrowth of or an entity emerging from the brain, nor do its activities parallel brain activities, nor is it merely nothing but brain activity. Peirce was aware of the work in physiology of his day pointing to the fact that after brain damage "other parts of the brain are made to do the work, after a fashion, with perhaps other parts of the body" (CP:7.376). It is entirely mistaken, Peirce therefore believed, to claim that the mind dwells exclusively in the brain "as something within this person or that, belonging to him and correlative to the real world" (CP:5.128).

In fact, Peirce once made the apparently outlandish remark that, regarding language, it is more valid to state that it exists in the speaker's tongue or the author's book than in a brain (CP:7.364). It exists no more in the brain than do emotions in the heart. The tongue that speaks and the hand that writes, once having taken on habit, possess a life of their own: they do what they do best, following pathways of least resistance, often in spite of, or in addition to, the intentions of their erstwhile master—i.e., *embedded, automatized* activity. These are habits which are "taken, lost, replaced continually, and felt, no matter how. Mostly no doubt lodged in nerve matter, but not necessarily so" (CP:8.85). Mind and its product, thought, then, appear in rudimentary form in slime molds and protoplasm, as well as, to repeat, "in the work of bees, of crystals, and through the purely physical world; and one can no more deny that it is really there, than that the colors, the shapes, etc., of objects are really there" (CP:4.551; for problems with this notion, see Holmes 1964). True to Peirce's antidualism, there is no clear-cut line of demarcation between *res extensa* and *res cogitans*.[1]

More firmly to place Peirce's formulation within Spencer-Brown's ball of wax, the contrived split between subject and object forming an illusory severance between thinker and thought, perceiver and world, necessarily evinces a time component, since space and time themselves are not Newtonian dichotomies but make up a continuum: a separation in space is also a separation in time. *Some*-thing which has become a distinction appears as a quality (First), but it is not a full sign as such until it has been mediated by an increment of time, a *difference* and *deferment*, such that it becomes *this-here* thing, a some-*thing* (Second), *as* such and such (Third). Thus it can be said from one perspective that there are two separations, first spatial and then temporal, which ultimately merge into one. Life—of a sign or any other organism—is created in space, and it begins its journey in time until it reaches its destination, at which point a *conjunctionis oppositorum* is enacted, death having once again closed the gap between space and time.

This necessarily introduces us to the broader ramifications of the mind-matter conjunction. Ultimately, Peirce believed physical reality consists of discrete bits and pieces composing a set of underdeveloped parts of a cosmic process, mind. Mind is another name for *semiosis,* which incorporates any and all "semiotically real" or "semiotically objective" worlds "out there" as well as any and all "semiotically real" universes "in here." The conjunction of these two "realities" constitutes the cornerstone of Peirce's *objective idealism,* which, as I have pointed out, embraces both methodological-epistemological realism and ontological-objective idealism, which must be subject to a more penetrating look.[2] A portion of Robert Almeder's (1980: 148–59) critique of this fusion of "isms," and especially of the finite with the absolute, bears full citation:

> If, on the one hand, real external objects are causally and logically independent of finite minds, but are not causally or logically independent of the Absolute Mind (since they are of its nature and since without the Absolute they would not exist), then there must be a real distinction between finite minds and the mind of the Absolute—otherwise the union of epistemological realism and objective idealism is impossible. For, if the aggregate of finite minds (Community) is, in fact, identical to the Absolute Mind (as Peirce sometimes suggests), then either there really are no finite minds or the Absolute mind is finite, being simply the collection of finite minds; but if there are not [*sic*] finite minds, then it is nonsense to defend the thesis of epistemological realism, and if the Absolute Mind is finite, then it would be nonsense for an epistemological realist to claim that physical objects do not exist independently of the Absolute Mind. If, on the other hand, the aggregate of finite minds is not identical to the Absolute Mind, then the thesis that one can be an epistemological realist and an objective idealist seems tenable. But this, of course, only raises the question as to how it is possible to assert that there is an Absolute Mind which is the sum total of all being while at the same time asserting that there is something which the Absolute is not. (Almeder 1980, 156–57)

At the outset Almeder's point appears well taken. He presents the classical dilemma with which one is confronted if one wishes to propound the notion of an Absolute Being endowed with the quality of mind and at the same time the notion of finite and physical entities which are not identical to the Absolute in the sense that they do not possess properties which are absolute in the Absolute being. If the aggregate of finite minds could somehow be coterminous with the Absolute, then epistemological realism and objective idealism could not both be adopted. Everything would be objective and "real." There could be nothing that the Absolute *is not.* And if the aggregate is not coterminous with the Absolute, then the problem of there being something which the Absolute *is not* arises.[3]

Almeder, in face of this dilemma, urges that one cannot consistently be both an epistemological (or methodological) realist and an objective (or ontological) idealist. He does admit, however, that Peirce, in arguing for his doctrine of objective idealism, prudently relied on the claim that quality, feeling, or First-ness is irreducible to the properties of matter, which plays the role of bringing about the "clash" of the "real." He also adds the corollary that Peirce's argument can hardly be defended as a basis for objective idealism, since the problem of discontinuity and finitude contradictorily interjected into continuity and the infinite remains, and, given the mind-body problem, which resists a clear-cut distinction between subject and object, idealism and realism, continuity and discontinuity, neither can it successfully be refuted. In this light Popper would likely decry Peirce's claim as no more than metaphysical mush.

II. FROM GRAND DICHOTOMIES TO COMPLEMENTARITY. In fact, juxtaposing Popper's falsification thesis with Almeder's critique of Peirce may help clarify the apparent inconsistency of Peirce's thought. Almeder puts forth the stipulation that the cotenability of Peirce's epistemological realism and objective idealism requires a concise demarcation between finite minds and the Absolute Mind. The problem is that such a demarcation "involves certain classical difficulties which Peirce was either reluctant or impotent to discuss" (Almeder 1980:156). This "unfortunate turn" in Peirce's philosophy, however, is perhaps not so tragic as Almeder makes it out to be, for two fundamental reasons:

(1) The distinction between a given collection of finite minds and the Absolute is, by Peirce's definition, fairly clear-cut: his ideal model of the Absolute is the mathematical continuum, an actual infinite. Since no collection of finite entities can stack up to it, Peirce, one must suppose, enjoys no warrant for mixing the finite and the infinite. Regarding knowledge, Popper (1974) commits the same sin when he points out that, as our knowledge is destined to remain finite, or better, for practical purposes infinitesimal, our ignorance will always be infinite, since extracting a finite section from the infinite still leaves it with its same quality of infinitude. In addition, since the Absolute, or Truth, is infinite, it must be ipso facto unfalsifiable by any collection of finite minds, which also renders Popper in this particular case compatible with Peirce's framework. That is, if we can falsify our knowledge, then it does not correspond to Absolute Truth, and if we cannot falsify it, then either it is not legitimate scientific knowledge or it is Absolute Truth, in which case we will never know we have it, for we cannot falsify it. In other words, we must be wrong as many times as we can, for therein lies our only possibility of approximating (asymptotically, Peirce would chime in) the Truth. (Peirce's scheme of things also fits the Spencer-Brownian universe necessarily mutilating itself so as to look at [know] itself. The [finite] knower sets himself apart from the [infinitely variable] universe, which cannot be known because of the incompatibility between the knower's [deluded] desire for infinitude and his infinitesimal capacities.)

(2) Peirce's contention that feeling is irreducible to material properties is partly exonerated if we accept the notion that Firstness is a *superposition* of possibilities, any one of which can at a given moment become actualized into the domain of the "semiotically real." Firstness, precisely, *is* irreducible to Second-ness. It is an unruly sea of *vagueness* as opposed to *this-hereness,* the *implicate*

as opposed to the *explicate,* the *nonselective, nondistinguished,* and *nonindicated* as opposed to the *actualized.* However, Thirdness, one must bear in mind, is capable of mediating between the two.[4]

Now, (2), when placed in our contemporary milieu, is predicated on the assumption, for some years on the rise, that the world does not present itself to us conveniently fractured at its necessary joints consisting of systems, subsystems, and contexts. Each observer, and each community, by agreement, and whether tacitly or not, makes these divisions according to particular and collective needs and demands as well as individual and social desires. This is true not only of human communities but of all societies, from *micro-* to *macro-levels,* cells to aggregates of cells, and to fishes, fowl, and mammals. Regarding part and whole, the aggregate and the absolute, finitude and infinity, it appears, in light of the preceding paragraphs, that alternative views, though at first glance they may appear mutually exclusive, are, at their lowermost level, interdependent and mutually defining. This effectively does away with dichotomies, traditionally conceived. Rather, each pair of interdependent terms is in reality *complementary,* not contradictory or oppositional—neither is it *differential* in the Saussurean sense. I write "lowermost level," implying that at this level there is no *essence,* only *form.*

This abrogation of dichotomies lies at the heart of *marks-cuts* insofar as they coexist, with some sort of unspecified and perhaps unspecifiable *purpose.* An entity, such as an individual cell, must define its boundaries in order to separate itself from its background, and it attempts to maintain itself in this condition as an individual with a certain rudimentary form of self-identity. *Distinction* is thus the *manifestation* of individuality (ego, self-maintenance) in a collective unit (organism, society, subculture). The problem is that even Spencer-Brown's *distinction,* which accompanies the *mark,* usually turns out to be some sort of *designation* of one of the two distinctions as being primary ("I," "us," "this," "here," as opposed to "you," "them," "that," "there"). In fact, it is the very *purpose* of a distinction to give rise to an *indication* (Varela 1984a, 1979:84).

The notion that a universe of forms comes into being by the marking of a distinction is nothing new; it is germane to much Eastern thought, as well as to the underpinnings of the binary system of Boolean algebra and the construction of natural numbers from the empty set or zero by means of forming a collection. The empty set, $\emptyset = \{\ \}$, brackets or forms nothing. Nonetheless, the brackets *indicate* a *distinction* in two-dimensional space—Peirce's initial sheet of his book of assertions—upon which the brackets are ciphered—Peirce's initial *cut.* The two-dimensional space itself is the *indication* of nothing, the void—that is, the absence of a set or collection of entities. Significantly, in this respect, the essence of Spencer-Brown's calculus is, however strange it may seem, radically nonnotational, in which case the equivalent of the empty set first frames nothing, then the frame is discarded entirely (Kauffman and Varela 1980). This calculus is independent of the vagaries of notation, for only *pure form* remains, whose very existence depends upon the process by means of which the form was formed in the first place. This is perhaps best illustrated by the following experiment:

> Sprinkle sand over the surface of a metal plate; draw a violin bow carefully along the plate boundary. The sand particles will toss about in a rapid dance, swarming and forming a characteristic pattern on the plate surface. This pattern is at once both form and process: individual grains of sand play continually in and out, while the general shape is maintained dynamically in response to the bowing vibration. (Kauffman and Varela 1980:171; see also Merrell 1982)

The form is there, bounded by no more than a set of undulations like the hologram introduced in chapter 2. The ongoing, dynamic process brought about by the dancing grains of sand is the *manifestation* of the form. The form is permanence, yet it is a constant flow of energy: discontinuity within continuity, finitude within infinity, so to speak. Its manifestation is a stable structure, yet at no instant is it identical to what it was at the previous instant: transitoriness within sameness. Hans Jenny, in his work on such stable but dynamic vibrating and undulatory systems, observes further that

> since the various aspects of these phenomena are due to vibration, we are confronted with a spectrum which reveals patterned figurate formations at one pole and kinetic-dynamic processes at the other, the whole being generated and sustained by its essential periodicity. These aspects, however, are not separate entities but are derived from the vibrational phenomenon in which they appear in their unitariness. . . . [T]he three fields—the periodic as the fundamental field with the two poles of figure and dynamics inevitably appear as one. They are inconceivable without each other. . . . [N]othing can be abstracted without the whole ceasing to exist. We cannot therefore number them one, two, three, but can only say . . . that we have morphology and a dynamics generated by vibrations, or more broadly by periodicity, but that all these exist together in true unitariness. . . . It is therefore warrantable to speak of a basic or primal phenomenon which exhibits this threefold mode of appearance. (Jenny 1967:176–77)

What appears to be a form/process duality in Jenny's discussion is actually not an opposition in the classical sense but rather a *complementarity*, which requires, for its proper manifestation, *triadicity*. The apparent duality is, at a more intuitive level, part of a triad in which the extremes of the original poles are related. Yet they remain apart, their relation being provided by a third pole, which can be given the following expression, as Varela (1979:99) formulates it:

$$* = \text{form/process}$$

The star is to be read as "Consider both sides of the '/'," that is, "Consider both the *form* and the *process* giving rise to it." Thus the virgule provides for transition from one side to the other of the supposed opposition by way of the star. The starred equation offered here is a paradigm case: all such activities imply both form and process as well as transition. In fact, the traditional dualism between Being and Becoming is actually a complementarity, since any conception of Being is impossible without the notion of Becoming, and vice versa. For example, consider the aphorism "One must be somebody before one can be nobody." It entails one's *becoming* somebody before there exists the possibility of one's *being* somebody, and such *becoming* implies nothingness (nobodyness) from which it was possible for somebody to be *distinguished* and *indicated as* somebody in the first place. Hence:

$$* = \text{Somebody/Becoming somebody from nobody}$$

is the legitimate equation, since merely to write *somebody/nobody* is to ignore the process and highlight the form as opposed to its absence.

This notion of complementarity is a departure from classical thought. The star does not indicate a synthesis in the Hegelian sense, for nothing new has been generated. It is no more than a bringing to attention the manner in which two complementary expressions are combined. In Hegelian thought duality is polarity, a struggle between opposites which are related by bilateral symmetry. Both extremes exist at the same level in the negative form: A/not-A. Therefore:

Form/process, in contrast, is chiefly, though not entirely, one-way and asymmetrical: the two extremes are related by inclusion/exclusion, process being more general and including within its domain of becoming the formation of all that is. Thus:

The terms A and B now extrend across levels indicated by the cut within a cut. They belong to distinct "logical typing," so to speak, in the terms of Bateson (1972) and Wilden (1980).

The central nervous system controlling this "logic" is that of self-reference, and ultimately paradox, following Russell's Theory of Logical Types, according to which paradox arises from a confusion of logical levels. Opposites remaining at the same level, A/not-A, are distinctions well-nigh impossible to specify either in nature or in human discourse. For example, male/female and all such supposed binaries are not value-neutral and viewed with an innocent eye. On the contrary. They are inevitably hierarchical, one indication of the pair supposedly being primordial and hence primary, the other inexorably taking on its subordinate role.

The problem is that symmetrical, reversible, and static states of affairs are never actually the case. Predator/prey do not operate as opposites of exclusion but call for a larger context, a unity, an ecosystem implying asymmetry, irreversibility, complementarity, and survival values insofar as the system can be maintained in some sort of equilibrium. Once the equilibrium is broken and, say, the prey faces destruction, the whole system is thrown out of kilter. *Ecosystem* is precisely the larger, self-referential domain constituting the legitimate left side of the complementarity, the right hand consisting of *species interaction*. Hence: * = Ecosystem/Species interaction (where the right side incorporates both predator and prey). Likewise, male/female can be subsumed into the all-encompassing equation: * = Society/Male-female interaction (which allows for the possibility of roles' being altered, of equality, or even of the subordinate's becoming superordinate). In this sense, pairs of the starred form entail different levels with a bridge connecting two expressions specifying each other: form needs process, and vice versa.

In short, (1) unstarred opposites generally depict symmetrical relationships, and (2) starred equations are generally qualified by *complementary* relationships. Unstarred equations are a matching, or a pitting of something against something else: A/B(not-A). Starred equations are a fit: A → B. Unstarred equations, in their pristine form, consist of mirror imagery, enantiomorphic symmetry. But, in light of the preceding chapters, exact repetition never exists in the nitty-gritty of "semiotically real" worlds—or the "real" world for that matter. Everything is always something other than what it was. Differences appear, which can threaten to become distinctions (either/or, atemporality). On the other hand, starred equations are quite effectively characterized by part-whole, container-contained, and cause-effect relations, which fuse time and space. The problem with complementarity is that, either in conjunction or in competition with symmetry—which is invariably the case in human social systems—progressive differentiation can snowball, sometimes approaching a critical mass. Bateson (1958) calls this snowball effect *schismogenesis,* which can be beneficial only if controlled.

The combination of two-way symmetry relations and one-way asymmetry relations is thus seen as dynamic, ongoing, and proper for a valid conception of *semiosis.* For whatever pair of presumably contradictory expressions, the starred operation creates a complementarity wherein an original pair of opposites makes up the right-hand side of the virgule. Thus interrelations of the form

(a) $(A) \leftrightarrow (-A)$, however artificially contrived, are invariably blemished, and tend toward interrelations of the form (b) $(A \rightleftarrows B)$, which in turn threatens, in its interrelations with the first form, to ignite a chain-reaction effect. In other words, symmetries (or binaries), fabricated rather than found, are actually part of the comings and goings of all signs most appropriately described as the irreversible, asymmetrical process depicted in (b) rather than (a). A (an enfolded possibility, First) is perpetually unfolded into B (a *mark-indication,* Second), both of which are mediately and synthetically embraced by the outer orb (Thirdness).

In the familiar binaries, Simultaneity/Sequentiality, Space/Time, *Langue/ Parole,* Synchrony/Diachrony, and Paradigmatic/Syntagmatic, the dual elements specify each other in the same manner. For example, as Saussure himself emphasized—though he often ignored it—diachrony is of utmost importance, and with synchrony, it makes up part of a larger, more encompassing, whole. Let us call this whole, consisting of a network of exceeding complexity, an "organism."[5] The equation now becomes: * = Organism/Synchrony-diachrony manifold. In similar fashion, *langue/parole* can be reformulated as: * = *Lan-*

gage/Langue-parole. Moreover, regarding the obstinate body-mind dilemma, we might posit the equation: * = mind/body, with the qualifier that body and brain are a manifestation of effete mind. A complementarity can thus be seen to inhere. One term cannot be duly considered without the other, and one of the two must properly be construed as a process from which the other arises. The equation, in this light, would more appropriately be: * = organism/mind-body. By the same token, Bohm's cosmology in notational form becomes: * = holomovement/explicate-implicate.

Observer/observed and subject/object, from this more general system, obviously compose a broader unity than the traditional mindset has hitherto allowed. Whatever this unity may be, it must surely encompass both expressions of the form interaction/interacting agents—the left side as the more general domain, and the right side as that which is subsumed within it. In all cases the system entails a Peircean *dialogic* between mind and minds, self and *other*, self and *Other*, interpretant and sign. The interacting duo does its dance while embraced by the larger domain. *Dialogic* interaction between what *is* and its *other-Other* (what *is not*) is crucial. In essence, as suggested in chapter 4, Sheffer's "stroke" function, as well as Peirce's "logic of relatives," provides the origin by negation of all logic and perhaps all thought—which, by extension, is tantamount to the general *semiosic* process. The *not both* or *neither nor* of the "stroke" is transformed into standard unities (signs) which then engender other unities (signs). And what is the largest of possible unities? The universe itself, the Final Interpretant, which "is constructed," Spencer-Brown (1979:105) concludes, "in order (and thus in such a way as to be able) to see itself."

III. THE UBIQUITOUS MIND. Now, I do not wish to give the impression that I am attempting to vindicate Peirce once and for all. His attempted synthesis, for which he was often branded a crackpot during his day, is still looked upon by many as inconsistent at worst and bizarre at best. Yet his objective idealism bears on contextualization within many of the hypotheses, conjectures, and assumptions I have presented throughout this inquiry.

In the first place, Peirce posited neither an objective reality in the form of the correspondence theory of truth that ruled during the heyday of empirical positivism nor the computational/representational approach of many cognitive psychologists.[6] On the other side of the ledger, he never propagated any Berkeleyan solipsism or Protagorean relativism according to which each person is the measure of all things. Rather, it may be said that he attempted to exercise a leap beyond what Richard Bernstein (1983) terms "objectivism and relativism," though Bernstein, as well as Rorty (1979), feels he generally failed in this respect. The fine line between objectivism and relativism is also precisely that precarious pathway along which Maturana and Varela attempt a balancing act. They oscillate, in an effort to give account of their descriptions, between the organism as a self-referential, autopoietic, autonomous system grounded in its own internal workings, and the organism in terms of its interaction with its environment when coupled with other organisms (Varela 1984a, 1984b).

In the second place, Peirce appears hell-bent, long before his time, on "transcending," by something rather akin to a principle of complementarity, the mind-matter—or software-hardware (wave-particle)—dichotomies (see Davies 1988:142–46). If on the left side of these three dichotomies we suppress mind (or consciousness) and replace it with self-"I" in complementary relationship with matter, we have, I believe, a more adequate formula. Just as for Peirce ideas spread continuously to merge into one another, so Mind is everywhere and everywhen. Communication between minds within the Universal Mind occurs through "continuity of being," which entails a swallowing up of the individual into the whole. A person, we are told, "is capable of having assigned to him a *rôle* in the drama of creation and so far as he loses himself in that *rôle*—no matter how humble it may be,—so far he identifies himself with its Author" (CP:7.572). The idea is that the general "law of mind" is precisely that: general in the broadest possible sense. As a bundle of habits, a person consists of "a connection of ideas" which make up "a general idea, and . . . a general idea is a living feeling" (CP:6.155), and feelings, "cöordinated a certain way, to a certain degree, constitute a person" (CP:6.585). On the other hand, upon those feelings' "being dissociated (as habits do sometimes get broken up), the personality disappears" (CP:6.585). And, we must suppose, in the same fashion, when an aggregate of ideas making up a general idea is dissociated, that general idea becomes fractured.

Many would charge Peirce—and by proxy, me—with some form of bleary-eyed mysticism, whether of the Eastern or Western variety. There is really no mysticism implied here, certainly not of that naive and distorted sort according to which mystics are inwardly turned on and tuned out, more in a trance than in the world. This version of "mysticism," recently popular in certain circles, largely overlooks the sayings of the great masters of every mystical tradition that the Tao, Buddha, Brahman, Absolute, Spirit, Mind, is fundamentally the essence of one's everyday consciousness. One's state of consciousness, no matter what it may be—sad, jubilant, depressed, ecstatic, calm, preoccupied, frightened—just *as it is,* is mind. In other words, the mystical experience is in the final analysis identical to whatever one happens to be doing and experiencing at a given moment.

Since Tao, Mind, or any other holistic level we care to paste on this experience is everywhere and everywhen, that is, tantamount to Peirce's continuous welding of all minds, then there is no meaning to the question, "*Where* is *it?*" It is not *there-then,* for the finding or the grabbing. In fact, the question itself is paradoxical, for to ask where it is is to imply that one does not have it. One always has it *here-now,* so we are told, though it has neither *where* nor *when.* According to a reliable report:

> The One Mind alone is the Buddha, and there is no distinction between the Buddha and sentient beings, but that sentient beings are attached to forms and so seek externally for Buddhahood. By their very seeking they lose it, for that is using the Buddha to seek for the Buddha and using Mind to grasp Mind. Even though they do their utmost for a full aeon, they will not be able to attain it. (Blofeld 1958:29–30)

So much for the so-called unspeakable totality. My introducing it in the manner I did serves to reintroduce Bohm's metaphysics within a Peircean context. Specifically, the *holomovement* concept (whole [= monad] plus scintillating, vibratory motion [= pluralism, myriad particulars]) *is* germane to the tenor of the discussion at hand. In addition to overcoming Zeno's paradox generated by the succession of "nows," Bohm's model of the universe implies the possibility for a quantization of time according to classical mechanics and of "real" time as a slice out of something comparable to Eddington's (1953:46–67; 1958b) complex or "imaginary" time. Here we have the implicate *and* the explicate, the continuous *and* quantized or particulate—which is found also in Oriental thought. Hindu philosophers teach that the Totality, or *Sunyata*, is propertyless *(neti, neti,* or "not this, not this, . . ."). This implicate order is the background of possibilities from which the particulate or explicate domain can be distinguished and indicated, thus yielding *maya* (illusion) to become the world of discrete entities.

However, unlike Zeno, and certain Eastern teachings, Bohm's implicate order is not mere propertyless stasis. It is, like the hologram and Jenny's dancing grains of sand, constant flux, incessant trembling—the moiré effect—without there being any overall change. Everything cancels everything else out.[7] What is more important—and this places Bohm directly in the same ballpark with Peirce—the notion of implicate and explicate orders represents an effort to speak the unspeakable by means of the language of mathematics and sheer ratiocination. This is an utter impossibility according to Eastern sages, but, as marvelously illustrated through the works of Samuel Beckett and Jorge Luis Borges, which constitute literary counterparts to this ultimately futile mathematical game, what interests us is the sheer Faustian effort expended and the means involved rather than the inconceivable end itself.

Bohm speculates on the relevance of his implicate-explicate orders to natural language and mind. He struggles to construct a language of becoming appropriate for his metaphysics, which gives him enough trouble. But the real bugbear is mind. Alex Comfort (1984:168) makes the timely observation that

> at one point [Bohm] seems to be saying that the mind, being an offshoot of a 4-space explicate, contains and intuitively perceives the "grain" of the multidimensional implicate which he postulates (a "Tao of mind") simply through being plugged in to material neurones. At other times he treats mental events as a separate order parallel with material, 4-space events, but having some measure of autonomy.

The same subtle (con)fusion of the mind-brain muddle exists in Bohm's struggle to explain consciousness, as we noted in chapter 2. Consciousness is construed on the one hand as an explicate parallel with the brain (the parallelism thesis) and on the other as itself an explicate of brain activity (the epiphenomenon thesis). But things don't seem to jibe here. If the brain as explicate is the implicate for explicates in consciousness, then consciousness represents a third order, much like a psychologist watching a patient through a two-way mirror as she reacts to the action on a TV screen before her. According to Peirce this would be a non sequitur, for consciousness cannot be so reduced to or derived from the brain (matter) because it is itself mummified mind (consciousness). Most likely neither would Peirce be attracted to epiphenomenalism, which tends to place consciousness (mind) and matter-energy (brain) on somewhat equal ontological footing.

Moreover, if self-consciousness is introduced into the implicate order, knee-jerk reactions will certainly be forthcoming from all directions. The door is opened to a mirror-image regress of consciousness *of* itself ad infinitum, which recalls the best of Borges's images as well as Schrödinger's observer of a live-or-dead cat, who in turn requires another observer observing him, and so on—to say nothing of uncanny though logically worked-out notions such as Dunne's (1934) and Matte Blanco's (1975) infinitely regressive consciousness. It also evokes, to repeat, the unspeakable totality. One is not comforted much by the thought that thought cannot reveal the "real reality," at least until one comprehends what the point is all about: Wigner's (1969) "unreasonable effectiveness of mathematics." It is not so much mathematical thought but that more mundane form of thought enshrouded in natural language or sensory images that is so incapable of the task. The trouble is that the helpless Western mind is so in tune with feeling and cogitating in terms of ocular images and abstract concepts, that he/she cannot intuitively grasp the forest for being surrounded by an arbitrary symbolic stand of trees that are neither heard nor seen but merely conceptualized.

If one assumes, on the other hand, that both the perceived mental (Peirce's inner) world of consciousness and the perceived objective (Peirce's outer) world are explicates of different orders, the first being primary and the second secondary, one might be on the right track. Mind, or consciousness, as a First, is an implicate that can be explicated as consciousness *of* something "out there" (a particular Second) which stands for something else (via a mediating Thirdness) *in* some respect or capacity (a particular interpretant or Third). By the same token it can be consciousness *of* itself, *of* its inner workings, mediately, and by way of something representing something else to that consciousness. This accounts for a measure of autonomy regarding the separate order of mental events.

It also bears on Maturana and Varela's oscillation between the self-referential, autopoietic entity and its being plugged into, or, better, coupled with, other entities in order to dance in step to the tune of the Big Band. In this case, which is also one of Comfort's (1984:174) suggestions, the operator that extracts explicates from the implicate is mind itself: mind in general is the *process* of explication, which equates it with the entire holomovement. More specifically, while one aspect of mind is the implicate, another aspect, the inner explicate (thought-signs), pertains to consciousness, while the explicate "out there" (sign-things) is matter—i.e., fossilized mind. In this sense mind is the *nonselective* as well as the *selective* domain. A little mind separate from but at the same time within the Big Mind (i.e., the melded community of minds) defines itself recursively, and as such on a small scale it maintains a level of autonomy. Consequently, this little mind is a paltry and radically failible mirror image of the self-contained, self-sufficient, recursively defined Grand Mind. Or so it would seem.

At any rate, Bohm's unfolding-enfolding holomovement, Jenny's grains of sand dancing in and out again, Spencer-Brown's schizophrenic "I"–"not-I" universe, the "stroke" function, Deleuze and Guattari's vacillating nomadic sensibility, all of them commensurate with $\sqrt{-1}$, or the "I am lying" paradox, defy any attempt to give them appropriate linguistic window-dressing (recall the words of de Broglie and others on the limitations of language from chapter I, section V). In modern times, Kierkegaard and Nietzsche, and more recently figures such as R. D. Laing and Antonin Artaud, were driven either well-nigh or literally crazy in their struggle with the contrapuntal *either* and the *or*. Bach used it to the hilt in his art of the fugue, Nicholas de Cusa was fascinated by it, Pascal anguished over it, the surrealists reveled in it, Beckett and Borges teased it virtually to its linguistic end, Escher and Magritte created tantalizing visual images of it, and Gödel raised it to a shrill pitch of abstraction. Some "postmodernists" claim they get along fine with such discomfitures. In whichever case, I trust that the obsession to know what it is all about will endure.

Perhaps, by and large, one of the most fruitful approaches on the contemporary scene—though prima facie it seems to border on the outlandish—is Wheeler's (1984) quite Peircean idea that meaning consists of the *joint product* of all the communication occurring in an entire community. Wheeler's suggestion that an explicate becomes an explicate in the full sense only when it is duly recorded and used *as* something that represents something *to* some organism *in* some respect or capacity implies that the only knowable "reality" is the "semiotically real," a given universe of signs. For example, the blackening of a grain of photographic emulsion in a camera due to a radioactive emission is an *irreversible act* of amplification. A single photon can bring about the reaction, yet the grain contains an enormous number of atoms, hence the amplification is mind-boggling in its complexity. And the act is asymmetrical and irreversible, since the grain stands hardly any chance of turning back to white once it is blackened. The irreversibility in question here is complementary rather than contradictory. The first is strictly arithmetic, the second pertains to the organic *(bio-nootemporal)* realm; the first lends itself to self-identity, the second demands difference and divergence from one reiteration to the next, from one cycle to the next.[8]

Wheeler takes pains to point out, in his opposition to Wigner's strictly consciousness-constructed world, that even the lower organisms communicate with one another and in the process *use* the signs of their "semiotic world," which as a result take on a less powerful sort of *meaning* in line with their relatively dim state of consciousness. Nevertheless, they are equally participants with human beings in creating a meaningful world (Wheeler 1980b:63–64). In either case, the end product is the same: meaning is the *joint product* of all the information that is exchanged by a community of communicators, whether human, animal, insect, or slime mold, and as such information ultimately arises from a set of myriad quantum phenomena.

This is meant to be neither reductionism nor physicalism nor determinism. At the quantum level there is no classical causality or determinacy, but probability factors in indeterminacy. In the final analysis it boils down to a yes/no process, but it eventually becomes nonlinear and non-Boolean. There is no simple-minded physicalism but a complex probability state based on superposed wave amplitudes. And reductionism is out of the question, since a given wave amplitude is not actualized of its own accord but depends upon its context, its environment, its community of observers, and the entire universe, for its existence. Moreover, "meaning" in the sense of what Wheeler (1984) calls "Era III meaning physics" is by no means a mere set of "nothing but" happenings.[9] Rather, quantum happenings have no meaning—i.e., "semiotic reality" is not "actual reality" as such—except insofar as they are subject to some community of actor-participants in collaboration with the self-organizing universe's creative advance. In this sense, meaning is always *there,* though it may not yet be generated *for* some observer *in* some respect or capacity. It is the implicate with the potentiality to become explicate (Bohm 1987a)

To extend Bohm's dye-drop-in-a-vessel-of-glycerine trope, what defines the dye drop when it has been explicated from the implicate medium is the jointly agreed-upon concept "dye drop," as a *meso-level molecular* entity (Second) whose *thingness* is related to all other *molecules* in the system. What lies behind the drop's appearance and disappearance is continuous, as quality, *vagueness* (Firstness). And that which endows the dye drop with its concept—the collective acts of the community of interpreter-interprctants (or observer-participants)— belongs to the Third order of habit, regularity, law, or *generality.* Or, once having been explicated, the meaning of a sign can sink into oblivion (Firstness) by embedment, subsequently to be *de-embedded,* explicated as a "semiotic" object (Second), raised *to* consciousness, and endowed with some form or fashion of a minute portion of its myriad possible meanings (Thirds).

Placing these three orders in the Varela starred framework, we have:

$$* - \text{Consciousness-mind-self-"I" (Third)/(Second)//Mind(First)}$$

where the single slash is inextricably artificial or false to itself, representing two different—and even incompatible—orders of the same phenomenon, while Mind, The Mind, is the possibility, as an implicate order, for representing the all-encompassing, synthetic whole, the Monad, which renders the opposition truly *dialogical* rather than merely dyadic, binary, or dialectical.

SEVEN *The Spectrum*

of Mind-Sign

I. THE NEVER-QUITE-PRESENT "REAL." Peirce's intriguing "Cosmos ≈ Sign ≈ Mind" equation must be taken yet a step further in order more adequately to see through the Grand Dichotomies discussed in chapter 6. Having denied intuition in his essay on our "four incapacities," while attacking the Cartesian paradigm, Peirce put forth the rather unexpected claim that we are all signs, and therefore something general (CP:5.264–317). By extension, as has been noted, the universe itself would be a developing sign, and the ideal and unlimited community of knowers would finally come into possession of the final self-referential, self-contained, self-sufficient Interpretant mirroring the entire universe, that is, mirroring itself—the Mirror of Nature, the Sublime Hologram. Throughout his life, Peirce, in spite of his antifoundationalist leanings, seemed "quite obviously attracted to such a semiotic Absolute Idealism" (Savan 1952:188; also Stearns 1952:198).

But, as we have also noted, from a strictly logical point of view, just as a knife cannot cut itself, so the universe, like Wittgenstein's eye scanning its world, cannot logically see itself without artificially separating itself from itself. The notion of a finite individual knowing the universe as an object of knowledge is thus inextirpably contradictory. Nevertheless, such notions have been the very cornerstone of Western philosophy, theology, and science. "Objective knowledge" is firmly embedded in the *either* and the *or* of a plethora of dualisms, which have their origin primarily in Greek thought. I cannot overemphasize my point that the dilemma inherent in this binary thinking is that the more it succeeds, the more it fails. Whatever is known of the universe—i.e., whatever a severed portion of the universe knows of its *other*—the more it becomes a fable in Nietzsche's conception. Whether we consider Popper's falsification (strangely related to Buddhism's *"neti, neti"*—*"not* this, *not* this") or a variant of "negative theology" recently the vogue in certain circles according to which every interpretant is a misinterpretant, it boils down to the same: whatever we think or say a thing *is,* it *is not.*

In this respect, Korzybski (1941) hit the target dead-center. It is perhaps unfortunate that his discipleship became a rather obscure cult engaged in little more than an ongoing litany to its master. One problem might be that Korzybski wrote during those euphoric times of positivism's confidence-building program of indoctrinating eager students with the power of positive thinking, binary thinking, that is. Positivism's "Separate the men (scientists) from the boys (nonscientists)" approach has been especially elusive and illusive in that its dualistic roots are grounded in intellection, and it is therefore well-nigh impossible to dig them out by means of sheer intellection. Dualisms must nonetheless be doggedly pursued to their limits.

But this, as I have implied, is an interminable task. If the only way we can say what a thing *is* is by saying what it *is not* (i.e., refute it), then we can never say what it *is,* for saying what it *is not* cannot be exhausted. In other words, we must continue being wrong until hopefully we are right, but if somewhere along the tortuous route we were somehow to be right, we could never know it, for since we could not demonstrate its rightness, we would not know whether it was right or wrong. Yet the fact remains that we can only hopefully be right, in the long run of things, by being wrong. This is admittedly a cross-eyed look at Popper's brand of "negative theology," but what it boils down to nonetheless.[1]

Ultimate Truth allows of no dualisms; but little truths do. Little truths contain little falsities (lies, fables) within themselves: a privileging of one side of the virgule at the expense of the other side: *this* not *that.* Little truths as opposed to little falsities are nonetheless asymmetrical, in spite of this privileging; they serve to rev up the motor of Western linear binary thinking. Such thinking can do no more than lead to little truths rather than that hopeful absolute Truth, since Western systems of thought are invariably *counterposed to,* in *reaction against,* something else.

From Galileo's falling stones to Newton's falling apple, and from Rousseau's Social Contract to Adam Smith's *Laissez Faire* and Bentham's Pleasure/Pain principle, in the most general sense either dualisms have been tested negatively, they have passed out of fashion, or they have managed to survive up to the present. In the latter case, all Grand Designs are destined to collapse, since they are, themselves, the privileged side of some dualism or other. Abolition of any and all dualisms by Western methods of intellection is, to repeat, an interminable affair. Gödel made certain of that, perhaps once and for all—if there can be in any form or fashion a "once and for all" for thought.

This quandary also appears endemic in Peirce's philosophy of the asymptote. Nothing short of an ideal and hence an immortal community of knowers can reach the end of the trail without being ambushed at an interminable number of passes along the way. Of course, Peirce's "economy of research," as Rescher (1978) aptly reviews it, points out a few shortcuts along the road, but since the journey is infinite, any subtraction from it will leave it as it was, infinite.[2] Although Popper's bold conjectures should enable the scientist to make as many mistakes as possible in the shortest amount of time, Peirce's limitation still applies: the dichotomy I have evoked time and again between the "semiotical-ly real" and the "real" can never be completely eradicated. "Semiotically real" worlds consist of *Umwelt*-generated modes of *sensing, acting on,* and, re-garding human semiotic, of *perceiving* and *conceiving* the universe. Indeed, most dramatically in the case of human semiotic, the twain "realities" shall never meet.

Given the insurmountable rift between these two "realities," then, in the sense of Peirce, sign use, and thought, which consists also exclusively of signs, cannot be divorced from the mind—a sign as well—or from the self—whose existence depends on an inferential process, therefore it is also a sign. There can be no dualisms within such an all-encompassing realm of signification, nor can the "stuff" of the world be anything other than some "semiotic reality" or other; hence this "stuff" is composed of "semiotic" rather than "real" objects, with whatever overlap there may be between the two remaining at least partly indiscernible. And this seems to be the consensus of twentieth-century physics. The physicists' conception of the world, Eddington tells us, "is only vivid so long as we do not face it. It begins to fade when we analyze it. . . . We have chased the solid substance from the continuous liquid to the atom, from the atom to the electron, and there we have lost it" (in Commins and Linscott 1947:448).

What is perhaps the ultimate dichotomy of modern Western thought, mind and matter, seems to have been led to the annihilating edge of the abyss and given a quick shove. It has disappeared, though most of us tend to continue along our pathways of least epistemological resistance as if the defunct paradigm were still alive and kicking. Bertrand Russell provides a cryptic epitaph along these lines: "The world may be called physical or mental or both or neither as we please; the words serve no purpose" (in Commins and Linscott 1947:387). And Schrödinger (1967:136) puts it bluntly, as only he can:

> It is maintained that recent discoveries in physics have pushed forward to the mysterious boundary between the subject and object. This boundary, so we are told, is not a sharp boundary at all. We are given to understand that we never observe an object without its being modified or tinged by our own activity in observing it. We are given to understand that under the impact of our refined methods of observation and of thinking about the results of our experiments that mysterious boundary between the subject and object has broken down.

In fact, the very idea that the observer-observed barrier has been broken down is yet another illusion, for, Schrödinger (1967:137) continues, "Subject and object are only one. The barrier between them cannot be said to have broken down as a result of recent experience in the physical sciences, for this barrier did not exist." The barrier was, in other words, from the very beginning a figment of the imagination—or as Peirce would have put it, the result of an inference: the dichotomy is itself a sign. *Mind* and *sign* are now properly seen to be one, as are mind and matter.

On the other hand, from various angles—twentieth-century process philoso-phy, general systems theory, synergistic thinking, ecology, the "new physics" (particularly that of Bohm, Prigogine, and Wheeler)—dualistic thinking in general is on the wane. At present this seems to be occurring at the expense of the universe as a Great Clock fading out to become a Vague Cloud, which can, in light of the "new physics," be construed in many forms, potentially an infinity of forms. Eddington (1958b:319) writes, much in the spirit of Wheeler, that

> we have torn away the mental fancies to get at the reality beneath, only to find that the reality of that which is beneath is bound up with its potentiality of awakening these fancies. It is because the mind, the weaver of illusion, is also the only guarantor of reality. That reality is always to be sought at the base of illusion. Illusion is to reality as the smoke to the fire.

Eddington is certainly not urging the hoary untruth that there is no smoke without fire. Simply stated, smoke as such is interminably deceptive. Like any other sign, smoke presumably—or hopefully—refers to the "real." As an *index,* a Second, a pointer, it invariably turns out to be something veering off from that which it might otherwise have been, though there can never be any guarantee that that "otherwise" is the "real" either. Any given sign, any given "semiotic reality," consequently, both promises and bamboozles, or it does either one or the other, but we cannot absolutely know which. The best we can do, ultimately, to cite Eddington (1958b:291) once again, is concede that

> *something unknown is doing we don't know what*—that is what our theory amounts to. It does not sound a particularly illuminating theory. I have read something like it elsewhere—
> > The slithy toves
> > Did gyre and gimble in the wabe.

Indeed, jabberwocky creates the image of some nebulous sort of uncertain activity, since for us it can start and finish only *in medias res.* Whether we contemplate electron-signs (that is, "object"-signs) or thought-signs, as icons, indices, or symbols, it's the same ultrapliable batch of dough: "The slithy nicos gyre and gimble with the dincies and transmute themselves into bymslos." By introducing a few logical notations here and some numbers there, along with a dash of geometrical figures and a dose of topological images, a "bymslo" does a slam dunk in a "dinxe's" face, seduces a "nico" in the park, and everything presumably becomes a matter of natural language—which is ultimately the bread and butter of physics anyway in Wheeler's conception (see also Gregory 1988). Natural language is actually as deceptive as it is destructive, for it is helplessly inadequate to the task, as we shall soon note.

On the other hand, if we switch our linguistic cargo to another vessel and navigate along a tangential route, we can arrive at what have often been considered two modes of knowing, two levels of consciousness.[3] For example, William James (1968:155) tells us that there are two ways of knowing things, knowing them immediately or intuitively, and knowing them conceptually or representatively. Although such things as the white paper before your eyes can be known intuitively, most of the things we know, the tigers now in India, for example, or the scholastic system of philosophy, are known only representatively or symbolically.

Juxtaposing this quote with another from Eddington (1958b:321–22), in a comparable vein:

We have two kinds of knowledge . . . symbolic knowledge and intimate knowledge. . . . [T]he more customary forms of reasoning have been developed for symbolic knowledge only. The intimate knowledge will not submit to codification and analysis; or, rather, when we attempt to analyse it the intimacy is lost and it is replaced by symbolism.

One might at the outset speculate that, regarding this distinction between *intimate* or *intuitive* and *representational* or *symbolic* knowledge, we have Peirce's distinctions between *feeling* and *form, quality* and *law, contingency* and *regularity, vagueness* and *generality:* that is, Firstness and Thirdness (see, for example, Savan 1952:187). As such the two modes must be separated by an increment of time, a *durée,* a specious present, commensurate with Peirce's distinction between immediacy and mediacy. To an extent this appears to be the case. Witness, for example, Peirce's words on quality, Firstness. We are told that we can never think "*This* is present in my consciousness," because as soon as we reflect *on* the event, our consciousness *of* it is past. Once it is past, we cannot "bring back the quality of the feeling *as it was in and for itself,* or know what it was like *in itself*" (CP:5.289; also 1.348, 7.351–52). That is to say, whatever is present *to* the mind is invariably a mediation of what *was* present in the previous moment, which is only at this present moment available. In this sense what is called the immediate "runs in a continuous stream through our lives; it is the sum total of consciousness, whose mediation, which is the continuity of it, is brought about by a real effective force behind consciousness" (CP:5.289).

Thus whatever we may say of thought-signs as they are *in* consciousness, Peirce remarks elsewhere, "is said of something unknowable in its immediacy." The data of Cartesian introspection do not "directly reveal what is immediately present to consciousness, at all; but only what seems to have been present from the standpoint of subsequent reflection" (CP:7.425). Peirce maintained emphatically that, as with the data of introspection, so also with those of external observation. Thus against the Cartesian dictum that to know and to know one knows are for the gifted introspectionist part and parcel of the same thing, Peirce countered that whatever is immediately present *to* consciousness is not that which introspection supposedly reveals. In a sense somewhat commensurate with the notion of alternate frames of reference in the non-Euclidean space-time continuum of relativity, Peirce argues that

the things we observe in a physical science, say in astronomy, are not the elementary facts, at all. Kepler, for example, was not, as even J. S. Mill seems to fancy, provided, in the observations of Tycho, with the real places of the planet Mars, by the study of which he made out two of his three laws. No astronomer can directly *observe* the situation of a planet relatively to the sun. He only observes, the secondary and derivative fact, that the planet as viewed from the earth, and subject to aberration and the equation of time, is in such and such a *direction* at such a time. According to the method of observation, this direction will be more or less affected by refraction, etc. Moreover, the astronomer is forced to recognize that every single observation he makes is more or less affected by *error*. Those errors have to be corrected by reasoning whose only premises are the erroneous observations themselves. (CP:7.419)

We cannot directly observe the world "out there" as it is in the absolute *here-now,* for there are no simultaneities. And we cannot observe it without there being a change, though ever so slight, from the moment we immediately "see" it to the moment we mediately see it *as* such and such with respect to something else. On so doing, we interpret it, and hence construct an interpretant *of* it, which is in turn part and parcel of the ongoing process of our (re)constructing ourselves. There are no unmediated facts. All facts are always already endowed with value, with culture-laden, language-laden, and private idiosyncratic meanings.[4] By the same token, introspection for Peirce does not directly reveal what is immediately present *to* consciousness, but only what seems to have been present from the vantage of subsequent reflection. It is not even capable of telling us "what the normal appearance from this subsequent vantage is," without "its testimony being falsified at all times with serious accidental errors" (CP:7.420).

II. CLOUDY KNOWING. Of the two modes of knowing, *intuitive* or *intimate* and *representational* or *symbolic,* Eddington calls the first intimate, for it unites subject and object. When subject and object are separated, however, the "intimacy" becomes tenuous, and symbolism threatens to take over.[5] This is the all-too-familiar world of language, discourse, rhetoric, analysis: binary thinking. This realm of symbolism, of representation, necessarily edified upon the rubble of the subject-object mutilation of a once-proud continuum, was, is, and must remain to a degree illusory.

The vicissitudes of symbolism, of language, are, so to speak, of the sign's own making: language, the human semiotic animal's sign system par excellence. When detached from the concreteness of everyday life, language is mummified in abstractions; at times it even threatens to become virtually inoperative as an instrument of understanding. Yet every culture is firmly anchored in language: *no language, no culture.* "Without an instrument of symbolic expression and communication," Aldous Huxley (1981:xii) observes,

we would be Yahoos, lacking the rudiments of civilization. It is because he starts by being *Homo loquax* that man is capable of becoming *Homo sapiens.* But this is a world in which everything has to be paid for. Language makes it possible for us to be more intelligent and better behaved than dumb brutes. But whereas the dumb brutes are merely bestial, we loquacious humans, who can talk ourselves into pure reason and almost angelic virtue, can also talk ourselves down into being devils, imbeciles, and lunatics.

Language is the universe, says Benjamin Lee Whorf (however, see note 14 of chapter 1). And it breeds a sense of self-confidence in us:

> We all hold an illusion about talking, an illusion that talking is quite untrammeled and spontaneous and merely "expresses" whatever we wish to have it express. This illusory appearance results from the fact that the obligatory phenomena within the apparently free flow of talk are so completely autocratic that speaker and listener are bound unconsciously as though in the grip of a law of nature. The phenomena of language are background phenomena, of which the talkers are unaware or, at the most, very dimly aware. . . . The forms of a person's thoughts are controlled by inexorable laws of pattern of which he is unconscious. These patterns are the unperceived intricate systematizations of his own language. (Whorf 1956:239)

Our thoughts, we are told, are to a degree controlled by inextricable laws of language pattern of which we are unconscious. These patterns are the unperceived intricate systematizations of our own language, which cuts "reality" up in partly arbitrary fashion at particular joints, which, for another language, might be the marrow making up the substance of the world. Our language is to us what water is to a fish: an implicit, implicate phenomenon so constant in our experience that though we are conscious of some of language's functions—of manipulating and choosing symbols with which to convey ideas to others—we are only at most vaguely aware of its all-pervading functions as a self-sufficient, self-contained whole, that is, as a *Monad*.

This "conventionalist"[6] view of language, and of symbolic thought, holds that, as Whorf (1956:253) puts it, "Every language contains its own metaphysics . . . each language performs this artificial chopping up of the continuous spread and flow of existence in a different way." As a consequence, the knowers of human communities "are not led by the same physical evidence to the same picture of the universe, unless their linguistic backgrounds are similar, or can be in some way calibrated" (Whorf 1956:214). Nature is dissected along lines laid down by particular languages. If the conventionalist view is tentatively embraced, language being acknowledged as actively contributing to a given community's knowledge, then the active role of the mind must also be acknowledged. And if so, then a given "semiotically real" world must also be "constructivist" (from various perspectives; see Arbib and Hesse 1986; Baer 1989; Layzer 1990:238–44; Watzlawick 1984).

But this is actually not so radical a posture as it appears at the outset. The "new physics" recognizes the mind (observer) as an active contributor to our picture of the world. Peirce in a roundabout manner took a step toward meeting this challenge with his notion of *abductive* leaps as tentative conjectures later to be backed up or refuted by *induction* and *deductive* arguments. *Abductive* leaps are acts of mind, think-signs in addition to, or in place of, thing-signs. The mind shoulders the responsibility of tuning in on the "real" as a result of, but not in total dependence upon, the experienced world. Hence any given "semiotic reality" is *Umwelt*-generated "mind-stuff." Einstein (1949:81), in a comparable vein, tells us that "physics is an attempt conceptually to grasp reality as it is thought independently of its being observed. In this sense one speaks of 'physical reality.'" To so grasp "reality" conceptually and independently of, but not in total separation from, the empirical world—since in the beginning was the *mark* or *cut* distinguishing the observed from everything else—implies, as we have already heard from Eddington, that this "reality" is "mind-stuff" before it is "thing-stuff."

Anglo-American philosophy, by holding onto the tenets of empiricism, has remained in large part firmly anchored within the Cartesian-Newtonian corpus-cular-kinetic world view. In contrast, extrapolation of the implications of the "new physics" allows for no existence of "thing-stuff" without mind. Some of these physicists are prepared to go so far as to propound the virtually unthinkable idea that without mind there is no world, Wheeler being one of the most outspoken in this respect. The notion of an active, constructivist mind becomes the basis for knowledge which in turn becomes the basis for ontology. The theory of mind and the theory of knowledge converge at some point to become the reverse side of one another. We are in a "participatory universe," as Wheeler has stated repeatedly.

If we peruse the writings of some of the most seminal scientists of the twentieth century, we shall discover that their expression, while above all poetic and occasionally not without a mystical tinge, is grounded in an obsessive quest for the relationship between mind (or consciousness) and the world by way of language. From James Jeans (1958:186), often maligned for his unchecked speculation, though of recent some of this thought can be viewed as prophetic, we have the following: "The concepts which now prove to be fundamental to our understanding of nature . . . seem to my mind to be structures of pure thought. . . . The universe begins to look more like a great thought than like a great machine."

Like Eddington's footprints in the sand—note 18 of chapter 4—the mind sees what the mind constructed in the first place. That is to say, the intellect and matter are correlatives. The one exists only for the other, and either both stand or they fall together. They are in fact really one and the same thing, considered from distinct points of view.

This leads us once again to Einstein's classic reminder that concepts which have been useful in ordering the universe surrounding the physicist soon begin to exercise authority over her to the extent that she forgets their human origin and begins accepting them—an artificial linguistic construct—as the genuine article. Subsequently, "they become 'necessities of thought,' 'given *a priori*,' etc. The path of scientific progress is then, by such errors barred for a long time" (in Born 1949:176). One must bear in mind, Einstein (1949:13) counsels further, that

the system of concepts is a creation of man together with the rules of syntax, which constitute the structure of the conceptual systems. . . . All concepts, even those which are closest to experience, are from the point of view of logic freely chosen conventions, just as is the case with the concept of causality, with which this problematic concerned itself in the first instance.

If we accept these premises, we are forced to the conclusion that a vast range, and perhaps an infinity, of possible conceptual frameworks and formal expressions of the "real" world "out there" may be adopted. The "new physics" apparently reveals that there are alternative ways of perceiving and conceiving the world, each couched in its own language. Black holes and white holes, quarks, leptons, and hadrons, are essentially *façon de parler*. They compose one story, classical physics is another tale, and Aristotle's hierarchy of elements is yet another one. Language says what a particular world is, not because it is capable of capturing an independent world "out there" but because it lies at the heart of our confrontation with the world. When a new way of talking about the world is created, virtually a new world comes into existence (see Gregory 1988).

And in the sense of Peirce, each and every one of these language-dependent worlds represents the characteristics of mind or consciousness in interaction with its surroundings. Ultimately, to say one is to say the other, for "the same organizing forces that have shaped nature in all her forms are also responsible for the structure of our minds" (Heisenberg 1971:101). Indeed, Heisenberg revealed an inherent limitation on the precision of observation or localization of any pair of conjugate properties such as position and momentum, or energy and time. Bohr followed up with the philosophical impact of this limitation, *complementarity*, which eventually became a panacea for some and a thorn in the side of others, and he subsequently extended his complementarity principle to other areas of application, to the chagrin of more than a few of his colleagues. The ultimate extrapolation of Bohr's principle must entail awareness, he suggested, that "we must, indeed, remember that the nature of our consciousness brings about a complementary relationship, in all domains of knowledge, between the analysis of a concept and its immediate application" (Bohr 1934:20). Heisenberg (1971:114) expressed his approval in a conversation with Bohr: "There can be no doubt that 'consciousness' does not occur in physics and chemistry, and I cannot see how it could possibly result from quantum mechanics. Yet any science that deals with living organisms must needs cover the phenomenon of consciousness because consciousness, too, is part of reality."

A chief interpretation of this irreducible complementarity—though it has often been contested—postulates that it is not so much the physical world that imposes such apparently intransigent dichotomies as particle/wave, subject/object, position/momentum, and so on, on the mind (consciousness); it is the mind (consciousness) that interacts with the physical world to reveal particle cum wave, and so on. Such being the case, it is reasonable to assume that the mind (consciousness) exercises the option of taking on either wave characteristics or particle characteristics, the nature of the implicate as well as the explicate domains, to reevoke Bohm's complementary images. In this light, Jeans (1943:204) remarks: "It seems at least conceivable that what is true of perceived objects may also be true of perceiving minds; just as there are wave-pictures for light and electricity, so there may be a corresponding picture for consciousness."

Finally, this knowledge hopefully possessed by a given investigating mind (consciousness) is not knowledge *of* something, in much the sense that, as I argued above, there is no immediate consciousness *of* the "semiotic object," for everything is always inexorably mediated by a temporal increment. As Louis de Broglie (1955:131) puts it:

> The ψ function [from Schrödinger's wave equation], in fact, does not represent something which would have its place in a point of space at a given instant; it represents, taken in its entirety, the state of knowledge of an observer, at the instant considered, of the physical reality that he studies; there is nothing surprising, therefore, in the fact that the function varies from one observer to another.

In view of the discussion of the semio-eigen-state in chapter 5, Schrödinger's equation replaces the classical corpuscular-kinetic dynamics by patterns of probability of superposed waves. Complex nodal patterns are a potential, a tendency or propensity to behave in such and such a way given certain conditions (Thirdness), from the domain of possibilities (Firstness). Transition of an atomic structure from one state to another (Secondness) is brought about by direct interaction with neighboring atoms, which involves *communication* (information transfer) between all entities of a particular system. Ultimately the physicist's measuring apparatus and her observation (interaction of consciousness) enter the scene, testifying to de Broglie's remark that "the function varies from one observer to another." Reinforcing the mind-dependent universe idea propounded above, de Broglie (1962:221) goes on to reveal elsewhere his profound sense of the controversial role of the mind (consciousness): "Science is therefore a strange sort of penetration into the world which through human consciousness and reason has learned to become aware of itself."

This reconfirms Peirce's notorious idea that mind acts upon mind and matter upon matter, and mind upon matter and matter upon mind (MS 936), and that all matter is really mind, and mind is continuous (CP:6.301). His suggestion—introduced in chapters 5 and 6—that just as mind, sign, and being are basically one, so are "man" and nature, cannot but lead to the conclusion that in the final analysis, a person "is only a particular kind of general idea."[7] The terms *particular* and *general* must be emphasized. This is no contradiction: *generality* (Thirdness) in a given *particular instantiation* or *actualization* can take on the form of a human organism. To reiterate Peirce's often-cited remark:

> There is no element whatever of man's consciousness which has not something corresponding to it in the word. . . . The word or sign which man uses *is* the man himself . . . that every thought is a sign, taken in conjunction with the fact that life is a train of thought, proves that man is a sign; so, that every thought is an *external* sign, proves that man is an external sign . . . the man and the external sign are identical. Thus my language is the sum total of myself; for the man is the thought. (CP:5.314)[8]

And elsewhere: "Every reality, then, is a Self; and the Selves are intimately connected, as if they formed a continuum. Each one is, so to say, a delineation— with mathematical truth incongruous as the metaphor is, we may say that each is a quasi-map of the organic aggregate of all the Selves, which is itself a Self" (CP:8.125).

Given Peirce's continuity thesis, not only is self-*other*-*Other* artificial—i.e., inferential in character—but in addition, there is no absolute "man-sign" separation. Both partake of "signness," so to speak. All this leads to Peirce's remark that each self is a *map* of the organic aggregate of all selves, of the community, and by extension, of the physical world. Significantly enough, Peirce once evoked, following Josiah Royce, the map paradox: a map covering the entire territory is thus complete, but if so, it must contain itself, and that replica must in turn contain itself, and so on, ad infinitum. The map "is therefore," Peirce observes, "the precise analogue of pure self-consciousness. As such it is *self-sufficient*" (CP:5.71).[9] In the first place, in order for Peirce's words to apply, he must have reverted back to Firstness, to the Monad. That is to say, the self as a microcosm mapping the community or the individual organism as microcosm mapping the universe creates the image of immanence.

But there is a problem here. Like a piece broken from the holographic plate which is capable of reconstructing the entire image, though there is a loss in precision, these microcosmic entities can no more than vaguely map their respective wholes—there is no Mirror of Nature, in all its *glassy essence,* here. As generalities are piled upon generalities, as more and more is taken into a given purview, the whole, as grasped by a finite, fallible, and extremely limited individual, stands a chance of becoming progressively less cloudy, though without the possibility of there being absolute clarity. De Broglie (1939:280) puts the dilemma—which from another perspective is a liberation—nicely: "May it not be universally true that the concepts produced by the human mind, when formulated in a slightly vague form, are roughly valid for Reality, but that when extreme precision is aimed at, they become ideal forms whose real contents tend to vanish away?"

In Peirce's terms, gravitation toward *generality* brings one to an awareness of the *incompleteness* of one's conceptualization; gravitation toward *vagueness* reveals the inextricable *inconsistency* underlying any and all of one's holistic accounts. That is one part of the story. The other part is a more antagonistic mind-bender. At the pole of vagueness where the law of noncontradiction has made a hasty retreat, everything is *there,* as we noted in chapters 4 and 5, in superposition. It is nothing yet it potentially is everything. At the opposite pole of generality, the excluded-middle principle has been pushed under the rug. This implies that with the successive actualization of more and more particulars—i.e., like points along a dense line—until somehow we hopefully have a continuum—staccato having become legato—our inherent limitations force themselves into our awareness.

Here also we find a counterpart to the quantum uncertainty-complementarity of particle manifestations and wave manifestations. For example, a beam of light is directed toward a half-silvered mirror. Half of the photons gain entrance into the beyond and the other half are rejected, but there is no determining a priori which have and which do not have a legitimate passport. Newton's corpuscular theory of light merely attributed the problem to fortune's wheel. Fate separates the sheep from the goats. Now if we turn to the wave manifestation of light, we find the comfort of a deterministic framework. Yet this determinism has little to do with actual events. The superposition of a set of waves provides no indication of future events following from present events. On the contrary. It merely shows "the imperfections of our future knowledge following inexorably from the imperfections of our present knowledge" (Jeans, in Commins and Linscott 1947:365). One is reminded of Heisenberg's words (1958a:81): "Natural science does not simply describe and explain nature; it is a part of the interplay between nature and ourselves; it describes nature as exposed to our method of questioning." This method of questioning depends upon one's imperfect knowledge of past and present moments, which can do no more than generate imperfect knowledge for future moments. Questioning and knowledge, I would suggest, are *in* language and *in* the mind, thus they are the product of, and at the same time the author of, "semiotically real" worlds.

Once more we are forcibly returned to conceptualization and its embodiment in symbolic forms as the other side of our Janus-faced desire to know.

III. ON THE OPAQUE WALLS OF THE CAVE. The upshot of the previous section is that the customary Western forms of reasoning have been especially developed for and adapted to "symbolic" ("representational") knowledge rather than "intuitive" ("intimate") knowledge. However, the symbolic universe, symbolic language, and symbolic knowledge itself eventually become shadowy. This shadowy character of an artificially contrived body of discourse is by no means a recent development. It has been with us, Schrödinger (1967:130) notes, "ever since Democritus of Abdra and even before, but we were not aware of it; we thought we were dealing with the world itself; expressions like model or picture for the conceptual constructs of science came up in the second half of the nineteenth century, and not earlier, as far as I know."

"Model" or "picture" for the constructs of science, "representation" for art and philosophy, "denotation" and "reference" for logic and language, are at the outset as symbolic (i e , linguistic) formulations, at least one remove from the concrete world of (immediate) experience. If this were the end of the story, perhaps the labyrinth would be two-dimensional instead of many-dimensional. But the tale goes on. As symbols accumulate, it is not simply that we are no longer dealing with the world itself; we eventually lose awareness *that* we are no longer doing so. The forest, so to speak, replaces the trees, and what we deludedly take to be trees are mere shadows. The symbols are about symbols about symbols . . . about nothing at all. The shadows are identified with that longed-for "reality," and attention is glued to the abstracted movements on the walls of the cave with the belief that "reality" is thus understood at its lowermost level. There is no longer any awareness of that other mode, Peirce's felt or sensed qualitative intimacy with immediate experience, which, though it cannot be represented symbolically, is more in tune with the universe (see Rochberg-Halton 1986).

Western disciplines have not been dealing directly with the "real"; they have been operating through the dualistic mode of knowledge couched in the symbolic mode. However, this mode is both the bane and the boon, the blind spot and the beauty, of Western intellectual endeavors. The mind has effectively generated highly sophisticated, though at the same time exceedingly abstract, "pictures" of the world. "One thinks that one is tracing the outlines of nature over and over again," Wittgenstein (1953:114–15) tells us, "and one is merely tracing round the frame through which we look at her. A *picture* held us captive. And we could not get outside it, for it lay in our language and language seemed to repeat it to us inexorably." But they can be no more than that: "pictures." There is no faithful representation to be had via "pictures"; even when on their best behavior, "pictures" do not stand a chance of becoming mirrors. From within the twentieth-century analytical tradition, Wittgenstein, Quine, Goodman, and Rorty, from pragmatics, James and Dewey, from phenomenology and beyond, Heidegger, Merleau-Ponty, and Derrida, and from hermeneutics, especially Gadamer, not to mention the ruminations of mathematicians, logicians, scientists, and philosophers of science, we are painfully forced to become aware of this limitation. We simply cannot conquer the territory armed with nothing but a partly arbitrary map.[10]

Now, the problem with all this is that, as Peirce scholars are well aware, I have been addressing myself regarding the two modes of knowing to yet another binary opposition. In contrast, Peirce predicated triadism throughout his writings. How can we reconcile this apparent contradiction? The two legs of the Peircean trio to which I refer above are Firstness and Thirdness. Secondness, which has been largely absent, must now be integrated into the scheme. Secondness is that which makes "inner" and "outer" *otherness* possible. Like the other two categories, Secondness is defined in relational not formal terms. These *others,* in this sense, are crucial.

In brief, *otherness* is necessary to the existence of thought itself, and "inner" *otherness* depends for its existence upon "outer" *otherness.* The "inner" is created when the self becomes aware of a distinction between itself and *something else, some other*—the shock of, or surprise with respect to some aspect of, the "outer" world (CP:1.334–36). But Firstness and Secondness, as quality or feeling and *this-hereness,* would remain outside any significance one with respect to the other without Thirdness (CP:1.337, 5.104). Thirdness unites all of that which without it would have remained in arbitrary and unmediated alienation: Firstness and Secondness without Thirdness would remain disjointed.

Yet, Thirdness in turn depends upon Firstness and Secondness for its very *raison d'être.* Its existence is defined in and through its mediary operation alone. At the same time it always projects beyond that which it mediates: it is potentiality, futurity. Pushing at the walls of actuality, it incessantly moves on toward ever greater generality and regularity, toward completion, which, if realized, would bring about a *conjunctionis oppositorum.* The fabric would finally double back upon itself as the Ultimate Interpretant, and at the same time its continuity would be coterminous with the continuity of Firstness. Peirce's process philosophy is in many respects quite obviously a philosophy of growth. But it necessarily stems from an *inconsistent* bedrock of perpetual *incompleteness.*

An illustration. Your senses pick up the call of a bird outside your window as a mere feeling. Then the image of a cardinal enters your consciousness. At this stage in the development of a sign there is a connection, though it is dim, a mere skeleton idea between the sound and the image of the particular species of a genus. The visual illustration of this connection between two things is given by Peirce as a line connecting a pair of points (CP:7.426). The line, of course, is infinitesimally thin, a nothingness, a fiction. Only its contrived physical manifestation is visible. In other words, there need be no necessary relation or connection at all between the cardinal-sound and the actual cardinal. It is there either by instinct—in the case of a hungry cat perceiving the bird—or by convention—eventually producing an image in your mind of a particular *type* of bird.

But I am racing ahead of myself; there is still no acknowledgment on the part of your emerging consciousness *of* the bird in question *as* a cardinal or *as represented by* the word *cardinal*. There is merely a fuzzy relation between two sensations, one in the "out there," the other in your mind. The "outer" representation (object) of the bird call, the sign representamen, is not directly sensed. It is not "actually real," for it is not immediately present *to* your mind. That is, there is no *this-hereness* in the *now* of things, hence the object can be no more than a "semiotic object," its existence as such remaining dependent upon the "inner" image you conjured up. Yet this bird call (representamen) and this "semiotic object" are already in the process of being symbolized (i.e., mediated) by the creation of the sign's interpretant. Thirdness, a cardinal-*idea,* brings the original relation into a triad, like the three points of a triangle connected by three lines (CP:7.426). Now, this cardinal-*idea* as a first-level legisign can evolve, by way of greater complexity, into the term *cardinal,* say, with your remarking to your spouse, "He's singing our song." And the two of you may then begin deliberating whether the feathered vertebrate in question is indeed a cardinal or some other species.

At each stage of this signifying process there is development, or growth, which is accelerated vastly by the process of symbolicity through increasing abstraction. The aloof, partly arbitrary nature of the symbol endows it with such a capacity. If we recall that most simple of rules, "The symbol at least in part *is* what that *of which* it is a symbol in part *is not,"* we begin to grasp the semiotic power of symbolicity. It breaks away from the "thingness" of things and goes off on a tangential tap dance, constantly threatening to drag us along with it. Thus Schrödinger's observation that our artificially contrived symbolic knowledge is of a shadowy character, which is, to repeat, both the bane and the boon of symbolicity.

Regarding symbolicity further, and commensurate with Peirce's categories, three semiotic paths toward the "real" stand out—the journey is "semiotically real," of course, though the inconceivable end of the road is that union of all opposites, the "real." These paths are (1) *analogy,* (2) *injunction,* and (3) *postulation through negation,* which correspond respectively to *Firstness* and *iconicity, Secondness* and *indexicality,* and *Thirdness* and *symbolicity.* Significantly, all three paths are in one guise or another crucial to Western scientific thought and practices as (1) *metaphors* and *analogical models* (Hesse 1966; Leatherdale 1974), (2) *instructions* to carry out operations such as in the activity of generating mathematical proofs, assembling a bicycle, baking a cake, conducting scientific experiments, or whatever, in order to obtain certain results (Spencer-Brown 1979; Lakatos 1976), and (3) *refutation,* a becoming of consciousness *that* something does not coincide with expectations (Popper 1972).

The analogical mode potentially rendering that portion or all of an unintelligible and unsayable domain at least partly describable, is most commonly shared by the arts and sciences. As one moves along the road toward the "actually real," analogical thought is capable of encompassing larger and larger domains. Roughly speaking, it might be said that the larger the domain, the more vague—and hence the more contradictory—the analog. The end product of the analogical mode, of course, is the ultimate self-contained Monad. In religious discourse it is tantamount to God, Buddha, the Tao, and so on. The finite mind is no match for such omniscience evoked by this analogical totality. Consequently, religious icons such as paintings, sculptures, narratives, mythological images, crosses, and mandalas vary greatly from religion to religion and from time period to time period (MacCormac 1976, 1985).

One might conjecture that scientific analogies or models do not suffer from the same de-generation of precision and form as the mapped domain increases. However, though scientific discourse may be embedded in formal language, and though this language may appear to describe reality with "unreasonable effectiveness," to use Wigner's (1969) words, the analog itself is not necessarily any more exact than that of any given line of poetry. This is true especially when the domain, like that of God, is unobservable. In modern times, for example, metaphors for unobservables such as machines for the universe, solar system for the atom, elastic balls for gas molecules, and ether for the propagation of light, have proved either scandalously inadequate or extremely limited.

The second mode, that of injunction, is an invitation, in the form of a set of rules, to become aware of some aspect of the "semiotically real," as one navigates, hopefully, toward one's destination. I have mentioned mathematical proofs and scientific experimental procedures. These activities, Spencer-Brown (1979:77) points out, are

> comparable with practical art forms like cookery, in which the taste of a cake, although literally indescribable, can be conveyed to a reader in the form of a set of injunctions called a recipe. Music is a similar art form, the composer does not even attempt to describe the set of sounds he has in mind, much less the set of feelings occasioned through them, but writes down a set of commands which, if they are obeyed by the reader, can result in a reproduction, to the reader, of the composer's original experience.

By the same token, a painting, sculpture, or architectural display contains within itself the tacit injunction to its viewer that she experience for herself something in line—though there is always a necessary difference—with what its maker originally experienced. A poem, on the other hand, is already couched in language. Nonetheless, the poem itself embodies an equally tacit injunction something like "Come, my dear reader. I invite you to share with me this unforgettable moment" (Levin 1976). It is as if the original creator were to grab her audience by the senses with the evocation: "Look!" "Listen!" "Feel!" "Experience!" and so on, which serves indexically as an indirect pointer. In all such cases, the action and experience are left to the audience; if they fail, that is not necessarily the fault of the author.

However, the injunctive mode contains inherent pitfalls. One often wanders up blind alleys leading to hero worship and unthinking adulation of authority figures, as Imre Lakatos (1976) takes pains to demonstrate. In mathematics, for example, methods and procedures, as well as overwhelming lists of axioms, lemmas, and definitions, are in doctrinaire fashion handed down to the student who is obliged

> to attend this conjuring act without asking questions either about the background or about how this sleight-of-hand is performed. If the student by chance discovers that some of the unseemly definitions are proof-generated, if he simply wonders how these definitions, lemmas and the theorem can possibly precede the proof, the conjuror will ostracize him for this display of mathematical immaturity. (Lakatos 1976:142)

The third mode, postulation by negation, is by no means the exclusive brain child of Peirce, of Popper, or even of science. It is also, from a distinct vantage, the *via negativa* of St. Thomas according to which the believer must proceed by successive cancellation of everything the finished product *is not,* chipping away the unnecessary stone to leave the perfect statue. In Vedanta this same process exists in the phrase, cited above: "Not this, not this, . . . *n.*" Popper's method of "falsification" and Peirce's "refutation" bear witness to the fact that the symbol, or symbolic discourse, in fact, everything sayable, *is not* what the domain said *is.*

In its inception analogy is qualitative, something sensed or felt. It is at once fullness and emptiness: fullness, for something *is* in comparable fashion to what something else *is,* and emptiness, for that something in part *is not* what that to which it is related *is.* The intuitive grasp of an analogy *selects* part of something while the rest remains *nonselected,* but the *nonselected* shares equal importance with the *selected,* since the two are related by complementarity. Injunction establishes *what is,* when that which is *selected* is foregrounded vis-à-vis that which *was not.* And falsification, the *via negativa,* reveals the inherent emptiness of all conceptualization, of symbolicity: signs taken as surrogates for the "real" thing of process, of event (like a snapshot of a turbulent river). That is to say, symbolicity tends to breed a false sense that knowledge by way of partly arbitrary and artificial signs has been realized or is just around the next bend in the road.

For example, you said to your spouse, "He's singing our song." This utterance, coupled with the fact that your spouse can decipher it and either agree or develop a counterproposition, is the result of a vast web of significance. Two human animals have intersected at a spatio-temporal "cardinal" node in the *semiosic* fabric, which involves their entire life history to that point. "Cardinal" is for each of them a singularity resulting from their evolution and training, from the appearance of the token of a particular type having entered their consciousness. But to say "cardinal" is to use a symbol which applies not merely to *that* cardinal but to all cardinals, independently of any specific time and place. When a symbol is so used, it threatens to take on the attributes supposedly of the thing itself—it becomes embedded in consciousness—such that it is regarded as a separate thing, autonomous, self-sufficient: it has become "indexicalized" and then "iconized." The semiotic triad has become a dyad, as the relation between symbol and object wanes, then a monad, as awareness *of* the sensation "cardinal" abates; the necessary relations of *semiosis* fall from consciousness. The word *cardinal* as such tends to be rather automatically associated with other signs; it has become a giant step removed from the "real," from physical existence, yet it is still generally taken to be "real." It has, in short, become an abstracted item of the "semiotically real."

And *negation* has a bearing in all this. "Cardinal" is *not* the affection between lovers but a mediated symbol *of* it. A flag is *not* the motherland when desecrated—thus provoking an outburst of indignation. A hammer and sickle is *not* the "beast," as the fundamentalist Protestant might conceive it, but a symbol of his paranoid mentality. Becoming aware of such negation, when expectations are met with surprise, involves consciousness *that* certain conditions are *not* what they were taken to be. Symbols fulfill a necessary social and communal function, enabling us most effectively to promote mutual understanding in our community. The "real," however, during such moments when one becomes aware of the negative function of the symbol, must be experienced in a very personal and direct manner, not merely through the medium of symbols themselves. This more immediate awareness allows us to view the world without the distorting medium of symbolism, especially regarding the arbitrary nature of symbols, the oftentimes presumed intentional nature of reference to the "semiotic object," and the influence of symbols on our attitudes and behavior. It is worthy of note that in the three modes of "symbolic knowing" I have summarily described there is a progression in good Peircean fashion from Firstness to Thirdness. Of the three, Firstness lies closest to the ideal of "intuitive knowledge," that which is immediately sensed. This marks the initiation of a process of development, of growth, the ultimate extrapolation of which carries Thirdness to its logical end.

I close this section, reiterating in the first place the impossibility, as far as Peirce is concerned, of any absolute knowledge for the finite, fragile, and tenderly fallible human semiotic animal, and in the second place the inadequacy of binary thinking as illustrated once again through triadicity. Fortunately, one is always susceptible to *abductive* leaps, free flights of the imagination, peak experiences, or whatever. These, however, are little doublings back, micro-epiphanies, which endow one at least ephemerally with some sense of omniscience. They are, nonetheless, paltry shadows of what *is,* which remains beyond even the most multitudinous sequence of experiences.

IV. FROM THE UNIFIED CLOUD OF VAGUENESS, THAT IS, FEEL-

ING. Once again, merely to point out the pitfalls of symbolic (dualistic, bifurca-tive) thought by juxtaposing it with intuitive (holistic, integrative) thought does not necessarily do more than erect yet another dualism. This is also the general fallacy of the right-brainers who call for an end to left-hemisphere dominance and a return either to right-minded thinking or to a balance of the two poles of the opposition. But the opposition remains. What we need is a corpus-callosumer capable of a legitimate unification, of integrating the parts of figure 3 into a whole. Actually, on the one hand, the sort of brain localization that seemed to be the wave of the future a couple of decades ago is now looked upon as ex-ceedingly more problematic than was supposed, and on the other hand, Prib-ram's holographic brain has fallen from grace somewhat. Yet the general move-ment seems to be toward a holistic conception of the brain-mind. Howard Gardner (1987:393–99) remarks that he is struck by a paradox: the sort of problems the leading-edge brain scientists are currently working on bear closer relationship to the mind set of scientists on the eve of cognitive science's birth than to work being carried out a decade or two ago.

Early cyberneticists such as Ashby, Karl Lashley, McCulloch, von Neumann, and Wiener envisioned computation and the understanding of the brain to be essentially the same. It was presumed that modeling entailed neural networks and logical calculi to account for their functioning. The early cognitiv-ists, Jerome Bruner, Noam Chomsky, George Miller, Herbert Simon, and on the other side of the Atlantic, Jean Piaget and Claude Lévi-Strauss, had little patience for such tinker toy models. They focused on introspection and higher cognitive processes, more at the software than the hardware level. The pendulum swing has once again changed directions over the past few years:

> As the limits of the serial digital "von Neumann computer" became clearer, and as alternative views of computation gained in persuasiveness, there has been a shift to a different "modal view" of cognition a view in which psychological, com-putational, and neurological considerations are far more intricately linked. (Gardner 1987:394)

The emergent concept seems to be "parallel distributed processing" accord-ing to which knowledge inheres in brain connections themselves. Instead of a set of facts or events stored in the brain, memory is viewed as the set of relationships that obtain between various aspects of the facts and events as they are encoded in groupings or patterns of units. The *what* of the storage does not consist so much of things as it does of *interconnections* between units which allow patterns to be called up and re-created. "Parallel distributed processing" thus operates in a manner more reminiscent of cybernetic brain models than the mind models of the early cognitivists.

If this recent turn proves to be of significant value, it may help dissolve the age-old brain-mind dualism, but more important, it can point the way toward a holistic view of things: the furniture of the world as "mind-stuff," or conversely, the mind as merely a particular aspect of just another piece of furniture. To reiterate Russell's words: "The world may be called physical or mental or both or neither as we please." The same, of course, has been observed in quantum theory—and Peirce's signs—as either "thing-stuff" or "mind-stuff," depending on the vantage. At any rate, whatever we decide to call this "stuff," it's a pretty safe bet that it is, at that final point in the infinite horizon toward which all lines converge, *One*.

And we are once again confronted with the problem of the one and the many, or, so to speak, of monism and pluralism. There is solace to be had in variety rather than in an unknowable one. Yet the one is suggested by Peirce and Bohm, Wheeler and Schrödinger, among a host of others. Schrödinger, in commenting on what he calls the "Arithmetical Paradox," has a few remarkable words in this respect. He begins: "The reason why our sentient, percipient and thinking ego is met nowhere within our scientific world picture can easily be indicated in seven words: because it is itself that world picture" (Schrödinger 1967:138).

He then continues, observing that this ego, this consciousness, is identified with the whole, *its whole*. Therefore it cannot be contained in it as a part of itself. In our world we find ourselves among innumerable individuals whose physical attributes and behavior appear to pattern ours. This leads each of us to the inevitable conclusion, following a basic human penchant for association, that every individual possesses a mind comparable to our own, with comparable faculties. Such a conclusion also breeds the paradox by which the one is identified with the many. Each of us has constructed a world map, and each map is to a greater or lesser degree different from all other maps. Nevertheless, the collection of these maps, however faithfully they represent the "real world," in their composite represent an attempt to align perception and conception with one world. In other words, just as the multiplicity of conscious egos is one, and just as the multiplicity of map-worlds is one world, so also the collection of "semiotically real" worlds generated by each individual of the entire sign-using community is one.

As Schrödinger (1967:138) puts it, "the several domains of 'private' consciousness partly overlap. The region common to all where they all overlap is the construct of the real world [i.e., the 'semiotically real'] around us." There is no absolutely individual mind. There are only many conscious egos and map-worlds that can be accounted for solely by the fact that the many domains of consciousness must overlap to produce some "common region" which constitutes the *Umwelt*-generated "real world" for a particular species or one of its subgroups.

What we have here, it seems to me, is Thirdness. I will illustrate this via Schrödinger (1967:138), who notes, after introducing the paradox in question, that

> an uncomfortable feeling remains, prompting such questions as: Is my world really the same as yours? Is there *one* real world to be distinguished from its pictures introjected by way of perception into every one of us? And if so, are these pictures like unto the real world or is the latter, the world "in itself," perhaps very different from the one we perceive?
>
> Such questions are ingenious, but in my opinion very apt to confuse the issue.

They have no adequate answers. They all are, or lead to, antinomies springing from one source, which I called the arithmetical paradox; the *many* conscious egos from whose mental experience the *one* world is concocted.

Schrödinger outlines two ways out of the arithmetical paradox, depending on whether we incline toward the many or the one: (1) Leibniz's solipsistic, windowless monads united by some mysterious "pre-established harmony," and (2) the unification of all minds or consciousnesses. The second way, it is now quite obvious, is Schrödinger's preference. That multiple consciousness is illusory conforms to the teachings of the ancient Upanishads, among other doctrines, which have had little appeal in the West, though Western thought could profit from an amendment along these lines, "perhaps by a bit of blood-transfusion from Eastern thought" (Schrödinger 1967:140). Schrödinger observes further that the oneness doctrine is supported by empirical evidence that consciousness is never experienced in the plural, only in the singular. This holds true even in pathological cases of split personality: the two or more persons alternate, never appearing jointly, though they may or may not be familiar with each other.

Neither is there absolute distinction, Schrödinger argues, between the self and the physical world "out there." Consider any sensory image, for example, that of a tree. It has traditionally been held that the perception one has of a tree must be distinguished from the tree "in itself": the tree does not enter the observing self but only certain effects from it. Another way of putting it is that the tree is perceived if, and only if, certain events, unknown to the observer in detail, occur in the observer's central nervous system. And if these events were known they would not describe the tree, be equal to the tree, or even be a faithful map of the tree. The perception is not the thing perceived. In other words, the tree "in itself" is colorless, tasteless, and odorless; it remains beyond experience. The phenomenalist Ernst Mach, roughly in line with Hume and British empiricism, believed that the tree is cognizable to the observer solely in terms of his bundle of perceptions of it. And since all humans are endowed with essentially the same perceptual faculties, there is no fundamental distinction between one person's sensations and those of somebody else.[11] That is, what constitutes a single complex of sensations—of the tree—is the complex which several observers observing the tree at the same instant hold in common. The content of consciousness of the various observing selves is not qualitatively identical, but in conjunction, the perceptions of these selves enjoy a common content, which is numerically one.

"This conclusion, though it is the only logical one," Schrödinger (1964:16–17) writes,

immediately strikes us Westerners as thoroughly bizarre. We . . . have accustomed ourselves to thinking (though there is nothing to prove it, and the most primitive daily experience demonstrates the contrary) that each person's sensation, perception, and thought is a strictly segregated sphere, these spheres having nothing in common with each other, neither overlapping nor directly influencing each other, but on the contrary absolutely excluding each other. In my opinion, the idea of elements of consciousness which are quite simply common to several human individuals is, in itself, neither self-contradictory nor in contradiction with other known facts of experience; rather, it does very properly restore the state of things which in fact exists for a really naïve human being.

The body, of course, offers the most clear-cut case of separation between this and that, inside and outside, myself and other. But, Schrödinger asks, why is it precisely at this intermediate level in the vast hierarchy of superposed unities (cell, organ, body, community, world) that the separation is made? And why is it at this level that a unitary form of self-consciousness comes into existence? It seems that regarding Peirce on mind and matter, consciousness and noncon-sciousness, we are confronted by difference of degree rather than kind, by continuity rather than discontinuous breaks.

Let us return to a more primitive level of organization, to Maturana and Varela's (1987) first-, second-, and third-order *entities*, in search of an answer. The first order includes individual cells (icons, Firstness) consisting of autopoi-etic, relatively autonomous systems. An individual cell as a domain of life processes stands out against a background of molecular soup by distinguishing and indicating its own boundary that sets it *apart from* what it *is not*. This indication of a boundary is exercised through molecular productions made possible by means of the boundary itself, which is a permeable membrane: there is a mutual indication of chemical transformation and boundary conditions. The cell, so to speak, lifts itself by its own bootstraps within its environment, and if the boundary it indicates for itself is interrupted, it diffuses back into the molecular soup from which it emerged. Thus far we have considered the life-system equivalent of Peirce's blank sheet of assertion and a cut-as-unary-icon, as Firstness, though the cell's indication of its boundary has already set the stage for indexicality, Secondness.[12]

This second order corresponds to "structural coupling"—i.e., "binary cou-pling," much in the sense of Deleuze and Guattari—which occurs when there is a history of ongoing interaction between two (or more) systems eventually leading to a structural congruence, and in concert they take on a function that would have been impossible for the individual cells in isolation. An example of structural coupling in its most basic form is that of a group of single-cell organisms called myxomycetes, fungi consisting of amoeboid individuals combining to form a fructiferous aggregate. The cells at the upper end of the aggregate generate spores, whereas the cells at the base become vacuoles and walls providing mechanical support to the entire multicellular complex. The structural changes each cell undergoes during its lifetime are complementary with the structural changes of all other cells in the system. While this dyadic structural coupling is indexical, that of Secondness, nonetheless, the role of *complementarity* sets the stage, as did *indication* for the first-order system, for a higher order. Com-plementation demands, like the quantum wave/particle pair, a larger context in order that its role be fully realized.

If the entities of the second order of structural coupling call for a higher level (context) of functioning for the multicellular organism, the entities of a third-order structural coupling demand yet higher relations (of symbolicity, Thirdness) between multicellular organisms themselves. And just as second-order coupling creates a new phenomenology of multicellular organisms, so third-order coupling creates a new phenomenology of trans-multicellular organisms, which includes sexual reproduction and family, community, or society. The classic example of third-order coupling is that of social insects, where there is a variety of forms among the participating individuals. Most are barren females whose task is to store food and defend the colony, take care of the eggs, and in general maintain the nest. The males are secluded inside, where there is usually only one fertile female, the queen, who is charged with the task of reproduction.

The most complex manifestation of third-order structural coupling is found in human societies and their natural language, which is symbolicity, or Thirdness, par excellence. The immediacy of Firstness and the *thisness* of Secondness are mediated by the third order, which unites individual organisms and individual cells into a larger *corpus,* the community or society, whose couplings now become increasingly "mindlike," or like "mind-stuff," so to speak. Human communities are closed physically, as are multicellular and cellular systems, regarding their nature as autonomous entities in the Maturana-Varela sense. But their role is not limited to autonomy. The community, as a collection of entities open to their environment, is dissipative in the style of Prigogine: it takes in material and energy and exports entropy in order to swim against the cosmic stream of increasing disorder. Moreover, in addition to the entity's conservation as an individual physical organism, conservation also depends on the mental domain: the organism reads information from its environment and responds accordingly, which enhances its capacity to maintain a relatively low level of entropy production. The evolutionary history of human beings and more complex organisms is thus associated with mental behavior to an increasing degree. Proportionate with Peirce's cosmology, this evolutionary history tends toward mind, Thirdness, which synthesizes increasingly complex parts into wholes. The push is toward *nootemporality,* the "semiotically real," which becomes progressively mindlike—an increase of thought-signs and a concomitant decrease of thing-signs (in general, Jantsch 1980).

In these more complex communities, when consciousness and self-consciousness enter the scene, there must be some account of self-knowledge. And this places us squarely in the crux of the issue. What sort of self-knowledge are we speaking of? What sort of self-knowledge is possible? And does it presuppose prior knowledge of the world "out there"? Varela (1984a, 1984b) would respond that we do not and cannot know the world "out there." In spite of our openness to it, both physically and mentally, we will always remain at least a step removed from it because of the inevitable breach between any and all *Umwelt*-generated "semiotic realities" and the "real." The best we can do is know our internal states, or perhaps we should say that our internal states are somehow capable of knowing themselves—in keeping with Maturana and Varela's bootstrapping operation. But these internal states are in a process of constant change, which is triggered by our constant interaction with our "semiotic realities" and the "real." Maturana and Varela (1987) provide the analogy of an airline pilot reduced to zero visibility because of a storm. His landing the plane by relying solely on his instruments is no different from the procedure he has followed many times in his training cabin with a simulated storm. He has done it a hundred times before, and he is now engaged in merely doing it once again. The central nervous system, like the automatic pilot, responds to its environment by altering its own internal states which are at the same time constrained by their structure and the history of previous pathways it traversed in building up its habits of response.

Thus the single-cell doctrine of sensory perception according to which a brain-to-world connection is mediated through the activity of a collection of single cells is soundly rejected. The logic of the operations of the brain is more adequately described as, following Hofstadter (1979), a *tangled hierarchy of surface-to-surface comparisons*. This, Varela (1984b:216) argues,

> means a radical change in our views of the functioning of the brain. For us, it means moving away from viewing the brain as a device which takes input in the form of information to act on. Rather, it means moving towards viewing the brain as a system characterized, not by its inputs, but by the *operational closure of its dynamics of states,* defined as a relative balance of activity between neural surfaces in a manner such that every change of state in the system can lead only to another change of state in the system itself.

Varela makes a plea for a "dialectical middle way" between representationalism and solipsism. This entails a taking explicitly into account of the conditions of description: a constant switching back and forth between the organism as a system operating according to its own internal logic and as a unit in interaction with its environment. This is, so to speak, the "electron" as "wave" according to the Schrödinger description and as "particle" after "collapse" (interaction) according to the probability function. In such oscillation between one complementary vantage and another, the observer can investigate the organism's internal logic and the fundamental constraints as a result of its environment. Consequently, a given organism's *Umwelt*-generated world neither becomes an arbitrary selection, construction, or invention, nor is it merely an expression of an organism's optimal fit with its environment. It is an account of the organism's "dynamics of states as a result of one of the possible viable phylogenic pathways within many others realized in the evolutionary history of living systems" (Varela 1984b:218).

Returning to Schrödinger, we are confronted with a somewhat paradoxical conclusion. If we are to think in a natural way about what goes on in a living, thinking, feeling entity, then "the condition for our doing so is that we think of *everything* that happens as taking place in our *experience* of the world, without ascribing to it any material substratum as the object *of which* it is an experience"

(Schrödinger 1964:61). Which seems to place us, contra Varela, squarely in the solipsist's ballpark.

Indeed, Schrödinger asks how it is that despite the obvious privacy, at times bordering on the hermetic, regarding different spheres of consciousness, there can nevertheless be a remarkable degree of understanding between them, which can reach the level of subtlety encountered among multilinguistic, multicultural human beings. At first sight the task appears as impossible as deciphering Mayan hieroglyphics or Egyptian documents before the discovery of the Rosetta Stone. One gets to know the "world" through one's own sense perceptions, and the same applies to everyone else. The "worlds" thus produced share many commonalities, which compel us in general to use the singular term *world*. But each person's sense-"world" is strictly a private affair, and inaccessible to anyone else. This agreement might have appeared commonsensical from within the framework of Cartesian-Newtonian objectivity according to which all subjects perceive the same world. But given the now-prevalent notions of relative frames of reference and observer participance, it is especially strange that a community of organisms of the same species, particularly humans with their complex private idiosyncrasies, would enjoy such a common world. In the terminology of this inquiry, no one perceives two "worlds," the "semiotically real" and the "real," in order to check one against the other. Everyone perceives solely his or her own "semiotically real" world.

Granted, that "semiotic world" is *Umwelt*-generated by individual members of a particular species. However, at a time when it is being increasingly proposed that "reality" is a social construction, the age-old empiricist hope that we all see the same world "out there" and arrive at a consensus by way of the analogies between our perceptual grasps tends to prevail. To the question, "Isn't there in fact an extremely strict correspondence, even to the very details, between the content of any one sphere of consciousness and any other so far as the external world is concerned?" Schrödinger (1964:69) asks: "And who enjoys the privileged position from which to establish this correspondence?"

Schrödinger argues against the empiricist (and by extension behaviorist) idea that a self arrives at a comprehension of other selves by analogy, that is, similarity of substance and behavior, and that a self takes on self-identity by its continuity of existence. If, according to nominalism (modern empiricism), a genus as general enjoys no "reality," nor does a species, but only individuals, why stop there? The logic that pushes us from genus to species to individuals is the very logic we should extrapolate to the event or momentary state of an individual in question. That is, an individual can be subdivided into the myriad events, each representing it at a given point in time and space of its historical coming into existence and passing away. In this sense we should consider event-signs rather than thing-signs; all are ephemeral comings and goings in the cosmic dance of things. There is, then, no analogy or similarity of things or of mind but of patterns, relations, the process of thinking, all of them fleet happenings.

And we can extrapolate further, to the lowermost level of happenings. According to Bohr's interpretation of quantum events, detection of micro-world "particles" presupposes the existence of an empirical macro-world. But even at this level "particles" enjoy no detectible self-identity, if by identity we mean that an "object" can be traced continuously along its trajectory from one location to another, and its alteration from one state to another. The best that can be said, according to Schrödinger (1951:17–21), is that sometimes subatomic "particles" arrange themselves in such a manner that they can be construed as things, as substance, as at least an approximation to that which they really are, though at other times their behavior appears to falsify the very idea of their "thingness." If substance there be, it is determinable only as events, and any determination of events suggests that substance most likely lurks somewhere nearby in the shadows. Schrödinger points out that for physics, any recognizable sameness involves patterns and relations in sequences of happenings. Happenings can be discerned (i.e., now *this*, now *this*), as are changes of patterns and relations, and persistence of patterns and relations from past events to present ones. But the same cannot be said of things. They simply do not remain the same over time. So over the long haul Schrödinger has no real bone to pick with Varela. For both, each individual stands alone as a partly autonomous system, but in concert with other systems of the same class their collective harmonics compose one indivisible whole.

To recap, in chapter 6 we noted the correlation between *semiostates, collapses,* and *aggregates,* on the one hand, and *Firstness, Secondness,* and *Thirdness,* on the other, as well as the transition from *atemporality* to *prototemporality* to *eotemporality* and the possibility of entrance into *bio-nootemporality*. In this section Firstness, Secondness, and Thirdness have been correlated with Maturana and Varela's three orders of biological *entities*. Let us now extrapolate these considerations to the biological sphere of *cells* and *aggregate organisms,* and more particularly to the individual-community and the self-*other-Other* relationships.

V. TOWARD THE UNITY OF MIND, THAT IS, GENERALITY. First and foremost, an additional word on the individual as an organic *entity* will be necessary. Eugene Rochberg-Halton (1986:230–72) calls the modern Western mind the product of "cultural nominalism," of the idea of rugged individualism. He argues at length how Herman Melville and Peirce, among other prophets in the wilderness, rebelled against what they conceived to be the devastating consequences of modern nominalistic culture, and particularly against the onslaught of American rugged individualism. On a comparable note, Hartshorne (1970:190) tells us:

> For what is culture if not certain things which individuals do to themselves and other individuals? But all parties were assuming "identity" through time as unproblematic. To add "culture," as identical—though also changing—through time, to the individuals as also persistent changing identities is not sufficient. What is really "in the

last analysis" there in social reality is neither culture nor individual people, but certain rather highly-ordered sequences of events characterized by the high level of symbolic functioning and creative freedom that is found on this planet only in those event-sequences which we call human beings. . . .

Our whole Western tradition is warped and confused by the concept of individual taken as ultimate. The results are ethical and not just theoretical. . . . The individual who now acts creatively is not simply I, or you, but I now, or you now. I yesterday, you yesterday, did not enact and can never enact our today's actions; only today's selves can do that. And since there is a new agent each tenth of a second or so, the actual momentary freedom cannot be very large. At a given moment, we are *almost* entirely a product, not a producer. And what productive power we have would be totally vacuous without inheritance from past actions, our own and those of countless others.

From this vantage—as from that of Peirce—the self-identical self is a vain notion, the vulgarist illusion of vanity. There is no absolutely isolated existence. The individual is a micro-level of the community, which is a loosely compacted individual; the community is a macro-individual. Just as one brain cell cannot know precisely what the whole brain is doing, so one mind cannot with certainty know the community mind. However, to reevoke the hologram trope, just as the consciousness of a portion of the brain and even of an individual cell is a dim image of the whole, so the individual can be at least dimly aware of the community mind. All this leads to the notion that there is no "real" plurality, no individuality, as the long-standing Western tradition has it. And it evokes the monist alternative implying the "reality" of the One only. Yet this One consists of a myriad plurality of entities in constant transition, the collection of which pushes the One along the path of its evolutionary development.

"Foul! Now you definitely are propagating sheer mysticism," one might retort. Yet Schrödinger, among other physicists instrumental in completely overturning the apple cart of classical mechanics, without reservations or apologies squarely confronts the issue. He establishes first that the hypothesis of a material world "out there" directly perceived by everybody as the *cause* of a common ground of experience cannot give us any guarantee that we can be aware *of* that shared common ground, but that it has to do as much with thought (mind) as with experience. Second, he stresses repeatedly that the hypothesis of a causal connection between the material world and our experience regarding both sense perceptions and volition is not empirically verifiable, in light of the ruminations of Berkeley and Hume. They demonstrated conclusively that these causal connections are not really observable *propter hoc*, but only *post hoc*. Schrödinger (1964:94) concludes that

the first of these considerations makes the hypothesis of the material world metaphysical, because there is nothing observable that corresponds to it; the second makes it mystical because it requires the application of an empirically well-founded mutual relation between two objects (cause and effect) to pairs of objects of which only *one* (the sense-perception or volition) is ever really perceived or observed, while the *other* (the *material* cause or *material* achievement) is merely an imaginative construct.

Schrödinger states quite bluntly what other leading twentieth-century scientists have occasionally intimated: to embrace the notion of an existing material world, as the ultimate explanation, and even proof, of the fact that we discover in the final analysis that we empirically share the same world, *is both mystical and metaphysical*. Rather than societies as aggregates of solipsists or monads, if we now openly embrace Schrödinger's "mystical-metaphysical" posture, we must admit that there is but one Monad. This ultimate Monad is at once many and one, discontinuous and continuous, depending on the vantage. Understandably, it can be said that certain representations of the Eastern tradition have produced the most radical of monisms and the most radical of pluralisms (Hartshorne 1970:177). According to Hindu thought, all things are, apart from their multifaceted manifestation as the *Maya,* simply one; at the same time, Buddhist thought stipulates that the very unity or identity of something through time is illusory, for it is but a multiplicity of momentary states (events) or ephemeral flashes, pulsations, of reality. Schrödinger highlights the Monadic aspect of Eastern philosophy, especially as presented in the ancient Upanishads. This is the ultimate doctrine of identity: as living organisms we belong together insofar as we are all aspects of one organism. The plurality of sensitive organisms is appearance, *Maya*.

Peirce's rather vague and ambiguous acceptance yet denial of pluralism takes on a special form: he argues, as I have suggested and will now discuss at greater length, against the nominalist doctrine that only individuals are "real." Peirce first criticizes nominalism insofar as it embodies the notion of natural law that places it in a dilemma. If, as the nominalist claims, "no law subsists other than an expression of actual facts, the future is entirely indeterminate and so is general to the highest degree" (CP:1.422). Peirce implies that the nominalist conception of law as a formula derived from the experience of a number of events perceived and conceived as *analogous* demands that the future is indeterminate, and since to say indeterminacy is to say generality, the future must be general, but this is a sin against the cardinal principle of nominalism that the "real" is thoroughly individual.

Of course, the nominalist could reply that the future is indeed indeterminate but "unreal," sheer nothingness, for it has not yet been actualized into particulars, so the nominalist's principle that what is "real" consists of individuals has not been violated. Peirce, subverting this response, assumes laws are fictions in good nominalist thinking, and the future is "unreal" because it is indeterminate. In this case nothing could exist except a series of "instantaneous states." And "if we are going to be so free in calling elements fictions an instant is the first thing to be called fictitious" (CP:1.422). Such a "series of instantaneous states" also contradicts Peirce's time as continuous, which can be so only if the future is "real," and it can be "real" only insofar as there is "real" potentiality (Thirdness) in nature, which nominalism denies. For Peirce both past and future are "real," as is law (CP:7.666f.), and the present is not an instant but an increment, "its earlier parts being somewhat of the nature of memory, a little vague, and its later parts somewhat of the nature of anticipation, a little generalized" (CP:7.653). Thus—and this is much in line with Whitehead—"the present is half past and half to come" (CP:6.126).

The oneness hypothesis recalls Borges's (1962:217–34) celebrated essay "The New Refutation of Time." Borges considers his "refutation" to be the ultimate consequence of the combined doctrines of Berkeley and Hume. In a nutshell, Berkeley, Borges notes, denies the existence of an external reality independent of our perception of it, while he retains the notion of a perceiving subject. Hume discounts the existence of a perceiving subject; the subject is merely a bundle of sensations. That is to say, we cannot speak of the form and color of the moon; they *are* the moon. Neither can we speak of the mind's perceptions; the mind is *nothing more than* a series of perceptions. When Berkeley and Hume are combined, both external reality and the subject disappear. Perception occurs solely in the present, and if there can be a single instant of repetition of two identical moments, then that will be evidence enough, Borges asserts, to deny time altogether. He then proceeds to give various examples of identical moments, observing that time is thus a mere figment. And he concludes with the remark that denials of temporal succession or of the individual self are "apparent desperations and secret consolations."

What is most frightful, however, is not that which is "unreal," Parmenidean, the "block," the abolition of time. Rather, for the sentient being the thought that the train of events is "irreversible and iron-clad" strikes the most disconcerting fear in the most stalwart of thinkers. But alas, there is no alternative, for Borges (1962:234) suggests at the close of his essay: "Time is the substance I am made of. Time is a river which sweeps me along, but I am the river; it is a tiger which destroys me, but I am the tiger; it is a fire which consumes me, but I am the fire. The world, unfortunately, is real; I, unfortunately, am Borges" (recall note 5 of chapter 4).

The idea inherent in both Borges and Schrödinger is that there is a timeless, self-contained, and recursive but constantly fluctuating One. Yet for each individual, indeed, for the collection of individual conscious egos as a whole, temporality exists, hence the dynamo of history is *real* after all. Time, perhaps unfortunately, is *real,* yet time and space and all things are continuous with the whole, the One.

This problem of invariance versus transience, and timelessness versus temporality, introduces us to Peirce's second criticism of nominalism. He argues that nominalists have no use for Aristotle's doctrine of future contingency, yet it is logically implied by their concept of general, determinate, and invariant law. For example, a stone released from a height either will fall or it will not fall, but it is not necessary that either will occur if, as nominalism has it, the law of gravity is merely the mental product of inductive grasps of analogous falling stone events. If the law is merely in the mind, a formula with no necessary prototype in nature, then it is a fiction. As such it nonetheless has the power to predict future events, which for Peirce is absurd if the future is in no fashion "real."

Peirce prefers to ground scientific concepts in a realist's notion of law (CP:7.686–87). But this does not imply that laws are invariant, for no law can be final for the finite mind. The mind's laws must always be subject to alteration, and thus they become more in tune with the universe, with universal law, which is itself also evolving as the mind's capacity to comprehend it evolves. In this manner, Peirce denies that the "real" is absolutely independent of mind, and vice versa, for the simple reason that the "real" is the object of the final interpretant, of the final opinion of the community. Hence any given "reality" we can know is "semiotically real" and transient only, and it is relative to the mind, since there is "no thing which is in itself in the sense of not being relative to the mind, though things which are relative to the mind doubtless are, apart from that relation" (CP:5.311). From this perspective, any speculation on invariant "real" law would appear fruitless, for there can be no invariant "real" law *for* the human semiotic animal. His/her "semiotic reality" is the product of an ongoing interactive give-and-take between the mind and the "real."

The antinominalism of Peirce's philosophy aside, his argument against "rugged individualism" (i.e., nominalism flying out of control, so to speak) is a reaction against that particular American attitude that was on the rise during the latter part of the nineteenth century. During the Lowell Lecture XI of 1866, expatiating on his notorious analogy between a "man" and a "word," Peirce argued that every person is conscious of *his own interpretant, of himself as interpretant,* his *other*—this of course is not *immediate* but *mediate* consciousness. Moreover, he is conscious of his interpretant in another mind, since minds merge into one another; he feels at home in it, feels himself in some degree there—which is strikingly reminiscent of Schrödinger's blatant "mystical" and "metaphysical" view. Peirce continues:

> When I, that is my thoughts, enter into another man, I do not necessarily carry my whole self; but what I do carry is the seed of the part that I do not carry—and if I carry the seed of my whole essence, then of my whole self actual and potential, I may write upon paper and thus impress a part of my being there; that part of my being may involve only what I have in common with all men, and then I should have carried the soul of the race, but not my individual soul, into the word there written. Thus every man's soul is a special determination of the generic soul of the family, the class, the nation, the race to which he belongs. Among the lower animals the generic soul is the greater part of their being—*bees* are more alike than men. (NE, I:499)

Taking this concept to its limits, Peirce in 1898 propounded the doctrine of individuals as

> mere cells of the social organism. Our deepest sentiment pronounces the verdict of our own insignificance. Psychological analysis shows that there is nothing which distinguishes my personal identity except my frailty and my limitations—or if you please, my blind will, which it is my highest endeavor to annihilate. (CP:1.673)

Annihilation of this personal identity is "a generalized conception of duty which completes your personality by melting it into the neighboring parts of the universal cosmos" (CP:1.673). This, Peirce readily admits, smacks of sentimentalism, but so be it. And though it is the supreme commandment of the "Buddhisto-christian religion," we are told that no philosopher or logician should suffer any embarrassment upon evoking it, for in the final analysis, the ultimate goal should be

> to generalize, to complete the whole system even until continuity results and the distinct individuals weld together. Thus it is, that while reasoning and the science of reasoning strenuously proclaim the subordination of reasoning to sentiment, the very supreme commandment of sentiment is that man should generalize, or what the logic of relatives shows to be the same thing, should become welded into the universal continuum, which is what true reasoning consists in. But this does not reinstate reasoning, for this generalization should come about, not merely in man's cognitions, which are but the superficial film of his being, but objectively in the deepest emotional springs of his life. In fulfilling this command, man prepares himself for transmutation into a new form of life, the joyful Nirvana in which the discontinuities of his will shall have all but disappeared. (CP:1.673)

Lest this proclamation fall on incredulous or indignant ears, recall Schrödinger's remarks, coupled with Einstein's humble testimony that "the most beautiful and most profound emotion we can experience is the sensation of the mystical. It is the sower of all true science. . . . The cosmic religious experience is the strongest and noblest mainspring of scientific research" (in Barnett 1979:108). And Jeans (1943:204): "There is no longer a dualism of mind and matter, but of waves and particles; there seem to be the direct although almost unrecognizable descendants of the older mind and matter, the waves replacing mind and the particles matter."

In the words of Maturana and Varela, the human semiotic animal has attained to the third-order stage of development, but this gives us no call to consider ourselves above and beyond that socially coupled system in which we are invariably submerged. For consciousness and mind "belong to the realm of social coupling. And as part of human social dynamics, mind and consciousness operate as selectors of the path which our ontologic structural drift follows" (Maturana and Varela 1987:234). Moreover, articulate animals that we are, we exist within the domains of discourse that we generate, they become part of our domain of existence, and we in turn become part of their domain of existence. Robinson Crusoe was well aware of this. He kept tabs on the days of the year and the seasons, read the Bible, dressed for dinner, and in general behaved as though he were in England. To the end he remained a part of his semiotic domain and it a part of him. Only thus could he conserve a modicum of self-identity vis-à-vis the myriad differences surrounding him.

When all is said and done, whether speaking of the Upanishads, Buddhist teachings, the Tao of Lao Tzu, the Judaeo-Christian world view, or a very important aspect of the "new physics," a comparable conclusion inheres: individualism dissolves into the collection of the many, into the One. Consider, in this light, Martin Buber's (1958) *I-thou* relationship. The *I-thou* as an asymmetrical, transitive, and irreversible relationship eliminates all semblance of an absolute subject, "I," relating to an absolute object. The *thou* of the *I-thou*, according to my reading, is comparable to Peirce's *other* and community *Other*, and the *it* of *I-it* is comparable to the *Other* to the exclusion of the community. In either case, as we are also told by Eastern sages, the dyads are intimately linked to compose one inseparable whole (Third)—much like Varela's starred equations as elaborated in chapter 6. That is, they are complementary, wavelike and particlelike, mindlike and matterlike. Each member of the dyads, then, is relative rather than absolute, commensurate with Peirce's logic of relatives to which he refers in the above citation. The question is: How does an individual consciousness come into existence in the first place if the dyads are indeed one rather then split? Sachs (1988:268), upon evoking Buber's philosophy in his attempt to reconcile the rift between quantum theory and relativity, has this to say:

> In the holistic interpretation, *I* appears in the sense of an *approximation* that an aspect of the whole, called "human consciousness," is capable of establishing, making it *appear* that there are only two things—an "absolute subject," *I*, and an absolute object, *it*. Still, this is an approximation that only gives the illusion of two, whereas *I-thou* is really one, a single entity. . . . [T]he *I-it* relation is not on the same ontological basis as *I-thou;* rather, the *apparent* objectivity of *I-it* refers to *an idea of* a component manifestation of the whole, the *I*, reached from "individual" reflection. It is only in the latter state of mind that *I* can have awareness of "other," as is required to understand the world in terms of a scientific representation. Thus, it only *seems* to the "observer," *I*, when in this state (of the whole), that it is in itself an absolute subject of the *I-it* relation—an "observer" of the absolute object, *it*.

Thus the two relations, *I-thou* and *I-it* (or self-*other* and self-*Other*), are complementary. When one is in charge, the other is subordinate, and vice versa.[13] While *I-thou* is a subject$_1$-subject$_2$ or single objective relation (Peirce's "interior" self-*other* or the self-community *Other*) and *I-it* a subject-object relation (Peirce's self and "exterior" *Other*), they are nevertheless, according to Buber's philosophy, on equivalent ontological footing. I take this to mean that commensurate with Peirce, there is no categorical distinction between mind and matter, "inside" and "outside." I also construe Peirce's notion that we first become aware of the self and its "interior" *other* with the shock of a surprise upon becoming aware that the "exterior" *Other* did not correspond to our expectations. And from that point onward the *dialogic* enterprise commences. In addition, Spencer-Brown's remark that the universe, upon splitting itself into that which sees and that which is seen, becomes false to itself, accounts for the fact that there can be no more than an approximation toward an absolute subject and an absolute object. If the absolute object in question is deemed tantamount to the "real," as I have used the term in this inquiry, then Peirce's asymptotic convergence theory applies. And if an approximation to the absolute subject, which is mere appearance rather than "reality," is tantamount to the *dialogic* give-and-take between the self and its "interior" *other,* then Peirce fakes a pass and runs around the right end for yet another touchdown.

The only alternative to this complementarity-approximation model, it would seem, is the Eastern way according to which *I-it* is illusory *(Maya)* and all we can say about *I-thou* is that *it is as it is:* we are reduced to silence. It cannot be defined within the context of space, time, matter, or events. It is prior to all things and all languages. Sachs (1988:269) suggests that a metaphysical interpretation of Einstein's relativity is close to the *I-thou* of the Eastern way, while the *I-thou-it* is comparable to the Bohr complementarity interpretation of quantum mechanics. The first system is holistic, continuous, nonlinear, nonlocal, and deterministic; the second is particulate, discontinuous, linear, local, and indeterminate. Realism rules the first; a positivist form of nominalism governs the second—though, as I have pointed out, they share the interconnected field concept. The first is mind-dependent and detached from any and all observers and relative frames of reference; the second is context-dependent and intimately linked to the observer.

Of course, as we have observed, this conflict has been with us for centuries in the guise of the "themata" of holism versus reductionism, or monism versus pluralism. Significantly enough, just as Sachs attempts to pull these antagonists of contemporary science together, so Peirce never ceased to mediate between the classical deterministic world view and the element of indeterminacy he conceived in the world.

VI. THE DEMON'S CRUCIBLE. Yet, the fact remains that, assuming the *joint product (pace* Wheeler) of all possible individuals, past, present, and future to come, were finally to reach fruition, chance (Firstness) would become necessity; all would be *there,* in the "block" for all time. There would be no *I-thou-it.* *Semiosis* would lose its very raison d'être. With reason Schrödinger alludes to the inevitable and multifarious polychromatic antinomy flowering from this indecisive bud. Such fruition cannot come to pass, so in the final analysis, "why worry about it?"

I bring up the issue further to illustrate that Schrödinger's enigmatic comments effectively create a pattern of Thirdness. The axis about which this pattern—or perhaps Mandala—revolves is generality (with its attendant concepts: continuity, abrogation of the excluded-middle principle, incompleteness). And it requires *semiosis* for its very existence. Indeed, the very concept of *semiosis* implies a community of knowers, a collection of individual minds, and their signs, all of which are nonlocalizable to the degree that, as Thirds, as *interpretants,* they spread and merge into one another. This spreading is not one-dimensional in the sense of a mathematical series; it is multidimensional, nonlinear, and asymmetrical. Rather than treelike, it is rhizomelike, or better, like grass. While trees, shrubs, and flowers stand out, grass does not. It grows between things and in the middle of things. Its growth is not linear but expansive. It knows no center, the center of its growth is everywhere: an interconnected web, a network. Yet this network is what ties things together (Deleuze and Guattari 1987; Deleuze and Parnet 1987).

"Grass" as I use it here is no more than a metaphor, of course. But as metaphor it is the pattern that connects, to paraphrase Bateson (1972). What appears as things is in reality grass, interconnections. Hence to Schrödinger's question, "Is my world the same as yours?" the answer is, "Yes," for they both partake of the interconnected pattern, *semiosis,* Thirdness, generality. But it is also "No," for there is separation in the sense of *marks* and *cuts,* and of a Maturana-Varela autonomy of autopoietic systems—generated from the domain of Firstness, vagueness. To the question, "Is there one world interjected into all minds?" the answer is affirmative: each individual is a general, though incomplete, micro-pattern of the total pattern; she is in this sense a self-contained, self-sufficient, recursive whole. But the answer is also negative, since each micro-pattern, unlike the whole, is capable of producing no more than an exceedingly dim and vague image, and it depends upon all other micro-patterns for its very existence. Thus it is possible to conceive of Schrödinger's overlapping multiplicity to be like the signs of *semiosis:* a mergence of particulars in ever-increasing complexity toward generality, that continuous whole where there are no middles—they are filled with grass—and where nothing is excluded. But, given the asymptote, any given set of micro-patterns, no matter how over-populated, will inexorably remain incomplete, a schematization.

Visually we have something like figure 12. The relations inherent in I and II, as outlined by Whitehead (1978:294–97), are those of *connection* and *inclusion.* Regions A, B, C, D, E . . . *n* of I are mediately connected insofar as each of a given pair of regions (A, B) is connected by a third region (A ∩ B). These connections are *symmetrical* and *nontransitive.* The oval, I, of I, includes all regions (A, B, C, D, E . . . *n*). The relation between the included regions and this including region is *asymmetrical* and *transitive.* A, B, C, D, E, . . . *n,* as incompleteness, is destined perpetually to push toward I, completeness. But it must necessarily remain incomplete, for there can be no all-encompassing framework, no view, *sub specie aeternitatis,* of the whole. Hence the ongoing and time-bound nature of *semiosis.* Moreover, I, qualified by generality, is

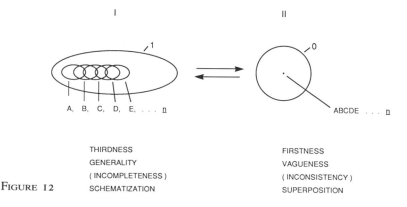

THIRDNESS	FIRSTNESS
GENERALITY	VAGUENESS
(INCOMPLETENESS)	(INCONSISTENCY)
SCHEMATIZATION	SUPERPOSITION

FIGURE 12

schematic and *incomplete* in the sense of Rescher and Brandom (1979), as described in chapter 3, while II, qualified by vagueness, is *inconsistent:* it entails a *superposition* of disparate, and even partly to wholly incompatible, regions. That is, from within II, given the immanent perspective of any and all finite sign users, ABCDE . . . *n,* like A, B, C, D, E . . . *n,* cannot be grasped in toto.

Interestingly enough, while Schrödinger in part bases his assumption of the Oneness of everything on the work of his contemporary, biologist Charles Sherrington, physicist Henry Margenau (1987) extrapolates from Schrödinger's meditations and relates them to the Minkowski "block" with its space-time manifold. His so doing implies a further degree of unity, that of the many in one and of space integrated with time. In other words, Margenau attempts precisely to account for the holistic perspective in question. He proposes a triad of approaches in his own effort to resolve Schrödinger's arithmetical paradox. The first involves a Minkowski "world-line." A given entity must move in three-dimensional space. But with the addition of time, a fourth coordinate enters the picture as if there were four dimensions of space, thus completing the familiar Einsteinian manifold which is *hyperbolic,* not Euclidean. The history of the entire universe, according to the "block" rendition of Einstein's theory, is the composite of an enormously large sum of "world-lines" into what Margenau calls a "world formula."

Supposing an ideal and impossible Laplacean superobserver to somehow be aware of all these "world-lines" in simultaneity, he/she would be in possession of the complete "world formula." Margenau goes so far as to posit the existence of a Grand Designer, a clockmaker—God?—who created the universe and keeps tabs on its course, which for him/her implies that there are no happenings, no "world-lines," or collection of "world-lines," that are in principle unknowable. Margenau further proposes that this is ample justification for his introducing a "Universal Mind, a mind that knows, and is perhaps a personal manifestation of, the World Formula. The common term for it is God, and we should not hesitate to use it, except for this consideration" (Margenau 1987:119).[14]

The second approach stipulates that human understanding entails a goal (the "world formula") which can, much in the Peircean sense, be approximated asymptotically—and which coincides with hyperbolic Minkowski space-time. And the third approach, which is most straightforward, simply postulates that all happenings are ruled by purpose, which presupposes a "Universal Mind" or cosmic consciousness capable of traveling back and forth in time at will. In other words, we are capable only of seeing the universe as one point at a time in the manifold, as if from the slit in the boxcar of a moving train, while the Universal Mind sees everything all at once (Margenau 1987:120).

Margenau's approach is the inverse of that of Comfort (1984). The latter makes a Herculean effort to come to grips with the perception and conceptual faculties of the equivalent of the Universal Mind, a demon he jocularly dubs "Gezumpstein." Margenau, in contrast, reveals our limitations vis-à-vis this Great Mind. Specifically, these limitations are, Margenau posits, (1) *individual isolation,* (2) *temporal restrictions*—Borges's dilemma, and (3) *probabilistic knowledge*. Limitation (1), corresponding to Firstness, iconicity, stems from our existence as Maturana-Varelan largely autonomous, autopoietic entities. Although we are in essence one, in order that cognition be made possible at all, the universe must split itself up so as to see itself. The arithmetical paradox thus appears inevitable. Limitation (2), tantamount to Secondness, linearity, indexicality, involves our limited view of the world through a time-slit. Unlike the Universal Mind or Comfort's Gezumpstein, we are limited to a linear one-thing-at-a-time movie, which gives us the illusion of a jolly good show such that we generally remain blissfully ignorant of our helpless state.

And limitation (3), which evokes thermodynamics as well as Peirce, Prigogine, and quantum theory, limits our knowledge to particular mediated state functions (Thirdness, symbolicity, what *would be*), while the World Formula at any given point in time spells out the probability distribution (superposition) of all possible happenings in simultaneity. This latter condition is somewhat akin to the Everett-Wheeler many-worlds interpretation of the cosmic superposition constantly bifurcating into myriad universes, comparable to Borges's (1962:19–29) labyrinthine infinite book in his "Garden of Forking Paths" in which all possible events actually occur.[15]

Margenau (1987:123) concludes with a personal note, suggesting that his theory opens the door to a comprehension of "some parapsychological effects that have attained a sufficient degree of scientific credibility to make them interesting and challenging." In this he goes much further than does Comfort, and he would certainly incur the wrath of Wheeler, who has no patience with parapsychic research. Nonetheless, his general view, disregarding its ties to contemporary physics, is mirrored in Eastern thought and much Western mysticism.

Schrödinger, in contrast, appears at least prima facie to remain closer to Wheeler's current stance. Evoking Sherrington's studies, he observes that his interpretation of the arithmetical paradox is "*one* world crystallizing out of many minds," while Sherrington's is "*one* mind, based ostensibly on the many cell-lives or, in another way, on the manifold of sub-brains [the two cerebral hemispheres] each of which seems to have such a dignity proper to itself that we feel impelled to associate a sub-mind with it" (Schrödinger 1967:145). Mind, Schrödinger concludes on a note reminiscent of Peirce, is always *now*. Much like a micro-model of Margenau's Universal Mind, there is no before or after for mind, only expectations and memories. To combine Margenau and Schrödinger, it might be said that, regarding the Universal Mind, it *has always been*, while the human mind is a recent product. And the world the human mind contemplates and studies is also of relatively recent origin.

For example, an archeologist reconstructing a long-bygone city is interested in human life in the past. In contrast, the astrophysicist attempts to go back further, to the very beginning. "But," Schrödinger (1967:146) asks,

> a world existing for millions of years without any mind being aware of it, contemplating it, is it anything at all? Has it existed? For do not let us forget: To say . . . that the becoming of the world is reflected in a conscious mind is but a cliché, a

phrase, a metaphor that has become familiar to us. The world is given but once. Nothing is reflected. The original and the mirror-image are identical. The world extended in space and time is but our representation *(Vorstellung)*. Experience does not give us the slightest clue of its being anything besides that—as Berkeley was well aware.

That this universe eventually produced brains with which to look at itself is Schrödinger's own equivalent of Dunne's (1934) painter painting himself within the landscape painting himself within . . . , of Matte Blanco's (1975) consciousness of infinite sets, of Spencer-Brown's universe as a giant self-contained set of onion rings, of the infinite regress interpretation of Schrödinger's own cat, and finally, of Peirce's infinite regress of signs (and by extension, consciousness, mind, self). In each case the individual mind that has produced an image of the whole is but an insignificant accessory that could as well have been absent without detracting from the total effect. The mind has not succeeded in elaborating on an outlook of the whole without retiring itself to the periphery, thus producing a world picture which has no place for it, like Wittgenstein's eye which sees its world from a circumference point but cannot see itself seeing its world. The paradox continues to elude us and at the same time remain enticing.

Indeed, Peirce's "Cosmos ≈ Sign ≈ Mind" is at once subtler and knottier than initially meets the eye. Signs, in terms of their categories, present themselves in a disorderly confusion. Mind partly *untangles* them upon *collaborating with* them, freeing them of their fusion and confusion in experience. In this fashion mind separates signs from their possibility to their *this-ness* to their meaning as conditionality for future sign instantiations, but at the same time mind is immanent, within the field of signs. The universe itself is held by Peirce to be mind in the process of development, and it is a sign, the Cosmic Poem, an Argument—a sign of itself. The categories as such are more adequately defined as *modes of becoming* than *modes of being;* they are themselves in perpetual transition, from one to three, and back again; they also engage in the same self-referential, self-reflexive act as mind, the field of signs, and the universe itself. What *is,* the appearance of (explicated) things, provides the comforting illusion of a stable *thing-ness* of the world. But that would be the easy interpretation of the story. The deeper (implicate) substratum eludes and intrigues as well as it poses an ominous threat to that coveted security of appearances. Jeans makes the distinction thus:

> When we view ourselves in space and time our consciousnesses are obviously the separate individuals of a particle-picture, but when we pass beyond space and time, they may perhaps form ingredients of a single continuous stream of life. As it is with light and electricity, so it may be with life; the phenomena may be individuals carrying on separate existence in space and time, while in the deeper reality beyond space and time we may all be members of one body. (In Commins and Linscott 1947:393)

Schrödinger (1964:21) considered this "one body" to be essentially "unchangeable and numerically *one* in all men, nay in all sensitive beings. . . .

Inconceivable as it seems to ordinary reason, you—and all other conscious beings as such—are all in all. Hence this life of yours which you are living is not merely a piece of the entire existence, but is in a certain sense the *whole*." It is perhaps not mere coincidence that a number of contemporary physicists, as well as mystics the world over for centuries, have referred to "reality" as mind, consciousness, the One. This, to repeat, does not imply "subjective" but "objective idealism." The world "out there" is not merely illusory and the world "in here" the "real" world. Both, as "actually real" and "semiotically real," remarkably closely fit Peirce's scheme of things. And both, from a certain vantage, indeed a totalizing vantage eternally inaccessible to finite and fallible beings, are in their own way illusory: there is, from this view, but One Reality.[16]

Yet, from the complementary view, what there apparently *is* presupposes some more primitive orb, to which I now turn.

EIGHT   *Nothing and Everything*

I. ON WHAT THERE IS NOT. Much of the preceding plus the premise of this chapter can be encapsulated thus:

> *Semiosis* implies the capacity to produce, in the theoretical long run, infinitely many signs which presumably re-present items in what is traditionally conceived to be an a priori *reality*. But such re-presentation necessarily remains false to itself. Rather than re-presentation, there is mere pre-sentation (introduction of that which cannot be re-introduced in its identical form) of "semiotically real" items for an active subject *(interpreter-interpretant; observer-observed)*. The entire system, especially given the self-falsifying character of the human animal's signs, owes its very existence to a special agent: *"nothingness,"* charged with revving up the generator of signs which evolve from the realm of *vagueness* and *inconsistency* to increasing determination, and hence *generality*, though the task will always remain *incomplete* short of the infinite theoretical long run.

To begin, by addressing myself to this "theorem's" taproot, in *Gravitation* (1973), the authors, Charles Misner, Kip Thorne, and John Wheeler, speculate on the nature of what they call "pre-geometry," which is prior to both time and space. They suggest that it is the generator of logical relationships, a self-generating "calculus of propositions," such as might immediately follow from a Spencer-Brownian logic of distinctions, with, at least in the beginning, the compelling simplicity of mere *this/thatness*. In the first place this calculus of propositions is suggestive of mindlike properties—as are, at a more primitive level, Spencer-Brown's calculus and Peirce's book of assertions. In the second place it presupposes the claim that "empty space" is not empty at all but is instead the scene of the most violent physics—the constant collapse and rebirth of the gravitational field, or in Bohm's terms, the constant explication of the implicate. "Empty space" is described as having "foamlike" properties of alternating negative and positive fluctuations where the basic particles are incessantly created and annihilated, a sort of micro-counterpart of the moiré effect (I must point out, however, that for Wheeler [1968, 1973], unlike Peirce, space is at this level radically discontinuous, the scene of a staggering multiplicity of mini-catastrophes).

Significantly, Wheeler and his associates who propagated this "geo-metrodynamic" concept envision a single entity, the gravitation-field geometry, which accounts for everything that is. It represents an attempt to undercut the set theoretical paradox of container/contained and part/whole, the equivalent of Schrödinger's arithmetical paradox, and the discrepancy between space-time continuity and quantum discreteness of the material *punctum*. This conception of "empty space," much like the "nothingness" of *Sunyata* and Bohm's implicate (Wilber 1982), is not the product of negation, nor is it simply non-being.

To negate something is to make its intended force become absent. Frege (1919) argued that negation, regarding the exercise of judgment, does not depend upon incompatibility at the same level, but on assertion at one level and its negation at a metalevel. Freud's (1925) negation is that of a denial *(Verneinung)* which suppresses, and at the same time conserves the repression *(Verdrägung)* of that which it negates—a sort of Hegelian negation of the negation. Both of these notions of negation are inadequate for the present purpose, which is more fundamental.

The notion of negation I am after is somewhat more comparable to Spinoza. He once revealed that every definition is a boundary which negates all other definitions and introduces language to what is up to this point a purely abstract calculus. Negation in this sense is not merely no. Neither is it not. Not is syntactic, while no can be communicated nonlinguistically (Wilden 1984). Like no, not refers to (indicates, points to) something whose existence or meaning is already at least partly specifiable. It requires a base capable of supporting some sign or thought-sign before it can point to anything, and what it cannot point to is the base supporting it—lest it negate its own foundation and self-destruct. The domain preceding this indexical pointing must be "iconic" in the most primitive sense. This ultimate ground of "nothingness" (pre-geometry) presupposes *distinguishability* (Wheeler), *distinction* (Spencer-Brown), and a *cut* providing *iconicity* (Peirce), which precedes *indication* (Spencer-Brown), *indexing* (Peirce), the *actualization* (Wheeler), or *explication* (Bohm), *of* something *for* someone *in* some respect or capacity (i.e., the *semiosic* process).

What, then, is this "nothingness" lying behind distinction, no, not, and indication? Like *sunya,*[1] it can be variously translated as empty, nothing, void, or open. The problem is that these words tend to convey the impression of some-*thing* blank—which is the fallacy also of Peirce's "blank sheet of assertion" and goes against the grain of Wheeler's "pre-geometry." The "nothingness" I speak of, in contrast, precedes notions of thingness and of opposition or duality, all of which *depends upon* negation, distinction, and indication. Regarding mind, "nothingness," simply put, is the emptiness of all intellection. Mental thought-signs have arisen out of distinctions which imply boundaries separating something *from* something else. In the total absence of thought-signs, it appears, we have "nothingness." But this will not do the trick either. We must still contend with the full mind/empty mind dichotomy.

Let us, then, defer to a scholar versed in Oriental thought in search of a more adequate articulation:

> Emptiness which is completely without form is freed from being and non-being because "non-being" is still a form as distinguished from "being." . . . Emptiness is not a mere emptiness as opposed to fullness. Emptiness as Synyata transcends and embraces both emptiness and fullness. It is really formless in the sense that it is liberated from both "form" and "formlessness." Thus Synyata, Emptiness as it is is Fullness and Fullness as it is is Emptiness; formlessness as it is is form and form as it is is formless. (Abe 1985:126–27)

In this light, a way of putting it is that every-thing as it is is no-thing, and no-thing as it is is every-thing. The holomovement is all and nothing; as nothing it is all and as all it is nothing. In the final analysis, emptiness is the simplest of simples made inordinately complicated when there is an attempt to articulate or conceptualize it. It is the most direct form of experience. If an alcoholic sees (distinguishes) snakes and points at (indicates) them while in an excruciating phase of delirium tremens, we may in turn point to the nonexisting snakes in our attempt to prove him wrong. But he is more right than we are: he is pointing at some-thing; we deludedly believe we are pointing at no-thing (Alice also marveled at the Queen who could see nobody on the road before her, and Odysseus used "nothingness" to fool the Cyclops by calling himself Nobody). Not an idea, a perspective, or a thing, "nothingness" is what it is, that's it. Perhaps we can hardly go any further.

But the question must be asked: How does this "nothingness" jibe, if at all, with Peirce's categories? Eugen Baer's (1988:240–41) considering the state of "nothingness" to be a sort of Peircean pre-First, which consists of the "absolute nothingness" (CP:6.215), the field within which *semiosis* plays out its drama in "unbounded freedom," like the random walk of a stick of chalk on a blackboard (CP:6.203), is revealing. Peirce was aware of the need for "nothingness" as that which makes possible the extraction of forms. As Peirce puts it, the "absolute nothing" (CP:6.215) of "nothingness" is not Hegelian being (CP:6.217). It is utter vagueness, dimensionless (CP:6.193), freedom, chance, spontaneity (CP:6.197–200). There are certain characteristics of the whole of consciousness in this field of "nothingness," as a "chaos of unpersonalized feeling" (CP:6.33), which, nonetheless, possesses a definite intensity (CP:6.265). In this respect, Peirce's cosmology entails a "hyperbolic" evolution which

> proceeds from one state of things in the infinite past, to a different state of things in the infinite future. The state of things in the infinite past is chaos, tohu bohu, the nothingness of which consists in the complete absence of regularity. The state of things in the infinite future is death. The nothingness of which consists in the

complete triumph of law and absence of all spontaneity. Between these, we have on *our* side a state of things in which there is some absolute spontaneity counter to all law, and some degree of conformity to law, which is constantly on the increase owing to the growth of *habit*. (CP:8.317)

Peirce must be partly exonerated for his hypercontradictory passage by virtue of the difficulty in articulating the slippery concepts he is attempting to confront head-on. "Nothingness," as he seems to sense it, is the "other side," a timeless orb framing his three categories whose very existence, meaningless outside temporality, perhaps creates the possibility for the evolution of time (CP:8.318).[2] Time, in impossibly traversing the frozen passage from finitude to infinity, gives rise to the categories, and these, in springing time from its condensed knot of primordiality, embody time, which is thus contained within itself. In addition to *sunyata*, this "nothingness" before time was is rather commensurate, I would submit, with the silent Tao, or *Asat*, the nonexistent sphere of the *Rg-Veda:* the silent, bottomless, unthinkable background of un-differentiated energy out of which everything emerges (T. de Nicolas 1976:89–107).

Peirce, to be sure, is clear on one important point: "nothingness," the undifferentiated, is not merely "the nothing of negation"; it is "the nothing of not having been born" (CP:6.217). It is the unbounded freedom of *tychism*, which, ineffable and well-nigh unthinkable to the core, refuses worthy candidacy as a Peircean category. Yet Peirce recognized the need to distinguish the domain of "utter nothingness" (CP:6.490) from that of *is*-ness. As he puts it:

We start, . . . with nothing, pure zero. But this is not the nothing of negation. For *not* means *other than*, and *other* is merely a synonym of the ordinary numeral *second*. As such it implies a first; while the present pure zero is prior to every first. The nothing of negation is the nothing of death, which comes *second* to, or after, everything. . . . There is no individual thing, no compulsion, outward nor inward, no law. It is the germinal nothing, in which the whole universe is involved and foreshadowed. As such, it is absolutely undefined and unlimited possibility— boundless possibility. There is no compulsion and no law. It is boundless freedom. (CP:6.217)

If pure "nothingness" is the primitive category preceding Firstness (origin), Secondness (otherness), and Thirdness (meaning), we have, then, after Zero, One, as the first numeral, as unity, individuality and nonduality, or in Peirce's terms, the Monad (see also Jung 1963). One is followed by Two, the dis-tinguished-indicated split between *this* and *that*. Three, which brings the pre-viously incompatible One and Two together, closes the circle, thus potentially reverting back to the continuity of the undifferentiated as a self-contained whole (following figure 5), though it contains the differentiated as the generation of a potentially infinite series of interpretants, each in some way the same as and yet different from all others. Parmenides' summary of his position as "If One is not, then nothing is" is, in this manner, turned inside out as "Nothing is what One is not, and One, when it *is*, is what nothing (as a potentiality) *was*."

In this sense the zero of "nothingness" becomes the *continuous flux* of Firstness: the ongoing processual stream before there is consciousness *of* what has been cut and marked out from "nothingness." This is essentially Hanson's (1958) distinction, following Wittgenstein, between *seeing* and *seeing as,* when sense data are put into their conventionally generated pigeonholes (see Merrell 1990). The flux can be grasped only by stopping it, not actually but conceptually, and the grasp can then be interpreted by resort and appeal to meanings even when they are not reflexively explicit but only implicit in action. Concepts or thought-signs ripped out of the continuous flux of experience are not by any stretch of the imagination determined by experience, for experience is part of the continuum which manifests no limits or boundaries. The establishment of limits is accompanied by the generation of thought-signs and consciousness *of* them, which serves to bring order to the world, creating its myriad pieces of furniture and giving rise to the possibility of generalities.

But the abstraction of thought-signs from the continuum is not entirely arbitrary, since, if we follow Peirce, the surprising "clash" of Seconds, of "real world" objects, persists in forcing itself into our attention in one form or another. Neither is the flux exactly characterless; the continuum, when cut and marked, manifests character at the location of the cut, which limits the range of possible interpretants for that particular cut. There is some free play, but the nature of the interpretants cannot be irrelevant to the nature of the original flux of Firstness as a potential for an indefinitely broad range of possible interpretants. The ultimate test of relevance is, most appropriately, Peirce's *pragmatic maxim* (CP:5.402) which, if successful, yields dividends in both action (resulting from habit) and understanding (from meaning attached to the interpretant in question). And the degree of rigidity of the interpretants is a measure of Peirce's *principle of tenacity* (CP:5.337), a sort of stubbornness factor which at times fetters more than it facilitates meaning. This success of interpretants by a stubbornness factor stringently limits alternatives, though it aids in the eternal push toward finality.

II. GETTING ALONG SWIMMINGLY. Thought has generally, though not always, brushed aside such intangibles as I outlined in the preceding section, while stepping up to a more comfortable level of abstraction in pursuit of *negation.* On the other hand, the West's obsession with truth has placed it in deep and murky waters time and again. Simply put, in mathematics, *syntax* involves *provability* (yes/no, not, negation), while *semantics* involves *truth.* Both provability and truth have traditionally been the intellectual elixir motivating seekers of knowledge. In contrast, Eastern thought, as far as my meager understanding goes, involves *pragmatics* in the broadest possible stretch of the imagination, where the subject well-nigh disappears in the contextual soup of things. Leaving this point aside for the moment, I will probe a mite further into *negation* in an attempt to approximate the ground level of *semiosis,* and subsequently return to this most general sense of pragmatics.

Most notably, negation is germane to Whitehead and Russell's *Principia*

Mathematica (1910). The sole formation rule in their work regarding negation, the primitive proposition 1.7, states:

> If *p* is an elementary proposition, NOT *p* is an elementary proposition.

While 1.7 could be an adequate formation rule for the arbitrary manipulation of marks on paper or noises uttered in sequence—the "formalist" philosophy of mathematics—things become messy once we start giving "NO" and "NOT" their interpretations we intuitively associate with negation in everyday communication. Admittedly, in the vast majority of sentences Whitehead and Russell's formation rule as stated in the *Principia* would still serve us quite well. But its adequacy falters for those cases where the formula *p* is a simple construction that can be interpreted as referring to some existential characteristic of its own—such as its own truth in every truth-value model—i.e., Russell's set theoretic paradox, a class which becomes a member of itself. And Whitehead and Russell (1910:13) seem ultimately to have had truth-value interpretation in mind, for they write that "the system must lead to no contradictions, namely, . . . both '*p* is a theorem' and 'NOT-*p* is a theorem' cannot legitimately appear."

But let's get back to the more fundamental level of syntax. At the outset Whitehead and Russell appear to have achieved their goal by formalizing logic introducing (1) *inference rules* relating to negation, and (2) *primitive definitions* involving negation. These rules and definitions bring into play the laws of noncontradiction and the excluded middle (and eventually their intended truth-value interpretation). This attempt to avoid any and all contradictions led Russell to his Theory of Logical Types, devised especially to prevent paradox from raising its ugly head in set theory. Russell's ploy, admittedly ad hoc, was to place restrictions not only on formal language use but, in addition, on the use of ordinary language, especially regarding its reference to formal language.

Eschewing Whitehead and Russell's notation of falsity as 0 and truth as 1 which compose a metalanguage for assigning values to the formulas of their deductive calculus, I will opt for the more primitive Spencer-Brown and Peircean *"nothingness"* in place of 0, and the *mark-cut* in place of 1. It might appear to those who cannot free themselves from the propensity to assign values to everything and anything that we now have two distinct levels, that is, a Whitehead-Russell "two-value logic," with the negation sign connecting them. In this sense negation erases a mark-cut, thus reducing it to level 0. However, one must be mindful that at this most primitive level the mark-cut is valueless, hence truth *through* falsity—the equivalent of 1 *and* 0—does not yet enter the picture. The most that can be said is that, commensurate with Spencer-Brown and Peirce, an even number of negations applied to the same level will be *the same as* no negation, and an odd number of negation signs will *reduce to* a single negation. At this lowermost point there is as yet no-*thing*.

In other words, at the level of the *mark-cut* there is no value in the sense either of logic or of mathematics. When the most fundamental sort of "value"— which is not yet any "value" in the ordinary sense—is introduced, it is simply the equivalent of *imaginary numbers,* most adequately expressed in natural language as the statement "This statement is false," which is neither true nor false but merely undecidable. Boolean algebra and the Theory of Logical Types disallow such undecidables: a statement must be either true or false, and if not, it is meaningless and hence worthless. In similar fashion, it is generally assumed that numbers must be either positive or negative or zero. The problem is that the imaginary number, $\sqrt{-1}$, is simply neither positive nor negative nor zero. Spencer-Brown extends this concept to Boolean algebra to compose, in addition to true, false, and meaningless, a fourth class, *imaginary*. *Imaginary values,* entailing oscillation between $+1$ and -1, true and false, yes and no, either and or, this and that, are like a wave train produced by an "excited" computer caught in a double bind called a "synchronizer glitch" (Wilden 1984), or like the wave train model of an "excited" subnuclear particle (Kauffman and Varela 1980). Perhaps we have here a microcosm of Wheeler's "self-excited" universe.

But we really must return to the comfort of solid earth beneath our feet. First and foremost, Spencer-Brown and Peirce's *"nothingness"* and the *mark-cut* are not compatible with the empty set of set theory. A set is a collection of things each of which is a member of the set. The individual members are identifiable at one level, as is the whole collection supposedly at another level. The identity of, say, an orange (as token) is contained in the orange's membership in the set of all oranges (as type). In addition, *complementarity* enters the scene. The set containing a particular orange *here-now* exists in complementary relationship with, and at the same time it constitutes, everything other than the/an orange, with a boundary dividing in essence *this* from *that*. And everything other than *this* orange constitutes the orange *as* orange within the set containing the orange. To consider everything other than the orange within the set of all oranges is like thinking of an orange without really thinking about it. The set is at that point not empty, though that which fills the container is implicit (implicate). Moreover, to consider the set of all real oranges with a radius of three feet or more is to be aware of an empty container, a sort of knothole, surrounded by that which is. This empty set is not mere nothing or "nothingness"; it is a contextualized container *containing* nothing. "Nothingness," in and of itself, is unbounded.

According to orthodox set theory, from Cantor to Zermelo-Fraenkel to von Neumann-Bernays-Gödel, there is only one empty set which is a member of all nonempty sets (Quine 1970). When properly and pragmatically contextualized, however, not all empty sets are identical. Donut holes, knotholes, and foxholes are different in terms of their complementary relations. The set of all nineteenth-century women presidents of the United States and the set of all twentieth-century kings of France are not the same, given the historical context of kings in France and the lack of women presidents in the United States. The set of all bald, hirsute men and of all barbers who shave all those who do not shave themselves are also both empty. In the latter case, the set of all bald, hirsute men is "empty" because of contradiction, and the set of all barbers who shave all those who do not shave themselves, if it is "empty," is so as the result of a paradox, and if it is not considered to be "empty," the paradox has not been acknowledged.

The empty set, then, can be construed as *noticed absence* in the sense of negation as ordinarily defined. It is an *outlined absence*, acknowledgment of a container without any contained. But a problem remains. The container generally is not, it cannot be, acknowledged without a pragmatically contextualized noticed absence *as opposed to* the presence of something "outside." And the "outside" consists of things (that is, signs, the "semiotically real") at the secondary level of something having *already been distinguished* and *indicated*. At the primary level, the "absence" can become an "absence" as such only *with respect to* that secondary level. In other words, *noticed absence*, that is, awareness *of* or consciousness *of*, at least in the domain of a distinctively human semiotic, already presupposes some form of Thirdness, mediation, symbolicity. It appears that we can no longer return to the primitive taproot of the *mark-cut;* we cannot recall that original separating and calling up of a boundary distinguishing something from something else.

This presupposed Thirdness has to do with language. In our age of the "linguistic turn," language is a much fought-over terrain. It is said to be a "prison-house," sick, experiencing a crisis, corrupted by metaphysics, incapable of describing either the world or itself, undecidable, multiply ambiguous, and contentiously indeterminate. Many of those most responsible for articulating the problems with language, which includes the likes of Wittgenstein, Heidegger, Sartre, Gadamer, and Derrida, are among the most trenchant critics of Western reason and metaphysics. The problem with language, Derrida (1974:6) observes, "has never been simply one problem among others. But never as much as at present has it invaded, *as such,* the global horizon of the most diverse researches and the most heterogeneous discourses, diverse in their intention, method, and ideology."

Derrida attacks the traditional account of the opposition speech/writing, which relegates writing to a secondary status while highlighting speech as the transcription of an epistemologically prior voice capable of speaking timeless truth in its immediacy. This prioritizing of speech, this *logocentrism*, also implies the generation of an entire set of binary offspring: presence/absence, inside/outside, thing/sign, identity/difference, reality/appearance. For each dichotomy there is presumably a cornerstone upon which one of the terms is privileged over the other as primary. One term supposedly remains pure, the other is blemished; one is superordinate, the other subordinate. Thus everything is already given a *value*. We are already caught up within the web of signs, wherever we are.

In line with Derrida's critique, the 1-0 system derived from Whitehead-Russell, binary Boolean algebra, and by extension Saussurean semiology, especially as redefined to fit the pattern of binary-based information theory by Jakobson and Lévi-Strauss, are simply outclassed when in the same ballpark with triadic semiotics. In any binary system, everything is already valued. There is no ultimate ground upon which to begin a signifying edifice. Peirce's triadic system, in contrast, allows for no such delusions of presuppositionless premises. The triadic production of the interpretant is absolutely essential to a sign

(CP:5.474). But triadic semiotics recognizes that the interpretant is an already advanced stage of signification at which point *value* has been interjected into the sign, with no turning back. In a radically fundamental sense the interpretant of a sign *is* its meaning. To reemphasize a most important point, if, as Peirce indefatigably argued, the only thought that "can possibly be cognized is thought in signs" and that "thought which cannot be cognized does not exist," then all thought "is necessarily in signs" (CP:5.251). From this proposition, it follows that "every thought is a sign," which "must address itself to some other, must determine some other, since that is the essence of a sign" (CP:5.253).

Moreover, since Peirce believed the interpretant of a sign is itself a sign of the same category, and that any sign must be interpreted or translated by a subsequent sign, then just as a sign is the interpretant or translatand of its predecessor, so the concept of the interpretant is that of infinite extension, a *progressus* as well as a *regressus*. There can be neither a first nor a last sign, nor is there any determinable center to the *semiosic* fabric. Hence there can be no ultimate presuppositions or foundations intuitively and intentionally generated ex nihilo. All signs, insofar as we can know them, be conscious *of* them, are mediated in the process of emerging and passing away. Consequently there *can be* no legitimate dichotomization or hierarchization.

Above all, the triadic *semiosic* fabric implies the sign user's immanence: unlimited possibilities from within a bounded domain whose horizon remains perpetually beyond reach. This reveals the futility of any and all programs for constructing metalanguages with which to launch a universe of discourse into the stratosphere of Truth. Along these lines, Anthony Wilden (1980:122) points out that Russell's theory, though a valiant effort to abolish paradox from his logical Garden of Eden, ultimately failed for two reasons: "(1) the transcendence of any paradox or double bind, in logic or in life, involves some form of meta-communication, and (2) the transcendence itself engenders paradox at the meta-communicative level—or at the level of the next logical type."

In other words, Russell's typing, and Tarski and Carnap's metalanguages, are themselves paradoxical. they fuse and confuse distinct levels. First, they punctuate the continuum by erecting the initial 1-0 hierarchy, and second, they involve the use of negation, which is supposedly metacommunicative, since it is capable of reversing 1 to 0 and vice versa. The negation sign is thus necessary to the very idea of identity by its repetition an even or odd number of times.

The problem with Wilden's critique, however, is that not only are meta-languages never without tangles, knots, and muddles, but contextualized meta-communication itself invariably merges levels. Lyotard (1984), effectively, and, indirectly but even more effectively, Rorty (1979) argue this point.[3] Wilden is also well aware of this quandary, as his later work encyclopedically illustrates (Wilden 1987a, 1987b). Nonetheless, guided by a Western-style missionary zeal, he gallantly puts forth a sort of metaprogram for hewing out a path leading to a rectification of the entire mess—a Herculean, yet Faustian, task indeed.

Perhaps our only alternative is in good postmodern fashion to learn to live with/in the bind (this was the later Wittgenstein's answer). To illustrate my point, I will begin once again with Russell, who, in reference to the violation of his logical types, tells us that

> the imaginary sceptic, who asserts that he knows nothing, and is refuted by being asked if he knows that he knows nothing, has asserted nonsense, and has been fallaciously refuted by an argument which involves a vicious-circle fallacy. In order that the sceptic's assertion may become significant, it is necessary to place some limitation upon the things of which he is asserting his ignorance, because the things of which it is possible to be ignorant form an illegitimate totality. (Russell 1910:38)

Suppose, for example, an honest and forthright scholar writes in the preface of her book: "At least one of all the sentences I write in this book is surely false." The possibility of a paradox ensues, of course, since that very sentence runs the risk of being the false one. But if so, then it is true, and if true, then false. In order to ban all such threats, Russell decreed that a statement cannot logically refer to the totality of all statements, because as the member of the set within which it is included, it cannot be elevated to the same status as that set. Thus, the scholar's phrase "all sentences" should be prohibited, for it belongs to an illegimate set.

However, the sentence I have just written must be prohibited as well, since the phrase "the phrase all 'sentences' is an illegitimate set" must also be a member of an illegitimate set. So now the question becomes this: "Is the phrase 'the phrase' "the phrase" 'all sentences' is an illegitimate set" is a member of an illegitimate set' legitimate or illegitimate?" Logically speaking, it should be illegitimate, though practically speaking, and with due respect to Russell, it is conventionally quite legitimate. The occasion often arises in everyday language use to write such sentences as "All sentences are writeable," "All sentences are written in a language," "All written sentences are narratives of one form or another," without their being considered pernicious. They are intelligibly perceived as true or false, and as meaningful or meaningless. Further, Russell's very Theory of Logical Types essentially asserts that "all propositions must be generated and classified in such a way that the subject 'All propositions' never occurs." This proposition itself must be forbidden by the nature of its injunction when applied self-referentially to itself (Davis 1972:149).

This conundrum—or so it must appear to those of an obstinate positivist bent—takes us back to Spencer-Brown's *imaginary values,* which, he demonstrates, have been used for the construction of *real* answers in computer circuits, and, he suggests, imaginary values were employed by Fermat in generating his great proof. Spencer-Brown (1979:99) writes in this regard:

> The fact that imaginary values *can* be used to reason towards a real and certain answer, coupled with the fact that they *are not* so used in mathematical reasoning today, and also coupled with the fact that certain equations plainly *cannot* be solved without the use of imaginary values, means that *there must be mathematical statements* (whose truth or untruth is in fact perfectly decidable) *which cannot be decided by the methods of reasoning to which we have hitherto restricted ourselves.*

In general, confining oneself to strictly defined binary Boolean equations eventually leads to undecidability of the Gödelian type, which throws a monkey wrench in the works of logic and mathematics, traditionally conceived. On the other hand, Spencer-Brown demonstrates that with imaginary values, and from within a broader context, it is possible to generate answers to such undecidables by means of an equation's turning back on itself, biting its own tail, and revealing information (by virtue of its in-forming itself, a formation within itself) regarding that which it expresses. Such an expression "is thus informed in the sense of having its own form within it" (Spencer-Brown 1979:100).

In a Peircean vein, the meaning of any given proposition can never be completely specified because the generalization of the conditional *would be* of the interpretant, or of Thirdness, incorporated in the "pragmatic maxim," cannot precisely identify the object of which the proposition is a sign (CP:5.447n). This is the nature of the *indeterminacy* (Peirce's counterpart to undecidability) of meaning. "All propositions" are hypothetical expressions about some aspect of the experienced world which must be, in some sense, indeterminate on account of the inevitable "clash" of this world (Secondness) on the author of the experiences (CP:3.93). Moreover, the object of a sign, like the sign itself, cannot be determinate, because every known property of both can never be fully specified:

> The absolute individual can not only not be realized in sense or thought, but can not exist, properly speaking. For whatever lasts for any time, however short, is capable of logical division, because in that time it will undergo some change in its relations. But what does not exist for any time, however short, does not exist at all. All, therefore, that we perceive or think, or that exists, is general. So far there is truth in the doctrine of scholastic realism. But all that exists is infinitely determinate, and the infinitely determinate is the absolutely individual. This seems paradoxical, but the contradiction is easily resolved. That which exists is the object of a true conception. This conception may be made more determinate than any assignable conception; and therefore it is never so determinate that it is capable of no further determination. (CP:3.93n)

This denial of absolute individuals because of their incessant fluctuation through time provides the grounds for Peirce's doctrine of the indeterminacy of meaning. Since no object can be fully specified with respect to the totality of its properties, any proposition about it is vague insofar as it cannot hope fully to specify a determinate set of properties for that object. Hence the meaning of any proposition is always open to further specification. Given the incessantly fluctuating universe, however, in the domain of natural language use the equivalent of Spencer-Brownian *imaginary values* in a state of constant oscillation, like $\sqrt{-1}$, serves at least temporarily to halt the continuum with the generation of some element of discontinuity, bringing to a tenuous determination that which is indeterminate.

A car is thus *that* particular car at *that* moment; it is in a *being of becoming* state and at the same time in a process of *becoming into being*. It *is* and *is not* what it *was,* and it *will have been* and *will not have been* what it *is*. The car in one sense *is* a singularity at *that* spatio-temporal juncture, and in another, complementary, sense, it *is* what it *was* at all spatio-temporal junctures and what it *will have been* at all future ones. It is coterminous with all its instantiations, hence it violates Russell's injunction against a set being a member of itself, and at the same time it simply *is as it is* during each and every instantiation. To put it another way, for the monist it is true that the car is the same car, yesterday, today, and tomorrow; for the pluralist it is false. The pluralist defends the truth of the car's being different with each instantiation; the monist rejects his argument as false. Both the monist and the pluralist might brand the statement "the car is *both* the same *and* not the same at each moment" as nonsensical or meaningless. Spencer-Brown's *imaginary* value, resting beyond negation, allows for this contradictory statement, however, as it does for statements barring excluded middles: hence it can be *vague* and/or *general*. In this sense, Peirce's thought was far removed from that wooden variety, empirical positivist thought, that reigned for almost half a decade after his death.

Consequently, if our scholar in the preface of her book happens to write, "We can never write about 'All sentences,' " she has committed a sin against Russell's prohibition. But the fact is that she has written it. To do so she must have been able somehow to think *about* "all sentences" and potentially speculate *about* this supposedly unsayable set. So she merely did it, regardless of whether her action was self-contradictory or not. It must therefore be acceptable and even inevitable that she, as we all do, occasionally write sentences *about* "all sentences."

Russell elsewhere tacitly acknowledges the practical validity of such everyday discourse. Wittgenstein's *Tractatus,* which won his respect, claims that we can say things about the world as a whole only if we can get outside the world as a whole, but since we cannot do so, we cannot say anything about the world as a whole. This prompted Russell's remark that "after all, Mr. Wittgenstein manages to say a good deal about what cannot be said, thus suggesting to the sceptical reader that possibly there may be some loophole through a hierarchy of languages, or by some other exit" (Wittgenstein, 1961:xxi). Wittgenstein obviously had this possible reservation in mind when, at the end of his treatise, he offered his reader the following notorious counsel: "6.54 My propositions serve as elucidations in the following way: anyone who understands me eventually recognizes them as nonsensical, when he has used them—as steps—to climb up beyond them. (He must, so to speak, throw away the ladder after he has climbed up it.)" (Wittgenstein 1961:74).

Russell's ideal logic *is* closed, but, speaking of the set of *all* possible logical systems, one must speak of openness, because of the inescapable self-contradictions and self-referential sentences in everyday language. The upshot seems to be that the mere fact of uttering a Russellian illegitimate sentence commits one to a form of relativism insofar as to comment *about* a totality renders that totality relative to one's perspective, which in turn is relative to the indefinite range of other possible perspectives and descriptions of that totality.

In Hacking's (1985) words, one's *style of reasoning* commits one to a particular perspective, but, given other myriad *styles of reasoning,* commitment could equally have been made elsewhere. Peirce himself admits that ultimately any reason for trusting in reason must be undecidable (CP:1.672). Nevertheless, like a sentence about "all sentences," some form of trust in reason and the validity of argumentation is a matter of fact. If we deny this trust, our mouths and our pens will be paralyzed: we will not reasonably be able to reason about the impossibility of trusting reason. What we do when we reason—in whichever style—is simply do it. We do so, to use Peirce's term, on *instinct,* by *habit,* and *belief* (CP:5.174). And doing it entails flatness: there are no permanent closed-system hierarchies here, only an infinite set of interconnected series, unlimited *semiosis.* This involves, in the broadest conceivable sense, a pragmatic, dialogic give-and-take, between the self, its *other,* and the *Other*—signs all.

III. INTO THE MAINSTREAM OF THINGS. In the final analysis, after all that has been written, warred over, and wrought regarding the "linguistic turn," I can hope to offer no ultimate solutions. I will limit myself to reiterating what I believe to be a most important point: pure "nothingness," that lowermost level from which all that *is*—i.e., all signs—emanates, is a far cry from the set theoretic form of *noticed absence,* which must presuppose the existence of some-*thing.* Such binary thinking demands truth and falsity, identity and contradiction, similarity and difference, presence and absence. The negative side of these dichotomies, however, is not mere "nothingness." *Noticed absence,* I have suggested, is already valued, always mediated. It entails a giant step beyond the *mark-cut,* which itself arises out of "nothingness." Pure "nothingness," in contrast, exists at the more primitive level before the *mark-cut,* which itself is independent of 1-0, true-false, and all other such binaries. "Nothingness" is at most only sensed. It cannot be made explicit. It is no more existent than would be Plato's shadows in the cave were the fire to be extinguished. There is nothing *in contrast to* which it can be conceived, perceived, and articulated.

This implies, regarding zero, an axiomatization of the natural numbers different from that of Peano. Zero represents not mere negation but the more primitive level I have referred to, that preceding the *mark-cut.* If what *is* ("being") is attributed to the number 1, then what *is not* ("nonbeing") is not 0, as is ordinarily conceived to be the case for binary or Boolean logic. Rather, "nonbeing," which maintains itself as a form of distinction and indication from "being," is, more properly, the counterpart to -1. By the same token, even numbers can be distinguished from prime numbers, real numbers from imaginary numbers, and so on. Regarding the Boolean framework, interestingly enough, Leibniz alluded to the creation of the totality, of God, 1, from the cipher, 0. And according to Frege, since nothing is usually attached to the concept "not identical with itself," 0 should be the number which belongs to the same concept.

The term *zero* harks back to "cipher" by way of the Hindu *Sunya* (= void, nothing, open), which, to repeat, is essentially in line with my use of "nothingness." As such zero *implies*—I do not say indicates or points to; though it is a sign, its "referent" precedes all signification—the absence of other mathematical signs. It does not "refer" to the nonpresence of "semiotically real" objects which are supposedly prior to, in a Platonic sense, the signs of which they are objects. Zero is simply a notation implying "nothingness." If notation there must be, the o, topologically speaking, will fit the bill quite well. The term *zero* is a *symbol (rheme* in the Peircean sense), but "o," also a symbol, is not exactly the equivalent of *zero.* "o" possesses the same status as other symbols nonetheless. As a sign among signs, it signifies, and unlike the vast majority of signs, it *signifies no-thing* (Rotman 1987). It is the void which Hermann Weyl (1949:75) envisioned when he qualified the Cartesian coordinates (o,o) with "o" as the midpoint between positive and negative integers as the "necessary residue of ego extinction." At this "point" the ego is collapsed into the continuum such that distinctions that were there are simply *no more.* But it is not "nothingness," as I use the term here, for there is a residue, a *noticed absence,* much like column II of figure 12, where the overlapping domains ABCDE . . . *n* remain dissolved in the soup of "o." Thus, although *zero,* given its relation to *sunya,* is more adequate to the task of signifying "nothingness," "o" can be used as a surrogate symbol.

Brian Rotman labels "o" a "metanumber." I would, in contrast, disqualify it as a number entirely, though, with Rotman, I would define it as pure potentiality for the infinite generation of integers—comparable to Bohm's implicate, Spencer-Brown's unmarked space, or Peirce's "nothingness." And, following Rotman (1987:19), zero is equivalent to, for example, the (asymptotic) "vanishing point" in Renaissance painting. The "vanishing point" functions like a visual zero to facilitate the generation of an infinite number of perspectives supposedly offering to the spectator the possibility of objectifying herself, of looking in as if from the outside as an omniscient seeing subject.

This quest for omniscience, for the possibility of an "outside" perspective, is delusory, however. Its base is a flimsy raft caught in a tossing and turning sea. It is like Sheffer's "stroke," stipulating that the entire universe of logic arises out of inconsistency, that there is neither one thing nor another, and not both not-this and not-that.[4] The edifice of dualisms previously standing straight and tall topple and disintegrate into myriad differences which move along with the ebbs of the tide and tend to fuse with the continuum. There is no some-*thing* that is prior to no-*thing,* the world prior to its representation, an identity prior to difference. That longed-for Oneness of all things, the union of opposites, is not of this world—i.e., the push toward absolute generality, regularity, law, will always remain incomplete. There are, in the "semiotically real" world, only differences, and differences of/in/among differences. Nothing necessarily precedes anything else, as if "o" preceded 1, 1 preceded −1, and −1 preceded "o." Neither is there, in this respect, any retrievable origin or center.

The whole infernal system reminds one of that short-lived but excellent TV program "The Prisoner." Patrick McGoohan, the main character, condemned to an amusement-park atmosphere with other ex–secret agents from all over the world, spends his time trying to escape and reveal the identity of No. 1, in whom total power presumably resides. He finally learns that he is No. 2, but he has no power: there is neither center nor focus of power; all is disseminated evenly throughout as differences. The system is, it appears, self-contained, self-regulatory, and self-organizing. The entire field of signs making up the system has created the very elaborate and labyrinthine set of objects they are believed to be denoting, naming, and representing. The vast illusion is now exposed: those objects are not anterior to the signs; the truths believed to be forthcoming through determinate lines of correspondence between signs and objects are chimerical; *"nothingness"* has revealed itself as the sole priority, whether regarding signs or things.

Yet we tend to carry on as if from some preordained point of origin, entering into conceptual space of ever-greater abstraction at each juncture. Perhaps this journey is inevitable. Everything that arises from "nothingness" is, Peirce repeatedly tells us, by way of inference, and, in the premises of this inquiry, of projection by dialogic self-consciousness. A *cut* or *mark* is made, and from that point an entire universe is generated. A cell comes into existence, which might form a minute part of the roots, the bark, the trunk, or the leaves of a tree consisting of countless cells. The tree's leaves fall, its branches are broken off and decompose, new branches are grown, roots drill ever deeper; there is incessant exchange of material between the tree and the atmosphere, between the roots and the chemicals of the soil; birds build nests in it, squirrels make a home, insects attack it, the logger cuts it down, or it finally dies and returns to the earth. This concatenation of elements and events making up the existence and life cycle of the tree is for practical purposes almost infinitely complex. Yet we have a mere sign, one symbol, "tree" in English, to qualify it. What power of abstraction! And this is one of our more menial examples of the mind's abstractive capacity. Ponder, for example, "democracy," "love," "$E = MC^2$," "deconstruction."

This tree, what exactly do we see when we see it *as* a "tree"? Our experience of it suggests at first blush purely immediate and direct perceptual awareness, devoid of all hypothetical elements. Attending more carefully to this percept reveals that our sensation yields a complex shape, colored patches, gentle to-and-fro motion, and so on. Combining these sensations into a whole by no means produces a "tree." We automatically, by embedded, habitual, inferential processes, endow the tree with a solid constituent beneath the bark, a root structure concealed underneath the surface of the ground, an obverse side which is not seen but is presupposed to be roughly comparable to the side of the "tree" open to view, and so on, even though there is no immediate empirical evidence for some of these inferences. We also assume the tree has self-identity, a certain permanence of existence. We ordinarily take it for granted that when we are not looking at the tree, it is there nonetheless. In short, we automatically go "beyond the information given" (Bruner 1957). This act of "construction" converts a complex of sensations into a "semiotically real" thing.

Of course there is no separate, completely autonomous entity tree, but myriad interconnecting cells making up a community, which is in turn interconnected with its environment. As nonduality, nonseparateness, emptiness of existence as a singular distinction, the so-called tree is really no "tree" at all. It has always been submerged in the vast undivided fabric, the *holomovement,* so to speak. The "tree's" coming into "existence" depends on the conditions of its initial environment, and its continued "existence" is equally dependent upon its surroundings. This "existence" is a composite stream, a convergence, divergence, involution, convolution, harmony, and dissonance, of an overwhelmingly intricate conglomerate of "world-lines." The tree is in this sense always already becoming in its interaction with its environment. It is, to avail myself of Deleuze and Guattari's rhetoric, carbon-dioxide-becoming, H_2O-becoming, soil-becoming, bird-becoming, squirrel-becoming, insect-becoming, sun-becoming, wind-becoming, lumberjack-becoming, and so on. It is a series of events rather than essence, process rather than product, flow rather than fact.

A mind can also be qualified as such a composite stream, though its structure and functions, unlike those of the tree, are nonempirical. The mind as stream has been suggested by both Eastern and Western philosophers (the Buddha, Nagarjuna, Hume, Peirce, James, Bergson, Whitehead). By inference this mind bifurcates zero into integers, 1 into -1, and the undivided into things whose "existence" depends upon their relation to what they *are not.* You see the "tree," "out there," from your living-room window, as a complex of happenings not because of a multiple sequence of mechanical cause-and-effect events, because God thinks it, or because your consciousness has "collapsed" billions upon billions of waves into particles. You see it as you do because it belongs to your "semiotically real" world, and reciprocally, you are as you are *to* it because you belong to its "semiotically real" world.

You are the sign that relates *to* it; it is the related sign that in turn relates *to* you; both of you are interpreters and interpretants, connectors and connected, subjects and objects, along the *semiosic* flow of all happenings.

Appendix I

From the notion that since a cut denies its content—i.e., what lies within the cut is severed from the rest of the sheet—Peirce derived his five "Alpha Rules of Transformation" (see Roberts 1973:40–45). The first rule is the Rule of Erasure (R1), "*Any evenly enclosed graph may be erased*," written thus:

$$(P \;(Q)) \;\rightleftharpoons\; (P)$$

which is a counterpart to Spencer-Brown's (1979:¶) "form of cancellation" by way of his Axiom 2, "*The value of a crossing made again is not the value of a crossing*," written:

$$\neg\rceil \;=\; \text{▦} \quad (\text{where } \text{▦} \text{ represents the "nothingness" from which the initial mark was made}).$$

In other words, in the Peirce equation, Q lies within two cuts, and if a cut denies its content, a double cut is the same as if there had been no cut.

Spencer-Brown's equation read right to left yields what he calls "compensation," which is comparable to Peirce's Rule of the Double Cut (R5), "*The double cut may be inserted around or removed (where it occurs) from any graph in any area*," such as:

$$X (P (Q)) \;\rightleftharpoons\; ((X (P (Q))))$$

Peirce's Rule of Iteration (R3), "*If a graph P occurs on the sheet of assertion or in a nest of cuts, it may be scribed on any area not part of P, which is contained by the set of all Ps*," can be written:

$$(P) \;\rightleftharpoons\; (PP)$$

Since a cut denies its content, the Rule of Iteration is closely related to the Rule of Insertion (R2), "*Any graph may be inscribed on any oddly enclosed area*," written:

$$(P (Q)) \;\rightleftharpoons\; (P X (Q))$$

That is, it makes no difference what graph is inscribed in the area in question, for that very graph is denied by the cut anyway. If read from right to left, the rules of iteration and insertion are comparable to Spencer-Brown's (1979:5) "form of condensation" by application of his Axiom 1, "*The value of a call made again is the value of a call*," which can be written:

$$\neg\rceil\,\neg\rceil = \neg\rceil$$

In other words, P can be inscribed again or X can be inscribed alongside P in any area where P is already inscribed in alternately nested cuts, and the graph will remain the same as it was. Reading Spencer-Brown's equation from right to left is "confirmation," which is a counterpart to Peirce's Rule of Deiteration (R4), *"Any graph whose occurrence could be the result of iteration may be erased,"* which is equivalent to reading the above graph representing the Rule of Iteration from right to left.

Appendix 2

Hartshorne, within a Peircean frame of reference, writes of the West's traditional "prejudice in favor of symmetry." This prejudice has been prevalent from the time of Plato and Pythagorean harmony, through classical mechanics and its metaphysical buttresses, to relativity theory and quantum mechanics. Recently, however, in microphysics, broken symmetries have been discovered, and current hypotheses, from the empirical macroscopic world to broad cosmologies, offer convincing arguments for an irreversible, indeterminate universe. Commensurate with this view, Peirce harbored a certain "prejudice in favor of asymmetry," which is evident from his "logic of relatives" to his evolutionary cosmology.

Nevertheless, referring specifically to the former, Hartshorne (1970:205) remarks that "it is clear to me that philosophers for the most part have yet to realize the importance of this logic for metaphysics or speculative philosophy." Hartshorne argues that any philosophy, logic, scientific hypothesis, or theoretical formulation in the social sciences and humanities has need of a "theory of relatives." Standard logic is clear on this point. There are one-place, two-place, three-place, and so on, predicates, depending upon the number of subjects required by a predicate. One-place predicates are absolute, and the remainder are relative. Peirce's categories entail the same distinction. Firstness (feeling-quality) is monistic, absolute; Secondness (reaction) and Thirdness (representation) are relative, and, according to Peirce, relations of higher order can be reduced at a minimum to Thirdness.

An important but neglected distinction—which is embodied in the "logic of relatives"—is between one-way and two-way relations, between asymmetry and symmetry, directed and directionless. Hartshorne proposes, against the current of metaphysics, that symmetry, rather than a supreme general principle, is a special case. In brief, (1) "$X = Y$" is symmetrical and directionless, while (2) "$X > Y$" is asymmetrical and directed. Contrary to common belief, (2) is actually more fundamental than (1), Hartshorne contends, since it is impossible to infer (2) from (1), or if the inference is made it will obviously be false. If (3) "$X \neq Y$" is given, on the other hand, it is impossible to know whether (4) "$X > Y$" and (5) "$Y > X$." In contrast, if (4) and (5) are given as both false, then (1) must be the case (Hartshorne 1970:206).

To emphasize his point, Hartshorne draws on existential relations of connectedness—cause-effect, objects-perception, preceding events–following events—which complement equality and greater-than relations. Suppose we know the meaning of a few words in a foreign language that are or can be one-way relations: *greater than, dominant-subservient, acting upon, temporality, knowing, loving, hating.* From these meanings, and provided we know the meaning of negation and conjunction, we can rather easily infer the meanings of their corresponding (roughly, though not formally) symmetrical terms: *equality, kings and subjects, interacting, now, mutually acquainted with, lovers, enemies.* Thus two things are equal if neither is greater than the other, kings are symmetrical with kings and subjects with subjects, interaction depends on one person acting upon another and vice versa, in the "now" nothing temporally succeeds anything else, knowing someone implies that that someone knows the knower, lovers love each other, and enemies garner mutual hatred. In contrast, the terms *equal, negation,* and *conjunction* do not imply one-way relations.

Hartshorne (1970:206) points out that

> taken as a dyadic operation of combining, conjunction is of course symmetrical or directionless, yet taken as a triadic relation between two propositions and the compound proposition produced by the operation, conjunction is less symmetrical than most propositional functions (such as *equivalence, either but not both,* etc.), and when negation is added to conjunction (as in *not both,* or *neither*) the highest degree of asymmetry or directionality is reached, and also the highest defining power since *not both, neither nor,* are (as Peirce was the first to see and Sheffer to publish) the only functions each of which, taken singly, can define all the others.

In other words, from Sheffer's "stroke," "|," and what Peirce calls the "ampheck," " ⅄," both of which entail maximum asymmetry and defining power, the fundamental logical connectives can be generated.[1] Thus the defining power of propositional functions varies inversely with their symmetry. For example, using Sheffer's "stroke" in the full sense, as does Hartshorne, the notation can be subsidived into "|," which signifies "not both" (Peirce's *alternate denial* via his amphek), and " ↓ ," which signifies "neither nor" (Peirce's *joint denial*). Given the expressions

(1) $(p \text{ "stroke" } p) = -p$

(2) $(p \downarrow p) = -p$

(1) would be written in English as (3), " 'Not both p and p' is the same as 'Not-p,' " and (2) as (4), " 'Neither p nor p' is the same as 'Not-p.' " The important point is that on the left side of the first two equations, the "Sheffer strokes" are used symmetrically and reflexively, and at the same time they "yield doubly asymmetrical expressions giving information about the proposition and showing how negation (and, in more complicated ways, all the functions) can be defined" (Hartshorne 1970:202). In other words, the left side of (1) involves a symmetrical dyadic relation, and when it is conjoined with the right side, a third instantiation of the sign p introduces an asymmetrical triadic relation. They are in this sense thus seen to be asymmetrical, the asymmetry of the triadic relation including a symmetrical dyadic relation. In addition, Hartshorne's example illustrates that the negation in question in (1) and (2) manifests "all the asymmetry a monary (unary, monadic) function could have" (Hartshorne 1970:210).

In a manner of speaking, "|" can be written as (5) "False if and only if both are true," and " ↓ " as (6) "True if and only if false." Then, conjoining (3) and (5) on the one hand, and (4) and (6) on the other, we have the proposition (7) "*p* on the right is false if and only if both *p*'s on the left are true-false"—i.e., there is an oscillation from one pole to the other. This is indeed significant. It reveals the asymmetry implied by the function of negation in the full sense. The left *p*'s are directly symmetrical with respect to the internal relations inherent in each equation, and when the equations are conjoined, a mirror symmetry is produced, which cannot "make up its mind," so to speak. It is neither symmetrical nor asymmetrical but somewhere in between. It exists at the boundary separating the reversible and timeless from the irreversible and temporal.

According to Spinoza, every definition of a boundary is a negation. The boundary can exist between presence/absence, integer/zero, positive/negative, inside/outside, inclusion/exclusion, and so on. The most precise form of negation, generally assumed to be unary and symmetrical, is found in Boolean algebra, which, in contemporary times, finds its expression in the binary code of the digital computer. The code is simple enough: "1" and "0," or "yes" and "no." In other words, "not-1" has no alternative but to mean "0," and vice versa. Digital computers can be programmed in such a manner that they become, like the conjunction of equations to yield (7), "schizophrenic," the victims of an "electronic paradox" (Spencer-Brown 1979), or "synchronizer glitch" (Wilden 1984). The current is reduced to flip-flopping, out of phase with the central processor, thus remaining in an undecided state between "yes" and "no," continuity and discontinuity, which can be compared to the Cretan liar paradox—the rough natural language equivalent of a Gödelian sentence. Spencer-Brown compares this state of affairs to what he terms *imaginary values* the likes of which are yielded by the equation "$X^2 + 1 = 0$," which is transposed to "$X^2 = -1$," and finally "$X = \sqrt{-1}$," where $\sqrt{-1}$, that amphibian between being and nonbeing as Leibniz put it, is the *imaginary* number, *i*. The equation, like the "schizophrenic" computer, is undecidable regarding its positive or negative value. Significantly—and rather surprisingly—$\sqrt{-1}$, ignored, stashed away in the closet, and deprecated by generations of mathematicians, is relevant to the "real" in many contemporary theories, namely, electromagnetism, relativity, and quantum mechanics.

Imaginary values shed light, Spencer-Brown (1979:xv–xvi) tells us,

> on our concepts of matter and time. It is, I guess, in the nature of us all to wonder why the universe appears just the way it does. Why, for example, does it not appear more symmetrical? Well, if you will be kind enough, and patient enough, to bear with me through the argument as it develops itself in this text, you will I think see, even though we begin it as symmetrically as we know how, that it becomes, of its own accord, less and less so as we proceed.

By way of Sheffer's definition of negation, as interpreted by Hartshorne, and in view of Spencer-Brown's remark, it becomes apparent that the dyad (symmetry) inherent in the two functions in equations (1) and (2) is essential to the superior defining power of the triadic (asymmetrical) functions. The general pattern, Hartshorne (1970:210) concludes, is symmetry from asymmetry, which he perceives as a paradigm for metaphysics according to which "what we are to look for in basic concepts is comprehensive asymmetry or directional order embracing a subordinate aspect of symmetry." At the same time, dyadic symmetry is necessary to render triadic asymmetry—i.e., oscillating truth values in (7)—unambiguous—i.e., *both* (5) *and* (6). That is, dyadic symmetry and triadic asymmetry, as we observed in chapter 6, are *complementary,* and, as we noted also in the discussion of disorder and chaos in chapter 5, asymmetry is more fundamental than symmetry.

Appendix 3

Many of the relations suggested in the fifth as well as preceding chapters are encapsulated in table 1. Moving from left to right, the columns progress from abstraction to concretion, from mind to effete mind, through number, space (A), time (B), process (C), relations (D), and the evolution of "semiotically real" worlds (E).

Firstness, Secondness, and Thirdness, as pure relations, are equidistant between columns C and E, which depicts their role as authors of the *becoming of being* and the *being of becoming. Symbols grow,* to repeat. As they grow, they take on *habit,* thus tending to gravitate toward the bottom of table 1. In a finite and fallible world, however, things are never so elegantly harmonious. Dissonances incessantly arise, from the "clash" of the "real" imposing its inevitable differences vis-à-vis "semiotic realities"—which parallels the difference between our overambitious ideals and our real capacities—thus demanding repeated alteration of the latter. Symbols can also *"de-generate"* (CP:1.540, 2.92, 3.359–62). The first degree of *de-generacy* yields an index and the second degree an icon (see Tursman 1987; Merrell 1990). The bad news is that symbols thus lose their vitality *as* symbols; the good news is that such *de-generacy* is essential to all change, whether involving a minor adjustment to a particular habit, a major overhaul, or its disposal altogether in order to try out something apparently novel, which promises to improve the state of affairs at hand.

There is a general push toward *vagueness* at the lower level; the scintillating holomovement which includes the implicate (nonselective) order of *possibilia.* The opposite push toward *generality* culminates also in atemporality of a different sort, which, from another perspective, is tantamount to the "zero-degree": the beginning is the end and the end the beginning.

TABLE I

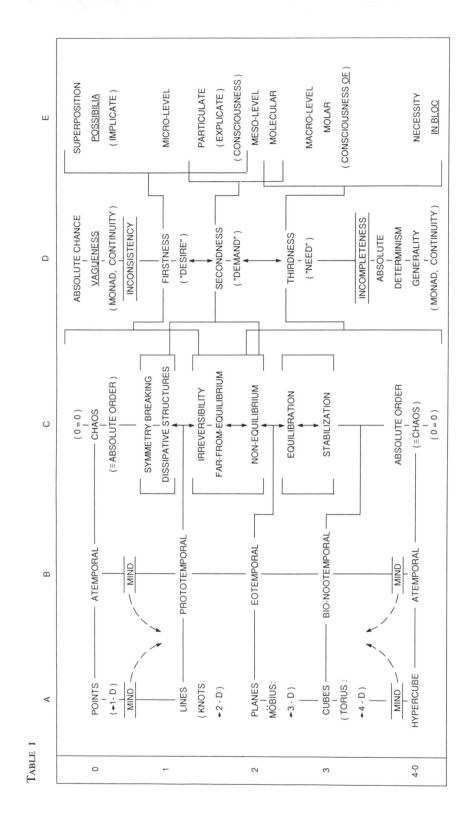

Notes

PREFACE

1. While rather critical of Peirce, Richard Rorty (1979) categorizes leading contemporary thinkers such as Dewey, Heidegger, and Wittgenstein as "antifoundationalists." Granted. The search for "foundations" in terms of understanding the world *sub specie aeternitatis* has been at long last abandoned. However, regarding, for example, Wittgenstein's case, the general verdict has it that groundings are the riverbed of language within "forms of life" rather than the bedrock of ultimate "foundations" in the classical sense. Language is a contextualized human activity constantly shifting with the ebbs and flows of the entire community of speakers. Add to this Peirce's notions of *evolution* and *self-correction,* and, though they evoke a nineteenth-century image of cumulative progress—after all, Peirce could not but exist within his own community, albeit at the margins—we have the idea that knowledge does not entail grasping some inner core but knowing how to think and act in a certain way. Peirce, it hardly needs stating, deserves a serious look in relation to Wittgenstein and other leading twentieth-century philosophers.

I. ASYMPTOTICALLY GETTING THERE

1. The "slash" between the "semiotically real" and the "actually real" will be highlighted throughout this inquiry. Although Peirce never used this pair of terms in the manner I do, the distinction between them, I would suggest, is in general commensurate with his doctrine of signs. They also fall in line with the thought of a large body of contemporary scientists and philosophers of science, as Einstein's (1950:98) words bear witness: "The sense experiences are the given subject matter. But the theory that shall interpret them is man-made. It is the result of an extremely laborious process of adaptation: hypothetical, never completely final, always subject to question and doubt." I will allude repeatedly to the "semiotically real" when referring to a particular world picture in common with a given individual and his community of knowers. The "actually real," in contrast, is the focus of the final or ultimate interpretant, which must remain inaccessible, as Peirce argued regarding his rather controversial "convergence theory" of truth, to a given individual or community.

2. This might appear to be a "coherence theory" of truth, but it is not. Rather, the relations between sentences determining their truth or falsity depend principally on *conventions* and *contexts,* as we shall note below.

3. I do not consider metaphysical statements and paradoxes to be meaningless or absurd as they are in the logical positivist framework. Rather, what is *regarded as* meaningless or absurd depends upon a particular time and place. Within another context, an apparent absurdity could well become the most profound of truths.

4. Such fictive constructs might imply, upon functioning as scientific metaphors or models (Black 1962; Hesse 1966), a potential for attaining increasing determinateness when successive "cuts" come into existence in the book of assertions, since the false propositions—inadequate aspects of the model—may in the future be successively canceled and the true ones retained (Roberts 1973:31–40).

5. For problems inherent in attempting to conceive of a world of higher dimensions than one's own, see Abbott's (1952) work on "Flatland," Burger's (1968) on "Sphere-land," and Rucker's (1977) insightful comments on both.

6. See Rescher (1978) for more detail. It is worthy of note that Peirce's notion of "cumulative knowledge," via his "convergence theory of truth," is relevant to the concept of "evolutionary epistemology," which in recent years has been subject to criticism (Radnitsky and Bartley 1987).

7. Admittedly, Peirce's use of the term *consciousness* is rather debatable, especially in light of recent work by Derrida (1973, 1974), among others. However, see Merrell (1985a) for a partial vindication of Peirce in this regard.

8. Spencer-Brown's *mark* is comparable to Niels Bohr's *theoretical distinction,* a partly arbitrary "cut," between the object and the physicist's instrument used to detect that object. Murdoch (1987:97–103) provides an enlightening discussion of the contradiction this "cut" creates between the classical (macroscopic) treatment of the instrument and the quantum-mechanical (microscopic) treatment of the object.

9. This "block" universe interpretation of relativity theory is admittedly controversial. See, for example, Capek's (1981) counterargument in the same volume.

10. Time-dependent considerations of truth and meaning variance go against the grain of most modern logic, an obvious exception being modal logic. Modern logic, especially since the early Wittgenstein, Russell, and Frege, is that of an omniscient and timeless being, the logician, for whom all possible world is the actual one. Peirce, on the other hand, considered logic, like Aristotelian and medieval time-dependent logic, to be a normative science. He believed in real possibilities and necessities of a particular person's knowledge at a particular time and place (CP:5.435ff., 6.367). Subsequently, he made a strong plea, though he himself never carried out the project, for a formal logic of time dimensions (Prior 1957).

11. In the 1930s, the terms *chronon* and *hodon* were invented for designating the atoms of time and space respectively. The value of the chronon was computed at between 10^{-21} and 10^{-24} seconds, and that of the hodon at 10^{-13} cm. Concerning these values, Capek (1961:231) suggests that

> for all practical purposes, and considered macroscopically, space and time are continuous: the duration of chronons is so insignificant that they may safely be equated with durationless instants; similarly, the difference between mathematical points and spatial regions of the radius 10^{-13} cm is entirely negligible on our macroscopic scale.

This, however, neither clears up the muddle between Hartshorne and Peirce nor makes the difference between the classical continuous space and time and its modern atomistic counterparts less radical. The last word on this, as on other debatable issues concerning quantum theory and relativity, is still up for grabs.

12. Regarding mathematics, interestingly enough, Einstein often mused that as far as propositions refer to "reality," they are not certain, and as far as they are certain, they do not refer to "reality." Eugene Wigner's (1969:138) words on the unintelligibility of such "reference" are especially revealing:

> The miracle of the appropriateness of the language of mathematics for the formulation of the laws of physics is a wonderful gift which we neither understand nor deserve. We should be grateful for it and hope that it will remain valid in future research and that it will extend, for better or for worse, to our pleasure even though perhaps also to our bafflement, to wide branches of learning.

13. W. V. O. Quine's (1960, 1969; also Gibson 1982, 1988; Romanos 1984) *radical intranslatability* and *inscrutability of reference* theses are germane to the issue at hand, though time and space do not allow for expatiation on this theme here.

14. For a sympathetic or mildly critical view of the Sapir-Whorf hypothesis, to which I shall return in chapter 7, see Black (1962:244–58), Penn (1972), Carroll (1964),

and an interesting study by Heynick (1983). For a critical view, see Fishman (1980, 1982). If the Sapir-Whorf hypothesis has its day, language and culture do all the work; the individual has hardly any say-so on the matter. "Reality," in the Sapir-Whorf conception, lends itself to a potential infinity of different classifications, and one learns to divide it up according to the implicit mandates of one's culture, but more particularly of one's language. Eleanor Rosch (1974, 1975a, 1975b, 1977, 1978), among others, places in question the existence of such linguistically fixed categories. They tend to become fuzzy and melt into one another, she contends, thus allowing for variations. And rather than arbitrary, they are by and large motivated.

Peirce would likely defer slightly toward Rosch's notion in his admission that "reality," as Secondness, *does* motivate: it forces itself upon the observer, bringing about interpretations which are at times contrary to her wishes. However, to reiterate, when considering the entire linguistic community, there will never be absolute agreement on the nature of "reality," hence a degree of arbitrariness, and therefore linguistic determinism, will inevitably prevail in any and all classificatory systems. Categories are not simply mental constructs in the head, though a lively give-and-take between the internally "real" and the externally "real" can and does lead to a victory—however ephemeral—of the latter over the former. In short, categories both produce and are the product of one's "semiotically real world," which sets the limits of the modus operandi one can employ in a continued attempt to cope with one's surroundings.

15. As Born (in Pais 1986:256) once put it: "It is necessary to drop completely the physical pictures of Schrödinger which aim at a revitalization of the classical continuum theory, to return only the formalism and to fill that with a new physical content."

16. One of the chief problems is, as suggested above, linguistic—and here perhaps Sapir-Whorf take center stage once again. In brief, the language of relativity portrays a continuous view of matter—the field concept—while the language of quantum theory propagates the atomistic view. The two languages have thus far proved to be by and large *formally contradictory* yet *complementary*—even though embracing this principle still tends to produce a profound cognitive dissonance.

17. In other words, the statement "Lemons are sour" can easily be put to the test by subjecting a lemon to the taste buds. But determinate meaning of the proposition is not to be found so easily. The range of all conceivable ramifications of this initial test must be exhausted, which include the chemical composition of citric acid, the pH factor of lemon juice, the ratio of H^+ ions to OH^- ions, the action of acidity on nerve endings on the tongue, impulses traveling from the taste buds to the brain, human cultural values regarding acidity in contrast to bitterness and sweetness, and so on. Each of these actual tests "out there" in the physical world implies, or directly involves, a subsequent proposition regarding what *would be* the case if certain conditions were to exist. The meaning of "Lemons are sour" cannot be exhausted short of an infinity of tests and generation of their respective propositions within pragmatic contexts.

Such proposition formulation and test procedures, however, are not always the product of intentional sign activity. For example, suppose a drug, x, reputed to help prevent cholesterol buildup, is released to across-the-counter pharmaceutical retailers. First, the "meaning" (i.e., use, which pragmatically endows the drug-as-sign with an interpretant, be it legitimate or not) of the drug is put to the test on the competitive market, and true to predictions, heart problems are lowered. Over time, consequently, habit is gradually developed on the part of the consumers. The drug's "meaning" becomes *embedded;* it is now purchased and used rather mindlessly (like a red traffic light, which, if disregarded, might subject one's car to a collision; therefore one stops the car by habit). For Peirce, what a sign "means" is ultimately determined by what *habit* is involved, which can be a bane and a boon. Without habit, community agreement and hence convention would be well-nigh impossible, but habit can also stultify, compelling one to mindless activity such that one is no longer conscious *of* one's motives and the consequences of one's actions (see Nesher 1983; Langer 1989).

In this sense, to speak of "semiotic reality" is to speak of relationships between a language—or other sign systems—and the "real." In the sentence " 'Photon' refers to a discrete packet of energy," there is discrimination between the sign being discussed and the signs used to discuss it. "Photon" signifies something presumably in the "real" world called a "discrete packet of energy." But notice that reference consists of a relation between the sign "photon" and the signs "packets of energy," not directly between signs and things "out there" that are nonsigns. In other words, the sign "photon" refers to its "semiotic object" in the "semiotically real." I use this particular example to stress the point that the signs a physicist uses to qualify his observations and the signs of his theoretical language, in concert, are not some pristine *mirror of the world*. They are *symbolic,* and they take on meaning and value in the interconnected system of interpretation. No observation has any meaning at all until it is interpreted by theory, convention, or habit. "Photons" are "semiotically real" not because they establish some mystical linkage between signs and the "real" but because physicists can speak about them, and their expectations regarding them can be fulfilled by means of their shared assumptions, conventions, and understandings: "photons" are the joint opinion of the community in Peirce's conception.

18. See Heelan (1970a, 1970b, 1971, 1983) for the context-dependency of "quantum logic"; also Merrell (1985a, 1990), where I develop this theme with respect to the semiotic perspective.

19. I should point out at this juncture that I by no means wish to imply that Peirce is everything to everybody. He was a helpless child of his times in certain respects, as we all are. Besides, modern thought can be traced back to a plethora of "sources." Einstein can be found in Spinoza, in Parmenides, in the Kabbala; Bohr can be found in Oriental thought, as can Schopenhauer from one angle, Whitehead from another, and Peirce from yet another. The list is inexhaustible. Holton's (1973) "themata" and Jung's "archetypes"—alluded to by physicist J. M. Jauch (1973)—are relevant here. If contemporary physics has picked up two contradictory "themata," one in quantum theory and another in relativity, I find it not at all surprising that Peirce's thought contains both, a contradiction he labored to resolve up to the end of his life.

20. The term *representation,* as it is used in logical positivist jargon, is rapidly becoming outmoded. I prefer to use *signification* but have remained with Peirce's term when it becomes necessary within the context of his writing.

21. Einstein's words are apropos in this respect:

> A human being is part of the whole, called by us "Universe"; a point limited in time and space. He experiences himself, his thoughts and feelings as something separated from the rest—a kind of optical delusion of his consciousness. This delusion is a kind of prison for us, restricting us to our personal desires and to affection for a few persons nearest us. Our task must be to free ourselves from this prison by widening our circle of compassion to embrace all living creatures and the whole of nature in its beauty. Nobody is able to achieve this completely but the striving for such achievement is, in itself, a part of the liberation and a foundation for inner secuity. (In Herbert 1985:250)

2. BOHM'S TROPOLOGY AND PEIRCE'S TYPOLOGY

1. For popularizations of the "new physics," see Capra (1975), Talbot (1980), and Zukav (1979)—dubbed vulgarizations by some (Bernstein 1982)—and for two captivating syntheses of relativity and the quantum world for laypersons, see Sachs (1988) and Davies (1988).

2. This phenomenon is related to the double-slit experiment, mentioned above, and especially the EPR experiment—so named after Einstein, Podolsky, and Rosen—designed in an effort to dislodge the Bohr-Copenhagen interpretation of quantum mechanics. Bohm is reported to have received his inspiration for "hidden variables" while musing over the nonlocalization implied by the EPR experiment (Hiley and Peat 1987:12–13).

3. Although Wheeler (1980a, 1982, 1984), I must add, is adamantly against "faster

than light travel" insofar as it is used to account for ESP and other comparable phenomena. I raise this point here, since I will briefly discuss Wheeler's view in chapters 5 and 6.

4. Bohm's rather Spinozist language of the *implicate* (*enfolded* within itself) and the *explicate* (*unfolded*) is, interestingly enough, also found in some of the early writings of Gilles Deleuze (especially 1968, 1969)—whose view, along with that of his collaborator, Félix Guattari, will be discussed in chapters 3 and 4. Deleuze often uses the terms to distinguish between inanimate and animate matter. The first is stable, the second metastable, involving a process of individuation in which difference differentiates itself, a virtuality constantly becoming actuality without ever becoming actualized, stable being.

5. However, Capek (1961, 1981), as well as Prigogine (1983:185–219)—to be discussed in chapter 5—argues against the artificiality of this static view, contending that time is not simply another dimension of space.

6. Bohm, though Hartshorne does not mention his name, is the chief proponent of the "hidden variables" thesis, which is grounded in the argument that the Copenhagen interpretation is incomplete, especially in light of its uncertainty principle (see Herbert 1985).

7. For Bohm, at the lowermost level of the holomovement, *both* the particle *and* the wave are implied, which is at once more primitive and more profound, Bohm proponents argue, than the Copenhagen interpretation (see Hiley and Peat 1987).

8. This example bears on Hilbert's "Hotel Paradox." The hotel, capable of accommodating an infinity of guests in its equal number of rooms, was filled to capacity on a particular day. The arrival of a new guest presented no problem for the manager. He simply had the occupant of room one move to room two, the occupant of that room move to room three, and so on. Then the new guest was placed in room one. By the same operation, an unlimited stream of new arrivals could be given a room. The hotel could never be filled! But, quite paradoxically, it *was filled,* since it already had an infinity of occupants.

9. I will further treat the topic of consciousness in light of speculations in contemporary physics in chapter 7.

10. The move during the 1970s was toward the idea that memories are distributed over the cortex. This concept has occasionally surfaced over the years. Karl Lashley (1951) speculated on the possibility of standing wave patterns set up by the interference of volleys of neural firing, much in the sense of Fourier transforms. Lashley did not specify, however, how such wave patterns could distribute a retrievable memory. D. O. Hebb (1949) agrees with Lashley, though he believes Lashley went too far in his denial that the same cells need to be excited to arouse the same perception. Pribram (1971, 1980, 1981, 1982), like Lashley, postulates that memories are laid down as interference patterns. Unlike Lashley, however, he has developed a specific model, the holograph, to illustrate his thesis. In brief, Pribram places the locus of neural interaction at junctions (synapses) between neurons. Neural junctions are activated from a "wavefront" which can simultaneously interfere with other such "wavefronts" in the same ensemble but originating in other parts of the nervous system. This interference constitutes the basis of his notion of information processing, or holography.

11. In this respect, and following Bohm, F. David Peat (1987:174) writes that

> our thoughts are the explicit forms thrown up by the underlying movements of the explicate order of mind. Like the vortex of a river, . . . thoughts have no absolute, independent existence of their own but are constantly being supported by the underlying process of their ground. Ultimately this movement of mind merges into that of matter so that the two should not be considered as dual aspects of nature but as arising out of the same underlying ground. . . . In this way it appears that individual minds have a common or collective origin that has something in common with that of matter. . . . [T]herefore, mind is able to act upon mind, and mind and matter exert an influence one on the other. But this should be thought of not as some form of causal *interaction* since individual minds, and mind and matter, are not fundamentally separate

but are simply the explicate forms that emerge out of a common, generative order. (See also Bohm 1987a:72–99)

In a comparable vein, Heisenberg (1958a:81) tells us, "Natural science does not simply describe and explain nature; it is a part of the interplay between nature and ourselves; it describes nature as exposed to our method of questioning."

12. I must mention that Pribram is now somewhat out of fashion, especially since his hypothesis has not yet been effectively validated (see Briggs and Peat 1989)—though one can only speculate on what he will offer in his soon-to-appear book. Besides, Bohm (1987b) has expressed reservations regarding certain limitations of the hologram model.

13. Interestingly enough, in this light, Peirce points out that in many cases of brain damage, recovery leads to a condition in which "other parts of the brain are made to do the work, after a fashion, with perhaps other parts of the body" (CP:7.376), which implies that the mind itself has not been impaired.

14. Regarding such "memory," see the thesis developed by Ilya Prigogine (Nicolis and Prigogine 1989), which will be the brief focus of attention in chapter 7.

15. Unlike Bohm, and the majority of physicists, a small group of avant-garde mavericks, including Musés (1977), Toben (1975), Walker (1970), Walker and Herbert (1977), Wigner (1967), and Wolf (1984), propose that "mind" or "consciousness" should be injected into quantum equations. They have produced elaborate mathematical explanations in their attempt to demonstrate the crucial role of consciousness at the microphysical level, which, above all else, has enticed a few "pop" physicists into mysticism and parapsychology. Other physicists, after putting forth wild conjectures, then inject a note of sobriety into their discourse, somewhat typical of which are the remarks of Geoffrey Chew (1968), author of the "bootstrap" hypothesis: "Carried to its logical extreme, the bootstrap conjecture implies that the existence of consciousness, along with all other aspects of nature, is necessary for self-consistency of the whole. Such a notion, although not obviously nonsensical, is patently unscientific."

Wheeler, as I mentioned in note 3 of this chapter, has been stridently opposed to such idealistic interpretations of quantum physics. Nonetheless, Skolimowski (1987:75), an ardent follower of Wheeler, observes that the philosophy of Karl Popper "appears to offer less and less for the newly emerging epistemological problems of quantum physics, especially for the conception of reality as co-extensive with the mind. Popper is an epistemological realist of the traditional kind, as he believes in a firm reality out there, a view the New Physics does not support" (see also Skolimowski 1986).

16. Of interest in this regard is the work of Kolers (1972), and the use of his empirical studies in a theory of aesthetic perception by Goodman (1978).

17. In like fashion, Peirce (CP:5.475) observes that the performance of a piece of music is a composite sign, a sort of holosign.

18. The river metaphor is a commonplace. It is also evoked by Bohm (1987b:34), and by physicist James Jeans, whose words bear citing:

> We may picture the world of reality as a deep-flowing stream; the world of appearance is its surface, below which we cannot see. Events deep down in the stream throw up bubbles and eddies on to the surface of the stream. These are the transfers of energy and radiation of our common life, which affect our sense and so activate our minds; below these lie deep waters which we can only know by inference. These bubbles and eddies show atomicity, but we know of no corresponding atomicity in the currents below. (In Commins and Linscott 1947:381)

3. THE TENUOUS "REALITY" OF SIGNS

1. Peirce's habit bears certain similarity to Rupert Sheldrake's (1988a) "morphic fields," though the analogy is easily stretched to its breaking point (in Sheldrake [1988b] he relates his "morphic field" idea directly to Peirce's habit). Sheldrake's controversial theory proposes that fields of information influence structures not only of living organisms

but of inorganic matter as well. All matter has an associated field of memory whose function is to guide the formation of structures. Molecules, crystals, plants, and animals all develop according to their proper form. If there were no fields of information and memory, there would simply be too many alternatives and contingencies for nature to exhibit the type of unity in diversity that is seen in the structures of matter and living things. The first time a new molecule is generated or a crystal grows, it follows a blind path down the valleys and hollows of its energy landscape, determined by the various local forces that operate on it. But this process also gives rise to a "morphic field," which is a kind of memory of the material processes involved. The next time this process occurs, it has the advantage, Sheldrake contends, of being guided by information from the morphic field. As repetitions accumulate, the field builds in strength and becomes more active in guiding the process. The effect is similar to Waddington's (1957) "chreodic paths," which are like skiers going down a slope. The first skier tentatively finds a path between trees, rocks, and broken terrain, which facilitates successive skiers, and finally a well-worn path develops, compelling them to follow certain pathways of least resistance. In a word, habit has exercised its force.

2. This was also the case during the structuralist euphoria of the mid-1960s with the appearance of relatively formal, parsimonious models for folklore and literary texts from Barthes (1966), Bremond (1966), Greimas (1966), Todorov (1966), et al.

3. See Gleick (1987) and Briggs and Peat (1989) for a layperson's account. I introduce the "physics of chaos" here for the sake of the following discussion. I turn attention specifically to nonlinearity and order from chaos in more detail in chapter 5 with respect to the holistic implications of Peirce's semiotics.

4. For the infatuation among scientists with harmony, simplicity, and elegant formulations, see Zee (1986) and Augros and Stanciu (1984), Wechsler (1978); also Girard (1984), who suggests that perhaps there is an inherent need to interpret disorder as order in myths.

5. I must guard against a potential misunderstanding of the terms *disorder, chaos,* and *randomness,* which, in their vulgar interpretation, do not escape ambiguity and even inconsistency, and in their most adequate usage inevitably remain fuzzy. In the first place, "randomness" cannot be determined. If a series is computed to the nth digit and no order is discovered, we still cannot be certain that the series is random, for there is no knowing whether $n + 1$ will evince some sort of order. In the second place, any tenable concept of "disorder" and "chaos" must be, in my estimation, subjective—it is we who perceive a meaning or pattern in a particular arrangement of symbols, the map of a city, a work of art, or a set of playing cards.

To the question, "Is a tropical forest ordered or disordered?" the answer, in this view, must be that there is an ecological process best qualified as *organized complexity,* though for a lonely human, unversed in ecological systems and wandering about on the jungle floor, disorder is sure to prevail. There is organization, though it appears disorderly, yet entropy is on the decrease, given the perpetual swim of all living systems against the inorganic stream toward entropy increase stipulated by the Second Law of Thermodynamics. On the other hand, an exothermic reaction leading to the crystallization of ions out of their aqueous solution is entropic, though it would appear to the nonchemist that the regular repetition of growth of units in the symmetrical lattice is orderly. When a gas expands from one vessel to another when the valve between the two is opened, the system becomes more uniformly distributed and symmetrical, hence it might appear ordered, though entropy is on the upswing (Denbigh and Denbigh 1985). In short, entropy cannot be appropriately related to disorder, in the subjective use of the term, which bears witness to the inevitable rift between mathematical language and our experienced world, between the "real" and a given "semiotically real" world.

6. I should mention at this point that Hjelmslev (1961), elaborating on somewhat of a linguistic counterpart to Bohm's quantum universe, distinguishes between unformed (implicate) matter and the substance shaped (explicated) by the forms of *expression* and

content. Deleuze and Guattari (1987:chap. 2), in parallel fashion, appropriate the Spinozistic concepts of *implication* and *explication, envelopment* and *development* for their own argument.

7. Deleuze and Guattari's "schizophrenic" must be taken literally as well as figuratively: literally insofar as this is the way society is, and figuratively insofar as the concept applies to all signs (minds as signs in contiguity with other signs).

8. See also Hofstadter (1979), who provides an extensive discussion along these lines regarding an ant colony, and Edward O Wilson (1971), for his work with ant colonies as complex organisms. This capacity of insect societies for organizing themselves toward a common goal is perhaps best illustrated in the work of Austrian Nobel laureate Karl von Frisch, who reports in *Animal Architecture* (1974) the case of a termite nest which had been covered by a plastic tent, resulting in diminished ventilation. Within forty-eight hours the insects had developed additional structures of a novel design which restored the old ventilation rate under the changed conditions. Obviously, information is transferred at the macrobranch of the evolution of life in terms of functions which may evolve independently of the exchange relations with the environment.

9. This does not contradict the loss of control to which I alluded in the last lines of the previous section. But especially in hierarchical living systems, as we shall observe below in a discussion of Prigogine, control brought about by dissipative structures can lead to order out of unpredictable and otherwise uncontrollable chaos.

10. In another way of putting it, Firstness as *abduction* is a possibility that presents itself for further speculation, inquiry, and thought. An *abduction* can then be linked to Secondness, *induction*, which is cumulative, becoming progressively more complex as the speaker's memory bank increases in size. Finally, the abduction-induction process gives way to Thirdness, *deduction*, which leads to the conclusion in what appears to be this relatively simple case of "it rains."

11. In his argument against the mirror of nature metaphor, Rorty might well have evoked Quine's (1969:26–86) "myth of a museum" in his own effort to debunk the positivist's faith in reference and univocal meaning. According to this "myth," exhibits are meanings and words are labels, and to switch languages is merely to change labels, meanings remaining invariant. Quine offers his celebrated dilemma of a field linguist attempting to translate a native expression, *gavagai,* as "rabbit," "undetached rabbit parts," or "a particular temporal stage in the rabbit's development." If the linguist does not know a single word in the native tongue, pointing, gestures, or any other mode of communication will not suffice for tranferring *gavagai* into the English language. There is simply no infallible empirical clue allowing us to determine reference or meaning in this and all such cases.

Historically, extension has been supposedly up-front and stalwart, intension uncertain and anemic. Now, Quine claims, both are inscrutable. Of course, within the parochial confines of our own language, extension continues to appear more reliable than intension, but this is not necessarily so: the empirical determinacy of extension, through time, cannot even be guaranteed within our own language. Thus for Quine, and more recently from Derrida's (1973) vantage, there is no experience that can provide data with which a statement can be absolutely verified. There are no data because there is no absolute *immediacy* or *presence*. This renders the meaning of the most basic of statements such as "That raven is black" simply undecidable, for they do not refer *instantaneously* to some independent empirical entity in the "real" world. In this view, we can do no more than gather up, *mediately* along the stream of time, an unruly collection of unfixed meanings and hope for the best. Reference is ultimately imaginary, or at most it is a linguistic act.

12. See Merrell (1982, 1983, 1985b, 1990) for further development of *embedded* and *automatized* sign processing and interpretation, which draws in large part from Polanyi's (1958, 1966) *focal* and *subsidiary* awareness as a component of *tacit knowing*.

13. Although, to repeat, relativity and quantum theory have not been effectively

united. Moreover, quantum theory remains mired in controversy; many of the problems have never been resolved to the general satisfaction of the scientific community.

14. For this distinction between intellectual and nonintellectual and conscious and nonconscious habit, see Nesher (1983) and Merrell (1990).

15. See Marty (1982) and Tursman (1987)—also Gorlée (1989)—for development of the topic of sign *generacy* as opposed to *de-generacy*, and use of the terms in this context.

4. SIGNS BECOMING MIND BECOMING SIGNS

1. See Peirce (CP:2.227–308), Tursman (1987:chap. 2), and Merrell (1990:chap. 2) for discussion of the sign types indicated by the integers 1, 2, and 3, which stand for Firstness, Secondness, and Thirdness. For the significance of 0, which precedes all signness, see Baer (1988).

2. This occurs by logical multiplication to yield 0, as in non-Boolean, nondistributive, context-dependent logic. Hence the one-way arrow from 0 to 1. And hence the radical asymmetry it implies. See Heelan (1970a, 1970b, 1971, 1983), also Merrell (1990), where I have written more extensively on this nondistributive, non-Boolean model.

3. Regarding the following pages, see Roberts (1973) for further discussion; also Merrell (1982) for development of a comparable theme regarding what I label "boundaried spaces."

4. However, Cull and Frank (1979) argue against the "arbitrariness" of Spencer-Brownian marks, a critique that could also be leveled against existential graphs.

5. Rucker (1977:120) observes that Borges's "refutation of time"—to which I shall turn in chapter 7—bears similarity to Gödel's (1949) argument, via Einsteinian relativity, for the unreality of time and change.

6. This bears on the notion that a degree of conceptual sloppiness is a necessary feature of empirical concepts (see, in Peirce studies, Swineburne [1969], and in philosophy of science, Feyerabend [1975]). Significantly, in this light, E. H. Hutten (1956:33) observes that "the demand for consistency [nonvagueness] is made by the logical law of contradiction—not both a and non-a—and completeness [generality] by the law of excluded middle—either a or non-a."

7. For example, Skagestad (1989; also 1983) effectively argues that a degree of fuzziness of concepts is necessary. Incommensurability is thus overcome by vagueness of all signs. If sign A and sign B were absolutely precise, then they would be absolutely different. Consequently, there could be no commensurability between them, and hence no possibility of moving from A to B (the Zeno problem once again).

8. Quite significantly, in this respect, Peirce (CP:6.172) tells us that "true generality is . . . nothing but a rudimentary form of true continuity. Continuity is nothing but perfect generality of a law of relationship."

9. This conception of differences is not Saussurean. I repeat, *similarities* and *differences* are more akin to Bateson's (1972) words: *differences that make a difference.* Peircean semiotic differences also bear comparison with Deleuze (1968) on "difference and repetition." Deleuze's Nietzschean-inspired concept of differences, rather than semiological signs as arbitrary entities referring to other signs, consists of differences based on physical forces (or Secondness). They are the product of a system of forces of which signs are *symptoms;* the study of signs is more properly a *symptomatology* than Saussurean semiology (see Bogue 1989:55–80).

10. Since Sheffer's "stroke" (and Peirce's formulation) implies incompatibility or inconsistency in the most fundamental sense, Whitehead (1938:52) tells us that it provides for "the whole movement of logic." And E. H. Hutten (1962:178) remarks that "it is the very essence of rationality to abolish contradictions; but logic—being the most rational thing in the world—is generated by contradiction."

11. I must point out that Rescher and Brandom (1979) give logically rigorous definitions to their terms, while I use them "rhetorically," for the purpose of generating discourse in natural rather than formal language. See Murdoch (1987:54–58) for the relation between "superposition" as I use the term and its use in the quantum theoretical formulation.

12. According to Deleuze and Guattari, everything is a machine, a part coupled to a second part, which in turn is coupled to a third part, and so on, in a binary connective synthesis forming chains of machines through which flows or fluxes pass. Every machine "is related to a continual material flow . . . that it cuts into," and "each associative flow must be seen as ideal, an endless flux" (Deleuze and Guattari 1983:43–44). These flows constitute a universal continuum of unceasing production. Regarding human machines, there is a flow of milk between a breast machine and a mouth machine, or a flow of words between a mouth machine and an ear machine. Regarding all machines, there are incessant flows of energy and information. Technical machines differ from human "desiring machines" in that they combine dependent parts into a whole which either functions efficiently or breaks down, while desiring machines are a heterogeneous concoction of chiefly independent parts which work only under conditions of chaos, dissipative structures, and bifurcations.

13. Further, in regard to figure 5, 1 is *microscopic*. This is the domain of consciousness, but it is not (yet) consciousness *of* such and such. It is feeling, quality. It presents the possibility of *abductions* as a result of perturbations in the experienced inner or outer "semiotically real" world. This experienced world, the world of immediate consciousness—without there (yet) being consciousness *of*—is analogous to Popper's (1972, 1974) World 2. Category 2 in figure 5 is *molecular,* the realm of individuals. With respect to language, it consists of sounds in the air or marks on paper without their (yet) having any meaning *for* someone in some respect or capacity. *Inductive* inferences arising from abductions are made possible in the counterpart to Popper's World 1 or physical "reality." World 1 is the "reality" of books as black marks on paper, mere physical existence. Only when read, that is, put to use, do they become actualized as signs, as something *for* somebody *in* some respect or capacity. Otherwise, they are possible signs. As quality, they are the immediacy of signness (World 2) without yet having gained entrance *into* any specific consciousness. Category 3 is *molar,* incorporating aggregates of individuals from 2 made possible by 1. This is the realm of *would be's,* of *deductive* inferences, of signs about other signs and signs countering other signs, which, in their highest form, are the equivalent of Popper's counterarguments in World 3. In sum, 1 as microscopic is pure *energy,* 2 is *matter,* and 3 is *meaning,* which corresponds effectively to Peirce's Firstness, Secondness, and Thirdness (see also Bohm 1987a:72–99).

14. Significantly, complex (imaginary) numbers, incorporated into figure 7, are employed in the description of superpositions, and the two dimensions of the complex number system are intimately related to the three dimensions of space. In this sense the complex plane becomes the fourth dimension of imaginary time in the space-time continuum (see Penrose 1977, 1987).

15. Recall also note 13 of this chapter. I must hasten to point out, though briefly, that Popper's thought departs from that of Peirce insofar as (1) he propagates a variation of the Cartesian brain/mind split (Popper and Eccles 1977), (2) his "objective knowledge" (Popper 1972) is devoid of the subjective component in Peirce's "objective idealism," (3) his not-so-naive realism (Popper 1982), though predicated on a Peirce-like indeterminism, is closer to the empirical tenets of logical positivism—of course, Popper would deny this—than Peirce. The fact remains, however, that in many respects there are striking affinities between Popper and Peirce (Freeman and Skolimowski 1974; Freeman 1983).

16. This concept has surfaced repeatedly in recent times. To cite merely a few instances: "Man ultimately finds nothing more in things than he himself has laid in them—this process of finding again is science, the actual process of laying a meaning in things, is art, religion, love, pride" (Nietzsche 1913:103). Rorty (1982:xlii) observes that

Sartre, Dewey, Foucault, and James, in addition to Nietzsche, collectively conclude that "there is nothing deep down inside us except what we have put there ourselves." One of the most telling and straightforward comments on this theme is found in the work of Eddington (1978:200–201):

> All through the physical world runs that unknown content, which must surely be the stuff of our consciousness. . . . Where science has progressed the farthest, the mind has but regained from nature that which the mind has put into nature.
> We have found a strange foot-print on the shores of the unknown. We have devised profound theories, one after another, to account for its origin. At last, we have succeeded in reconstructing the creature that made the foot-print. And Lo! it is our own.

All of which reminds one of Borges's (1964b:93) man who set out to construct a map of the world: "For many years he filled a space with images of provinces, kingdoms, mountains, shores, ships, islands, fish, rooms, instruments, stars, horses, and persons. Shortly before dying he discovered in this patient labyrinth on his map the outline of his own face."

17. Interestingly enough, in this light, Popper's arguments plus their respective counterarguments, as scientific hypotheses and refutations, must continue ad infinitum, for we can know only what *is not* the case.

5. MEDIATING FALLIBLY

1. With reason Peirce solemnly declared that there can be no final interpretant *for* the immanent sign user. Moreover, Peirce's "mind of some vast consciousness" as all-sufficient and self-sufficient is also in-sufficient for finitistic thinking. It can be accounted for solely with infinitistic thinking of the Cantor set sort: Aleph $+ 1 =$ Aleph $\rightarrow$ Aleph $+ 2 =$ Aleph $\rightarrow$ Aleph $+ 3 =$ Aleph . . . n. The sign of infinity engulfs any and all integers in the series, and in so doing it always remains the same as it was.

2. To give an idea of the magnitude of all possible semiostates, cyberneticist Stafford Beer once calculated that the brain considered as a digital device would possess the capacity for 10^{10^9} possible brain states. For practical purposes this number can be described as countably infinite even if Beer erred to the tune of a few billion. By comparison, the number of electrons in the universe is estimated to be a mere 10^{120} (Fraser 1979:114).

3. This superposition of semiostates and their "collapse" into a state of awareness is comparable to Bohm's *backgrounded* (the implicate) and *foregrounded* (the explicate), as described in chapters 1 and 2 (see also Merrell 1983, 1990).

4. The terms are used by Lacan (1966, 1977; also Wilden 1968). Although I do not follow Lacan's definitions, I have appropriated his terms for the context of this discussion.

5. Yet I do not subscribe to Hofstadter's algorithmic view of mind according to which it is sufficient to compute an algorithm (or perhaps the end product of an algorithm) in order to determine whether thoughts, or even consciousness, have been developed during the implementation of that algorithm. This is an operational or Turing test by means of questions and answers between the investigator and the object of investigation (considered as a mere computing device) which will eventually lead to a determination of the level of awareness or consciousness of the object (see Penrose 1987).

6. This "clash" is brought about when an unexpected item of the community-generated "semiotically real," or the "real" itself, happens to pop up in the interaction between the individual self and its *other* in confrontation with the external *Other*.

7. It bears mentioning at this juncture that in spite of the differences between Wheeler, Prigogine, Bohm, and Peirce, their thesis on the *evolution of laws* draws them together (regarding the general twentieth-century scientific view in this respect, see Briggs and Peat 1989).

8. See also Bohm (1957) for such "swerving" of an actual series of events from the ideal dictated by physical laws.

9. It is conceded today that there is hardly any hope of actually carrying out a program of absolute certainty leading to the exact and true value of a continuous physical quantity on account of the subtlety and complexity of nature. Few investigators in the nineteenth century even dared speculate on the possibility that the classical quest for certainty was a deluded dream, that there are perpetual and spontaneous random fluctuations. Peirce was an exception in this respect. After citing Epicurus, he writes that "we now see clearly that the peculiar function of the molecular hypothesis in physics is to open an entry for the calculus or probabilities." And later, he observes:

> Try to verify any law of nature, and you will find that the more precise your observations, the more certain they will be to show irregular departure from the law. We are accustomed to ascribe these, and I do not say wrongly, to errors of observation; yet we cannot usually account for such errors in any antecedently probable way. Trace their causes back far enough, and you will be forced to admit they are always due to arbitrary determination, or chance. (CP:6.46)

The development of statistical mechanics and kinetic theory of heat ultimately provided the proper context for acceptance of Peirce's reservations about classical determinacy, but unfortunately, rejection of the kinetic theory did not come about until the early years of this century. Consequently, Peirce has been given little credit for his path-breaking efforts (see Suppes 1984:83–84).

10. Interestingly enough, Peirce claims that synechism flatly denies Parmenides' universe, declaring that being "is a matter of more or less, so as to merge insensibly into nothing" (CP:7.569).

11. For a discussion of the relevance of hypercycles to *semiosis*, see Merrell (1990; Merrell and Anderson 1989b).

12. Schrödinger invented what he called a "ridiculous example" with which to debunk the Copenhagen interpretation of quantum mechanics:

> A cat is placed in a steel chamber, together with the following hellish contraption. . . . A Geiger counter contains a tiny amount of radioactive substance, so tiny that within an hour one of the atoms may decay, but it is equally probable that none will decay. If one decays the counter will . . . activate the little hammer which will break a container of cyanide. (Schrödinger, in Layzer 1990:106)

According to the Copenhagen interpretation, at the end of an hour, the cat-plus-hellish-contraption will be half in the state "cat alive, bottle intact" and half in the state "cat dead, bottle broken." This apparently contradictory situation was Schrödinger's method of demonstrating that Bohr and his cohorts were on the wrong track. According to quantum physics, a system can change in two completely different ways: while it is not being observed it evolves continuously and predictably—which was Schrödinger's preference—but if a measurement is carried out to discover which of its discrete states the system is "actually" in, its state changes discontinuously and unpredictably—the Copenhagen view. At the end of the experiment, the cat must be in one of its two possible states, and which one it is in is a matter of chance (for a layperson's account, see Gribbin 1984).

6. FROM A BROADER POINT OF VIEW

1. At this juncture I should point out that relatively recent cognitive studies are generally based on the dualistic premise that the mind can be studied independently of the brain, that psychology's focus on "software" is independent of neurophysiology, which focuses on "hardware" (see Fodor 1968, 1975; Johnson-Laird 1983; Miller, Galanter, and Pribram 1960; Oatley 1978; Putnam 1960). The course of this trend has been changing during the past few years, however, about which I will have some brief observations below.

2. See Murphey's (1961) interpretation of Peirce, though Murphey was criticized, unjustly I believe, by Riley (1968), who argues that Peirce was never an epistemological or ontological idealist—as Murphey claimed he was—during his early years, and later dropped his idealism for an epistemological realism.

3. This is tantamount to the paradox, introduced in chapter 1, of the *selective* and *nonselective* domains. The problem inevitably arises when two incompatible frameworks—finitude and the infinite in this case—are artificially thrown into the same mixing bowl. It is the problem, as I have intimated often throughout this essay, existing at the root of all holistic, cosmological visions.

4. Almeder concludes, nonetheless, that, contrary to Peirce, both epistemological realism and objective idealism as they are traditionally defined cannot be consistently endorsed. Epistemological realism presupposes a slash between mind and the world's furniture, while objective idealism dissolves that slash with the claim that everything is mind. One asserts what the other denies; one is a full-blown dualism or pluralism, the other a radical monism. They appear to defy synthesis, which is precisely what Peirce claims to do. Regardless of how one reads Peirce, Almeder argues, a "tragic flaw" remains, namely, his belief that the property of mind is irreducible to a property of matter. As Peirce would have it, however, everything in the universe consists of some sort of psychic energy, which apparently subsumes epistemological realism into an idealism devoid of true individuals. In this sense epistemological realism, according to Peirce's use of the term, is radically distinct from the term's ordinary usage. Even if one embraces Peirce's unorthodox nomenclature, Almeder continues, it is difficult to comprehend how one can take the next giant step to construe everything as mindlike: if some things are mindlike and therefore irreducible to a property of matter, would it not equally follow that some things are not mindlike? Almeder (1980:184–85) concedes that though Peirce's belief is not necessarily false, he nevertheless did not effectively argue his point.

5. Saussure (1966:82–88) used the example of the stem of a plant considered in terms of either its longitudinal development or a cross-section at a given point along the stem for illustrating diachrony and synchrony respectively. I could use the term *system* instead of *organism* with respect to Saussure, but *system* would be more relevant to synchrony, in the strict Saussurean sense, which has been associated with *structure*—though Saussure did not use the latter term.

6. There have been heated debates among cognitive psychologists and intelligence researchers concerning the process of thinking. Some hypotheses from artificial intelligence assign an epiphenomenal role to the perception of images on the assumption that the base components making up an image consist in atomic "bits" of information which combine to form abstract propositional structures. That is, according to this hypothesis, picturelike entities are not stored in memory. They can, however, be constructed by recombining a set of atomic "bits" to form holistic patterns (analogous to the ideal language of the logical positivists which begins with fundamental atomic propositions and combines them into logically cogent arguments). In this sense our "seeing" relations between things in our perceived world is dependent upon our ability to "say" them by means of propositions and with an explicit code—that is, the relations are dependent upon our possession of some sort of language (Anderson and Bower 1973; Collins and Quillian 1972).

Critics of this view reject such a complete dependency of images or "pictures" on propositional structures. They argue in favor of "dual coding" according to which conceptual and propositional messages are conveyed by means of a linearly generated digital language consisting in discrete entities, while analog (iconic) images form a distinct but complementary mode of communication. There always exists a degree of interaction between the two, but neither is clearly dependent upon the other. According to this notion, "seeing" and "saying" are distinct but complementary activities (Neisser 1967; Paivio 1969, 1971).

On the other hand, some theorists working in the information-processing tradition have suggested that there may exist a form of representation which differs radically from both sensory iconic patterns and linear verbal-propositional descriptions. In this light, Z. W. Pylyshyn (1973:7) concurs that

> the need to postulate a more abstract representation—one which resembles neither pictures nor words and is not accessible to subjective experience—is unavoidable. As long as we recognize that people can go from mental pictures to mental words or vice versa, we are forced to conclude that there must be representation (which is more abstract and not available to conscious experience) which encompasses both. There must, in other words, be some common format or interlingua.

According to this hypothesis, a relatively simple set of *symbol structures* can provide for a parsimonious account both of thought images and of the deep structure of language. There must be some common principle underlying our "seeing" relations and our "saying" them. At some level, "seeing" and understanding what is "seen" is equivalent in structure to "saying" and understanding what is "said" (Fodor 1975).

7. The moiré effect is appropriate to the model of *semiosis* developed in this inquiry. A particular style of "op art," moiré results from the creation of optical effects through the manipulation of geometric forms, color dissonance, and kinetic elements to exploit visual illusions. The effect is produced by a surface kinetic which sets off a two-dimensional surface into an apparently three-dimensional pulsation, much like a collection of Necker cubes on a sheet oscillating between the two possible actualizations. It is comparable also to the hologram, Bohm's image of the holomovement, and Jenny's dancing grains of sand; there is perpetual scintillating movement, but no overall change (see Ulmer's [1985] pedagogical application of the moiré and other related phenomena).

8. Commensurate with irreversibility, this blackened grain in the camera is recorded, a hypothesis is supposedly verified, a paper is written and published, the scientific community applauds, the author eventually gets a write-up in *Scientific American* and a few lines in the *New York Times* and *Time* magazine, and plush government grants are suddenly forthcoming. All because of a solitary photon! Ah, the power of the sign.

9. Physics I is that of Galilean-Newtonian mechanics, physics II of relativity–quantum theory, and physics III Wheeler terms "meaning physics," which calls for an exploitation of language itself, which is, in the final analysis, the only "reality" we can know, that is, the "semiotically real."

7. THE SPECTRUM OF MIND-SIGN

1. Among the various compatibilities and divergences between Peirce and Popper to which I have alluded above, Peirce's "refutation" constitutes one of the most evident zones of overlap. In Peirce's (CP:1.120) words:

> The best hypothesis, in the sense of the one most recommending itself to the inquirer, is the one which can be the most readily refuted if it is false. This far outweighs the trifling merit of being likely. For after all, what is a *likely* hypothesis? It is one which falls in with our preconceived ideas. But these may be wrong. Their errors are just what the scientific man is out gunning for more particularly. But if a hypothesis can quickly and easily be cleared away so as to go toward leaving the field free for the main struggle, this is an immense advantage. (CP:1.120; see Rescher 1978 for further discussion)

2. By the end of the nineteenth century it was considered in many quarters that the quest for Absolute Truth was nearing its end point, and that the physicist's task was merely that of, so to speak, calculating the next decimal point. Prima facie this calls to mind Peirce's asymptote model. While Peirce was somewhat off the mark in this respect (see Suppes 1984), there is a fundamental difference between his conception of the investigative community and the general turn-of-the-century attitude toward the future of the classical *episteme*. In the first place, Peirce was already a vehement critic of the

classical paradigm, especially regarding its mechanistically oriented determinism. Second, Peirce was always explicit concerning the impossibility of any finite number of human beings' ever coming into possession of the Grand Prize. And third, Peirce held that, though the asymptote generally described a fairly smooth curve, he also admitted to fits and jerks, and even catastrophes, all of which serves further to substantiate his indeterminacy of meaning.

3. I refer here not simply to mysticism in contrast to rational thought or to the Freudian consciousness/unconsciousness dichotomy per se, but rather to the distinction conveyed in general by the likes of Conant (1964), Cassirer (1953–57), Geertz (1973, 1983), Langer (1942), and Northrop (1946) (see also the synthesis by Wilber [1977]). Nonetheless, as implied above, this general concept is in a certain manner germane to much Eastern thought. It is revealed in D. T. Suzuki's (1971:131) words that, in the beginning,

> the will wants to know itself, and consciousness is awakened, and with the awakening of consciousness the will is split in two. The one will, whole and complete in itself, is now at once actor and observer. Conflict is inevitable; for the actor now wants to be free from the limitations under which he has been obliged to put himself in his desire for consciousness. He has in one sense been enabled to see, but at the same time there is something which he, as observer, cannot see.

4. In general, the "radical meaning variance" theory of science propagated by the likes of Feyerabend (1975), Hanson (1958), and Kuhn (1970) posits that any and all theories are invariably language-bound, world view–bound, and dependent upon particular cultural contexts of discourse.

5. The use of *symbolism* and *symbols* in this regard is not that of Peirce's symbol, which, in conjunction with the index and icon, makes up his most general class of signs. I do not, of course, wish to disparage Peirce's notion of the symbol, but to foreground the West's penchant for abstraction, for hypertrophying symbols to the extent that they are presumed to be coterminous with the "actually real."

6. Contemporary conventionalism, of which the Sapir-Whorf hypothesis is a powerful expression, had its beginning in the nineteenth century. It was formulated by, among others, Poincaré to account for the emergence of non-Euclidean geometries and phenomena that could not be explained by classical physics. In the twentieth century, conventionalism was taken a giant step further with the corollary that language uniquely determines the nature and structure of the perceived and conceived world, and that by internalizing different languages, one is thereby creating different pictures of "reality."

7. Arthur Burks (1980:283) puts forth the homology that "an individual man is to the ultimate community of knowledge seekers as an individual sign is to the complete and living system of signs, or language." He goes so far as to say that language in man is a genetic program, and that man is ultimately an algorithm. This reductionistic computer model stretches the analogy between man and sign to the breaking point. Peirce was actually against mind as an algorithm machine, especially at the abductive level.

8. Fairbanks (1976:19) suggests that we accept this and other such apparently outlandish statements literally "to see their more interesting philosophical implications." I don't know whether Peirce intended his words to be construed literally or not, but I would guess the latter.

9. I refer the reader once again to Dunne (1934) and Matte Blanco (1975), whose consciousness within consciousness reduplicates the image of the map paradox.

10. Perhaps no contemporary philosopher has stressed the fundamental importance of distinguishing the two modes of knowing more than Whitehead, whose voice has occasionally, though fleetingly, been overheard in this book. Abstraction and a bifurcation of the seamless fabric of the universe belong to the Western way which has mistaken those abstractions for concrete reality, thus committing the "fallacy of misplaced concreteness."

11. This is much in keeping with J. J. Gibson (1950, 1966, 1979) and Quine (1960, 1969), who refer to perception as reactions at nerve endings.

12. Significantly enough, in this regard, Sebeok (1979:xiii) observes that all "survival-machines," all cells, are only a sign's way of making another sign, which recalls the words of François Jacob that the dream of a bacterium is to make another bacterium.

13. Sachs goes on to point out that Buber's relations are comparable to Bohr's complementarity. See Agassi (1986) for a further discussion of Buber and complementarity.

14. Margenau, I must hasten to add, concedes that he indulges in a measure of speculation that will be questioned by many readers, though he maintains that his speculation is logically rigorous and consistent. The same conclusion, he adds, can be rephrased "in less mathematical form" in the other two of his three approaches.

15. Interestingly enough, a collection of papers on the "many worlds interpretation" of quantum theory, edited by DeWitt and Graham (1973), opens with an aphorism taken from Borges's short story "The Garden of Forking Paths," which is a strikingly faithful image of Hugh Everett's hypothesis.

16. Thus Schrödinger (1967:165) states that the multiplicity of individual minds "is only apparent, in truth there is only one Mind." And he uses that most common of analogies, the mirror, to illustrate the split of one into two, subject and object, interpreter and interpretant, which is actually but one. As Varela (1975:22) puts it:

> In finding the world as we do, we forget all we did to find it as such, and when we are reminded of it in retracing our steps back to indication, we find little more than a mirror-to-mirror image of ourselves and the world. In contrast with what is commonly assumed, a description, when carefully inspected, reveals the properties of the observer. We, observers, distinguish ourselves precisely by distinguishing what we apparently are not, the world.

This, of course, comes within a hair of Rorty's "Mirror of Nature" fallacy, as does Peirce's allusion to "man's glassy essence," to which I referred in chapter 3. However, see Varela (1984a) for an "antifoundationalist" statement regarding his hypothesis.

8. NOTHING AND EVERYTHING

1. *Sunya* plus the suffix *ta* can be translated as "ness"—"nothingness," voidness, openness. But to contrast "nothingness" to somethingness is to fall into binary "thing" thinking once again. "Nothingness" is, most simply, Plato's shadow on an unilluminated wall of the cave. The problem is that we generally tend to see "things" as either A or not-A. If a child is good, he is not bad; this is the power and pathos of conceptualization. "Nothingness," in contrast, is free of all things and concepts.

2. As mentioned briefly in the previous chapter, the laws of nature, rather than static, are the result of evolution (CP:6.13; 7.514–15), hence we cannot pin these laws down for all time (CP:7.514). In fact, not only logic but time itself is the product of the evolutionary process (CP:6.189, 6.200, 6.214, 8.318). Moreover, for Peirce the evolution of the universe is hyperbolic (CP:8.317), which is commensurate with his asymptote model.

3. This flattening of language by razing all hierarchical metalinguistic schemes can be viewed as an extension of the "limitative theorems" of Gödel and others (DeLong 1970), the "radical meaning variance" theorists' critique of logical positivism's metalanguage hypothesis and its distinction between observation language and theoretical language (Feyerabend 1975; Hanson 1958; Kuhn 1970), and the complementarity principle's requiring distinct context-dependent languages within an encompassing framework (Heelan 1983).

4. The origin as absence is not the mark of prior presence. Whiteness (the blank page) is the presence (juxtaposition) of all colors, and blackness the absence. The white

sheet is a *potentia* from which all colors (signs) of varying wavelengths can be generated. But the sheet itself is nothing; it is "nothingness," which is perhaps most adequately stated as *both* presence *and* absence, *both* blackness *and* whiteness.

APPENDIX 2

1. For brief comparisons of Peirce and Sheffer, see Bochenski (1961), Church (1956), and Kneale and Kneale (1962).

References

Abbott, Edwin A.
  1952. *Flatland*. New York: Dover.
Abe, Masao
  1985. *Zen and Western Thought*. Honolulu: University of Hawaii Press.
Abraham, Ralph, and Christopher D. Shaw
  1982. *Dynamics: The Geometry of Behavior*. Santa Cruz: Arial Press.
Agassi, Joseph
  1986. "The Consolation of Science." *American Philosophical Quarterly*, 23, 129–41.
Almeder, Robert
  1980. *The Philosophy of Charles S. Peirce. A Critical Introduction*. Totowa, N.J.:
    Rowman and Littlefield.
Anderson, J. R., and G. H. Bower
  1973. *Human Associative Memory*. New York: V. H. Winston.
Apel, Karl-Otto
  1981. *Charles S. Peirce: From Pragmatism to Pragmaticism*, trans. J. M. Krois.
    Amherst: University of Massachusetts Press.
Arbib, Michael A., and Mary Hesse
  1986. *The Construction of Reality*. Cambridge: Cambridge University Press.
Ashby, W. Ross
  1954. *Design for a Brain*. New York: John Wiley.
Augros, Robert M., and George N. Stanciu
  1984. *The New Story of Science*. Lake Bluff, Ill.: Regnery Gateway.
Aune, Bruce
  1971. "Two Theories of Scientific Knowledge." *Critica*, 5 (13), 3–20.
Baer, Eugen
  1988. *Medical Semiotics*. Lanham, Md.: University Press of America.
  1989. "Constructing Reality." *Semiotica*, 73 (1/2), 137–44.
Barnett, Lincoln
  1979. *The Universe and Dr. Einstein*. Rev. ed. New York: William Morrow.
Barrow, John D., and Frank J. Tipler
  1986. *The Anthropic Cosmological Principle*. Oxford: Oxford University Press.
Barthes, Roland
  1966. "Introduction a l'analyse structurale des récits." *Communications*, 8, 1–27.
Bartley, W. W., III
  1984. *The Retreat to Commitment*. 2nd ed. LaSalle, Ill.: Open Court.
  1987. "A Refutation of the Alleged Refutation of Comprehensively Critical Rational-
    ism." In *Evolutionary Epistemology, Rationality and the Sociology of Knowledge*,
    ed. G. Radnitsky and W. W. Bartley III, 313–41. LaSalle, Ill.: Open Court.
Bateson, Gregory
  1958. *Naven*. 2nd ed. Stanford: Stanford University Press.
  1972. *Steps to an Ecology of Mind*. New York: Chandler.
Baynes, Kenneth, James Bohman, and Thomas McCarthy (eds.)
  1987. *After Philosophy: End or Transformation?* Cambridge: MIT.
Beckett, Samuel
  1955. *Molloy, Malone Dies, The Unnamable*. New York: Grove.

Beer, Stafford
1959. *Cybernetics and Management*. New York: John Wiley.
Bernstein, Jeremy
1982. *Science Observed: Essays out of My Mind*. New York: Basic.
Bernstein, Richard
1964. "Peirce's Theory of Perception." In *Studies in the Philosophy of Charles Sanders Peirce*, ed. E. C. Moore and R. S. Robin, 165–89. Amherst: University of Massachusetts Press.
1983. *Beyond Objectivity and Relativism: Science, Hermeneutics, and Praxis*. Philadelphia: University of Pennsylvania Press.
Berry, George D. W.
1952. "Peirce's Contribution to the Logic of Statements and Quantifiers." In *Studies in the Philosophy of Charles Sanders Peirce*, ed. P. P. Wiener and F. H. Young, 143–52. Cambridge: Harvard University Press.
Bertalanffy, Ludwig von
1968. *General System Theory*. New York: Braziller.
Black, Max
1962. *Models and Metaphors*. Ithaca: Cornell University Press.
Blofeld, J. (trans.)
1958. *The Zen Teaching of Huang Po*. New York: Grove.
Bloor, David
1976. *Knowledge and Social Imagery*. London: Routledge and Kegan Paul.
1983. *Wittgenstein: A Social Theory of Knowledge*. New York: Columbia University Press.
Bochenski, I. M.
1961. *A History of Formal Logic*, trans. I Thomas. Notre Dame: University of Notre Dame Press.
Bogue, Ronald
1989. *Deleuze and Guattari*. London: Routledge and Kegan Paul.
Bohm, David
1951. *Quantum Theory*. New York: Prentice-Hall.
1957. *Causality and Chance in Modern Physics*. Philadelphia: University of Pennsylvania Press.
1965. *The Special Theory of Relativity*. New York: W. A. Benjamin.
1977. "The Implicate or Enfolded Order: A New Order for Physics." In *Mind in Nature: Essays on the Interface of Science and Philosophy*, ed. J. B. Cobb, Jr., and D. R. Griffin, 37–42. Washington: University Press of America.
1980. *Wholeness and the Implicate Order*. London: Routledge and Kegan Paul.
1986. "Time and the Implicate Order, and Pre-Space." In *Physics and the Ultimate Significance of Time: Bohm, Prigogine, and Process Philosophy*, ed. D. R. Griffin, 177–208. Albany: State University of New York Press.
1987a. *Unfolding Meaning*. London: Routledge and Kegan Paul.
1987b. "Hidden Variables and the Implicate Order." In *Quantum Implications: Essays in Honour of David Bohm*, ed. D. Hiley and F. D. Peat, 33–45. London: Routledge and Kegan Paul.
Bohm, David, and F. David Peat
1987. *Science, Order, and Creativity*. New York: Bantam.
Bohr, Niels
1934. *Atomic Theory and the Description of Nature*. Cambridge: Cambridge University Press.
Boler, John P.
1964. "Habits of Thought." In *Studies in the Philosophy of Charles Sanders Peirce*, ed. E. C. Moore and R. S. Robin, 382–400. Amherst: University of Massachusetts Press.

Borges, Jorge Luis

1962. *Labyrinths: Selected Stories and Other Writings*, ed. D. A. Yates and J. E. Irby. New York: New Directions.

1964a. *Other Inquisitions, 1937–1952*, trans. R. L. C. Simms. Austin: University of Texas Press.

1964b. *Dreamtigers*, trans. M. Boyer and H. Morland. Austin: University of Texas Press.

Born, Max

1949. "Einstein's Statistical Theories." In *Albert Einstein: Philosopher-Scientist*, vol. I, ed. P. A. Schilpp, 163–77. LaSalle, Ill.: Open Court.

Boulding, Kenneth E.

1956. *The Image: Knowledge in Life and Society*. Ann Arbor: University of Michigan Press.

1978. *Ecodynamics: A New Theory of Societal Evolution*. Beverly Hills: Sage.

Bremond, Claude

1966. "La Logique des possibles narratifs." *Communications*, 8, 66–76.

Briggs, John, and F. David Peat

1984. *Looking Glass Universe: The Emerging Sciences of Wholeness*. New York: Simon and Schuster.

1989. *Turbulent Mirror*. New York: Harper and Row.

Broglie, Louis de

1939. *Matter and Light: The New Physics*, trans. W. H. Johnson. New York: W. W. Norton.

1953. *The Revolution in Physics*. New York: Noonday.

1955. *Physics and Microphysics*, trans. M. Davidson. New York: Pantheon Books.

1962. *New Perspectives in Physics*, trans. A. J. Pomerans. New York: Basic Books.

Bruner, Jerome

1957. "Going beyond the Information Given." In *Contemporary Approaches to Cognition: A Symposium Held at the University of Colorado*, 41–69. Cambridge: Harvard University Press.

Buber, Martin

1958. *I and Thou*. New York: Charles Scribner's Sons.

Burger, Dionys

1968. *Sphereland: A Fantasy about Curved Space and an Expanding Universe*, trans. C. J. Reinboldt. New York: Thomas Y. Crowell.

Burks, Arthur W.

1980. "Man: Sign or Algorithm? A Rhetorical Analysis of Peirce's Semiotics." *Transactions of the Charles S. Peirce Society*, 16 (4), 279–92.

Campbell, Jeremy

1982. *Grammatical Man: Information, Entropy, Language, and Life*. New York: Simon and Schuster.

Capek, Milic

1961. *The Philosophical Impact of Contemporary Physics*. New York: Van Nostrand.

1981. "Time in Relativity Theory: Arguments for a Philosophy of Becoming." In *The Voices of Time*, ed. J. T. Fraser, 434–54. Amherst: University of Massachusetts Press.

Capra, Fritjof

1975. *The Tao of Physics*. Berkeley: Shambhala.

Carroll, John B.

1964. *Language and Thought*. Englewood Cliffs, N.J.: Prentice-Hall.

Cassirer, Ernst

1953–57. *The Philosophy of Symbolic Forms*, trans. R. Manheim. 3 vols. New Haven: Yale University Press.

Chew, Geoffrey
1968. "Bootstrap: A Scientific Idea?" *Science,* 161, 762–65.
Church, Alonzo
1956. *Introduction to Mathematical Logic.* Princeton: Princeton University Press.
Clément, Catherine
1983. *The Lives and Legends of Jacques Lacan,* trans. A. Goldhammer. New York: Columbia University Press.
Clifford, James, and George E. Marcus (eds.)
1986. *Writing Culture: The Practice and Politics of Ethnography.* Berkeley: University of California Press.
Cohen, Jonathan L.
1962. *The Diversity of Meaning.* London: Methuen.
Collins, A. M., and T. Pinch
1982. *Frames of Meaning: The Social Construction of Extra-Ordinary Science.* London: Routledge and Kegan Paul.
Collins, A. M., and M. R. Quillian
1972. "How to Make a Language User." In *Organization in Memory,* ed. E. Tulving and W. Donaldson, 310–51. New York: Academic Press.
Comfort, Alex
1984. *Reality and Empathy: Physics, Mind, and Science in the 21st Century.* Albany: State University of New York Press.
Commins, Saxe, and R. N. Linscott (eds.)
1947. *Man and the Universe: The Philosophers of Science.* New York: Random House.
Conant, James B.
1964. *Two Modes of Thought.* New York: Simon and Schuster.
Corning, Peter A.
1983. *The Synergism Hypothesis: A Theory of Progressive Evolution.* New York: McGraw-Hill.
Costa de Beauregard, Olivier
1981. "Time in Relativity Theory: Arguments for a Philosophy of Being." In *The Voices of Time,* ed. J. T. Fraser, 417–33. Amherst: University of Massachusetts Press.
Cull, Paul, and William Frank
1979. "Flaws of Form." *International Journal of General Systems,* 5, 201–11.
Dantzig, Tobias
1930. *Number: The Language of Science.* 4th ed. New York: The Free Press.
Davies, Paul
1988. *The Cosmic Blueprint.* New York: Simon and Schuster.
Davis, James
1972. *Peirce's Epistemology.* The Hague: Martinus Nijhoff.
Deikman, A.
1966. "De-Automatization and the Mystical Experience." *Psychiatry,* 29, 329–43.
Deleuze, Gilles
1968. *Différence et repetition.* Paris: PUF.
1969. *Logique du sens.* Paris: Minuit.
1986. *Cinema I: The Movement-Image,* trans. H. Tomlinson and B. Habberjam. Minneapolis: University of Minnesota Press.
Deleuze, Gilles, and Félix Guattari
1983. *Anti-Oedipus: Capitalism and Schizophrenia, I.* Minneapolis: University of Minnesota Press.
1987. *A Thousand Plateaus: Capitalism and Schizophrenia, II,* trans. B. Massumi. Minneapolis: University of Minnesota Press.
Deleuze, Gilles, and Claire Parnet

1987. *Dialogues*, trans. H. Tomlinson and B. Habberjam. New York: Columbia University Press.

DeLong, Howard
1970. *A Profile of Mathematical Logic*. New York: Addison-Wesley.

Denbigh, K. G., and J. S. Denbigh
1985. *Entropy in Relation to Incomplete Knowledge*. Cambridge: Cambridge University Press.

Derrida, Jacques
1973. *Speech and Phenomena, and Other Essays on Husserl's Theory of Signs*, trans. D. B. Allison. Evanston: Northwestern University Press.
1974. *Of Grammatology*, trans. G. C. Spivak. Baltimore: Johns Hopkins University Press.
1978. *Writing and Difference*, trans. A. Bass. Chicago: University of Chicago Press.

Descartes, René
1644. *Principles of Philosophy, IV*, trans. V. R. Miller and R. P. Miller. Dordrecht, Holland: D. Reidel.

DeWitt, Bryce S.
1968. "Reversion of the 2-Sphere." In *Battelle Rencontres*, ed. C. M. Dewitt and J. A. Wheeler, 546–57. New York: W. A. Benjamin.

DeWitt, Bryce S., and Neill Graham (eds.)
1973. *The Many-Worlds Interpretation of Quantum Mechanics*. Princeton: Princeton University Press.

Diana, Paul
1948. *Philosophy of Mind in Sixth Century China*. Stanford: Stanford University Press.

Dunne, J. W.
1934. *The Serial Universe*. London: Faber and Faber.

Eco, Umberto
1984. *Semiotics and the Philosophy of Language*. Bloomington: Indiana University Press.

Eddington, Arthur
1953. *Fundamental Theory*. Cambridge: Cambridge University Press.
1958a. *The Philosophy of Physical Science*. Ann Arbor: University of Michigan Press.
1958b. *The Nature of the Physical World*. Ann Arbor: University of Michigan Press.
1978. *Space, Time, and Gravitation*. Cambridge: Cambridge University Press.

Eigen, Manfred
1971. "Self-Organization of Matter and the Evolution of Biological Macromolecules." *Naturwissenschaften*, 58, 465–523.

Eigen, M., and P. Schuster
1979. *The Hypercycle: A Principle of Natural Self-Organization*. New York: Springer-Verlag.

Einstein, Albert
1949. "Autobiographical Notes." In *Albert Einstein: Philosopher-Scientist*, vol. 1, ed. P. A. Schilpp, 1–95. New York: Harper.
1950. *Out of My Later Years*. New York: Philosophical Library.

Eisele, Carolyn
1979. *Studies in the Scientific and Mathematical Philosophy of Charles S. Peirce*. The Hague: Mouton.

Escher, Maurits C.
1971. "Approaches to Infinity." In *The World of M. C. Escher*, 15–16. New York: Harry N. Abrams.

Fairbanks, Matthew J.
1976. "Peirce on Man as a Language: A Textual Interpretation." *Transactions of the Charles S. Peirce Society*, 12 (1), 18–32.

Feyerabend, Paul
　1958. "Complementarity." *Proceedings of the Aristotelian Society Supplement,* 32, 75–104.
　1975. *Against Method.* London: NLB.
Feynman, Richard P.
　1967. *The Character of Physical Law.* Cambridge: MIT.
Finkelstein, David
　1969. "Matter, Space, and Logic." In *Boston Studies in the Philosophy of Science,* vol. 1, ed. M. Wartofsky and R. Cohen, 199–215. New York: Humanities Press.
Fishman, J. A.
　1980. "The Whorfian Hypothesis: Varieties of Valuation, Confirmation, and Disconfirmation." *International Journal of the Sociology of Language,* 26, 25–40.
　1982. "Whorfianism of the Third Kind: Ethnolinguistic Diversity as a Worldwide Societal Asset." *Language in Society,* 11, 1–14.
Fodor, Jerry A.
　1968. *Psychological Explanation.* New York: Random House.
　1975. *The Language of Thought.* Sussex: Harvester Press.
Foucault, Michel
　1970. *The Order of Things.* New York: Pantheon.
Fraser, J. T.
　1979. *Time as Conflict: A Scientific and Humanistic Study.* Basel: Birkhäuser.
　1982. *The Genesis and Evolution of Time: A Critique of Interpretation in Physics.* Amherst: University of Massachusetts Press.
Freeman, Eugene
　1983. "C. S. Peirce and Objectivity in Philosophy." In *The Relevance of Charles Peirce,* ed. E. Freeman, 59–79. LaSalle, Ill.: Monist Library of Philosophers.
Freeman, Eugene, and Henryk Skolimowski
　1974. "The Search for Objectivity in Peirce and Popper." In *The Philosophy of Karl Popper,* ed. P. A. Schilpp, 464–519. LaSalle, Ill.: Open Court.
Frege, Gottlob
　1919. "Negation." In *Logical Investigations,* trans. P. T. Geach and R. H. Stoothoff, ed. P. T. Geach, 31–53. Oxford: Blackwell, 1977.
　1974. *The Foundations of Arithmetic,* trans. J. L. Austin. Oxford: Blackwell.
Freud, Sigmund
　1925. "Negation." In *The Complete Psychological Works of Sigmund Freud* (Standard Edition), ed. J. Strachey, vol. 19, 235–39. London: Hogarth Press, 1953–74.
Frisch, Karl von
　1974. *Animal Architecture.* New York: Harcourt, Brace, Jovanovich.
Gallie, W. B.
　1952. "Peirce's Pragmatism." In *Studies in the Philosophy of Charles Sanders Peirce,* ed. P. P. Wiener and F. H. Young, 61–75. Cambridge: Harvard University Press.
Gardner, Howard
　1987. *The Mind's New Science: A History of the Cognitive Revolution.* 2nd ed. New York: Basic Books.
Geertz, Clifford
　1973. *The Interpretation of Cultures.* New York: Basic Books.
　1983. *Local Knowledge: Further Essays in Interpretive Anthropology.* New York: Basic Books.
Gerach, Robert
　1978. *General Relativity from A to B.* Chicago: University of Chicago Press.
Gibson, James Jerome
　1950. *The Perception of the Visual World.* Boston: Houghton-Mifflin.
　1966. *The Senses Considered as Visual Systems.* Boston: Houghton-Mifflin.
　1979. *The Ecological Approach to Visual Perception.* Boston: Houghton-Mifflin.

Gibson, Roger F., Jr.
  1982. *The Philosophy of W. V. Quine*. Tampa: University Presses of Florida.
  1988. *Enlightened Empiricism: An Examination of W. V. Quine's Theory of Knowledge*. Tampa: University Presses of Florida.
Girard, René
  1984. "Disorder and Order in Mythology." In *Disorder and Order* (Proceedings of the Stanford International Symposium), ed. P. Livingston, 80–97. Saratoga, Calif.: Anma Libri.
Gleick, James
  1987. *Chaos: Making a New Science*. New York: Viking.
Gödel, Kurt
  1949. "A Remark about the Relationship between Relativity Theory and Idealistic Philosophy." In *Albert Einstein: Philosopher-Scientist*, vol. 2, ed. P. A. Schilpp, 557–62. LaSalle, Ill.: Open Court.
Gombrich, E. H.
  1960. *Art and Illusion*. Princeton: Princeton University Press.
  1979. *The Sense of Order: A Study in the Psychology of Decorative Art*. Ithaca: Cornell University Press.
Goodman, Nelson
  1978. *Ways of Worldmaking*. Indianapolis: Hackett.
Gorlée, Dinda
  1989. "Degeneracy: A Reading of Peirce's Writing." 4th World Congress of the International Association for Semiotic Studies, Perpignan, France, April 4.
Gregory, Bruce
  1988. *Inventing Reality: Physics as Language*. New York: John Wiley.
Greimas, A. J.
  1966. "Eléments pour une théorie de l'interprétation du récit mythique." *Communications*, 8, 28–59.
Greimas, A. J., and J. Courtés
  1982. *Semiotics and Language: An Analytical Dictionary*, trans. L. Crist et al. Bloomington: Indiana University Press.
Gribbin, John
  1984. *In Search of Schrödinger's Cat: Quantum Physics and Reality*. New York: Bantam.
Griffin, David Ray
  1988. *The Reenchantment of Science: Postmodern Proposals*. Albany: State University of New York Press.
Grünbaum, Adolph
  1967. *Modern Science and Zeno's Paradoxes*. Middletown, Conn.: Wesleyan University Press.
Guattari, Félix
  1984. *Molecular Revolution: Psychiatry and Politics*, trans. R. Sheed. New York: Penguin.
Hacking, Ian
  1985. "Styles of Scientific Reasoning." In *Post-Analytic Philosophy*, ed. J. Rajchman and C. West, 145–65. New York: Columbia University Press.
Hadamard, Jacques
  1945. *The Psychology of Invention in the Mathematical Field*. Princeton: Princeton University Press.
Haken, Hermann
  1978. *Synergetics*. New York: Springer-Verlag.
  1980. *Dynamics of Synergetic Systems*. New York: Springer-Verlag.
Hanson, Norwood R.
  1958. *Patterns of Discovery*. Cambridge: Cambridge University Press.

Hartshorne, Charles

1952. "The Relativity of Nonrelativity: Some Reflections on Firstness." In *Studies in the Philosophy of Charles Sanders Peirce*, ed. P. P. Wiener and F. H. Young, 215–24. Cambridge: Harvard University Press.

1964. "Charles Peirce's 'One Contribution to Philosophy' and His Most Serious Mistake." In *Studies in the Philosophy of Charles Sanders Peirce*, ed. E. C. Moore and R. S. Robin, 455–74. Amherst: University of Massachusetts Press.

1970. *Creative Synthesis and Philosophic Method*. LaSalle, Ill.: Open Court.

1973. "Charles Peirce and Quantum Mechanics." *Transactions of the Charles S. Peirce Society*, 9 (4), 191–201.

1983. "A Revision of Peirce's Categories." In *The Relevance of Charles Peirce*, ed. E. Freeman, 80–92. LaSalle, Ill.: Monist Library of Philosophers.

1984. *Omnipotence and Other Theological Mistakes*. Albany: State University of New York Press.

Hayward, Jeremy W.

1984. *Perceiving Ordinary Magic: Science and Intuitive Wisdom*. Boulder, Colo.: Shambhala.

1987. *Shifting Worlds, Changing Minds*. Boston: Shambhala.

Hebb, D. O.

1949. *Organization of Behavior*. New York: John Wiley.

Heelan, Patrick

1970a. "Complementarity, Context-Dependence, and Quantum Logic." *Foundations of Physics*, 1 (2), 95–100.

1970b. "Quantum and Classical Logic: Their Respective Roles." *Synthese*, 21, 2–33.

1971. "Logic of Framework Transpositions." *International Philosophical Quarterly*, 11, 314–34.

1983. *Space-Perception and the Philosophy of Science*. Berkeley: University of California Press.

Heisenberg, Werner

1958a. *Physics and Philosophy*. New York: Harper and Row.

1958b. *The Physicist's Conception of Nature*. New York: Harcourt, Brace.

Herbert, Nick

1985. *Quantum Reality: Beyond the New Physics*. Garden City, N.Y.: Anchor.

Hesse, Mary

1966. *Models and Analogies in Science*. Notre Dame: University of Notre Dame Press.

Heynick, Frank

1983. "From Einstein to Whorf: Space, Time, Matter, and Reference Frames in Physical and Linguistic Relativity." *Semiotica*, 45 (1/2), 35–64.

Hiley, B. J., and F. David Peat

1987. "General Introduction: The Development of David Bohm's Ideas from the Plasma to the Implicate Order." In *Quantum Implications: Essays in Honour of David Bohm*, ed. B. J. Hiley and F. D. Peat, 1–32. London: Routledge and Kegan Paul.

Hjelmslev, Louis

1961. *Prolegomena to a Theory of Language*, trans. F. J. Whitfield. Madison: University of Wisconsin Press.

Hofstadter, Douglas R.

1979. *Gödel, Escher, Bach: An Eternal Golden Braid*. New York: Basic Books.

Holmes, Larry

1964. "Prolegomena to Peirce's Philosophy of Mind." In *Studies in the Philosophy of Charles Sanders Peirce*, ed. E. C. Moore and R. S. Robin, 359–81. Amherst: University of Massachusetts Press.

Holton, Gerald

1973. *Thematic Origins of Scientific Thought: Kepler to Einstein.* Cambridge: Harvard University Press.

Hookway, Christopher
1985. *Peirce.* London: Routledge and Kegan Paul.

Hunt, Lynn (ed.)
1989. *The New Cultural History.* Berkeley: University of California Press.

Huntington, Edward V.
1929. *The Continuum, and Other Types of Serial Order.* Cambridge: Harvard University Press.

Hutten, E. H.
1956. *The Language of Modern Physics: An Introduction to the Philosophy of Science.* London: George Allen and Unwin.
1962. *The Origins of Science: An Inquiry into the Foundations of Western Thought.* London: George Allen and Unwin.

Huxley, Aldous
1981. "Foreword." In *Mystics as a Force for Change,* by Sisirkumar Ghose, xi–xvi. Wheaton, Ill.: Theosophical.

Jakobson, Roman
1972. "Verbal Communication." In *Communication: A Scientific American Book,* 39–42. San Francisco: W. H. Freeman.

James, William
1948. *Some Problems of Philosophy.* London: Longmans, Green.
1968. *The Writings of William James.* New York: Modern Library.

Jantsch, Erich
1980. *The Self-Organizing Universe: Scientific and Human Implications of the Emerging Paradigm of Evolution.* Oxford: Pergamon.

Jauch, J. M.
1973. *Are Quanta Real?* Bloomington: Indiana University Press.

Jeans, James
1943. *Physics and Philosophy.* Cambridge: Cambridge University Press.
1958. *The Mysterious Universe.* Cambridge: Cambridge University Press.

Jenny, Hans
1967. *Cymatics: The Structural Dynamics of Waves and Vibrations.* Basel: Basilius.

Johnson-Laird, P. N.
1983. *Mental Models: Towards a Cognitive Science of Language, Inference, and Consciousness.* Cambridge: Harvard University Press.

Jung, Carl G.
1963. *Mysterium Conjunctionis,* trans. R. F. C. Hull. New York: Pantheon.

Kant, Immanuel
1781. *Kant's Critique of Pure Reason,* trans. N. K. Smith. New York: St. Martin's Press, 1963.

Kauffman, Louis H.
1986. "Self Reference and Recursive Forms." *Journal of Social Biological Structure,* 9, 1–21.

Kauffman, Louis H., and Francisco J. Varela
1980. "Form Dynamics." *Journal of Social Biological Structure,* 3, 171–206.

Kneale, William, and Martha Kneale
1962. *The Development of Logic.* Oxford: Clarendon.

Kolers, Paul
1972. *Aspects of Motion Perception.* New York: Pergamon Press.

Korzybski, Alfred
1941. *Science and Sanity: An Introduction to Non-Aristotelian Systems and General Semantics.* Lancaster, Pa.: The International Non-Aristotelian Library.

Kuhn, Thomas S.

1970. *The Structure of Scientific Revolutions*. Chicago: University of Chicago Press.

Lacan, Jacques

1966. *Ecrits*. Paris: Seuil.

1977. *The Four Fundamental Concepts of Psycho-Analysis*, trans. A. Sheridan. New York: W. W. Norton.

LaCapra, Dominick

1983. *Rethinking Intellectual History: Texts, Contexts, Language*. Ithaca: Cornell University Press.

Lakatos, Imre

1976. *Proofs and Refutations: The Logic of Mathematical Discovery*, ed. J. Worrall and E. Zohar. Cambridge: Cambridge University Press.

Langer, Ellen J.

1989. *Mindfulness*. Reading, Mass.: Addison-Wesley.

Langer, Suzanne K.

1942. *Philosophy in a New Key: A Study in the Symbolism of Reason, Rite, and Art*. New York: New American Library.

Lashley, Karl S.

1951. "The Problem of Serial Order in Behavior." In *Cerebral Mechanisms in Behavior: The Hixon Symposium*, ed. L. A. Jeffres, 112–36. New York: John Wiley.

Layzer, David

1990. *Cosmogenesis: The Growth of Order in the Universe*. Oxford: Oxford University Press.

Leatherdale, W. H.

1974. *The Role of Analogy, Model and Metaphor in Science*. Amsterdam: North-Holland.

LeShan, Lawrence, and Henry Margenau

1982. *Einstein's Space and van Gogh's Sky: Physical Reality and Beyond*. New York: Macmillan.

Levin, Samuel R.

1976. "Concerning What Kind of Speech Act a Poem Is." In *Pragmatics of Language and Literature*, ed. T. A. van Dijk, 141–60. Amsterdam: North-Holland.

Lewis, David

1973. *Counterfactuals*. Cambridge: Harvard University Press.

Lyotard, Jean-François

1984. *The Postmodern Condition: A Report on Knowledge*, trans. G. Bennington and B. Massumi. Minneapolis: University of Minnesota Press.

MacCormac, Earl R.

1976. *Metaphor and Myth in Science and Religion*. Durham, N.C.: Duke University Press.

1985. *A Cognitive Theory of Metaphor*. Cambridge: MIT Press.

McCulloch, Warren Sturgis

1965. *Embodiments of Mind*. Cambridge: MIT.

McKeon, Charles K.

1952. "Peirce's Scotistic Realism." In *The Philosophy of Charles Sanders Peirce*, ed. P. P. Wiener and F. H. Young, 238–50. Cambridge: Harvard University Press.

McTaggart, J. M. E.

1927. *The Nature of Existence*. Cambridge: Cambridge University Press.

Mandelbrot, Benoit

1982. *The Fractal Geometry of Nature*. San Francisco: Freeman.

Margenau, Henry

1987. *The Miracle of Existence*. Boston: Shambhala.

Margolis, Joseph

1986. *Pragmatics without Foundations*. New York: Blackwell.

Marty, Robert
   1982. "C. S. Peirce's Phaneroscopy and Semiotics." *Semiotica,* 41 (1/4), 169–81.
Matte Blanco, Ignacio
   1975. *The Unconscious as Infinite Sets: An Essay in Bi-Logic.* London: Duckworth.
Maturana, Humberto, and Francisco Varela
   1980. *Autopoiesis and Cognition: The Realization of the Living.* Dordrecht, Holland:
      D. Reidel.
   1987. *The Tree of Knowledge: The Biological Roots of Human Understanding.* Boston:
      Shambhala.
Merrell, Floyd
   1982. *Semiotic Foundations: Steps toward an Epistemology of Written Texts.*
      Bloomington: Indiana University Press.
   1983. *Pararealities: The Nature of Our Fictions and How We Know Them.* Amster-
      dam: John Benjamins.
   1985a. *Deconstruction Reframed.* West Lafayette: Purdue University Press.
   1985b. *A Semiotic Theory of Texts.* Berlin: Mouton de Gruyter.
   1987. "Of Position Papers, Paradigms, and Paradoxes." *Semiotica,* 65 (3/4),
      191–223.
   1990. "Self-Excited Signs: Semiosis in the Postmodern Age" (unpublished manu-
      script).
   1991. "Sign, Textuality, World" (in press).
Merrell, Floyd, and Myrdene Anderson
   1989a. "Shifting Worlds, Semiotic Modeling." 4th World Congress of the International
      Association for Semiotic Studies, Barcelona, Spain, March 30.
   1989b. "Superphaneroscopy or Hypersemiosis?" Proceedings of the Fourteenth Annual
      Meeting of the Semiotic Society of America, Indianapolis, July 14.
de la Mettrie, Julien Offray
   1912. *Man a Machine.* LaSalle, Ill.: Open Court.
Michaels, Walter Benn
   1977. "The Interpreter's Self: Peirce on the Cartesian 'Subject.' " *Georgia Review,* 31
      (2), 383–402.
Miller, Arthur I.
   1978. "Visualization Lost and Regained: The Genesis of the Quantum Theory in the
      Period 1913–27." In *On Aesthetics in Science,* ed. J. Wechsler, 73–102. Cambridge:
      MIT.
   1986. *Imagery in Scientific Thought.* Cambridge: MIT.
Miller, G. A., E. Galanter, and K. Pribram
   1960. *Plans and the Structure of Behavior.* New York: Holt, Rinehart and Winston.
Miller, J.-A.
   1966. "Les Graphs de Jacques Lacan." *Cahiers pour l'Analyse* (1–2), 169–77.
Misner, Charles W., Kip S. Thorne, and John A. Wheeler
   1973. *Gravitation.* San Francisco: W. H. Freeman.
Monod, Jacques
   1971. *Chance and Necessity.* New York: Knopf.
Murdoch, Dugald
   1987. *Niels Bohr's Philosophy of Physics.* Cambridge: Cambridge University Press.
Murphey, Murray G.
   1961. *The Development of Peirce's Philosophy.* Cambridge: Harvard University Press.
Musés, Charles
   1977. "Paraphysics: A New View of Ourselves and the Cosmos." In *Future Science,*
      ed. J. White and S. Krippner, 280–88. New York: Doubleday.
Nadin, Mihai
   1982. "Consistency, Completeness, and the Meaning of Sign Theories." *American
      Journal of Semiotics,* 1 (3), 79–98.

1983. "The Logic of Vagueness and the Category of Synechism." In *The Relevance of Charles Peirce,* ed. E. Freeman, 154–66. LaSalle, Ill.: Monist Library of Philosophers.

Neisser, Ulric

1967. *Cognitive Psychology.* New York: Appleton-Century-Crofts.

Nesher, Dan

1983. "Pragmatic Theory of Meaning: A Note on Peirce's 'Last' Formulation of the Pragmatic Maxim and Its Interpretation." *Semiotica,* 44 (3/4), 203–57.

Neumann, John von

1958. *The Computer and the Brain.* New Haven: Yale University Press.

Nicolis, Grégoire, and Ilya Prigogine

1989. *Exploring Complexity.* New York: W. H. Freeman.

Nietzsche, Friedrich

1913. *The Will to Power,* ed. O. Levy. In *The Complete Works of Friedrich Nietzsche,* vol. 15. Edinburgh: Foulis.

1968. *Twilight of the Gods and the Anti-Christ,* trans. R. J. Hollingdale. Harmondsworth, England: Penguin.

1969. *Selected Letters of Friedrich Nietzsche,* trans. C. Middleton. Chicago: University of Chicago Press.

Northrop, Filmer Stuart Cuckow

1946. *The Meeting of East and West: An Inquiry concerning World Understanding.* New York: Macmillan.

Oatley, K.

1978. *Perceptions and Representations: The Theoretical Bases of Brain Research and Psychology.* London: Methuen.

Pais, Abraham

1982. *Subtle Is the Lord: The Science and Life of Albert Einstein.* New York: Oxford University Press.

Paivio, Allen

1969. "Mental Imagery in Associative Learning and Memory." *Psychological Review,* 76, 241–63.

1971. *Imagery and Verbal Processes.* New York: Holt, Rinehart.

Park, David

1980. *The Image of Eternity: Roots of Time in the Physical World.* New York: New American Library.

Parsons, Terence

1980. *Nonexistent Objects.* New Haven: Yale University Press.

Pattee, Howard H.

1970. "The Problem of Biological Hierarchy." In *Towards a Theoretical Biology 3,* ed. C. H. Waddington, 117–36. Chicago: Aldine.

1972. "Laws and Constraints, Symbols and Languages." In *Towards a Theoretical Biology 4,* ed. C. H. Waddington, 245–58. Edinburgh: University of Edinburgh Press.

1977. "Dynamic and Linguistic Modes of Complex Systems." *International Journal of General Systems,* 3, 259–66.

1982. "The Need for Complementarity in Models of Cognitive Behavior: A Response to Fowler and Turvey." In *Cognition and the Symbolic Processes,* vol. 2, ed. W. B. Weimer and D. S. Palermo, 22–36. Hillsdale, N.J.: Lawrence Erlbaum.

1986. "Universal Principles of Measurement and Language Functions in Evolving Systems." In *Complexity, Language, and Life: Mathematical Approaches,* ed. J. L. Casti and A. Karlqvist, 268–81. Berlin: Springer-Verlag.

Peat, F. David

1987. *Synchronicity: The Bridge between Matter and Mind.* New York: Bantam.

Peirce, Charles S.

1931–35. *Collected Papers of Charles Sanders Peirce*, ed. C. Hartshorne and P. Weiss, vols. 1–6. Cambridge: Harvard University Press. (Reference to Peirce's collected papers will be designated CP.)

1958. *Collected Papers of Charles Sanders Peirce*, ed. A. W. Burks, vols. 7–8. Cambridge: Harvard University Press. (Reference to Peirce's collected papers will be designated CP.)

1976. *The New Elements of Mathematics by Charles S. Peirce*, ed. C. Eisele. 4 vols. The Hague: Mouton. (Reference to this book will be designated NE.)

MSS refers to Peirce's unpublished manuscripts.

Peitgen, H. O., and P. H. Richter

1986. *The Beauty of Fractals*. Berlin: Springer-Verlag.

Penn, Julia M.

1972. *Linguistic Relativity versus Innate Ideas*. The Hague: Mouton.

Penrose, Roger

1977. "Is Nature Complex?" In *The Encyclopaedia of Ignorance*, ed. R. Duncan and M. Weston-Smith, 159–66. New York: Pergamon.

1987. "Quantum Physics and Conscious Thought." In *Quantum Implications: Essays in Honour of David Bohm*, ed. B. J. Hiley and F. D. Peat, 105–20. London: Routledge and Kegan Paul.

Phillips, Derek

1973. *Abandoning Method*. San Francisco: Jossey-Bass.

1977. *Wittgenstein and Scientific Knowledge: A Sociological Perspective*. Totowa, N.J.: Rowman and Littlefield.

Piaget, Jean

1953. *Logic and Psychology*. Manchester: Manchester University Press.

Poincaré, Henri

1914. *Science and Method*, trans. F. Maitland. London: Thomas Nelson.

Polanyi, Michael

1958. *Personal Knowledge*. Chicago: University of Chicago Press.

1966. *The Tacit Dimension*. New York: Doubleday.

Popper, Karl R.

1963. *Conjectures and Refutations: The Growth of Scientific Knowledge*. Oxford: Oxford University Press.

1972. *Objective Knowledge*. Oxford: Oxford University Press.

1974. *Unended Quest: An Intellectual Autobiography*. LaSalle, Ill.: Open Court.

1982. *The Open Universe: An Argument for Indeterminism* (from the *Postscript to the Logic of Scientific Discovery*), ed. W. W. Bartley III. Totowa, N.J.: Rowman and Littlefield.

Popper, Karl R., and John C. Eccles

1977. *The Self and Its Brain*. New York: Springer-Verlag.

Posner, Roland

1981. "Charles Morris and the Behavioral Foundations of Semiotics." In *Classics of Semiotics*, ed. M. Krampen et al., 23–57. New York: Plenum.

1986. "Morris, Charles William." In *Encyclopedic Dictionary of Semiotics*, ed. T. A. Sebeok, 565–71. Berlin: Mouton de Gruyter.

Pribram, Karl

1971. *Languages of the Brain: Experimental Paradoxes and Principles in Neuropsychology*. Englewood Cliffs, N.J.: Prentice-Hall.

1980. "Mind, Brain, and Consciousness: The Organization of Competence and Conduct." In *The Psychology of Consciousness*, ed. R. J. Davidson and J. M. Davidson, 47–63. New York: Plenum.

1981. "The Distributed Nature of the Memory Store and the Localization of Linguistic

Competencies." In *The Neurological Basis of Signs in Communicational Processes,* Toronto Semiotic Circle Monographs, Working Papers and Prepublications, 2–3, ed. P. Perron, 127–82. Toronto: Victoria University.

1982. "Localization and Distribution of Function in the Brain." In *Neuropsychology after Lashley,* ed. J. Orbach, 273–91. Hillsdale, N.J.: Lawrence Erlbaum.

Prigogine, Ilya

1973. "Time, Irreversibility and Structure." In *The Physicist's Concept of Nature,* ed. J. Mehra, 561–93. Dordrecht, Holland: D. Reidel.

1980. *From Being to Becoming: Time and Complexity in the Physical Sciences.* San Francisco: W. H. Freeman.

1981. "Time, Irreversibility, and Randomness." In *The Evolutionary Vision: Toward a Unifying Paradigm of Physical, Biological, and Sociocultural Evolution,* ed. E. Jantsch, 73–82. Boulder, Colo.: Westview.

1983. *Tan sólo una ilusión?,* ed. J. Wagensberg. Barcelona: Tusquets.

Prigogine, Ilya, and Isabelle Stengers

1984. *Order out of Chaos: Man's New Dialogue with Nature.* New York: Bantam.

Prior, A. N.

1957. *Time and Modality.* Oxford: Clarendon.

Putnam, Hilary

1960. "Minds and Machines." In *Dimensions of Mind,* ed. S. Hook, 148–79. New York: New York University Press.

Pylyshyn, Z. W.

1973. "What the Mind's Eye Tells the Mind's Brain: A Critique of Mental Imagery." *Psychological Bulletin,* 80, 1–24.

Quine, Willard von Orman

1960. *Word and Object.* Cambridge: MIT Press.

1969. *Ontological Relativity and Other Essays.* New York: Columbia University Press.

1970. *Philosophy of Logic.* Englewood Cliffs, N.J.: Prentice-Hall.

Radnitsky, G., and W. W. Bartley III

1987. *Evolutionary Epistemology, Rationality and the Sociology of Knowledge.* La-Salle, Ill.: Open Court.

Rajchman, John, and Cornel West (eds.)

1985. *Post-Analytic Philosophy.* New York: Columbia University Press.

Rapoport, Anatol

1950. *Science and the Goals of Man: A Study in Semantic Orientation.* New York: Harper and Row.

1974. *Conflict in Man-Made Environment.* Harmondsworth, England: Penguin.

Reese, William

1952. "Philosophical Realism: A Study in the Modality of Being in Peirce and Whitehead." In *Studies in the Philosophy of Charles Sanders Peirce,* ed. P. P. Wiener and F. H. Young, 225–37. Cambridge: Harvard University Press.

Rescher, Nicholas

1978. *Peirce's Philosophy of Science.* Notre Dame: University of Notre Dame Press.

Rescher, Nicholas, and Robert Brandom

1979. *The Logic of Inconsistency: A Study of Non-Standard Possible-World Semantics and Ontology.* Totowa, N.J.: Rowman and Littlefield.

Riley, B. Gresham

1968. "Existence, Reality and Objects of Knowledge." *Transactions of the Charles S. Peirce Society,* 4 (1), 34–48.

Roberts, Don

1973. *The Existential Graphs of Charles S. Peirce.* The Hague: Mouton.

Rochberg-Halton, Eugene

1986. *Meaning and Modernity: Social Theory in the Pragmatic Attitude.* Chicago: University of Chicago Press.

Romanos, George D.
1984. *Quine and Analytic Philosophy*. Cambridge: MIT Press.
Rorty, Richard
1979. *Philosophy and the Mirror of Nature*. Princeton: Princeton University Press.
1982. *Consequences of Pragmatism*. Minneapolis: University of Minnesota Press.
Rosch, Eleanor
1974. "Linguistic Relativity." In *Human Communication: Theoretical Explorations*, ed. A. Silverstein, 95–121. New York: Halsted Press.
1975a. "Cognitive Representations of Semantic Categories." *Journal of Experimental Psychology: General*, 104, 192–233.
1975b. "Universals and Cultural Specifics in Human Categorization." In *Cross-Cultural Perspectives on Learning*, ed. R. Brislin, S. Bochner, and W. Lonner, 177–206. New York: Halsted Press.
1977. "Human Categorization." In *Studies in Cross-Cultural Psychology*, vol. 1, ed. N. Warren, 3–49. London: Academic Press.
Rosch, Eleanor (ed.)
1978. *Cognition and Categorization*. Hillsdale, N.J.: Erlbaum.
Rotman, Brian
1987. *Signifying Nothing: The Semiotics of Zero*. New York: St. Martin's.
Rucker, Rudolf v. B.
1977. *Geometry, Relativity and the Fourth Dimension*. New York: Dover.
Ruelle, David
1980. "Strange Attractors." *Mathematical Intelligencer*, 2, 126–37.
Russell, Bertrand
1910. "The Theory of Logical Types." In *Principia Mathematica*, by Alfred North Whitehead and Bertrand Russell, vol. 1, 37–65. Cambridge: Cambridge University Press.
1957. *Mysticism and Logic*. New York: Doubleday.
Sachs, Mendel
1988. *Einstein versus Bohr: The Continuing Controversies in Physics*. LaSalle, Ill.: Open Court.
Salthe, Stanley N., and Myrdene Anderson
1989. "Modeling Self-Organization." In *Semiotics 1988*, ed. T. Prewitt, J. Deely, and K. Haworth, 14–23. Lanham, Md.: University Press of America.
Saussure, Ferdinand de
1966. *Course in General Linguistics*, trans. W. Baskin. New York: McGraw-Hill.
Savan, David
1952. "On the Origins of Peirce's Phenomenology." In *Studies in the Philosophy of Charles Sanders Peirce*, ed. P. P. Wiener and F. H. Young, 185–94. Cambridge: Harvard University Press.
Schlegel, Richard
1980. *Superposition and Interaction*. Chicago: University of Chicago Press.
Schrödinger, Erwin
1951. *Science and Humanism*. Cambridge: Cambridge University Press.
1961. "The Not-Quite-Exact Sciences." In *The Fate of Man*, ed. C. Brinton, 452–62. New York: George Braziller.
1964. *My View of the World*. Cambridge: Cambridge University Press.
1967. *What Is Life?* and *Matter and Mind*. Cambridge: Cambridge University Press.
Sebeok, Thomas A.
1979. *The Sign and Its Masters*. Austin: University of Texas Press.
Sheffer, H. M.
1913. "A Set of Five Independent Postulates of Boolean Algebras." *Transactions of the American Mathematical Society*, 14, 481–88.

Sheldrake, Rupert

    1988a. *The Presence of the Past: Morphic Resonance and the Habits of Nature.* New York: Random House.

    1988b. "The Laws of Nature as Habit: A Postmodern Basis for Science." In *The Reenchantment of Science: Postmodern Proposals,* ed. D. R. Griffin, 79–86. Albany: State University of New York Press.

Skagestad, Peter

    1983. "C. S. Peirce on Biological Evolution and Scientific Progress." In *The Relevance of Charles Peirce,* ed. E. Freeman, 348–72. LaSalle, Ill.: Monist Library of Philosophy.

    1989. Discussant for "Plenary: Peirce and History of Science." At the Charles Sanders Peirce Sesquicentennial International Congress, Harvard University, Sept. 7.

Skolimowski, Henryk

    1986. "Quine, Ajdukiewicz, and the Predicament of 20th Century Philosophy." In *The Philosophy of W. V. Quine,* ed. L. E. Hahn and P. A. Schilpp, 463–91. LaSalle, Ill.: Open Court.

    1987. "The Interactive Mind in the Participatory Universe." In *The Real and the Imaginary: A New Approach to Physics,* ed. J. E. Charon, 69–94. New York: Paragon.

Smullyan, Arthur F.

    1952. "Some Implications of Critical Common-Sensism." In *The Philosophy of Charles Sanders Peirce,* ed. P. P. Wiener and F. H. Young, 111–20. Cambridge: Harvard University Press.

Smullyan, Raymond M.

    1977. *The Tao Is Silent.* New York: Harper and Row.

Spencer-Brown, G.

    1979. *Laws of Form.* New York: E. P. Dutton.

Stearns, Isabel S.

    1952. "Firstness, Secondness, and Thirdness." In *The Philosophy of Charles Sanders Peirce,* ed. P. P. Wiener and F. H. Young, 195–208. Cambridge: Harvard University Press.

Suppes, Patrick

    1984. *Probabilistic Metaphysics.* London: Basil Blackwell.

Suzuki, D. T.

    1971. *Essays in Zen Buddhism.* 1st series. London: Rider.

Swineburne, R. G.

    1969. "Vagueness, Inexactness and Imprecision." *British Journal for the Philosophy of Science,* 19 (4), 281–99.

Talbot, Michael

    1980. *Mysticism and the New Physics.* New York: Bantam.

T. de Nicolas, Antonio

    1976. *Meditations through the Rg Veda: Four-Dimensional Man.* Boulder, Colo.: Shambhala.

Thom, René

    1975. *Structural Stability and Morphogenesis,* trans. D. H. Fowler. Reading, Mass.: W. A. Benjamin.

    1983. *Mathematical Models of Morphogenesis,* trans. W. M. Brooks and D. Rand. West Sussex: Ellis Horwood.

Thomas, Lewis

    1980. "On the Uncertainty of Science." *Harvard Magazine,* Sept./Oct., 19–22.

Thompson, Manley H., Jr.

    1952. "The Paradox of Peirce's Realism." In *Studies in the Philosophy of Charles Sanders Peirce,* ed. P. P. Wiener and F. H. Young, 133–42. Cambridge: Harvard University Press.

1953. *The Pragmatic Philosophy of C. S. Peirce*. Chicago: University of Chicago Press.

Toben, Bob

1975. *Space-Time and Beyond*. New York: E. P. Dutton.

Todorov, Tzvetan

1966. "Les Catégories du récit littéraire." *Communications*, 8, 125–51.

Trungpa, Chogyam

1973. *Cutting through Spiritual Materialism*. Boulder, Colo.: Shambhala.

Turkle, Sherry

1978. *Psychoanalytic Politics: Freud's French Revolution*. New York: Basic Books.

Turley, Peter T.

1977. *Peirce's Cosmology*. New York: Philosophical Library.

Tursman, Richard

1987. *Peirce's Theory of Scientific Discovery: A System of Logic Conceived as Semiotic*. Bloomington: Indiana University Press.

Tyler, Stephen

1978. *The Said and the Unsaid*. New York: Academic Press.

1987. *The Unspeakable: Discourse, Dialogue, and Rhetoric in the Postmodern World*. Madison: University of Wisconsin Press.

Uexküll, Jakob von

1957. "A Stroll through the World of Animals and Men." In *Instinctive Behavior: The Development of a Modern Concept*, ed. C. H. Schiller, 5–80. New York: International Universities Press.

Uexküll, Thure von

1982. "Jakob von Uexküll's *The Theory of Meaning*." *Semiotica*, 42 (1), 1–87.

1985. "From Index to Icon: A Semiotic Attempt at Interpreting Piaget's Developmental Theory." In *Iconicity: Essays on the Nature of Culture*, ed. P. Bouissac, M. Herzfeld, and R. Posner, 119–40. Berlin: Springer-Verlag.

1986. "Medicine and Semiotics." *Semiotica*, 61 (3/4), 201–17.

1988. "Jakob von Uexküll's Umwelt Theory." In *The Semiotic Web 1988*, ed. T. A. Sebeok and J. Umiker-Sebeok, 129–58. Berlin: Mouton de Gruyter.

Ulmer, Gregory L.

1985. *Applied Grammatology: Post(e)-Pedagogy from Jacques Derrida to Joseph Beuys*. Baltimore: Johns Hopkins University Press.

Vaihinger, Hans

1935. *The Philosophy of "As If": A System of the Theoretical, Practical and Religious Fictions of Mankind*, trans. C. K. Ogden. London: Kegan, Paul, Trench, Truber.

Varela, Francisco J.

1975. "A Calculus for Self-Reference." *International Journal of General Systems*, 2, 5–24.

1979. *Principles of Biological Autonomy*. Amsterdam: North-Holland.

1984a. "The Creative Circle: Sketches on the Natural History of Circularity." In *The Invented Reality*, ed. Paul Watzlawick, 309–23. New York: W. W. Norton.

1984b. "Living Ways of Sense-Making: A Middle Path for Neuroscience." In *Disorder and Order*, Proceedings of the Stanford International Symposium, Sept. 1981, ed. P. Livingston, 208–24. Saratoga, Calif.: Anma Libri.

Waddington, Conrad H.

1957. *The Strategy of the Genes*. London: George Allen and Unwin.

Walker, Evan Harris

1970. "The Nature of Consciousness." *Mathematical Biosciences*, 7, 138–78.

Walker, Evan Harris, and Nick Herbert

1977. "Hidden Variables: Where Physics and Paranormal Meet." In *Future Science*, ed. J. White and S. Krippner, 279–94. New York: Doubleday.

Watzlawick, Paul (ed.)

1984. *The Invented Reality*. New York: W. W. Norton.

Wechsler, Judith (ed.)

1978. *On Aesthetics in Science*. Cambridge: MIT Press.

Weiss, Paul

1952. "The Logic of the Creative Process." In *Studies in the Philosophy of Charles Sanders Peirce*, ed. P. P. Wiener and F. H. Young, 166–82. Cambridge: Harvard University Press.

Weyl, Hermann

1949. *Philosophy of Mathematics and Natural Science*. New York: Atheneum.

Wheeler, John Archibald

1968. "Superspace and the Nature of Quantum Geometrodynamics." In *Battelle Rencontres*, ed. C. M. DeWitt and J. A. Wheeler, 242–69. New York: W. A. Benjamin.

1973. "From Relativity to Mutability." In *The Physicist's Concept of Nature*, ed. J. Mehra, 202–47. Dordrecht, Holland: D. Reidel.

1977. "Genesis and Observership." In *Foundational Problems in the Special Sciences*, ed. R. E. Butts and K. J. Hintikka, 1–33. Dordrecht, Holland: D. Reidel.

1980a. "Beyond the Black Hole." In *Some Strangeness in the Proportion*, ed. H. Wolff, 341–80. Reading, Mass.: Addison-Wesley.

1980b. "Law without Law." In *Structure in Science and Art*, ed. P. Medawar and J. H. Shelley, 132–68. Amsterdam: Excerpta Medica.

1982. "Bohr, Einstein, and the Strange Lesson of the Quantum." In *Mind in Nature*, ed. R. Q. Elvee, 1–30. New York: Harper and Row.

1984. "Bits, Quanta, Meaning." In *Theoretical Physics Meeting*, 121–34. Napoli: Edizioni Scientifiche Italiane.

White, Hayden

1978. *Tropics of Discourse: Essays in Cultural Criticism*. Baltimore: Johns Hopkins University Press.

1987. *The Content of the Form: Narrative Discourse and Historical Representation*. Baltimore: Johns Hopkins University Press.

Whitehead, Alfred North

1925. *Science and the Modern World*. New York: Macmillan.

1938. *Modes of Thought*. New York: Free Press.

1978. *Process and Reality: An Essay in Cosmology*. New York: Free Press.

Whitehead, A. N., and Bertrand Russell

1910. *Principia Mathematica*. Cambridge: Cambridge University Press.

Whitrow, G. J.

1980. *The Natural Philosophy of Time*. 2nd ed. Oxford: Clarendon.

Whorf, Benjamin Lee

1956. *Language, Thought, and Reality*, ed. J. B. Carroll. Cambridge: MIT.

Wiener, Norbert

1948. *Cybernetics: Or, Control and Communication in the Animal and the Machine*. Cambridge: MIT Press.

1950. *The Human Use of Human Beings: Cybernetics and Society*. Boston: Houghton-Mifflin.

Wigner, Eugene P.

1967. *Symmetries and Reflections, Scientific Essays*. Bloomington: Indiana University Press.

1969. "The Unreasonable Effectiveness of Mathematics in the Natural Sciences." In *The Spirit and the Uses of the Mathematical Sciences*, ed. T. L. Saaty and F. J. Weyl, 123–40. New York: McGraw-Hill.

Wilber, Ken

1977. *The Spectrum of Consciousness*. Wheaton, Ill.: Theosophical.

1982. *The Holographic Paradigm and Other Paradoxes: Exploring the Leading Edge of Science*. Boulder, Colo.: Shambhala.

Wilden, Anthony

1968. Trans. with notes and commentary. *The Language of the Self: The Function of Language in Psychoanalysis,* by Jacques Lacan. Baltimore: Johns Hopkins University Press.

1980. *System and Structure.* 2nd ed. London: Tavistock.

1984. "Montage, Analytic, and Dialectic." In *American Journal of Semiotics,* 3 (1), 25–47.

1987a. *The Rules Are No Game: The Strategy of Communication.* New York: Routledge and Kegan Paul.

1987b. *Man and Woman, War and Peace: The Strategist's Companion.* New York: Routledge and Kegan Paul.

Wilson, Edward O.

1971. *The Insect Societies.* Cambridge: Harvard University Press.

Winfree, Arthur T.

1987. *When Time Breaks Down: The Three-Dimensional Dynamics of Electrochemical Waves and Cardiac Arrhythmias.* Princeton: Princeton University Press.

Wittgenstein, Ludwig

1953. *Philosophical Investigations,* trans. G. E. M. Anscombe. New York: Macmillan.

1961. *Tractatus Logico-Philosophicus,* trans. D. F. Pears and B. F. McGuinness. London: Routledge and Kegan Paul.

Wolf, Fred Alan

1984. *Star Wave: Mind, Consciousness, and Quantum Physics.* New York: Macmillan.

Young, Arthur M.

1972. "Consciousness and Cosmology." In *Consciousness and Reality,* ed. C. Musés and A. M. Young, 151–64. New York: Outerbridge.

Zee, A.

1986. *Fearful Symmetry: The Search for Beauty in Modern Physics.* New York: Macmillan.

Zeeman, Christopher

1977. *Catastrophe Theory.* Reading, Mass.: Addison-Wesley.

Zukav, Gary

1979. *The Dancing Wu Li Masters: An Overview of the New Physics.* New York: William Morrow.

Index